WHEN we build, let us think that we build forever. Let it not be for present delight nor for present use alone. Let it be such work as our descendants will thank us for; and let us think, as we lay stone on stone, that a time is to come when those stones will be held sacred because our hands have touched them, and that men will say, as they look upon the labor and wrought substance of them, "See! This our father did for us."

—*John Ruskin.*

12, 13, 17.

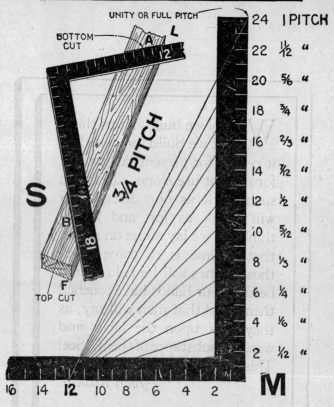

UNITY OR FULL PITCH

24 1 PITCH

22 1½ "

20 ⅚ "

18 ¾ "

16 ⅔ "

14 7/12 "

12 ½ "

10 5/12 "

8 ⅓ "

6 ¼ "

4 ⅙ "

2 1/12 "

BOTTOM CUT

A L

12

3/4 PITCH

S

B

18

F

TOP CUT

M

16 14 12 10 8 6 4 2

How to Use the Steel Square

The lines radiating from division **12** on the tongue of the square to various points on the blade to be seen in fig. **M**, are inclinations corresponding to the various roof pitches.

The **12** inch mark on tongue and mark on blade opposite roof pitch desired is used to obtain cuts for *common rafters*. For octagon, or hip rafters use mark 13, or 17 respectively. In fig. **S**, the square is seen applied to a rafter with the 12 in. mark on tongue and 18 in. mark on body at the edge of the rafter corresponding to ¾ pitch of common rafter.

The inclinations A, and B, of the tongue and body of the square with the edge LF, of the rafter give the correct angles for bottom and top cuts for ¾ pitch when placed in position; that is, when A is horizontal and B, vertical or plumb.

AUDELS CARPENTERS AND BUILDERS GUIDE #1

A PRACTICAL ILLUSTRATED TRADE ASSISTANT

ON

MODERN CONSTRUCTION

FOR CARPENTERS - JOINERS - BUILDERS - MECHANICS

AND

ALL WOOD WORKERS

EXPLAINING IN PRACTICAL, CONCISE LANGUAGE AND BY WELL
DONE ILLUSTRATIONS, DIAGRAMS, CHARTS, GRAPHS AND
PICTURES, PRINCIPLES, ADVANCES, SHORT CUTS-BASED ON
MODERN PRACTICE-INCLUDING INSTRUCTIONS ON HOW
TO FIGURE AND CALCULATE VARIOUS JOBS

BY

FRANK D. GRAHAM-Chief ◆ THOMAS J. EMERY-Associate

Theo. Audel & Co., Publishers
49 West 23rd St., New York 10, N.Y.

CARPENTERS AND BUILDERS GUIDE #1

COPYRIGHT, 1923, 1939, 1945, 1951

BY

THEO. AUDEL & CO.

NEW YORK

All Rights Reserved

Printed in the United States

Foreword

"The Audel's Guides to the Building Trades" are a practical series of educators on the various branches of Modern Building Construction and are dedicated to Master Builders and their Associates.

These Guides are designed to give technical trade information in concise, accurate, plain language.

The Guides illustrate the hows and whys, short cuts, modern ways and methods of the foundation principles of the art.

Each book in the series is fully illustrated and indexed for readiest form of reference and study.

The Guides will speak for themselves—and help to increase the reader's knowledge and skill in the Building Trades.

—Publishers.

How to Use This Table

By the intelligent use of the **Table of Contents** the reader will have no difficulty in finding any **desired item,** and if he will carefully read the table he will be amazed at the vast amount of information to be found in this book, and will in this way find numerous items he would like to look up.

This book is made up of several chapters with contents as indicated by the chapter heading. Each chapter is referred to by a number as indicated at the extreme left and the pages covered are given at the extreme right.

Finally, if an item is not found in one Guide, look for it in one of the other volumes of the set. Thus, for example, the *steel square* is explained in **Guide No. 1,** and its application to roof framing treated at length in **Guide No. 3.**

Get the habit of using this Table of Contents. It will quickly reveal a vast mine of valuable information.

TABLE OF CONTENTS

Chapter   Pages

1—Woods . . . .   1 to 22F

Classification—mode of growth—grain—lumbering—logging—sawing—defects—seasoning
—kilns—selection—properties of wood—preservation—decay—laminated wood—plywood
—paper-faced plywood—wood-fiber boards—
rigid boards—wood-base plastics.

2—Nails . . . .   23 to   58

History—sizes—classification—tables—holding power—selection—spacing—how to drive
nails.

3—Screws . . . .   59 to   74

Classification—material—wood screws—length
—shape of head—shape of point—thread—
how to put in wooden screws—strength of
screws—lag screws—how to put in lag screws
—strength of lag screws—safe loads for lag
screws.

4—Bolts . . . .   75 to   84

Kinds of bolts—history—proportions and
strength—U. S. standard thread—tables—
strength of bolts.

5—Work Bench . . . .   85 to   94

How to build—bench attachments—bench
hooks—vises.

Table of Contents

Chapter	Pages

6—Carpenters' Tools . . . . 95 to 98

Selection—guiding and testing tools—marking tools—measuring tools—holding tools—toothed cutting tools—sharp edge cutting tools—rough facing tools—smooth facing tools—boring tools—fastening tools—sharpening tools.

7—Guiding and Testing Tools . . . . . 99 to 128

Straight edge—try square—mitre square—framing square—combination square—shooting board—mitre box—mitre shooting board—level—plumb bob—plumb rule.

8—Marking Tools . . . . 129 to 136

Classification—chalk line—marking—scriber—compasses and dividers.

9—Measuring Tools . . . . 137 to 154

Various folding rules—rules with attachments—board measure—lumber scales—decimal log scale—log tables—marking gauges—double bar gauge—slide gauge—butt gauge.

10—Holding Tools . . . . 155 to 164

Horses—clamps—vises.

11—Toothed Cutting Tools . . . . 165 to 178

Saws—saw teeth—setting the saw—cross cut and rip saws—action of the rip saw—angles of saw teeth—files and rasps.

Table of Contents

Chapter		Pages

12—Circular Saws . . . . **179 to 190**

Construction—tilting arbor saw—ripping operation — cross-cutting operation — mitering operations—grooving operations—dado head—power and speed of saw— rules for calculating the speeds of saws and pulleys—rim speed.

13—Band Saws . . . . **191 to 204**

Construction—band saw guides—straight cutting operation—ripping—re-sawing—cutting circular arcs and segments—multiple sawing operation—designating number of teeth to the inch—cutting to length by the use of mitre gauge and stop rod—method of cutting short pieces to length using square board or fence—use of mitre clamp attachment—method of assembling multiple sawing operations—pointers on band saw operation.

14—Jig Saws . . . . **205 to 212**

Construction—component parts of jig saw—driving mechanism — tension mechanism — guides and saw blade—various items produced by means of jig saw cutting—operation—blades to use.

15—Saw Filing . . . . **213 to 236**

Sharpening handsaws — jointing — shaping — setting—filing—method of holding file when filing handsaw—cross cutting saws—rip saws—dressing the saw—**filing band saws**—refitting band saws — brazing—**filing circular saws**—jointing — shaping — setting — filing — swage set—spring set—gumming—small circular rip

Table of Contents

Chapter		Pages

saws—small circular cut off saws—fine tooth cut off saw — **large circular saws** — inserted tooth saws—inserting new teeth.

16—Sharp Edge Cutting Tools . . . . . . 237 to 250

Paring chisel— firmer chisel—framing or mortise chisel — corner chisel — tang and socket chisels—butt, pocket and mill chisels—how to select chisels—how to use chisels—how to sharpen chisels—draw knife.

17—Rough Facing Tools . . . . 251 to 256

Hatchet—broad hatchet or hand axe—adze.

18—Smooth Facing Tools . . . . 257 to 290

Spoke shave—jack plane—fore plane—trying and jointer planes — smooth plane — block plane—moulding and special planes—rabbet or rebate plane — fillester plane — grooving plane—router—rounds and hollows—nosing and scotia planes—chamfer plane—plane irons or cutters—bevel of the cutting edge—double irons — plane mouth — how to use a plane— sharpening planes—adjusting the cutter—how to plane — jointing — scrapers — sharpening scraper blade for heavy work.

19—Boring Tools . . . . 291 to 304

Brad awls—gimlets—augers—how to sharpen augers—twist drills—hollow augers—spoke pointers—counter sinks—reamers.

20—Fastening Tools . . . . 305 to 312

Hammers—screw drivers—wrenches—how to use a monkey wrench.

Table of Contents

Chapter   **Pages**

21—Sharpening Tools . . . . **313 to 322**

Grind stones—use of water on grind stones—
truing a grind stone—tool rests—abrasives—
grinding wheels—oil stones—directions for installing and using emery wheels—natural oil
stones—artificial oil stones.

22—How to Sharpen Tools . . . . **323 to 328**

Grinding—honing—points on oil stones—how
to repair a broken oil stone—how to clean an
oil stone.

23—How to Use the Steel Square . . . . **329 to 376**

Application of the square—scales or graduations—scale problems—angle table for square
— square and bevel problems — table for inscribed polygons—table of chords or equal parts
—main or common rafters—rise per foot run
—pitch table—hip (and valley) rafters—jack
rafters—cripple rafters—finding rafter lengths
without aid of tables—rafter tables—to find
the length of a common rafter—reading length
of rafter per foot run—table of octagon rafters
—table of angle cuts for polygons—table of
brace measure—octagon table or eight square
scale—Essex board measure table.

24—Joints and Joinery . . . . **377 to 414**

Straight joint—dowel pin joint—square corner
joint — mitred corner joint — feather joint —
splice joint—housed butt or rabbetted joint—
compression scarf joint—tension scarf joint—
bending scarf joint—compression and tension
scarf joint—tension and bending scarf joint—
mortise and tenon joints—cutting the mortise
—cutting the tenon—making pins—draw boring

Table of Contents

Chapter   **Pages**

—common dovetail joint—compound dovetail
joint—spacing—position of pins—lap or half-
blind dovetail joint—blind dovetail joint—
tongue and groove joint.

24A—Cabinetmaking Joints . . . . 414-1 to 414-32

Tools—bench—glued joints—rubbed joints—
gluing up—bevelled joints—cutting the bevel
— plowed and tongued joints — hidden slot
screwed joints—dowelled joints—placing the
dowels—dowel template—halved and bridle
joints—bridle or open tenon joints—mortise
and tenon joints—laying out mortise and tenon—cutting the shoulder—dovetail joints—
the angle of dovetails—bevelled dovetailing—
setting out a diminished dovetail—mitred joints
tonguing a mitre—screwed mitre joint—framing joints—hinging and shutting joints.

24B—Wood Patternmaking . . . 414-33 to 414-68

Patternmaker's tools — paring chisel — trade
terms—lumber—glue—shellac or pattern varnish — pattern colors—dowel pins—fillets —
split or parted pattern—cores, core prints and
core boxes—green sand core—core prints—core
boxes—draft—shrinkage—finish—blueprints
—shrinkage rule—pattern joinery—butt joints
—checked joint—half-tapped joint—splined
joint—rabbet joint—dado joint—mortise and
tenon joint—dovetail joint.

25—Furniture Suggestions . . . . 415 to 430

Tool box—book rack—cabinet wall shelf rack
—bracket shelf—flower box—cedar chest—
hall chair—tabouret—cupboard—framing for
drawers—home made couch.

CHAPTER 1

Woods

Wood.—This is one of the most common of building materials and a general knowledge of the structure and characteristics of the various woods used in building operations is an absolute necessity to the carpenter. Wood may be classed

1. With respect to its mode of growth as

   a. Exogeneous (outside growing)
   b. Endogeneous (inside growing)

2. With respect to its density, as

   a. Soft
   b. Hard

3. With respect to its leaves, as

   a. Needle leaved (*conifers*)
   b. Broad leaved

4. With respect to shade or color

   a. White
   b. Yellow
   c. Red
   d. Brown
   e. Black, etc.

5. With respect to grain, as

   a. Straight

  b. Cross
  c. Fine
  d. Coarse

6. With respect to the nature of the surface when sawed, as

  a. Plain (ex.: white pine)
  b. Grained (ex.: oak)
  c Figured or marked (ex.: bird's-eye maple)

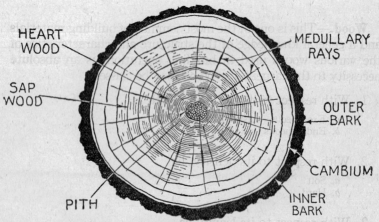

Fig. 1.—Cross section of an oak nine years old showing: pith; concentric rings comprising the woody part, cambium, and the bark. The arrangement of the wood in concentric rings is due to the fact that it was formed gradually, one layer being added each year, and for this reason the rings or layers are sometimes called annual rings. The wood nearest the center is considerably darker in color than that which is on the outside nearer the bark; it is called the *heart wood* to distinguish it from the other, which is called the *sap wood*. **Only the heart wood should be used for building work.** The reason the heart wood is the harder is because it is older and has therefore been compressed more and more each year. It requires from 9 to 35 years to transform sap wood into heart wood according to the nature of the tree, those which harden in the shortest time being the most durable.

In addition there are numerous woods such as the bamboos, palms, rattans, etc., which may be classed as *tropical*.

Mode of Growth.—The wood used in building is obtained

from trees of the class known to botanists as *exogens*, or those trees which grow larger by the addition each year of a layer of new wood on their outer surface. A transverse section of a tree of this class, as in fig. 1 shows it to consist of

1. Pith or medalla.
2. Annual rings or concentric layers of wood.
3. Medullary or rays.
4. Cambium.

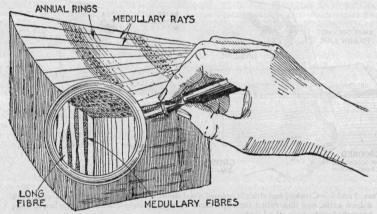

Fig. 2.—Highly magnified piece of wood showing detail of its structure. Wood is made up of bundles of fibres or long tubes, parallel to the stem of the tree which are crossed by other fibres that form the medullary rays, which pass from pith to bark and which serve to bind the whole together. There are also resin ducts and other fibres scattered through the trunk of the tree. In pine more than 15,000 pith rays occur on a square inch of section.

5. Bast or inner bark.
6. Corky layer or outer bark.

The pith is in the center of the tree and around it the wood is dispersed in approximately concentric rings; that part near the pith is hard and close in grain and from its position is termed heart wood.

The sap wood is made up of the outer layers or rings and these are softer than the heart and generally of more open grain. Each annual ring is made up of two parts, an *inner* soft portion, light in color, and an *outer* hard dark colored portion. The inner portion is formed early in the season and is termed *spring wood*, the darker part being called autumn wood.

At the end of the season (autumn) growth stops to be resumed the following spring and the rapid open growth of the spring against the slow and condensed growth of the summer gives rise to the peculiar marking or rings which indicates each year's increase.

The medullary rays extend radially from the center of the tree to the bark at right angles to the grain of the wood and serve during life to bind the whole

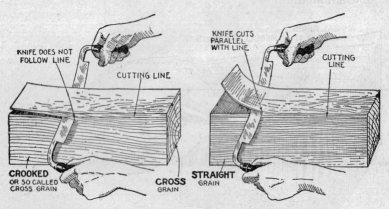

Figs. 3 and 4.—Crooked and straight grained wood showing results obtained in working as with a draw knife, and illustrating the importance of using straight-grained wood when it must be worked with sharp-edged tools.

together as well as to convey nourishment from one part of the tree to another. The width of the annual rings varies from 1/50 to 1/8 in. according to the character of the tree and the position of the ring.

As seen in fig. 1, there are in addition to the annual rings, radial lines or *medullary rays* which run from the center toward the bark at right angles to the annual rays.

Grain of Wood.—When the annual rings are large, the *grain* or marking which separates adjacent rings is said to be coarse; when small, it is called *fine grained*. When the direction of the fibres is nearly parallel with the sides and edges of the board it is said to be straight grained; when the lumber is taken from a crooked tree, it is said to be *crooked grained** as the grain follows the shape of the log whereas the board is sawed straight.

The importance of using straight grained wood where same must be worked is shown in figs. 3 and 4.

Lumbering.—The term lumbering is here used to denote the two operations which must be performed in preparing wood for commercial purposes, and known as

1. Logging.
2. Sawing.

Logging.—This comprises all the steps from felling the tree to the delivery of the logs at the saw mill. The logs are then sawed into board planks and timbers of certain dimensions and are piled and exposed to the air for a sufficient time to allow a large part of the water in them to evaporate, when the lumber is said to be weather dried and ready for shipment to the consumer.

Sawing.—The manner in which a log is sawed has an important bearing on its quality and behaviour. There are several methods, as

1. Plain or bastard (sometimes called *flat* or slash).
2. Quarter or rift.

   a. Radial
   b. Tangential
   c. Quarter tangential
   d. Combined radial and tangential

Plain or Bastard Sawing.—This consists in cutting entirely through

---

* NOTE—The term *cross grained* is generally used but the author prefers to confine that term to the case where the grain is at right angles to the edge of the board.

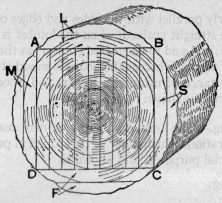

Fɪɢ. 5.—Plain or bastard sawing, sometimes called *flat* or *slash*. *In sawing,* the log is first squared by sawing off boards MS, and LF, giving the rectangular section ABCD, the object being to obtain a flat surface on which it may rest while being sawed. With this bedding it is not necessary to run each board by the edging saw to true the edges. The board MS, and LF, obtained in squaring the log, are of inferior quality, being nearly all sap, but are worth saving in the case of large logs.

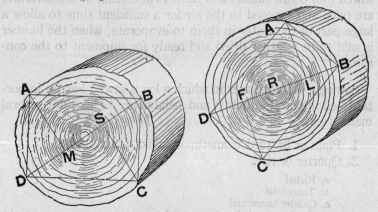

Fɪɢ. 6.—Method of squaring a log to obtain one heavy beam. *Rule: Divide longest diameter DB, into three parts by points M and S; erect perpendiculars on DB, at M and S, and join points thus obtained, giving the rectangle ABCD.*

Fɪɢ. 7.—Method of squaring a log to obtain a stiff beam. *Rule:* Divide longest diameter DB, into four parts by points FRL; erect perpendiculars to diameter DB, at L and F, and join points thus obtained giving the rectangle ABCD.

the log through a diameter and parallel chords, that is cutting through the log tangential to the annual rays, as in fig. 5. This is the cheapest way to cut logs both as to time and waste. Since logs are not always of circular cross section, it is a problem to obtain the most efficient square for cutting. Two methods of doing this are shown in figs. 6 and 7.

Quarter Sawing.—The four methods of quarter sawing are shown in fig. 8, each quadrant *a,b,c,d*, of the log illustrating one of the methods.

The radial method shown in quadrant *a*, is the best but gives the most waste. The cuts are taken along radii, or in the direction of the medullary rays. This method is the best not only on account of the handsomer surface

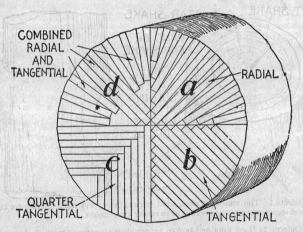

Fig. 8.—Various methods of quarter sawing. *a*, radial; *b*, tangential; *c*, quarter tangential; *d*, combined radial and tangential. Quarter or *rift* sawing and flat sawing (see fig. 5) give rise in the lumber trade to the terms *edge grain* and *flat grain* respectively.

but also because it will hold its shape better than when sawed by other methods. The reason for this is that the board shrinks most in a direction parallel with the annual rings, hence when radially sawed this shrinkage is normal to the surface of the board and accordingly the warping is minimum.

Defects.—The various defects found in wood may be divided into two classes:

1. Those due to abnormal growth, as

    a. Heart shakes
    b. Wind shakes
    c. Star shakes
    d. Knots

2. Those due to deterioriation, as

    a. Dry rot
    b. Wet rot

Fig. 9.—Defects 1: The various shakes, wind or cup, heart, and star. Shakes are common defects and sometimes are so numerous as to render a log useless.

Fig. 10.—Defects 2: Hard knot and broken branch showing nature's method of covering the break, resulting in a *rhind gall* produced by the growth of fresh layers over the injury.

Fig. 9 shows the various shakes and fig. 10, knots.

Heart shakes are radial cracks wider at the pith of the tree than at the outer end. This defect is most commonly found in those trees which are old, rather than in young vigorous saplings; it occurs most frequently in hemlock.

A wind or cup shake is a crack following the line of the porous part of the annual rings and is curved by a separation of the annual rings. A wind shake may extend for a considerable distance up the trunk. Other explanations for wind shakes are: 1, expansion of the sap wood, and 2, wrenchings received due to high winds hence the name. Pine is especially susceptible to wind shakes.

A star shake resembles the wind shake but differs in that the crack extends across the center of the trunk without any appearance of decay at that point; it is larger at the outside of the tree.

Dry rot, so called, to which timber is so subject is due to fungi, the name being misleading as it only occurs in the presence of moisture and the absence of free circulation of air.

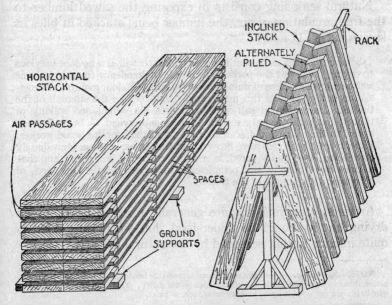

FIG. 11.—Horizontal stack of lumber for air drying. One end of the pile should be a little higher than the other so that rain water which falls on top or drives into the pile will drain. Each layer should be separated by three or four spacers so that the air will have free access to both sides of each board. The lowest layer should be well elevated above the ground to protect it from the dampness of the latter. It takes from one to three years to thoroughly season lumber depending upon the character of the wood, climatic conditions, etc.

FIG. 12.—Inclined stack of lumber for rapid drying. Note alternate placing of the lumber in the rack. Evidently water will drain very quickly.

Stacking and Seasoning of Lumber.—In preparing lumber for the market, it is necessary that it be seasoned, that is, the moisture should be expelled and the more thoroughly this is done the less liable is the lumber to shrink or decay. The various methods may be classed as

1. Natural.
2. Artificial.

Natural seasoning consists in exposing the sawed lumber to the free circulation of air, the lumber being stacked in piles as shown in figs. 11 and 12.

Some authorities claim that immersion in water will, if it be done previous to drying, wash out the pores and prevent the tendency to again become wet, and limit the time of immersion to from three to four months. Immersion in hot water does this more rapidly, but impairs the strength of the timber. Immersion in salt water increases the weight and solidity of timber, but unfortunately renders it more subservient to becoming wet again, so that this would scarcely be a fit method for the wood worker. Experiments, however, have proven that timber set in water immediately after being felled and squared, is less subject to split and decay, and that it dries more quickly and completely. Immersion has the fault, too, of decreasing the strength of the timber.

Artificial seasoning is quite generally resorted to for quick drying but it should be understood that wood thus dried is quite inferior to that seasoned by the natural method.

NOTE—*Seasoning.*—Condensation by heat increases the hardness of timber; it is a popular notion that increasing the hardness also increases its durability. This is an error. The safest way to protect the wood is by an exterior substance, as paint.

NOTE—To deprive wood of its moisture, one writer says: "1st. different woods and different thicknesses require different degrees of heat. 2nd. hard woods and thick pieces require a moderate degree of heat, say from 90 to 100 degrees. 3rd. the softer woods, as pine, may be safely exposed to 120 degrees, or even a higher temperature; when cut very thin and well clamped 182 or 200 degrees has been found to harden the fibres and increase its strength. 4th. mahogany boards one inch thick may be subjected with advantage to 280 or 300 degrees. This will heighten its color, beauty of grain and strength. A piece of this wood (San Diego mahogany) was deprived wholly of its moisture, amounting to 36 per cent., by exposure to a temperature of 300 degrees for 50 hours."

There are some woods into which rapid kiln drying vulcanizes, so to speak, the outside fibre sealing the moisture latent within, which when acted upon by the air and sun, taken from the heat and exposed to dampness, the moisture again becomes fluid, resumes its tendency to ferment. This is the explanation why so much used material warps after manufacture.

In artificial seasoning the lumber is stacked in a drying kiln, and usually exposed to steam and hot air. Sometimes the heat is supplemented by the use of an air pump. It is common practice to steam the timber first, which reduces its tendency to warp; this however reduces its strength. If not steamed the ends of the boards should be clamped before kiln drying to prevent splitting and warping. The best temperature to be employed depends upon the dimensions of the lumber and varies from 100° Fahr. for oak to 200° for pine.

The time required depends upon the thickness of the stock.

Hard woods are usually dried in air from three to six months and then placed in the drying tank from six to ten days. Boiling timber in water has much the same effect as steaming but is costly and probably weakening in its effect.

NOTE—*Seasoning* by passing smoke laden products of combustion from the furnace through a stack of lumber has been found successful and has an important preservative effect. A modification of this, known as the *M'Neill process* consists in exposing the wood to a moderate heat in a moist atmosphere charged with the products of the combustion of fuel.

NOTE—Seasoning by immersion in water is a slow method that answers well for wood to be used in water or in damp situations. It reduces warping, but renders the wood brittle and less elastic. It is important that the submergence be total, as otherwise there is great danger of fungus attack along the water line. Two or three weeks' water seasoning is often a good preparation for air seasoning, and it must be remembered that foreign timbers have often had some weeks or months of such treatment while being transported by water to the port of shipment. It is important that wood seasoned in this way be thoroughly dried before use, otherwise dry rot will set in. In Mauritius, Ebony, which is perfectly sound when freshly cut, is immersed immediately for 6 to 18 months, and then on being taken out is secured at both ends of the logs with iron rings and wedges. Soaking timber or burying it under corn were methods of seasoning practiced by the ancient Romans, who also steeped wood in oil of cedar to protect it against worms.—*Boulger*.

NOTE—Salt water makes wood harder, heavier, and more durable; and the rules of Lloyd's add a year to the term of classification of a ship if she be "salted" during construction, that is, having her timbers packed with salt. Salt water cannot. however, be applied to any timber intended for use in ordinary buildings as it gives the wood a permanent tendency to attract moisture from the air. Boiling in oil is an effective and strengthening, but costly, method of seasoning, employed in making wooden teeth for mortise gears. The wood is roughed out in blocks little more than the size of the finished work, and the oil kept at a temberature not exceeding 250° F.—*Boulger*.

Kilns.—There are two kinds of kilns used in air drying:

1. Natural draught
2. Induced draught.

Due to the slow circulation of the air in natural draught kilns the air will become charged to a much greater degree with moisture than if forced rapidly through as in the induced draught kiln. It is for this reason claimed that with natural draught, the boards will dry out from their centers, and since the moist

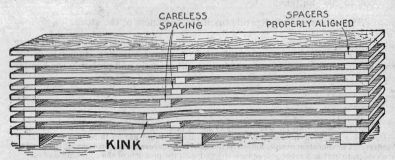

CARELESS SPACING   SPACERS PROPERLY ALIGNED

KINK

Fig. 13.—Placement of spacers in piling lumber. When the spacers are carelessly spaced so that they do not lie over each other, the weight must be supported by the board, which especially in the case of a high pile, is considerable and will in time cause the board to sag resulting in a permanent *kink*.

air keeps the outside of the boards moist, it will prevent case hardening.

In induced draught kilns, the air after passing over the lumber, and becoming charged with moisture circulates over cold condensing plates where it is relieved of its moisture, and after being reheated passes again over the lumber each time abstracting more moisture from the lumber. Since the cost of the blower and condensing equipment and operation of same is considerable, lumber to be dried in an induced draught kiln should first be well weather dried.

Selection of Lumber.—The selection of the kind and grade of wood to be used is always important. Consideration should be given to the prominence, character, location and strength of the wood needed for any work. It is possible at times to obtain just as satisfactory results with a very cheap low grade of wood as with an expensive high grade. Very often also a higher grade of a cheap wood can be used to better advantage than a lower grade of an expensive wood.

In general lumber is graded as follows:

Number 1.—This grade is practically perfect, though in large dimensions small blemishes may be allowed, restricted to one inch of sap, a small sound, or a small discoloration per board.

Number 2.—Two sound knots, an inch of sap and one other blemish are allowed.

Common boards.—This grade allows three or four sound knots per board but two-thirds of one side must be clear stock.

Culls.—This is the lowest grade. One-half of each board must be usable.

Knots, coarse grain and other defects may or may not reduce the strength of the timber, according to their location in the piece.

There is no objection to using a grade of lumber containing sound standard knots in work where stress is negligible, such as siding, trim, casing, partition, out-buildings, cabinets, closets, book-stalls, shelves, etc.

All sound knots should plane smooth, and in sound knotted woods, if all the knots be first coated with shellac and then the whole piece well painted with three or four coats of good paint, any appearance of knots will be obliterated, and the work in which they are placed will look as well, last as long and cost considerably less than if clear lumber be used.

Season checks in timber may or may not be a source of slight weakness, more injurious on the vertical than on the horizontal face of a stringer or joist, and their effect continues even after they have been closed up, as many do, and are no longer visible.

For framing where light stiff wood is wanted, the soft woods excel.   Also where heavy, steady loads are to be supported, yellow pine, spruce, etc., will answer as well as hard woods, which are costlier for the same amount of stiffness.

If small dimensions be desired, with moving loads or shocks to be encountered as in farm machinery, the hard woods should be used.   For engine bed foundations and the wearing and buffeting pieces in heavy construction work, oak, in most cases, is the best.   Heavy wood always surpasses in strength light wood of the same specie.

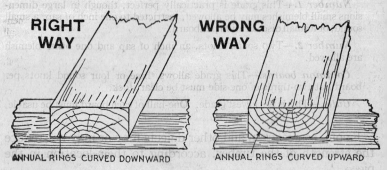

RIGHT WAY   **WRONG WAY**

ANNUAL RINGS CURVED DOWNWARD   ANNUAL RINGS CURVED UPWARD

FIGS. 14 and 15.—*Right* and *wrong* way to lay planks.   Regarding the annual rings as the more porous parts of the wood it must be evident that in the presence of water, any moisture entering the annual rings when they curve downward as in fig. 14, will tend to pass out through the lower side of the plank, whereas when they curve upward as in fig. 15, there is no outlet, hence they form moisture pockets which cause the wood to deteriorate more rapidly.

It should be noted that different kinds of wood may be used for the same purpose.

For example, the following are suitable for inside finish and trim and can be readily used: White pine, white wood, fir, cypress, chestnut, North Carolina pine and long leaf yellow pine.   For outside work, woods that are not easily affected by the weather should be used, such as white pine, cypress cedar, fir, spruce and long leaf yellow pine.   Spruce and long leaf yellow pine are not good woods for outside trim, etc., as spruce will show bad checks after being exposed for a short time, and yellow pine will not take a fine paint finish. However, both these woods are excellent for outside structural work, framing, etc., and both are strong and durable.

Cypress is undoubtedly a very good wood to use at the present time for trim, siding, etc., as it is more durable than most woods, and the price, grade for grade, is much lower than that of other wood suitable for outside finish.

Ordering Lumber.—Random widths should always be called for when ordering any kind of lumber, except white pine, yellow pine, North Carolina pine, cypress and spruce. Dealers stack the lumber in their yards in this way; consequently, if lumber of one width and one length is specified, it is necessary for the dealer to sort over many thousand feet of lumber to get the required widths and lengths, and very often he has to send the boards to a mill and have them ripped to get the widths wanted. Not only is the cost of handling and the mill work added to the price of the lumber, but the depreciation in value of the remainder of the lumber dealer's stock, together with the cost of any waste pieces made by ripping, which the buyer does not get, is also added. Therefore, unless a great many pieces of one size are to be used without cutting, specified sizes, other than those included in the respective grades, should not be called for.

As to cost, it should be noted that *wide boards cost more than narrow boards*, that is, one board $1'' \times 12'' \times 16'$ will cost more than two boards $1'' \times 6'' \times 16'$.

The standard lengths of lumber are multiples of 2 ft. running from 10 to 24 ft. for boards, fencing, joists, etc. Longer or shorter lengths are special. The standard widths are multiples of 1. All sizes 1 in. or less in thickness being counted in estimating cost as 1 inch thick.

Properties and Uses of Woods.—Certain kinds of wood are more desirable for some purposes than others, hence to properly select the kind of wood to use for a given job, the properties or characteristics of the various woods available should be known. These are briefly given in the accompanying list:

Properties of Woods

White Ash.—Heavy, hard, very elastic, coarse grained, and compact. Tendency to become decayed and brittle after a few years. Color, reddish-brown, with sap wood nearly white. Used for interior and cabinet work, but unfit for structural work.

Red Ash.—Heavy, compact, and coarse grained but brittle. Color, rich brown, with sap wood a light brown sometimes streaked with yellow. Used as a substitute for the more valuable white ash.

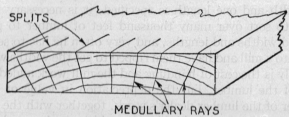

SPLITS

MEDULLARY RAYS

Fig. 16.—Board with splits along the medullary rays, this condition being known as *honeycombed*. It is caused by too rapid kiln drying. Previous natural drying or steaming will prevent this.

Green Ash.—Heavy, hard and coarse grained, brittle. Color, brown, with lighter sapwood. Used as a substitute for white ash.

Balsa.—Extremely light, about half the strength of white pine. Appearance like poplar. Used for heat insulation and, when water proofed, for life preservers.

White Cedar.—Soft, light, fine grained, and very durable in contact with the soil; lacks strength and toughness. Color, light brown, darkening with exposure. Sap wood very thin and nearly white. Used for water tanks, shingles, posts, fencing, cooperage, and boat building.

Red Cedar.—Strong pungent odor repellant to insects. Very durable and compact, but easily worked and brittle. Color, dull brown tinged with red. Used as posts, sills, ties, fencing, shingles and lining for chests, trunks and closers.

Chestnut.—Light, moderately soft, stiff, and, of coarse texture. Shrinks and checks considerably in drying; works easily. Durable when exposed to weather. Color, heart wood dark and sap wood light brown. Used for cabinet work, cooperage, railway ties, telegraph poles, and exposed heavy construction.

Cypress.—One of the most durable of woods, light, hard, close grained but brittle. Easily worked, polishes highly and gives a satiny gloss. Color, bright clear yellow with nearly white sap wood. Used for interior finish and cabinet work, but used as extensively in the South as pine is in the North.

White Elm.—Heavy, hard, strong and tough and very close grained. Difficult to split and shape, but warps badly in drying. Capable of high polish. Color, light clear brown often tinged with red and gray, with broad whitish sapwood. Used for car, wagon, boat, and ship building, bridge timbers, sills and ties, and furniture, also barrel staves.

Greenheart.—Very heavy, strong, durable heart wood, dark green to dark chestnut. Color, free from knots. Used for ship building, docks, implements, rollers.

Gum.—Heavy, hard, tough, compact and close grained. Tendency to shrink and warp badly in seasoning. Not durable if exposed. Takes high polish. Color, bright brown tinged with red. Used in the manufacture of furniture, wagon hubs, hat blocks.

Hickory.—Medullary rays very numerous and distinct. Heaviest, hardest, toughest, and strongest of American woods. Very flexible. Color, brown, with very thin but valuable sap wood nearly white. Used for carriages, sleighs, handles, and bent wood implements. Unfit for building material because of extreme hardness and liability to attack of boring insects.

Hemlock.—Brittle, splits easily and likely to be shaky. Soft, light, not durable, with coarse and uneven grain. Color, light brown tinged with red and often nearly white. Used for cheap rough framing timber.

Locust.—Heavy, hard, strong and close-grained. Very durable in contact with ground. Hardness increased with age. Color, brown and rarely light green, with yellow sapwood. Used for posts and turned ornaments.

Lignum Vitae.—Exceedingly heavy, hard, resinous, difficult to split and work, and has a soapy feeling. Color, rich yellow brown varying to almost black. Used for small turned articles, tool handles, and sheaves of block pulleys.

Hard Maple.—Heavy, hard, strong, tough, and close-grained. Medullary raks small but distinct. Curly and circular inflexion of fibers gives rise to "curly maple" and "bird's eye maple." Susceptible of good polish. Color, very light brown to yellow. Used for flooring, interior finish, and furniture.

White Maple.—Fine grained, hard, strong and heavy. Characteristics of grain the same as hard maple and more marked. Light colored. Used for flooring and furniture.

Mahogany.—Strong, durable, and flexible when green, but brittle whe dry. Free from shakes and less liable to attacks of dry rot and worm Rapid seasoning causes deep shakes. Color, red brown or various shad and degrees of brightness, often varied and mottled. Inferior qualiti contain large numbers of gray specks. Used for interior finish, hand rails patterns, etc.

White Oak.—Heavy, strong, hard, tough, and close grained. Checks if not carefully seasoned. Well known silver grain and capable of receiving high polish. Color, brown, with lighter sap wood. Used for framed structures, ship building, interior finish, carriage and furniture making.

Chestnut Oak.—Very durable in contact with soil. Color, dark brown. Used for railroad ties.

Live Oak.—Very heavy, hard, tough, and strong. Difficult to work. Color, light brown or yellow, with sap wood nearly white.

Red and Black Oak.—More porous than white oak and softer. Color, darker and redder than white oak. Used for interior finish and furniture.

Palmetto.—Light but difficult to work when dry. Very durable under water and less subject to attacks of teredo. Color, light brown, with dark colored fibers. Used for wharf piles, canes and handles.

White Pine.—Light, soft and straight grained and easily worked, but not very strong. Color, light yellowish brown often slightly tinged with red. Used for interior finish and pattern making.

Red Pine. (*Norway Pine.*)—Light, hard, coarse grained, compact, with few resin pockets. Color, light red, with a yellow or white sap wood. Used for all purposes of construction.

Yellow Pine. (*Long Leaf.*)—Heavy, hard, strong, coarse grained and very durable when dry and well ventilated. Cells are dark colored and very resinous. Color, light yellowish red or orange. Cannot be used in contact with ground. Used for heavy framing timbers and floors. As house sills, sleepers, or posts it rapidly decays.

Yellow Pine. (*Short Leaf Pine.*)—Varies greatly in amount of sap and quality. Cells broad and resinous, with numerous large resin ducts. Medullary rays well marked. Color, orange, with white sap wood. Used as a substitute for long leaf pine.

Oregon Pine. (*Douglas Fir.*)—Hard, strong, varying greatly with age, conditions of growth and amount of sap. Durable but difficult to work. Of two varieties, red and yellow, of which yellow is the more valuable. Color, light red to yellow, with white sap wood. Used in all kinds of construction.

Poplar. (*White wood.*)—Soft, very close and straight grained, but brittle and shrinks excessively in drying. Warps and twists exceedingly, but when dry will not split. Easily worked. Color, light yellow to white. Used in carpentry and joinery.

Redwood. (*California.*)—Light, soft, coarse grained, and easily worked. Durable in contact with soil but brittle. "Shrinks lengthwise as well as crosswise." Color, dull red, resembling pine. Used for railroad ties, fence posts, telegraph poles, and general building material.

Alaska Spruce. (*Sitka Spruce.*)—Light, soft, medium strength. Heart wood, light, reddish brown; sap wood white, trees very large. Used for general structural purposes, also for air plane frame work.

NOTE—*Pine*—In the selection of pine, it is considered under two classes: *soft* and *hard*, although it grows in many varieties throughout the U. S. The white pine or softer varieties are used for all kinds of outside finishing lumber. Of the 10 different varieties of hard pine only five are of practical importance to the builder and that most generally used we speak of, *Georgia Pine.* White is most popular in the market. It is light, soft and fairly strong and whitish in color, is stronger than hemlock and is much used for framing when the sizes in which it can be had meet the requirements. It is also used for flooring, and sometimes for other interior finish when a very light natural wood finish is required or to mix with darker woods. Commonly called yellow pine. This is the heavier, and Carolina pine which is lighter. The trees grow very large enabling large timber for massive structural work. They are also both used for interior finish lumber where natural finish is required. Especially for flooring, ceilings and dados.

NOTE—*In ordering pine lumber*, great care is necessary to make sure that the purchaser and seller have the same wood in mind when they apply a particular name to it. White pine, soft pine, and pumpkin pine are terms used in the Eastern States for the timber taken from the white pine tree, while on the Pacific coast the same terms refer to the timber of the sugar pine. The name yellow pine when used in the East is generally applied to the pitch or southern pines, but in the West it refers to the bull pine. Georgia pine or long leaf pine is a term applied to the southern hard pine which grows in the coast region from North Carolina to Texas and which furnishes the strongest pine lumber on that market. Pitch pine may refer to any of the southern pines or to pitch pine proper, which is found along the coast from New York to Georgia and in the mountains of Kentucky.

Red Spruce —Light, soft, close and straight grained and satiny. Color, light red and often nearly white. Used for piles, lumber, and framing timber, submerged cribs and cofferdams, as it well resists decay and the destructive action of crustacea.

White Spruce.—Similar to black variety, but not so common. Color, light yellow, sap wood indistinct. Used as lumber for construction.

Tamarack. (*Larch.*)—Wood like pine in appearance, quality and uses. Used for telegraph poles, railway ties and in ship building.

White Walnut. (*Butternut.*)—Light, soft, coarse grained, compact, and easily worked. Polishes well. Color, light brown, turning dark on exposure. Used for interior finish.

Black Walnut.—Heavy, hard, strong and checks if not carefully seasoned. Coarse grained but easily worked. Color, rich dark brown with light sapwood. Used for interior finish and cabinet work.

Preserving Methods.—It is said that the average life of timber used in the United States and subject to decay is eight years. The first essential to successful preservation is good seasoning. The various preservation processes may be divided into two general methods:

1. External
2. Internal.

That is, the wood may be treated with a preservative coating (as paint) which will penetrate the fibres, or it may be impregnated by some chemical compound at a pressure sufficient to

NOTE—*Best time for cutting timber.* The time of felling has to do with how well wood seasons, and the time or season for felling depends upon the tree's genus. Generally winter or summer is best for then they contain less sap. For all but the resinous woods winter is the best time, except trees from which the bark is to be taken such as oak, then, of course, the spring is better, for the more sap there is in the tree the easier it is to remove the bark.

NOTE—*To distinguish kiln dried from natural dried lumber.* Take a piece of the lumber and saw across the grain. If kiln tried, especially if the process has been hurried by induced draught drying, the core will be moist and the sawdust will pack, and the end will have the appearance of steel case hardened on the surface. If thoroughly dried by natural seasoning the sawdust will be light and fluffy and will readily fall from the cut during the sawing operation

cause it to permeate the wood thoroughly. This latter treatment enables the wood to resist better the elements and to keep away insects.

Some of the numerous methods are here given:

Allardyce Process.—This treatment consists in impregnating the timber with a 2% zinc chloride solution followed by an injection of about 3 lbs. of creosote oil per cubic ft. of wood. The Card treatment injects both elements in the one treatment.

Lowery Process.—Selected air seasoned timber of same species and density is run into the retort on cars, but no compressed air is used. The cylinder is filled from the charging tank with creosote oil at a temperature of 200° F., and pressure is applied until the timber takes up oil to a predetermined amount. The pressure is then released and the oil drained off and a strong quick vacuum is substituted to recover the free oil.

Bethel Process.—The green or partially seasoned timber on buggies is run into metal cylinders 8 to 9 ft. in diameter and 150 ft. long and the doors or heads bolted. The charge is then subjected to live steam raised to 20 lbs. per sq. in. in 30 to 50 minutes and maintained at this pressure from 1 to 5 hours. A vacuum of 18 to 26 in. is then created and maintained for at least ½ hour, when creosote oil is introduced at a temperature of about 160° F. A pressure of 150 to 200 lbs. per sq. in. is then applied until the timber has absorbed about 5 lbs. of oil per cu. ft.

Burnett Process.—This method of treatment is essentially the same as that previously described, except that zinc chloride is used as the preservative.

Card Process.—In this treatment, patented by J. P. Card in March, 1906, the timber is thoroughly air seasoned and run into the retorts, where it is subjected to a vacuum of 22 to 26 ins. for one hour. The liquid solution, consisting of an emulsion of chloride of zinc with 20% of creosote oil, is then introduced into the tanks at a temperature of 180° and under a pressure of 125 lbs. per sq. in., maintained from 3 to 5 hours.

Non-Pressure Processes.—Preservatives of a penetrating nature, as tar oils, carbolineum, spirittine, etc., may be applied to the outside of wood either by spraying, by brush application, or by immersion in an open tank. The wood must be absolutely dry and seasoned so as to absorb a sufficient quantity of the preservative. All tar oil products should preferably be applied hot. Alternate hot and cold baths are occasionally employed. The timber, first peeled and thoroughly seasoned, is immersed in the preservative at about 200° F. for 5 to 6 hours, to drive off all the moisture.

Kyan's Process.—The timber is steeped in a solution of corrosive sublimate, 1 part of bichloride of mercury to 99 parts of water for a period (at least 5 to 10 days) sufficient to insure thorough penetration of the preservative. Sublimate is comparatively insoluble in water and remains in timber for a longer time than salts like zinc chloride.

Decay of Lumber.—The life of timber depends upon the methods employed in felling, seasoning and working. It is claimed that hewed lumber is more durable than sawed lumber because the hewing process closes the cells and prevents the absorption of moisture. There are numerous causes for the decay of wood, such as

1. Alternate moisture and dryness
2. Bacteria and fungi.
3. Insects and worms
4. Heat and confined air

Timber kept constantly immersed may soften and weaken but will not decay; oak, birch, elm and elder in this condition possess great durability. Well seasoned wood in a uniform state of moisture or dryness and well ventilated should never decay.

The two forms of decay in timber are *dry rot* and *wet rot.*

The cause of dry rot is fungus growth, and this takes place most readily when the wood is subjected to alternate moisture and dryness.

Wet rot sometimes takes place in a growing tree, caused by the tree becoming saturated with water as when located in a bog or swamp.

Modified Forms of Wood

Many new so called modified classes of wood have been developed in recent years. The principal objective has been to make of wood a material less subject to dimensional changes, such as are caused by shrinking and swelling with changes in moisture content, and to obtain a material with more uniform strength properties in all directions. A great deal of research has also been devoted to finding ways of utilizing sawdust shavings and other waste products of the woodworking industries.

The resultant products range from *plywoods* surfaced with special plastic materials to *wood fiber boards* made by very much the same pulping processes as are used in the paper industry and compressed in presses to the desired density.

Laminated Wood.—Laminated wood may be defined as wood built up of plies or laminations that have been joined together either with glue or mechanical fastenings. The term is most frequently applied where the laminations are too thick to be classified as veneer and when the grain of all laminations are generally parallel. Members made of laminated wood may be used with the width of the laminations either vertical or horizontal.

Plywood.—Plain plywood is usually made of an *odd number of thin plies* (veneers) glued together so that the grain of each ply is at right angles to that of the adjacent ply or plies. In three-ply plywood, the outside plies are termed "faces" or "face and back" and the center ply is the "core."

In the panels with five plies, the center ply is the core, and the inner plies (the grain of which is usually at right angles to the faces and the core) are called *cross-bands*. For plywood used in home construction, the veneer usually ranges from $\frac{1}{16}$ to $\frac{3}{16}$ inch in thickness.

The chief advantage of plywood as compared with solid wood are its more nearly equal strength properties along the length and width of the panel, greater resistance to checking and splitting, very small changes in width and length with the change in moisture content, and the fact that it can be produced in much wider sizes than solid wood.

The principle of plywood construction lends itself to many unusual combinations of wood. Flooring panels of considerable size are sometimes made, using relatively inferior grades of wood for the body of the panel, to which an excellent floor surface is bonded consisting of birch veneer or veneers of other hard species of wood, as well as vertical grain Douglas-fir, in thicknesses of one-eighth inch or more. The purpose is to provide a floor with better wearing qualities than rotary-cut veneer offers.

A special type of Douglas-fir wall paneling material has recently been made from plywood that has a face of somewhat thicker veneer than the back. This face is scored to a depth of about one-sixteenth inch with many close grooves, oriented so as to run parallel to the grain direction of the face ply. This plywood is used on exterior walls with the scoring running vertically, either in full sized panels or in strip form applied as lap siding. It is also being used for interior walls. The scoring is said to be effective in breaking up the rather pronounced grain pattern of the Douglas-fir, in making the small face checks that sometimes occur on Douglas-fir less noticeable, and in making any dirt pattern that might develop less evident.

Resin-impregnated Paper-faced Plywood.—Several types of plywood faced with resin impregnated paper have been produced in recent years. The face material used on these panels generally consists of one or more sheets of paper impregnated with 25 to 50 per cent of thermosetting, phenolic-type resin. The paper plastic material, when properly molded to the surface of the plywood, forms an integral part of the panel and cannot be peeled off.

One such type of faced paneling consists of Douglas-fir plywood faced with a dark brown paper plastic that gives it the appearance of a hardboard panel. The purpose of the facing material is to prevent surface checking of the plywood, to mask the grain of the wood, and to provide a readily paintable surface.

Another type of faced panel consists of Douglas-fir faced with a dense, brittle paper plastic, the chief quality of which is its high resistance to the passage of moisture. It also provides a smooth, abrasion-resistant surface on the wood. A variety of dark colors is possible. Panels of this type have found uses as drainboards and table tops. Hardwood plywood panels faced with this type of paper plastic have also been produced in limited quantities for use where such special properties as low water absorption and abrasion resistance are useful.

Wood-fiber Board Materials.—Various types of fibrous board materials have in recent years come into increasing use in housing. While their primary purpose in most cases has been to provide thermal insulation, some of these have gained a place in low cost housing as semi-structural or curtain-wall materials in interior partitions and ceilings. A few have been demonstrated to be suitable for exterior wall covers from the standpoint of durability under outdoor exposure. Some pre-fabricators make extensive use of these products.

In general, four types of fibrous materials are manufactured, *rigid boards*, *semi-rigid sheets*, *flexible mats*, and *fill-type insu-lation*. Of these, only the rigid boards generally are used in themselves for structural purposes. Some semi-rigid types, however, are finding structural application when used as the core material in a sandwich type of product with stiff faces. The flexible mats and fill-type materials are used only for insulation.

Rigid Boards.—Besides wood fiber, rigid board materials are made from *waste paper*, *cork*, *bagasse*, *wheat straw*, *corn stalks* and *screenings* from paper mills. Their manufacture closely resembles that of paper. The wood fibers used for paper are also used for production of these boards. The wood chips are softened by mild chemical treatment or steaming under pressure and fiberized in attrition mills, or the untreated wood in the form of short logs or blocks is mechanically reduced to a fibrous condition in pulpwood grinders.

These fibers, in a water suspension, are then run over a paper machine and reduced to a wet mat. This mat is compressed under rollers or in a hydraulic press and then finally dried in a dryer similar to those used to dry veneer. Depending upon the pressure exerted upon it by the press, a hard, smooth board with varying porosity is produced.

Rigid boards produced in this manner are known as homoge-neous boards. Other types of rigid boards are of laminated construction, either several thin homogeneous boards pressed or glued together, or many sheets of paper laminated to form a board three-sixteenths inch thick or thicker. They are made in panels ranging in size from 4 by 6 feet to 12 by 12 feet.

Other Fiber Materials.—The semi-rigid boards and flexible sheet materials are prepared in the fibrous condition in much the same way as the rigid boards. The flexible materials usually consist of a loosely aggregated mat covered on both sides with paper or fabric. The raw materials used in their manufacture include *wood fibers*, *hair*, *grass*, *kapok* or mineral substance. Flexible insulators are usually called *"blanket"* or *"batt"* types of insulation.

Fill insulation consists of granulated shredded or powdered material either in bulk or in the form of batts. Various materials are used, including *shredded vegetable fiber*, *gypsum*, *limestone* or other *rock*, *slag*, *charcoal*, *bark*, *sawdust*, *shavings*, *grain hulls*, *shredded paper*, and *diatomaceous earth*.

Wood-base Plastics.—The word *"plastic"* has in recent years become a broad, generic term including many kinds of materials that can under certain conditions be molded to desired shapes. Under this loose definition, wood itself is a plastic material, since it can be softened by hot water or steam to a certain degree of moldability. True plastics, however, are in general materials that can, at some stage of their production, be pressed to given shapes without acquiring stresses that remain in the finished product and affect its strength or stability of form.

The most common plastics available today consist of *synthetic resins* with or without some filler material such as *wood flour*. Other widely used plastics are *cellulose derivatives*, such as *cellulose nitrate* and *acetate*, which are largely made from *wood pulp*. Common examples of such plastics are tool handles of various sorts, automobile steering wheels, washing machine agitators and toys. Their nature, properties, and above all their cost, do not lend them to wide utility as housing materials.

Among materials that hold promise of ultimate usefulness in housing, although at present still in the experimental stage of their development, are a number of wood base laminates (modified woods and paper base laminates) that because of their improved moldability, fall within the broad category of plastics. Among these are such non-proprietary products as *impreg, compreg, staypak, staybwood, acetylated wood, papreg,* and various commercial densified stabilized and resin-treated products.

CHAPTER 2

Nails

Early Attempts at Nail Making.—Up to the end of the Colonial period, all nails used in the United States were hand made.

They were forged on an anvil from nail rods which were sold in bundles. These nail rods were prepared either by rolling the malleable iron into small bars of the required thickness, or by the much more common practice of cutting plate iron into strips by means of rolling shears.

Just before the war of the Revolution, the making of nails from these rods was a household industry among the New England farmers. The struggle of the Colonies for independence intensified inventive search after short cuts to mass production of material entering directly or indirectly into the prosecution of the war; thus came about the innovation of cut nails made by machinery. With its coming the household industry of nail making rapidly declined. At the close of the 18th century 23 patents for nail making machines had been granted in the United States and their use had been generally introduced into England, where they were received with enthusiasm.

In France, light nails for carpenter's use were made of wire as early as in the days of Napoleon I, but they were made by hand with a hammer. The hand made nail was pinched in a vise with a portion projecting. A few blows of a hammer

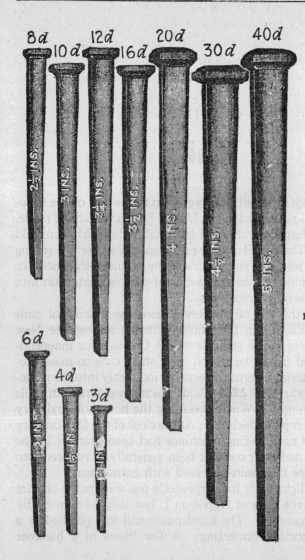

FIGS. 17 to 26.—*Cut nails* showing *actual sizes*, Cut nails have considerably greater holding power than wire nails. Cut nails made from iron are generally preferred for use in exposed positions. There are three regular shapes of cut nails known as 1, common, 2. finish, and 3, casing. The common nails are used for rough work; finish nails for finished work, and casing nails for flooring, matched ceiling and sometimes for pine casings, although the

flattened one end into a head. The head was beaten into a counter sunk in the vise, thus regulating its size and shape.

In the United States wire nails were first made in 1851 or 1852 by William Hersel of New York.

In 1875 Father Goebel, a Catholic priest, arrived from Germany and settled in Covington, Ky., and began the manufacture of wire nails which he had learned in his native land. In 1876 the American Wire and Screw Nail Co. was formed under Father Goebel's leadership. As the production and consumption of wire nails increased, the vogue of cut nails which dominated the market until 1886 declined.

The approved process of the earlier days of the cut nail industry was as follows: Iron bars, rolled from hematite or magnetic pig were faggotted, that is piled so as to break joints, reheated to a white heat, drawn, paned through a nail plate train and the sheets of the required width and thickness allowed to cool. The sheet was then cut across its length (its width being usually about a foot) into strips a little wider than the length of the required nail. These plates heated by being set on their edge on hot coals, were seized in a clamp and fed to the machine, end first. The pieces cut out, slightly tapering, were squeezed and headed up by the machine before going into the trough.

The manufacture of tacks frequently combined with that of nails, is, for all that, a distinct branch of the nail industry, affording much room for specialties. Originally it was also a household industry carried on in New England well into the 18th century. The wire pointed on a small anvil, they placed in a vise worked by the foot, which clutched it between jaws

heads are rather too large for finish work. Although the wire nail is the prevailing type, cut nails are beginning to return to favor because of their superior holding and lasting qualities.

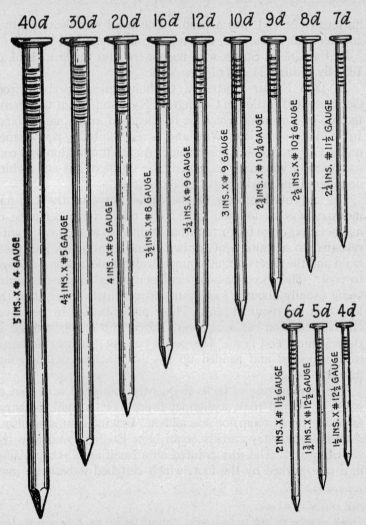

40d

30d

20d

16d

12d

10d

9d

8d

7d

5 INS. X # 4 GAUGE

4½ INS. X # 5 GAUGE

4 INS. X # 6 GAUGE

3½ INS. X # 8 GAUGE

3¼ INS. X # 9 GAUGE

3 INS. X # 9 GAUGE

2¾ INS. X # 10¼ GAUGE

2½ INS. X # 10¼ GAUGE

2¼ INS. X # 11½ GAUGE

6d

5d

4d

2 INS. X # 11½ GAUGE

1¾ INS. X # 12½ GAUGE

1½ INS. X # 12½ GAUGE

Figs. 27 to 38 —*Common wire nails:* the standard nail for general use. Regularly made in sizes from 1 in. (2d) to 6 ins. (60d)

furnished with a gauge to regulate the length. A certain portion was left projecting, which was beaten by a hammer into a flat head. For many years Taunton, Mass., was the centre of the tack industry.

Antique pieces of furniture are frequently held together with iron nails driven in and countersunk holding very firmly. These old time nails were made of wrought iron, four square and tapered something like a brad, but with a head which, when driven in, held with great firmness.

Modern Methods.—The raw material of the modern wire nail factory is hand drawn wire in bundles, just as it comes from the wire drawing block. The stock is low carbon Bessemer or basic open hearth steel, stiffened by drawing two to five drafts from the rod, or, in small gauge, from the last annealing point. The wire, feeding from a loose reel passes between straightening rolls into the gripping dies where it is gripped a short distance from its end and the nail head formed, by an upsetting blow from a heading tool. As the header withdraws, the gripping dies slack up and the straightener carriage pushes the wire forward the length of the nail. The cutting dies advance from the sides of the frame and clip off the nail, at the same time forming its characteristic chisel point. The gripping dies have already seized the wire again and an ejector flips the nail out of the way just as the header comes forward and heads the next nail. All these motions are induced by cams and eccentrics on the main shaft of the machine and the speed of production is at the rate of 150 to 500 complete cycles per minute. At this stage the nails are covered with a film of drawing lubricant and oil from the nail machine and their points are frequently adorned with whiskers—a name applied to the small diamond shaped pieces stamped out when the point is formed—which are occasionally encountered on the finished nail by the customer.

Cut Steel Nails and Spikes

Approximate Number Per Pound

(According to the Hand Book of the Cambria Steel Co.)

Sizes	Length, inches	Common	Clinch	Finishing	Casing and box	Fencing	Spikes
2d	1	740	400	1 100	....	....	....
3d	1¼	460	260	880	....	....	....
4d	1½	280	180	530	420	....	....
5d	1¾	210	125	350	300	100	....
6d	2	160	100	300	210	80	....
7d	2¼	120	80	210	180	60	....
8d	2½	88	68	168	130	52	....
9d	2¾	73	52	130	107	38	....
10d	3	60	48	104	88	26	....
12d	3¼	46	40	96	70	20	....
16d	3½	33	34	86	52	18	17
20d	4	23	24	76	38	16	14
25d	4¼	20	....	....	....	....	....
30d	4½	16½	....	....	30	....	11
40d	5	12	....	....	26	....	9
50d	5½	10	....	....	20	....	7½
60d	6	8	....	....	16	....	6
......	6½	....	....	....	....	....	5½
......	7	....	....	....	....	....	5

Sizes	Length, inches	Barrel	Light barrel	Slating	Sizes	Length, inches	Flat grip, fine	Edge-grip, fine
....	⅝	750	....	....	......	¾	1 462	......
....	¾	600	....	....	......	⅞	1 300	......
....	⅞	500	....	....	2d	1	1 100	960
2d	1	450	....	340	3d	1⅛	800	750
....	1⅛	310	400	....	4d	1⅜	650	600
3d	1¼	280	304	280				
....	1⅜	210	....	....	Tobacco		Brads	Shingle
4d	1½	190	224	220				
5d	1¾	....	....	180	130		......	......
6d	2	....	....	....	97		120	......
7d	2¼	....	....	....	85		94	......
8d	2½	....	....	....	68		74	90
9d	2¾	....	....	....	58		62	72
10d	3	....	....	....	48		50	60
12d	3¼	....	....	....	....		40	......
16d	3½	....	....	....	....		27	......

These oily nails in lots of 500 to 5,000 lbs. are shaken up with sawdust in tumbling barrels from which they emerge bright and clean and freed of their whiskers, ready for weighing, packing and shipping.

The "Penny" System.—This method of designating nails originated in England. Two explanations are offered as to how this curious designation came about.

One is that the six penny, four penny ten penny, etc., nails derived their names from the fact that one hundred cost six pence, four pence, etc.

The other explanation, which is the more probable, is that one thousand ten penny nails, for instance, weighed ten pounds. The ancient as well as modern abbreviation for penny is *d*, being the first letter of the Roman coin denarius; the same abbreviation in early history was used for the English pound in weigh. The word *penny* has persisted as a term in the nail industry.

Kinds of Nails.—There is a great variety of nails, to meet the needs of all kinds of construction. They may be classed

1. With respect to cross sectional shape, as:

    a. Cut (rectangular)
    b. Wire (circular)

NOTE.—*How nails were named.* Several accounts are given to the origin of the terms "six penny," "eight penny," "ten penny," etc.; as applied to the various sizes of the old fashioned nails. According to one statement, when nails were made by hand, the penny was taken as a standard of weight, and six were made to equal the weight of a copper penny. Another explanation is that "ten penny" nails originally sold for ten pence a hundred, "six penny" nails for six pence a hundred, and so on. Of the ordinary "six penny" nails there are 80 to the lb.; of the "eight penny," 50; of the "ten penny," 44; and of the "twelve penny," 39 to the lb.—*The Irish Ironmonger.*

2. With respect to size (broadly speaking), as:

    a. Tacks
    b. Sprigs
    c. Brads
    d. Nails
    e. Spikes $\begin{cases} \text{ordinary} \\ \text{barge} \end{cases}$

3. With respect to material, as:

    a. Steel
    b. Brass
    c. Copper

4. With respect to finish, as:

    a. Plain $\begin{cases} \text{smooth} \\ \text{barbed} \end{cases}$
    b. Coated $\begin{cases} \text{cement} \\ \text{sterilized} \end{cases}$
    c. Galvanized
    d. Blued

5. With respect to service, as:

    a. Common
    b. Flooring
    c. Finishing
    d. Roofing
    e. Boat

Etc., etc.

Formerly cut nails were universally used, but today the wire nail is the prevailing form. However, cut nails are beginning to return to favor as they have holding power superior to wire nails and are more durable.

2. With respect to sizes of nails in general, the following definitions should be noted:

Tacks.—*Small sharp pointed nails, commonly with tapering sides and a thin flat head;* used chiefly in fastening down carpets. The regular length of tacks are from ⅛ to 1⅛ ins. The regular sizes are designated in ounces according to the following table:

Wire Tacks

Size Ozs.	Length Ins.	No. per Lb.	Size Ozs.	Length Ins.	No. per Lb.	Size Ozs.	Length Ins.	No. per Lb.
1	⅛	16,000	4	⁷⁄₁₆	4,000	14	¹³⁄₁₆	1,143
1½	³⁄₁₆	10,666	6	⁹⁄₁₆	2,666	16	⅞	1,000
2	¼	8,000	8	⅝	2,000	18	¹⁵⁄₁₆	888
2½	⁵⁄₁₆	6,400	10	¹¹⁄₁₆	4,600	20	1	800
3	⅜	5,333	12	¾	1,333	22	1¹⁄₁₆	727
...		....	..	..	....	24	1⅛	666

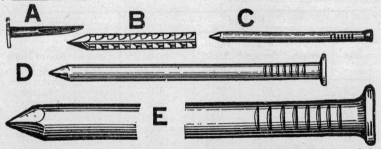

FIGS. 39 to 42.—Various nails grouped according to popular notion as to size in general; **A,** tack; **B,** sprig or dowel pin; **C,** brad; **D,** "nail"; **E,** spike.

NOTE.—*Cut versus wire nails.* Experiments were made at the Watertown Arsenal in 1893 on the comparative direct tensile adhesion, in pine and spruce, of cut and wire nails. The results are stated by Prof. W. H. Burr as follows: "There were 58 series of tests, ten pairs of nails (a cut and a wire nail in each) being used. The tests were made in spruce wood in most instances. The nails were of all sizes, from 1⅛ to 6 in. in length. In every case the cut nails showed the superior holding strength by a large percentage. In spruce, in nine different sizes of nails, both standard and light weight, the ratio of tenacity of cut to wire nail was about 3 to 2. With the 'finishing' nails the ratio was roughly 3.5 to 2. With box nails (1¼ to 4 inches long) the ratio was roughly 3 to 2. The mean superiority in spruce wood was 61%. In white pine, cut nails, driven with taper along the grain, showed a superiority of 100% and with taper across the grain of 135%. Also when the nails were driven in the end of the stick, *i.e.* along the grain, the superiority of cut nails was 100% or the ratio of cut to wire was 2 to 1. The total of the results showed the ratio of tenacity to be about 3.2 to 2 for the harder wood, and about 2 to 1 for the softer. and for the whole taken together. the ratio was 3.5 to 2."

Sprigs.—The name *sprig* is sometimes given to *a small headless nail;* usually called *barbed dowel pin.* Sprigs are made regularly in sizes ½ to 2 ins.; No. 8 steel wire gauge or .162 in. diameter.

Brads.—*Small slender nails with small deep heads;* sometimes having instead of a head, a projection on one side. There are several varieties adapted to varied requirements. Although brads are generally thought of

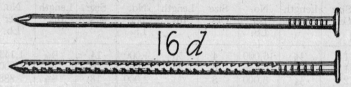

FIGS. 43 and 44.—Smooth and barbed box nails 16d size (full size). *Note* sharp point and thir flat head.

Common Brads

	PLAIN				COATED	
Size	Length Ins.	Gauge No.	Diam. Head Gauge	Approximate No. to Lb.	Gauge No.	No. of Nails in Keg
2d	1	15	12	876	6	82,400
3d	1¼	14	11	568	5	53,000
4d	1½	12½	9½	316	3½	30,000
5d	1¾	12½	9½	271	3½	26,100
6d	2	11½	8½	181	2½	17,200
7d	2¼	11½	8½	161	2½	15,500
8d	2½	10¼	7	106	11	9,400
9d	2¾	10¼	7	96	11	8,500
10d	3	9	6	69	10	6,250
12d	3¼	9	6	64	10	5,600
16d	3½	8	5	49	9	4,200
20d	4	6	3	31	7	2,625
30d	4½	5	2	24	6	2,040
40d	5	4	1	18	5	1,540
50d	5½	3	0	16	4	1,190
60d	6	2	00	11	3	910

Net weight of coated common brads per keg 70 lbs.

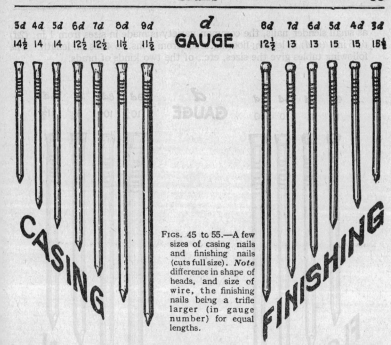

3d 4d 5d 6d 7d 8d 9d
14½ 14 14 12½ 12½ 11½ 11½

d
GAUGE

8d 7d 6d 5d 4d 3d
12½ 13 13 15 15 15½

CASING

FINISHING

FIGS. 45 to 55.—A few sizes of casing nails and finishing nails (cuts full size). *Note* difference in shape of heads, and size of wire, the finishing nails being a trifle larger (in gauge number) for equal lengths.

Flooring Brads

Size	Length Ins.	Gauge No.	Diam. Head Gauge	Approximate No. to Lb.	Gauge No.	No. of Nails in Keg
		PLAIN			COATED	
6d	2	11	6	157	12	14,500
7d	2¼	11	6	139	12	12,500
8d	2½	10	5	99	11	9,000
9d	2¾	10	5	90	11	7,800
10d	3	9	4	69	10	5,900
12d	3¼	8	3	54	9	4,300
16d	3½	7	2	43	8	3,450
20d	4	6	1	31	7	2,600

Net weight of coated flooring brads per keg 70 lbs.

as small slender nails, the common variety is made in sizes from 1 in. (2*d*) to 6 ins. (60*d*) in length; flooring brads from 2 ins. to 4 ins. in length. The following tables give the sizes, etc., of the two kinds of brads:

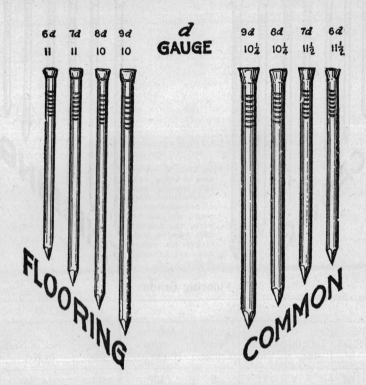

FIGS. 56 to 63.—A few sizes of flooring and common brads (cuts full size). *Note* difference in shape of heads and variations in gauge numbers for equal sizes.

Nails.—The term "nails" as popularly applied to *all kinds of nails except extreme sizes* such as tacks (small) brads, and spikes. Broadly speaking, however, it includes all of these. The most generally used are called *common nails*, and are regularly made in sizes from 1 in. (2*d*) to 6 in. (60*d*) according to the following table:

Common Nails

	PLAIN			COATED			
Size	Length Ins.	Gauge No.	Approximate No. to Lb.	Length Ins.	Gauge No.	No. of Nails in Keg	Net Wgt. Lbs.
2*d*	1	15	876	1	16	85,700	79
3*d*	1¼	14	568	1⅛	15½	54,300	64
4*d*	1½	12½	316	1⅜	14	29,800	61
5*d*	1¾	12½	271	1⅝	13½	25,500	70
6*d*	2	11½	181	1 /8	13	17,900	65
7*d*	2¼	11½	161	2⅛	12½	15,300	72
8*d*	2½	10¼	106	2⅜	11½	10,100	71
9*d*	2¾	10¼	96	2⅝	11½	8,900	68
10*d*	3	9	69	2⅞	11	6,600	63
12*d*	3¼	9	63	3⅛	10	6,200	80
16*d*	3½	8	49	3¼	9	4,900	80
20*d*	4	6	31	3¾	7	3,100	83
30*d*	4½	5	24	4¼	6	2,400	84
40*d*	5	4	18	4¾	5	1,800	82
50*d*	5½	3	14	5¼	4	1,300	79
60*d*	6	2	11	5¾	3	1,100	82

The count for coated common nails is the same for standard and countersunk heads.

Spikes.—By definition, an ordinary spike is *a stout piece of metal from* 3 *to* 12 *ins. in length and* ***thicker*** *in proportion than a common nail.* It is provided with a head and a point, and is frequently curved, serrated, or cleft to render extraction difficult; much used in attaching railroad rails to ties and in the construction of docks, piers, and other work requiring large timbers.

It should be noticed that spike and common nail sizes overlap—sizes common to both being from 3 in. to 6 in., the spike being thicker for equal sizes. There are two kinds of ordinary or round wire spikes classed with respect to the shape of the ends; as

1. Flat head, diamond point.

2. Oval head, chisel point.

The proportions for both kinds as regularly made are given in the following table:

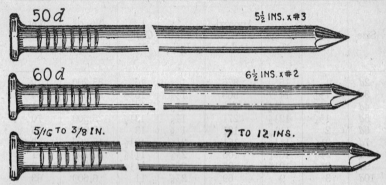

Figs. 64 and 65.—Two sizes of flat head diamond point ordinary spikes (full size).

Fig. 66.—A large flat head, diamond point spike.

Ordinary Spikes

Size	Length	Gauge No.	Deg. of Countersunk	Diam. Head	Head Rad. (oval)	Approximate No. to Pound
10d	3 in.	6	123	13/32	7/16	41
12d	3¼ "	6				38
16d	3½ "	5	123	7/16	7/16	30
20d	4 "	4	123	15/32	7/16	23
30d	4½ "	3	123	½	7/16	17
40d	5 "	2	123	17/32	7/16	13
50d	5½ "	1				10
60d	6 "	1	123	9/16	7/16	9
7 inch	7 "	5/16 inch	123	5/8	5/8	7
8 "	8 "	3/8 "	123	3/4	3/4	4
9 "	9 "	3/8 "				3½
10 "	10 "	3/8 "				3
12 "	12 "	3/8 "				2½

GALVANIZED WIRE

ROUND HEAD CHISEL POINT

ROUND HEAD BLUNT POINT

Figs. 67 to 69.—Various boat nails.

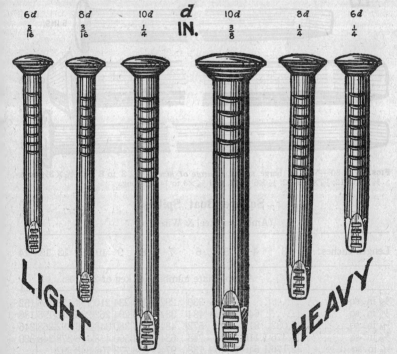

| 6d | 8d | 10d | *d* | 10d | 8d | 6d |
| 2/16 | 3/16 | 1/4 | IN. | 3/8 | 1/4 | 1/4 |

LIGHT

HEAVY

Figs. 70 to 75.—A few sizes of light and heavy boat nails, made regularly 1½ in. to 4 in. (4d or 20d). light gauge No. 1/8 to 1/4; heavy No. 1/4 to 3/8

Boat Spikes.—These are driven mostly in hard timbers, hence a clean cut sharp chisel point is necessary to facilitate this kind of work. They are regularly made according to the following table:

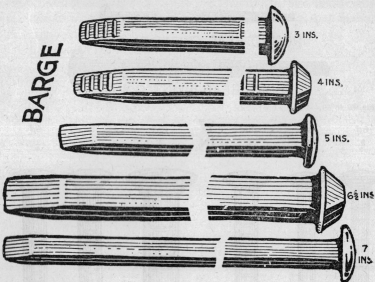

Figs. 76 to 80.—Various barge spikes. *Range of sizes:* ¼ × 3 to 8 ins.; ⁵⁄₁₆ × 3½ to 8; ⅜ × 3 to 12; ⁷⁄₁₆ × 6 to 12; ½ × 6 to 12, and ⅝ × 8 to 14 ins. long.

Square Boat Spikes

(American Steel & Wire Co.)

Length Inches....	3	4	5	6	7	8	9	10	11	12	13	14
	Approximate number per keg of 200 lbs.											
⅝ in. sq.........	....	....	....	330	292	260	234	210	194	178	166	152
½ in. sq.........	....	648	512	434	384	338	294	262	236	212	198	186
⁷⁄₁₆ in. sq.........	1,082	812	692	572	484	414	380	348	318	292	268	246
⅜ in. sq.........	1,476	1,110	920	748	634	554	500	458	416	378	348	320
⁵⁄₁₆ in. sq.........	2,176	1,646	1,386	1,138	974	858	778	708	648	592	...	...
¼ in. sq.........	3,400	2,600	2,040	1,748	1,456	1,294	...	...	...	...	...	...

3. With respect to material, most nails are made of steel wire. The grade of steel used is known as low carbon Bessemer or basic open hearth. Brass and copper nails are extensively used for the better class of boat building and refrigerator work.

4. With respect to finish, for ordinary work the plain, or barbed nail has sufficient holding power, but where extreme

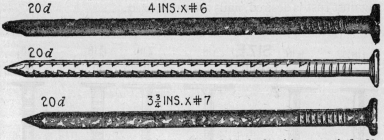

FIGS. 81 to 83.—Various nails grouped according to finish; fig. 81, plain or smooth; fig. 82, barbed; fig. 83, cement coated.

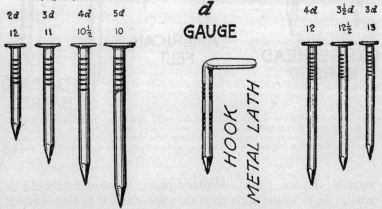

FIGS. 84 to 87, and 89 to 91.—A few sizes of slating and shingle nails (cuts full size) *Note* that the slating nails are considerably heavier than the shingle nails for equal sizes.

FIG. 88.—Hook head metal lath nails, semi-barbed (cut full size). This is a 1⅛ ×12 bright so-called smooth nail with a long thin at head, especially suitable for applying metal lath. It is also regularly made blued, galvanized and in other lengths. Approximate number per lb.: blued or bright 278; galvanized 213.

holding power is desired as in crating or boxing goods for shipment, cement coated nails are used.

The coating consists of resinous gums mixed by a secret process and put on the nails by baking which involves the use of quite complicated machinery. Coated nails are sometimes used in laying flooring to prevent springing. Where protection against rust is desired, nails are galvanized.

Lathers while at work have a habit of putting nails in the

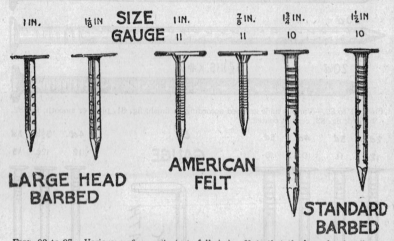

FIGS. 92 to 97.—Various roofing nails (cuts full size). *Note* that the large head nails are regularly made in lengths from ¾ to 1¾ ins. and in gauge numbers 8, 9, 9½, and 10 for each length. The American felt roofing nail has a large head especially adapting it for the roofing material for which it is intended. The head is reinforced on the shank so that it will not easily pull off.

mouth. Hence, from a sanitary point, blued nails should be used. In finishing such nails they are cleaned in hydrochloric acid which removes all dust, grease and injurious substances. They are then blued and put up in paper lined kegs, which insures delivery of the nails free from dust which might accumulate in transit.

5. With respect to service, there is a great multiplicity of uses for nails, hence the large variety regularly listed in manufacturers' catalogues. An idea of the extensive variety is had from an inspection of the

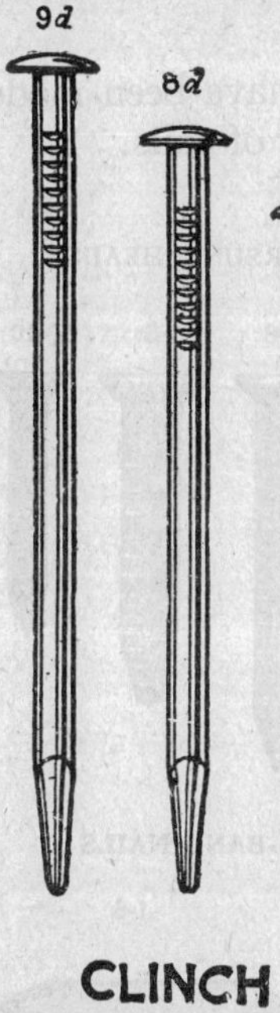

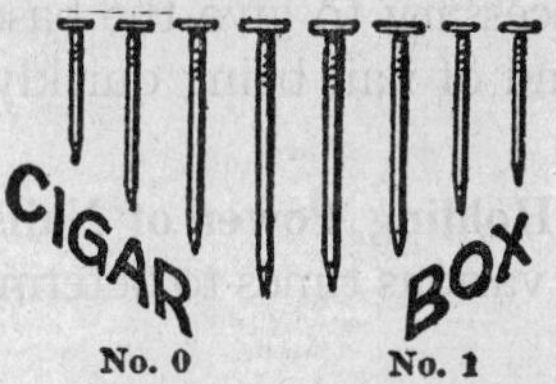

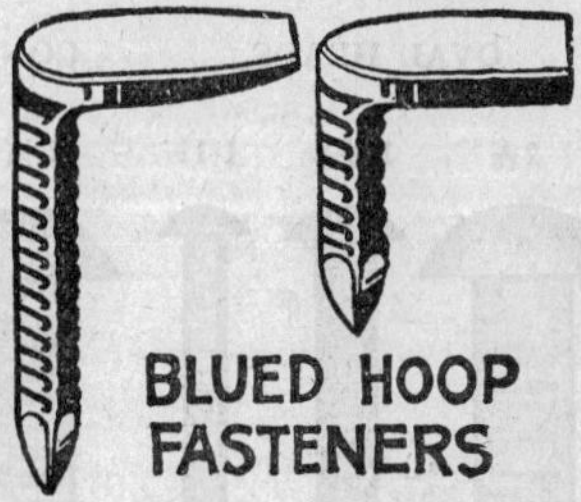

CIGAR BOX
No. 0   No. 1

BLUED HOOP FASTENERS

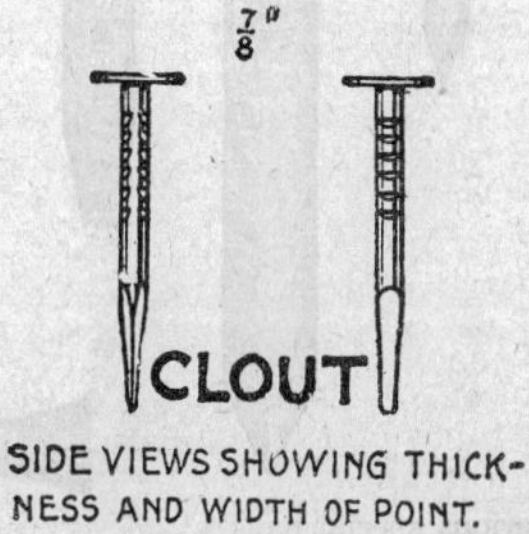

CLINCH

CLOUT
SIDE VIEWS SHOWING THICK-NESS AND WIDTH OF POINT.

BERRY BOX

FIGS. 98 to 115.—Miscellaneous nails (cuts full size). *Clinch nails* are regularly made in sizes from 1 in. No. 14 gauge to 4 in. No. 7 gauge (2*d* to 20*d*). *Cigar box nails* are made with short diamond point, or if so ordered with short needle point, bright, barbed or smooth. Made in sizes ½ in., ⅝ in., and ¾ in., of either No. 18, No. 19 or No. 20 gauge. Packed in kegs, 25-lb. boxes, and in 1-lb., 5-lb. or 10-lb. packages.. Made with either oval or flat heads. *Blued hoop fasteners* range in size from ⅜ to 1 in. long, No. 13 to 6 gauge. Kegs of 100 or 110 lbs. *Clout nails.* By definition, *a strong wrought nail with a large flat circular head and long sharp point*; used for securing leather and the like to wood, as in bellows, hand pump buckets, etc. Clout nails are regularly made in lengths ¾ to 1½ in., 15 to 13 gauge, 1,160 to 350 to the pound. *Berry box nails* range in lengths ¾ to 1¼ ins., 16 or 17 gauge; diameter heads 9 ga.

"Manufacturers' Standard Nail Card" as shown on page 53. Evidently to quote prices on the entire list of nails it is only necessary to give the base price, the price on any particular kind of nail being quickly figured, knowing the base.

Holding Power of Nails.—Numerous tests have been made at various times to determine the holding power of nails.

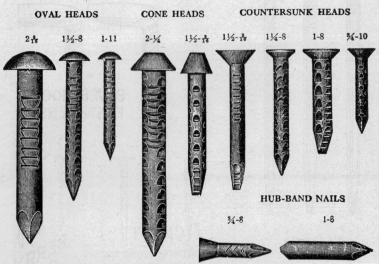

FIGS. 116 to 126.—Various special nails.

Tests at the Watertown Arsenal on different sizes of nails from 8*d* to 60*d*., reduced to *holding power per sq. in. of surface in wood*, gave average results in pounds, as follows: white pine wire, 167; cut, 405. Yellow pine wire, 318; cut, 662. White oak wire, 940; cut, 1,216. Chestnut, cut, 683. Laurel wire, 651; cut, 1,200.

A. M. Wellington found the force required to draw spikes $\frac{9}{16} \times \frac{9}{16}$ in., driven 4¼ inches into seasoned oak, to be 4,281 lbs., same spikes, etc., in unseasoned oak, 6,523 lbs.

"Professor W. R. Johnson found that a plain spike ⅜ inch square driven 3⅜ inches into seasoned Jersey yellow pine or unseasoned chestnut required about 2,000 lbs force to extract it; from seasoned white oak about 4,000 and from well-seasoned locust 6,000 lbs."

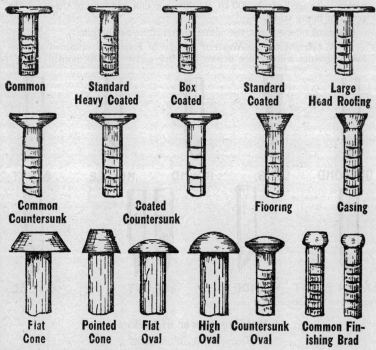

Common   Standard Heavy Coated   Box Coated   Standard Coated   Large Head Roofing

Common Countersunk   Coated Countersunk   Flooring   Casing

Flat Cone   Pointed Cone   Flat Oval   High Oval   Countersunk Oval   Common Finishing Brad

Figs. 127 to 143.—Various nail heads.

Experiments in Germany, by Funk, give from 2,465 to 3,940 lbs. (mean of many experiments about 3,000 lbs.) as the force necessary to extract a plain ½ inch square iron spike 6 inches long, wedge-pointed for one inch and driven 4½ inches into white or yellow pine. When driven 5 inches, the force required was about ¹⁄₁₀ part greater. Similar spikes $\frac{9}{16}$ inches square, 7 inches long, driven 6 inches deep, required from 3,700 to 6,745 lbs. to extract them from pine; the mean of the results being 4,873 lbs. In all cases about twice as much force was required to extract them from oak. The spikes were all driven across the grain of the wood. When driven with the grain, spikes or nails do not hold with more than half as much force.

Boards of oak or pine nailed together by from 4 to 16 ten penny common cut nails and then pulled apart in a direction lengthwise of the boards, and, across the nails, tending to break the latter in two by a shearing action, averaged about 300 to 400 lbs. per nail to separate them, as the result of many trials.

Chestnut offers about the same resistance as yellow pine.

A. W. Wright of the Western Society of Engineers obtained the following results with spikes driven into dry cedar (cut 18 months):

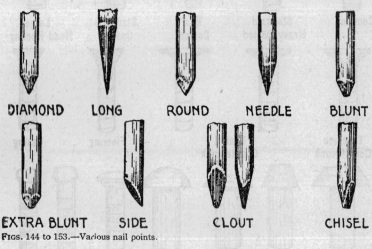

DIAMOND   LONG   ROUND   NEEDLE   BLUNT

EXTRA BLUNT   SIDE   CLOUT   CHISEL

FIGS. 144 to 153.—Various nail points.

Holding Power of Spikes
(Tested by A. W. Wright)

Size of spikes............	5×¼ in. sq.	6×¼	6×½	5×⅜
Length driven in........	4¼ in.	5 in.	5 in.	4¼ in.
Pounds resistance to drawing, Average lbs..	857	821	1,691	1,202
Max. lbs....	1,159	923	2,129	1,556
From 6 to 9 tests each, Min. lbs.............	766	766	1,120	687

Holding Power of Nails and Spikes
(Values given are in lbs. per in. of penetration)

Size	Cut Nails					
	Parallel to grain			Cross grain		
	Yellow Pine	White Pine	White Oak	Yellow Pine	White Pine	White Oak
6d.............	89	....	....	154	77	317
8d.............	206	89	520	327	211	630
10d............	222	108	580	324	181	650
20d............	320	148	692	407	298	800
50d............	439	170	820	570	316	991
60d............	445	200	950	639	324	1,040

Size	Wire Nails				
	Parallel to grain	Cross grain			
	White Pine	Cedar (dry)	White Oak	Yellow Pine	White Pine
6d..................	30	....	129	108	60
10d.................	50	....	390	132	70
60d.................	....	....	731	465	....
⅜ in................	370	283	1,188	590	450
⁷⁄₁₆ in..............	344	....	....	....	436
½ "	113	338	744	700	364

Selection of Nails.—On any kind of construction work an important consideration is the kind and size of nails to use. First, comes the finish, whether smooth, barbed or cement coated.

The holding power of cement coated nails, it was found, is considerably greater than that of the same sized smooth nails. In most cases the barbed nails have the least holding power. Thus nails can be graded as to holding power as follows: First, cement coated; second, smooth; third, barbed.

Next to be considered is the size of the nail in diameter.

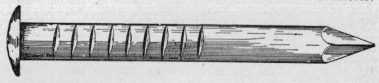

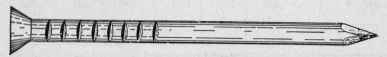

FIGS. 154 and 155.—Hinge nails. Fig. 154, oval head; fig. 155, countersunk head. *Range of sizes*, 1½ × ¼ to 4 × ⅜ inch (4*d* to 20*d*), 50 to 9 per lb. oval head per lb.; 82 to 19 countersunk head per lb. *In ordering* hinge nails, state whether oval or countersunk head, light or heavy, annealed or bright.

Short, thick nails work loose quickly. Long thin nails are apt to break at the joints of the lumber. The simple rule to follow is to use as long and thin a nail as will drive easily.

Definite rules have been formulated by which to determine the size of nail to be used in proportion to the thickness of the board which is being nailed as follows:

1. In using box nails in timber of medium hardness, the penny of the nail should not be greater than the thickness, in eighths of an inch, of the board into which the nail is being driven.

2. In very soft woods the nails may be one penny larger, **or** even in some cases, two penny larger.

Approximate Number of Wire Nails per Pound

American Steel & Wire Co.'s Steel Wire Gauge	LENGTH																											
	3/16	¼	⅜	½	⅝	¾	⅞	1	1⅛	1¼	1½	1¾	2	2¼	2½	2¾	3	3½	4	4½	5	6	7	8	9	10	11	12
⅜	....	....	....	....	....	....	....	29	26	23	20	17	15	15	12	11	11	8.9	7.9	7.1	6.4	5.2	4.5	4.0	3.4	3.2	2.9	2.7
3/16	....	....	....	....	....	....	....	43	38	34	29	25	22	20	18	16	15	13	11	10	9.0	7.6	6.5	5.7	5.0	4.5	4.1	3.8
1	....	....	....	....	....	....	....	47	44	40	34	29	26	23	21	20	18	16	14	12	11	9.3	8.0	7.0	6.3	5.7	5.2	4.7
2	....	....	....	....	....	....	....	60	54	48	41	35	31	28	25	23	21	18	16	14	13	11	9.3	8.1	7.2	6.6	6.1	5.6
3	....	....	....	....	....	....	....	67	60	55	47	41	36	32	29	27	25	21	18	16	15	12	11	9.4	8.3	7.6	7.1	6.6
4	....	....	....	....	....	....	....	81	74	66	55	48	41	37	34	31	29	25	22	20	18	15	13	11	9.8	8.9	8.1	7.5
5	....	....	....	....	....	....	....	90	81	74	61	52	45	41	38	35	32	28	24	22	21	18	16	14	12	12	11	9.6
6	....	....	....	213	174	149	128	113	101	91	76	65	58	52	47	43	39	34	29	26	24	20	18	16	15	13	11	11
7	....	....	....	250	205	174	148	132	120	110	92	78	70	61	55	51	47	40	35	31	28	24	19	18	16	14	13	12
8	....	....	....	272	238	198	174	153	139	126	106	93	82	74	66	61	56	48	42	38	34	28	24	21	19	17	15	14
9	....	....	....	348	286	238	213	185	170	152	128	112	99	87	79	71	67	58	50	45	41	34	29	25	23	21	19	17
10	....	....	....	469	373	320	277	242	216	196	165	142	124	111	100	91	84	71	62	55	49	42	36	31	27	25	23	21
11	....	....	....	510	417	366	323	285	254	233	200	171	149	136	122	111	103	87	77	69	61	52	44	39	35	31	29	26
12	....	....	....	740	603	511	442	397	351	327	268	229	204	182	161	149	137	118	103	95	87	71	63	56	50	45	40	36
13	....	....	1356	1017	802	688	590	508	458	412	348	297	260	232	209	190	175	153	138	123	110	93	....	....	....	....	....	....
14	....	2293	1664	1290	1037	863	765	667	586	536	459	398	350	312	278	256	233	201	176	157	140	117	....	....	....	....	....	....
15	....	2899	2213	1619	1316	1132	971	869	787	694	578	501	437	390	351	317	290	246	220	196	177	145	....	....	....	....	....	....
16	....	3932	2720	2142	1708	1414	1229	1099	973	872	739	635	553	496	452	410	370	318	277	248	226	....	....	....	....	....	....	....
17	....	5316	3890	2700	2306	1904	1581	1409	1253	1139	956	831	746	666	590	532	486	418	360	322	295	....	....	....	....	....	....	....
18	....	7520	5072	3824	3130	2608	2248	1976	1760	1590	1338	1150	996	890	820	740	680	585	507	448	412	....	....	....	....	....	....	....
19	....	9920	6860	5075	4132	3508	2816	2556	2284	2096	1772	1590	1390	1205	1060	970	895	800	....	....	....	....	....	....	....	....	....	....
20	18620	14050	9432	7164	5686	4795	4230	3596	3225	2893	2412	2070	1810	1620	1450	1315	1215	1035	....	....	....	....	....	....	....	....	....	....
21	23260	17252	12000	8920	7232	6052	5272	4576	4020	3640	3040	2665	2310	2020	1830	....	....	....	....	....	....	....	....	....	....	....	....	....
22	28528	21508	14676	11776	9276	7672	....	....	....	....	....	....	....	....	....	....	....	....	....	....	....	....	....	....	....	....	....	....
23	35864	27039	18026	13519	10815	9013	....	....	....	....	....	....	....	....	....	....	....	....	....	....	....	....	....	....	....	....	....	....
24	44936	34018	22678	17008	13607	11339	....	....	....	....	....	....	....	....	....	....	....	....	....	....	....	....	....	....	....	....	....	....
25	57357	43243	28828	21622	17297	14414	....	....	....	....	....	....	....	....	....	....	....	....	....	....	....	....	....	....	....	....	....	....

These approximate numbers are an *Average* only, and the figures given may be varied either way, by changes in the dimensions of the heads or points. Brads and no-head nails will run more to the pound than table shows, and large or thick-headed nails will run less.

Nails for Soft Wood Boxes

¼ in. thickness use 4*d* cement coated nails
⅜ " " " 5*d* " " "
7/16 or ½ " " " 6*d* " " "
9/16 or ⅝ " " " 7*d* " " "
⅞ " " " 8*d* " " "
1¼ in. thickness use special large 3*d* or regular 4*d* cement coated nails

Nails for Hard Wood Boxes

⅜ in. thickness use 4*d* cement coated nails
7/16 or ½ " " " 5*d* " " "
9/16 or ⅝ " " " 6*d* " " "
⅞ " " " 7*d* " " "

NOTE.—***Nailing boxes.*** The number of nails to be used for a given box is determined by adhering to the rule of spacing nails given on page 48, that is, the nails should be spaced approximately 2 ins. apart, except when nailing up boxes where sides, tops and bottoms consist of more than one piece. In such cases the narrow pieces should have at least two nails in each nailing edge and more if necessary to comply with the rule for two inch spacing referred to.

3. In hard woods, nails should be one penny smaller.

The kind of wood is, of course, a big factor in determining the size of nail to use. The dry weight is the best basis for the determination of its grain substance or strength. The greater its dry weight the greater its power to hold nails. However, the splitting tendency of hard wood tends to offset its additional holding power. Smaller nails can be used in hard than in soft timber. Positive rules governing the size of nail to be used as related to the density of the wood cannot be laid down. Experience is the best guide.

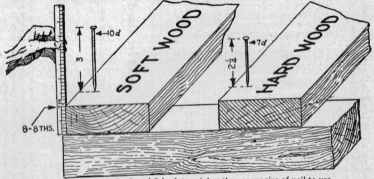

Fig. 156.—Application of rules 2 and 3 in determining the proper size of nail to use.

Spacing of Nails.—This has always been a perplexing problem. Six penny or smaller nails holding in the side grain should be driven about two inches apart, and the same size nails in end grain should be driven about one and three-quarter inch for each additional penny in size. This may seem too

NOTE.—*Sizes of Nails for Different Classes of Work.*—It is imperative for first-class work that nails of proper size should be used and to insure the best results it is well in certain classes of work to specify the sizes which are to be used. For framing, twenty penny, forty penny and sixty penny nails, or spikes are used, according to the size of the timber. For sheathing and roof-boarding, under-floors and cross bridging, ten penny common nails should be used. For over floors ten penny floor nails or casing nails should be used for jointed boards, and nine penny or ten penny for matched flooring, although eight penny nails are sometimes used. Ceiling when ¾ in. thick is generally put up with eight penny casing nails, and when thinner stuff is used, with six penny nails. For inside finish any size of finish nails or brads from eight penny down to two penny is used, according to the thickness and size of the moldings. For pieces exceeding 1 in. in thickness, ten penny nails should be used. Clap boarding is generally put on with six penny finish nails or casing nails. Four penny nails should be used for shingling and slating, and three penny for lathing. For slating, galvanized nails should be used, and they are also better for shingling.

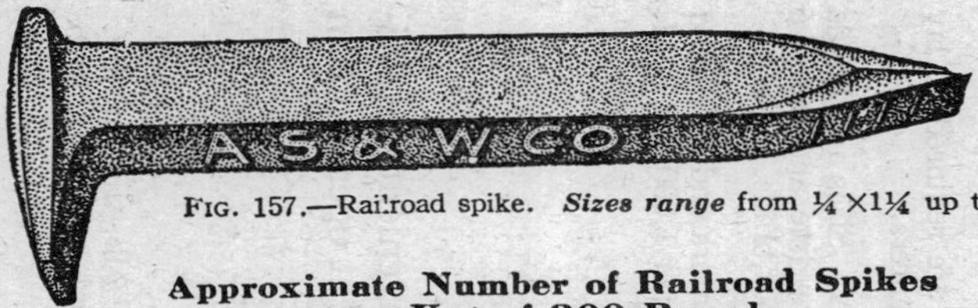

FIG. 157.—Railroad spike. ***Sizes range*** from ¼ X 1¼ up to 9/16 X 4½ and larger.

Approximate Number of Railroad Spikes to a Keg of 200 Pounds

Size, Measured Under Head	Average Number per Keg	Ties 2 Feet Between Centers, 4 Spikes per Tie, Makes per Mile—	Size, Measured Under Head	Average Number per Keg	Ties 2 Feet Between Centers, 4 Spikes per Tie, Makes per Mile—
5 x ½	460	4,592 lbs.—22.96 kegs	2½ x ⅜	1,600	1,320 lbs.— 6.60 kegs
4½ x ½	528	4,000 " —20.00 "	2¼ x ⅜	1,750	1,206 " — 6.03 "
4 x ½	592	3,568 " —17.84 "	2 x ⅜	1,902	1,112 " — 5.56 "
3½ x ½	660	3,200 " —16.00 "	4 x 5/16	1,630	1,308 " — 6.54 "
3 x ½	732	2,886 " —14.43 "	3½ x 5/16	1,810	1,168 " — 5.84 "
2½ x ½	814	2,596 " —12.98 "	3 x 5/16	2,066	1,024 " — 5.12 "
5 x 7/16	664	3,178 " —15.89 "	2½ x 5/16	2,380	888 " — 4.44 "
4½ x 7/16	712	2,966 " —14.83 "	2¼ x 5/16	2,760	766 " — 3.83 "
4 x 7/16	764	2,766 " —13.83 "	2 x 5/16	2,912	726 " — 3.63 "
3½ x 7/16	854	2,474 " —12.37 "	1½ x 5/16	4,200	504 " — 2.52 "
3 x 7/16	1,032	2,048 " —10.24 "	3 x ¼	3,266	646 " — 3.23 "
2½ x 7/16	1,210	1,746 " — 8.73 "	2½ x ¼	4,120	512 " — 2.56 "
5 x ⅜	908	2,326 " —11.63 "	2¼ x ¼	4,600	460 " — 2.30 "
4½ x ⅜	1,000	2,112 " —10.56 "	2 x ¼	4,778	442 " — 2.21 "
4 x ⅜	1,092	1,934 " — 9.67 "	1½ x ¼	6,000	352 " — 1.76 "
3½ x ⅜	1,200	1,760 " — 8.80 "	1¼ x ¼	7,920	266 " — 1.33 "
3 x ⅜	1,342	1,574 " — 7.87 "			

NOTE.—***Length of nail limited.*** There is a limit to the depth a long nail may be driven into any wood before it begins to bend. When a nail begins to bend it shows that a hole must first be made. The object of the hole is to reduce the friction so as to allow the nail to be driven without bending, but if made too large, the holding power of the nail will be reduced and clinching will be a very poor remedy.

close, but it is only about two-thirds the number that can be used in a board before excessive splitting takes place.

Wire Nails, Kinds and Quantities Required (according to American Steel & Wire Co.):

The following example on the use of the table will illustrate its usefulness:

> *Example.*—What size, kind and quantity of nails are required to lay 1×3 flooring for a hall 50×100, joists spaced 16 in. in centers.
>
> Referring to the table look in the fifth column headed "Sizes and Kinds of Materials," and find "Flooring, 1×3." Follow the line and the size and kind specified in the Trades names column is 8*d* floor brads.
>
> Continue on the same line, in the column for 16″ centers under "Pound per 1,000 feet B.M.," is found 32 lbs. of nails required per 1,000 feet B.M.
>
> B. M. in flooring 1 in. thick = 50 × 100 = 5,000.
>
> $$\text{Lbs. of nails } 32 \times \frac{5{,}000}{1{,}000} = 160 \text{ lbs.}$$

The following table will also be found convenient in estimating the quantity of nails required for different operations in house building:

Nail Table

For 1,000 shingles, allow 5 lb. four penny nails or 3½ lb. three penny.
" 1,000 laths, 7 lb. three penny fine, or for 100 sq. yd. of lathing, 10 lb. three penny fine.
" 1,000 sq. ft. of beveled siding, 18 lb. six penny.
" 1,000 sq. ft. of sheathing, 20 lb. eight penny or 25 lb. ten penny.
" 1,000 sq. ft. of flooring, 30 lb. eight penny or 40 lb. ten penny.
" 1,000 sq. ft. of studding, 15 lb. ten penny and 5 lb. twenty penny.
" 1,000 sq. ft. of 1 by 2½ in furring, 12 in centers, 9 lb. eight penny or 14 lb. ten penny.
" 1,000 sq. ft. of 1 by 2½ in furring, 16 in centers, 7 lb. eight penny or 10 lb. ten penny.

Wire Nails—Kinds and Quantities Required

(American Steel and Wire Co.)

Length in inches	Am. Steel & Wire Co.'s Steel Wire Gauge	Approx. No. to lbs.	Nailings	Sizes and Kinds of Material	Trade Names	Pounds per 1000 feet B. M. on center as follows: 12"	16"	20"	36"	48"
						Pounds				
2½	10¼	106	2	1 x 4 (I. Used square edge, as platforms, floors, sheathing, or shiplap. II. When used D. & M., blind nailed, only ½ quantity named required.)	8d common	60	48	37	23	20
2½	10¼	106	2	1 x 6	8d common	40	32	25	16	18
2½	10¼	106	2	1 x 8	8d common	31	27	20	12	10
2½	10¼	106	2	1 x 10	8d common	25	20	16	10	8
2½	10¼	106	3	1 x 12	8d common	31	24	20	12	10
4	6	31	2	2 x 4	20d common	105	80	65	60	33
4	6	31	2	2 x 6	20d common	70	54	43	27	22
4	6	31	2	2 x 8	20d common	53	40	53	21	17
4	6	31	3	2 x 10	20d common	60	50	40	25	20
4	6	31	3	2 x 12	20d common	52	41	33	21	17
6	2	11	3	3 x 4	60d common	197	150	122	76	61
6	2	11	2	3 x 6	60d common	131	97	82	52	42
6	2	11	2	3 x 8	60d common	100	76	61	38	34
6	2	11	3	3 x 10	60d common	178	137	110	70	55
6	2	11	3	3 x 12	60d common	145	115	92	53	46
2½	12½	189	2	Base, per 100 ft. lin.	8d finish	......	1	......	......	......
2½	10¼	106	2	Byrket lath	8d common	......	48	......	......	......
2½	12½	189	1	Ceiling, ¾ x 4	8d finish	18	14	......	......	......
2	13	309	1	Ceiling, ½ and ⅝	6d finish	11	8	......	......	......
2½	12½	189	2	Finish, ⅞	8d finish	25	12	......	......	......
3	11½	121	2	Finish, 1⅛	10d finish	12	10	......	......	......
2½	10	99	1	Flooring, 1 x 3	8d floor brads	42	32	......	......	......
2½	10	99	1	Flooring, 1 x 4	8d floor brads	32	26	......	......	......
2½	10	99	1	Flooring, 1 x 6	8d floor brads	22	18	......	......	......
4	6	31		Framing, 2 x 4 to 2 x 16	20d common	20	16	14	......	......
3½	8	49		requires 3 or more sizes	16d common	10	10	8	......	......
3	9	69		and vary greatly.	10d common	8	6	5	......	......
6	2	11		Framing, 3 x 4 to 3 x 14	60d common	30	25	20	......	......
2½	11½	145	2	Siding, drop, 1 x 4	8d casing	45	35	......	......	......
2½	11½	145	2	Siding, drop, 1 x 6	8d casing	30	25	......	......	......
2½	11½	145	2	Siding, drop, 1 x 8	8d casing	23	18	......	......	......
2	13	309	1	Siding, bevel, ½ x 4	6d finish	23	18	......	......	......
2	13	309	1	Siding, bevel, ½ x 6	6d finish	15	13	......	......	......
2	13	309	1	Siding, bevel, ½ x 8	6d finish	12	10	......	......	......
				Casing, per opening	6d and 8d casing.	About ½ pound per side.				
1¼	14	568	12" o. c.	Flooring, ⅜ x 2	3d brads	About 10 pounds per 1000 square feet.				
1⅛	15	778	16" o. c.	Lath, 48"	3d fine	6 pounds per 1000 pieces.				
⅞	12	469	2" o. c.	Ready roofing	Barbed roofing	¾ of a pound to the square.				
⅞	12	469	1" o. c.	Ready roofing	Barbed roofing	1½ pounds to the square.				
⅞	12	180	2" o. c.	Ready roofing (⅝ heads)	American felt roofing	1½ pounds to the square.				
⅞	12	180	1" o. c.	Ready roofing (⅝ heads)	American felt roofing	3 pounds to the square.				
1¼	13	420	.....	Shingles†	3d shingle	4½ pounds; about 2 nails to each 4 inches.				
1½	12	274	.....	Shingles	4d shingle	7½ pounds; about 2 nails to each 4 inches.				
⅞	12	180	4	Shingles	American felt roofing	12 lbs., ⅝" heads; 4 nails to shingle.				
⅞	12	469	4	Shingles	Barbed roofing	4½ lbs., ⅝" heads; 4 nails to shingle.				
1	16	1150	2" o. c.	Wall board, around entire edge	2d Barbed Berry, flat head	5 pounds, ⅝" heads; per 1000 square feet.				
1	15½	1010	3" o. c.	Wall board, intermediate nailings	2d casing or floor brad	2½ lbs., ⅝" heads; per 1000 square feet.				

†Wood shingles vary in width; asphalt are usually 8 inches wide. Regardless of width 1000 shingles are the equivalent of 1000 pieces 4 inches wide.

NOTE.—*Wire vs, Cut Nails,*—Whether wire or cut nails should be used may generally be left to the builder; but in places where there is any danger of the nails being drawn out either by the warping of the boards or from the pull of the nail, cut nails should be used, as they have greater holding power than the wire nails under certain conditions. It is generally understood that a wire nail will hold more firmly when barbed than when smooth.

#1 #2 #3 #4 #5 #6 #7 #8 #9 #10 #11 #12 #13 #14 #15 #16 #17 #18 #19 #20

Illustrations Full Size
STEEL WIRE GAUGE

Steel Wire Gauge No.	Sizes of Wire		Weight One Mile Pounds	Lbs. per Foot	Feet to Pound
	Common Fractions	Decimally			
1		2830	1128.0	2136	4.681
	⅝	.28125	1114.0	211	
2		.2625	970.4	.1838	5.441
	¼	.250	880.2	.1667	
3		.2437	836.4	.1584	6.313
4		.2253	714.8	.1354	7.386
	⁷⁄₃₂	.21875	673.9	.1276	
5		.2070	603.4	.1143	8.750
6		.1920	519.2	.0983	10.17
	³⁄₁₆	.1875	495.1	.0937	
7		.1770	441.2	.0835	11.97
8		.1620	369.6.	.070	14.29
	⁵⁄₃₂	.15625	343.8	.0651	
9		.1483	309.7	.0586	17.05
10		.1350	256.7	0486	20.57
	⅛	.1250	220.0	.0416	
11		.1205	.204.5	.0387	25.82
12		.1055	156.7	.0296	33.69
	³⁄₃₂	.09375	123.8	.0234	
13		.0915	117.9	.0223	44.78
14		.0800	90.13	.0170	58.58
15		.0720	73.01	.0138	72.32
16	¹⁄₁₆	.0625	55.0	.0104	95.98
17		.0540	41.07	.0077	128.6
18		.0475	31.77	.006	166.2
19		.0410	23.67	.0044	223.0
20		.0348	17.05	.0032	309.6

Standard Nail Card
Adopted August, 1920
Extras on Standard Wire Nails in Kegs

Common Wire Nails

2d	$1.45
3d	1.15
4d	.80
5d	.75
6d	.60
7d	.55
8d	.30
9d	.30
10d	.20
12d	.15
16d	.10
20d-60d	Base

Casing Nails

2d	$1.70
3d	1.35
4d	1.10
5d	1.05
6d	.75
7d	.70
8d	.50
9d	.50
10d	.35
12d	.30
16d	.20
20d-40d	.10

Finishing Nails

2d	$2.00
3d	1.55
4d	1.25
5d	1.20
6d	1.00
7d	.70
8d	.60
9d	.60
10d	.45
12d	.40
16d	.25
20d	.15

Flooring Brads

6d	$0.55
7d	.50
8d	.35
9d	.35
10d	.25
12d	.20
16d	.15
20d	.05

Common Brads

2d	$1.50
3d	1.20
4d	.85
5d	.80
6d	.65
7d	.60
8d	.35
9d	.35
10d	.25
12d	.20
16d	.15
20d-60d	.05

Shingle Nails

3d	$0.90
3½d	.75
4d	.70

Smooth Box Nails

2d	$1.65
3d	1.30
4d	1.05
5d	1.00
6d	.70
7d	.65
8d	.45
9d	.45
10d	.30
12d	.25
16d	.15
20d-40d	.05

Siding Nails

Same advance as Smooth Box Nails

Slating Nails

2d	$1.20
3d	.95
4d	.85
5d	.75
6d	.65

Barbed Roofing Nails
Regular Head

¾-inch	$1.55
⅞-inch	1.30
1 -inch	1.20
1⅛-inch	1.10
1¼-inch	.95
1⅜-inch	.90
1½-inch	.80
1¾-inch	.75
2 -inch	.65

Fence Nails

5d	$0.50
6d	.45
7d	.35
8d	.25
9d	.25
10d	.20
12d	.10
16d	.05
20d	Base

Hinge Nails
Bright

	Light	Heavy
4d	$1.00	$0.95
6d	.90	.85
8d	.75	.70
10d	.65	.65
12d	.60	.60
16d	.55	.55
20d	.50	.50

Annealed

	Light	Heavy
4d	$1.25	$1.20
6d	1.15	1.10
8d	1.00	.95
10d	.90	.90
12d	.85	.85
16d	.80	.80
20d	.75	.75

Boat Nails

25 cents per 100 lbs. over Hinge Nails

Fine Nails

2d	$1.95
3d	1.35
4d	1.05
2d, extra fine	1.95
3d, extra fine	1.55

Clinch Nails
Bright

2d	$1.55
3d	1.15
4d	.95
5d	.90
6d	.75
7d	.70
8d	.55
9d	.55
10d	.45
12d	.40
16d	.35
20d	.30

Barbed Car Nails
Bright

	Light	Heavy
4d	$0.95	$0.80
5d	.75	.70
6d	.70	.65
7d	.60	.60
8d	.50	.50
9d	.50	.50
10d	.45	.45
12d	.40	.35
16d	.35	.30
20d-60d	.25	.25

Annealed

	Light	Heavy
4d	$1.20	$1.05
5d	1.00	.95
6d	.95	.90
7d	.85	.85
8d	.75	.75
10d	.70	.70
12d	.65	.60
16d	.60	.55
20d-60d	.50	.50

Clout Nails
Bright Annealed

¾-in.	$2.15 $2.40
⅞-in.	1.90 2.15
1 -in.	1.65 1.90
1⅛-in.	1.50 1.75
1¼-in.	1.20 1.45
1⅜-in.	1.10 1.35
1½-in.	.85 1.10

Sterilized Blued Lath Nails

2d	$2.20
2d Light	2.20
3d	1.60
3d Light	1.80

Barrel Nails

⅝-inch	$2.25
¾-inch	1.90
⅞-inch	1.55
1 -inch	1.45
1⅛-inch	1.35
1¼-inch	1.15
1⅜-inch	.85
1½-inch	.80

Barbed Dowel Pins
No. 8 Gauge

⅝-inch	$1.75
¾-inch	1.50
⅞-inch	1.35
1 -inch	1.25
1⅛-inch	1.15
1¼-inch	1.10
1⅜-inch	1.05
1½-inch	1.00

Berry Box Nails
Smooth

	No. 16	No. 17
¾-in.	$1.90	$2.20
⅞-in.	1.75	2.05
1 -in.	1.65	1.95
1⅛-in.	1.55	1.85
1¼-in.	1.50	1.80

Barbed

	No. 16	No. 17
¾-in.	$2.15	$2.45
⅞-in.	2.00	2.30
1 -in.	1.90	2.20
1⅛-in.	1.80	2.10
1¼-in.	1.75	2.05

Spikes

All sizes to 9-inch $0.10
10-inch and larger ..... .25
Special gauges 10c additional.

Special Extras on Standard Wire Nails

Annealed Nails, 25c per 100 lbs. extra.
Blued Nails, 25c per 100 lbs. extra.
Barbing Nails, 25 cents per 100 lbs. extra (except as provided for above).

Special Heads, 15c per 100 lbs. extra.
Special Points, 15c per 100 lbs. extra.
Galvanizing All Standard Nails, at special prices.

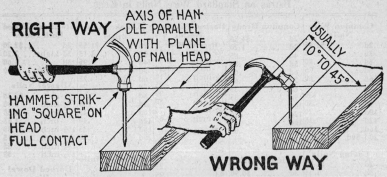

RIGHT WAY

AXIS OF HANDLE PARALLEL WITH PLANE OF NAIL HEAD

HAMMER STRIKING "SQUARE" ON HEAD FULL CONTACT

USUALLY 10° TO 45°

WRONG WAY

Figs. 158 and 159.--Right and wrong way to drive a nail. Hit the nail "squarely" on the head as in fig. 158; this means that *the handle should be horizontal when the hammer hits a vertical nail—not inclined, as in fig.* 159.

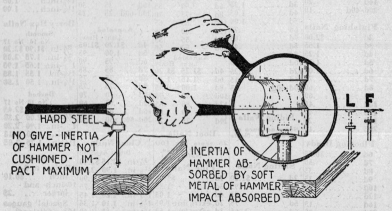

HARD STEEL

NO GIVE - INERTIA OF HAMMER NOT CUSHIONED - IMPACT MAXIMUM

INERTIA OF HAMMER ABSORBED BY SOFT METAL OF HAMMER IMPACT ABSORBED

L F

Figs. 160 to 163.—Why a cheap hammer should not be used. The force that drives the nail is due to the *inertia* of the hammer, and this depends upon the suddenness with which its motion is brought to rest on striking the nail. With hardened steel there is practically no give and all the energy possessed by the hammer is transferred to the nail. With soft and inferior metal all the energy is not transferred to the nail; hence the drive per blow is less as at F than with hardened steel, as at L.

Method of Driving Nails.—An advantage of wire nails is that it is not necessary to hold them in a certain position in driving to prevent splitting. However, in some instances it is advisable to first drill holes nearly the size of the nail before driving to guard against splitting. Also, in fine work where a

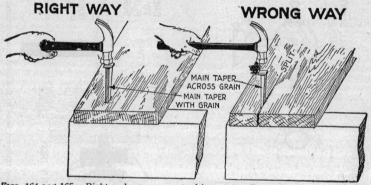

FIGS. 164 and 165.—Right and wrong ways to drive a cut nail.

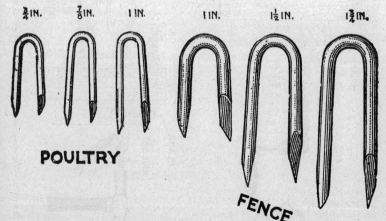

FIGS. 166 to 171.—A few sizes of poultry and fence wire staples. *Note* difference in gauge number as seen by comparing the 1 inch staples.

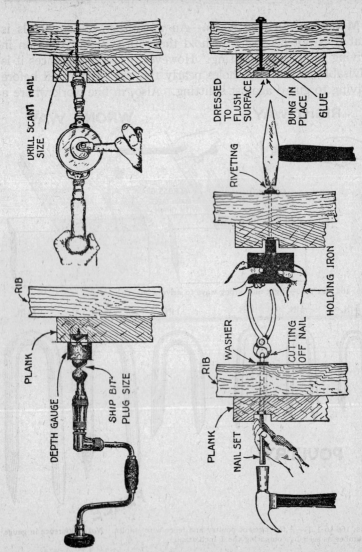

FIGS. 172 to 176.—Various operations in making a riveted copper fastened joint in fine boat construction.

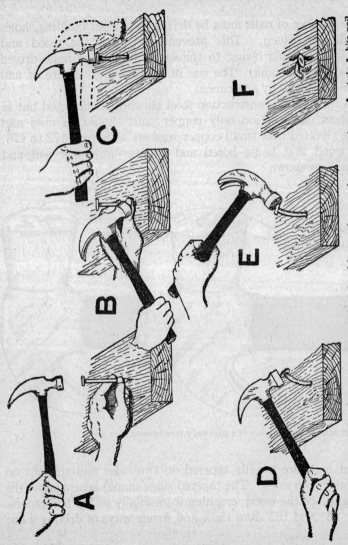

FIGS. 177 to 182.—How not to drive a nail, or method employed by greenhorns and some amateurs. **A**, *stroke 1*, hits nail (accident); **B**, *stroke 2*, hits thumb; **C**, *stroke 3*, oblique blow causes hammer to slide off nail and hit board (first dent); **D**, *stroke 4*, second oblique blow bends nail; **E**, *stroke 5*, side blow to straighten nail; **F**, appearance of nail and board after "driving."

large number of nails must be driven as in boat building, holes should be driven. This prevents crushing the wood and possible splitting owing to the large number of nails driven through each plank. The size of drill for a given size of nail should be found by experiment.

In cheap boat construction steel clinch nails are used but in the best construction only copper nails should be used and these rivetted over small copper washers as in figs. 172 to 176, the wood first being bored and counter-bored for nail and "bung" as shown.

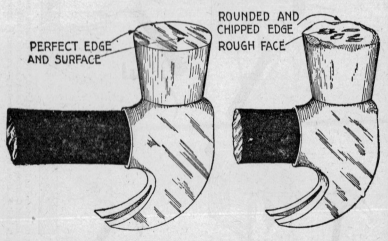

Fig. 183 and 184 —Appearance of a good and a poor hammer after use.

Cut nails are usually tapered on two sides and straight on the other two sides. The tapered sides should bear against the end grain of the wood crushing it gradually as the nail enters. Figs. 164 and 165 show right and wrong ways of driving a cut nail.

CHAPTER 3

Screws

In all branches of carpentry there are many instances where screws are used instead of nails, because: 1, of their greater holding power; 2, neater appearance; 3, less chance of injuring the material; and 4, ease of removing them in case of repairs.

There is a large multiplicity of screws for various uses, the particular kind here considered are those employed in wood construction known as "wood screws" although they are made of metal. By definition a wood screw is *a screw nail, having a right handed coarse thread to give a good grip, a gimlet point to enter the wood and a slotted head for the reception of a screw driver.*

Wood screws may be classed

1. With respect to the material of which they are made, as:

    a. Iron
    b. Steel
    c. Brass
    d. Copper
    e. Bronze

2. With respect to the shape of the head, as:

    a. Flat
    b. Round {ordinary / piano}
    c. Fillister {oval / countersunk}
    d. Oval
    e. Winged
    f. Bung {round / square}
    g. Pinched

    h. Headless
    i. Slotted (wood screws)
    j. Square (lag screws)
    k. Hexagonal
    l. Clove
    m. Grooved

3. With respect to the shape of the point, as:

   a. Gimlet
   b. Diamond
   c. Conical or Fetter

4. With respect to the thread, as:

   a. Standard
   b. Full length (felloe)
   c. Coarse (drive)

5. With respect to duty, as:

   a. So-called "wood" (light duty)
   b. Lag (heavy duty)

6. With respect to finish, as:

   a. Bright
   b. Blued
   c. Nickel plated
   d. Silver plated
   e. Brassed
   f. Bronzed
   g. Coppered
   h. Japanned
   i. Lacquered
   j. Tinned
   k. Galvanized

Material.—For ordinary purposes iron or steel screws are used. In boat building or other work where other metal than iron is desirable to avoid corrosion and where all the metal should be of the same kind to avoid electrolytic action, brass or copper screws are used. Where extra strength alloy is required bronze screws are used.

Wood Screws.—All screws which are turned by a screw driver are called "wood" screws as distinguished from those having square or hexagon heads turned by a wrench.

The term "wood" screws is ill advised and should never have been applied in the above sense, as all screws whether turned by a screw driver or wrench, and adapted to wood are wood screws.

Common wood screws (screws for use in wood) are regularly made in both iron and brass with three styles of head: flat, round and oval.

The use of oval heads is comparatively very limited, flat heads constituting fully four-fifths of the total demand, and round heads three-fourths of the remainder.

The sizes are designated by length in inches and by diameter in numbers of the American screw gauge. The length measurement includes the head of the flat heads, about half the head of the round heads, and the countersink portion of oval heads. Standard dimensions are shown on pages 62 and 63.

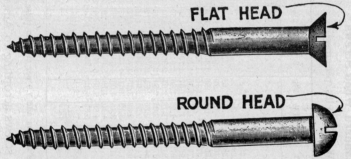

FLAT HEAD

ROUND HEAD

FIGS. 185 and 186.—Flat and round head wood screws with gimlet point—standard and much used forms of screw.

Wood screws are put up in paper boxes containing one gross each, excepting the larger sizes, mostly 3½ inches or more in length, which are in paper boxes containing a half gross or quarter gross, according to the size of the screws.

With exception of a few larger sizes, the paper boxes are wrapped, for the convenience in handling, and carried in stock in paper bundles of 10 gross, 5 gross, or 2½ gross, according to size.

Figs. 185 and 186 show most generally used forms of wood screw. Wood screws are regularly made in sizes ranging from ¼ in length gauge No. 0 to 6 ins. gauge No. 30, as shown in the following table as given by Southington Hardware Co.

Standard Wood Screws

(Weights in lbs. per gross)

Size	1/4	3/8	1/2	5/8	3/4	7/8	1	1 1/4	1 1/2	1 3/4	2	2 1/4	2 1/2	2 3/4	3	3 1/2	4	4 1/2	5	6
0	.024	.040																		
1	.037	.060	.07	.09																
2	.052	.085	.10	.12	.13	.15														
3	.070	.101	.13	.15	.17	.20	.26	.30												
4	.092	.13	.16	.19	.22	.26	.29	.37	.44											
5		.16	.20	.25	.29	.33	.38	.48	.56	.64	.73									
6		.20	.25	.30	.36	.41	.46	.59	.68	.79	.90	1.10	1.13	1.25	1.35					
7		.24	.31	.37	.43	.50	.56	.72	.82	.96	1.10	1.23	1.37	1.53	1.64					
8		.29	.37	.44	.56	.59	.67	.85	.99	1.15	1.32	1.46	1.64	1.82	1.96	2.25				
9		.34	.44	.52	.61	.70	.79	.99	1.17	1.35	1.54	1.71	1.93	2.12	2.29	2.63				
10			.51	.60	.71	.81	.92	1.16	1.36	1.57	1.78	2.00	2.24	2.46	2.67	3.07				
11			.58	.69	.82	.94	1.07	1.34	1.56	1.80	2.00	2.32	2.59	2.85	3.09	3.53	2.57			
12			.66	.79	.93	1.07	1.21	1.52	1.78	2.04	2.34	2.64	2.94	3.25	3.52	4.01	3.00			
13				.90	1.05	1.21	1.37	1.72	2.01	2.34	2.67	2.97	3.33	3.67	3.97	4.53	3.48			
14				1.03	1.18	1.36	1.54	1.93	2.26	2.63	2.99	3.33	3.72	4.10	4.44	5.08	4.01			
15					1.32	1.53	1.74	2.15	2.54	2.92	3.34	3.72	4.16	4.56	4.94	5.65	4.57	5.14	5.80	
16					1.47	1.71	1.92	2.39	2.82	3.25	3.73	4.14	4.62	5.06	5.98	6.28	5.75	6.25	7.34	8.60
17							2.12	2.65	3.13	3.61	4.13	4.58	5.13	5.61	6.07	6.95	7.10	8.09	9.04	10.70
18							2.34	2.95	3.45	4.00	4.53	5.05	5.65	6.18	6.70	7.68	8.67	9.89	11.10	12.90
20								3.50	4.10	4.78	5.40	6.03	6.70	7.36	7.98	9.13	10.40	11.80	13.40	15.40
22								4.13	4.86	5.60	6.35	7.04	7.90	8.55	9.35	10.70	12.20	13.30	15.50	18.30
24								4.86	5.65	6.52	7.39	8.26	9.13	10.01	10.81	12.20	14.15	16.20	18.15	21.20
26															12.50	14.40	16.25	18.60	20.80	24.40
28																	18.40	21.25	23.75	27.70
30																	21.00	24.30	27.30	31.80

For weight of Brass Screws add 7.9 per cent. to these weights.

The general properties of wood screws according to American Screw Co. standard is shown in figs. 187 and 188, and the table following:

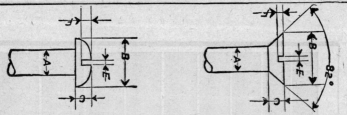

FIGS. 187 and 188.—Flat and round head screws. The lettered dimensions correspond to the letters to table below of American Screw Co. standard wood screws. *Threads per inch:* #0–32; #1–28; #2–26; #3–24; #4–22; #5–20; #6–18; #7–16; #8–15; #9–14; #10–13; #11–12; #12–11; #13–11; #14–10; #15–10; #16–9; #17–9; #18–8; #20–8; #22–7; #24–7; #26–6; #28–6; #30–6.

Standard Wood Screws

No.	A	FLAT HEAD				ROUND HEAD			
		B	C	E	F	B	C	E	F
0	.0578	.1105	.0303	.025	.0101	.1060	.0524	.025	.0314
1	.0710	.1368	.0378	.027	.0126	.1302	.0598	.027	.0359
2	.0842	.1631	.0454	.030	.0151	.1544	.0672	.030	.0403
3	.0973	.1894	.0530	.032	.0177	.1786	.0746	.032	.0448
4	.1105	.2158	.0605	.034	.0202	.2028	.0820	.034	.0492
5	.1236	.2421	.0681	.036	.0227	.2270	.0894	.036	.0536
6	.1368	.2684	.0757	.039	.0252	.2512	.0968	.039	.0580
7	.1500	.2947	.0832	.041	.0277	.2754	.1042	.041	.0625
8	.1631	.3210	.0908	.043	.0303	.2996	.1116	.043	.0670
9	.1763	.3474	.0984	.045	.0328	.3238	.1190	.045	.0714
10	.1894	.3737	.1059	.048	.0353	.3480	.1264	.048	.0758
11	.2026	.4000	.1135	.050	.0378	.3701	.1338	.050	.0803
12	.2158	.4263	.1210	.052	.0403	.3922	.1412	.052	.0847
13	.2289	.4526	.1286	.054	.0429	.4143	.1486	.054	.0891
14	.2421	.4790	.1362	.057	.0454	.4364	.1560	.057	.0936
15	.2552	.5053	.1438	.059	.0479	.4585	.1634	.059	.0980
16	.2684	.5316	.1513	.061	.0504	.4806	.1708	.061	.1024
17	.2816	.5579	.1589	.063	.0530	.5027	.1782	.063	.1069
18	.2947	.5842	.1665	.066	.0555	.5248	.1856	.066	.1114
20	.3210	.6368	.1816	.070	.0605	.5690	.2004	.070	.1202
22	.3474	.6895	.1967	.075	.0656	.6106	.2152	.075	.1291
24	.3737	.7421	.2118	.079	.0706	.6522	.2300	.079	.1380
26	.4000	.7948	.2270	.084	.0757	.6938	.2448	.084	.1469
28	.4263	.8474	.2421	.088	.0807	.7354	.2596	.088	.1558
30	.4526	.9000	.2573	.093	.0858	.7770	.2744	.093	.1646

Wood Screw Numbers

(American Screw Co. and Asa I. Cook Co. standard.　Illustrations full size)

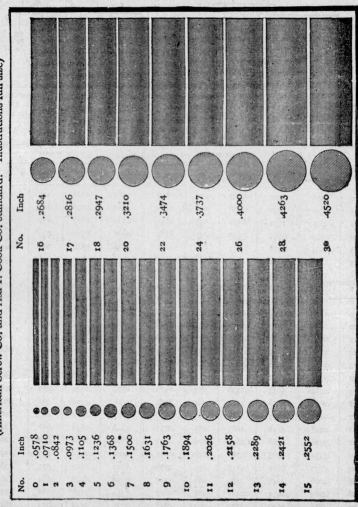

No.	Inch
0	.0578
1	.0710
2	.0842
3	.0973
4	.1105
5	.1236
6	.1368
7	.1500
8	.1631
9	.1763
10	.1894
11	.2026
12	.2158
13	.2289
14	.2421
15	.2552

No.	Inch
16	.2684
17	.2816
18	.2947
20	.3210
22	.3474
24	.3737
26	.4000
28	.4263
30	.4520

Length of Screws.—In ordering screws it is important to know what constitutes the length of a screw.

That is the over all length for instance of a 2 in. flat head screw is not the same as that of a 2 in. round head screw. To avoid confusion and mistakes, the length for various type of screw as graphically defined in figs. 189 to 192 should be carefully noted.

It should be noticed that, unlike the ordinary wire gauges, the 0 of the screw gauge indicates the diameter of the smallest screw, while the diameter of the screw increases with the number of the gauge.

Screw Gauge.—The accompanying table gives values for diameter of shank of the screw, being known by the gauge number.

A — Measure Over All.

B — Measure from Bottom of the Slot.

C — Measure from Edge of the Head.

D — Measure from the Bottom of the Head.

Figs. 189 to 192.—Various wood screws defining *the length of screw*. Avoid mistakes by remembering how to measure the different types.

Shape of the Head.—The buyer will find a multiplicity of head forms to select from, the variety of heads regularly carried in stock being great enough to meet every possible requirement as shown in figs. 189 to 192. However, in order to avoid possible disappointment where the supply base (small dealers)

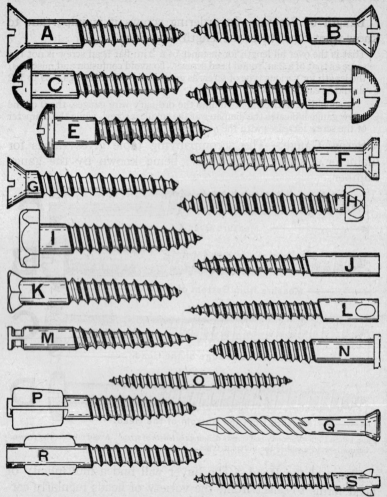

Figs. 193 to 211.—Various wood screws illustrating the multiplicity of thread shapes to meet all requirements. **A**, flat head; **B**, oval head; **C**, round head; **D**, piano head; **E**, oval fillister head; **F**, countersunk fillister head; **G**, felloe; **H**, close head; **I**, hexagon head; **J**, headless; **K**, square bung head; **L**, grooved; **M**, pinched head; **N**, round bung head; **O**, dowel; **P**, winged; **Q**, drive; **R**, winged; **S**, winged head.

is remote from large centers, it is better to select from these three forms of head, which may be regarded as standard:

1. Flat
2. Round
3. Fillister

the other forms may be regarded as special or semi-special, that is, carried by large dealers only.

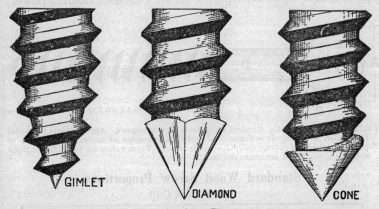

FIGS. 212 to 214.—Standard wood screw points. The gimlet point is an all turn or self feed point while the diamond and cone are for heavy duty work where the screw is partly driven and partly turned in inserting.

Flat heads are necessary in some cases as on door and blind butts, etc., where any projection would interfere with the working of the hinge; also on finish work where flush surfaces are desirable. The round and fillister heads are ornamental.

Shape of the Point.—There are three standard points as given in the classification: 1, gimlet; 2, diamond; and 3, cone. The gimlet point is the most common, being used on wood and coach screws. As the thread starts practically at the point the screw is easily started in the wood by pressing forward on the screw driver while turning, no driving being necessary

The diamond and conical points are used on screws when more or less driving is done before turning as on drive and lag screws.

The Thread.—For ordinary purposes the standard thread extending about two-thirds the length of the screw is used, as given in the table below.

In some cases, as felloe screws (fig. 199) the thread is extended full length or up to the head, to secure increased holding power,

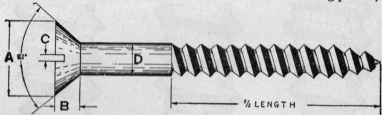

Fig. 215.—Asa S. Cook Co. standard proportions for wood screws. *Approximate formula:* D = 01325 N + .056; D = diameter of screw; N = number of screw; A = diameter of head; B = depth of countersunk; C = width of slot. These values for the different screw sizes are given in the accompanying table.

Standard Wood Screw Proportions

(Asa S. Cook Co.)

Screw Numbers	A	B	C	D	Number of Threads per Inch	Screw Numbers	A	B	C	D	Number of Threads per Inch
0	....	....	...	0.0578	30	13	0.4427	0.1286	0.055	0.2289	11
1	....	....	...	0.0710	28	14	0.4790	0.1362	0.057	0.2421	10
2	0.1631	0.0454	0.030	0.0841	26	15	0.5053	0.1437	0.059	0.2552	9.5
3	0.1894	0.0530	0.032	0.0973	24	16	0.5316	0.1513	0.061	0.2684	9
4	0.2158	0.0605	0.034	0.1105	22	17	0.5579	0.1589	0.064	0.2815	8.5
5	0.2421	0.0681	0.036	0.1236	20	18	0.5842	0.1665	0.066	0.2947	8
6	0.2684	0.0757	0.039	0.1368	18	20	0.6368	0.1816	0.070	0.3210	7.5
7	0.2947	0.0832	0.041	0.1500	17	22	0.6895	0.1967	0.075	0.3474	7.5
8	0.3210	0.0908	0.043	0.1631	15	24	0.7421	0.2118	0.079	0.3737	7
9	0.3474	0.0984	0.045	0.1763	14	26	0.7421	0.1967	0.084	0.4000	6.5
10	0.3737	0.1059	0.048	0.1894	13	28	0.7948	0.2118	0.088	0.4263	6.5
11	0.4000	0.1134	0.050	0.2026	12.5	30	0.8474	0.2270	0.093	0.4546	6
12	0.4263	0.1210	0.052	0.2158	12	...	...	....	....	....	...

as required for screws (called felloe screws) which secure the tire to the fellow or rim of wheel supported by the spokes.

How to Put in a Wood Screw.—First bore a hole slightly less than the diameter of the shank and about one-half its depth. Then put the screw in by turning with the screw driver; do not

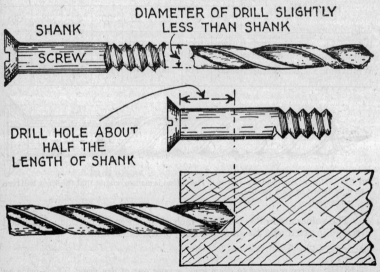

SHANK

SCREW

DIAMETER OF DRILL SLIGHTLY LESS THAN SHANK

DRILL HOLE ABOUT HALF THE LENGTH OF SHANK

FIGS. 216 and 217.—How to put in a wood screw showing approximate size of drill (or bit) and depth of hole. Of course exact size and depth will depend on kind of wood, whether cross or with grain, size of screw. *If screw turn too hard use soap.*

hammer. In the case of a large number of screws of the same size, it is well to experiment to determine the correct size of drill to use in boring the holes.

Strength of Wood Screws.—The following table gives the

safe resistance, or safe load against pulling out in points per linear inch of wood screws when inserted across the grain:

Safe Loads for Wood Screws

(Inserted across the grain)

Kind of Wood	Gauge Number							
	4	8	12	16	20	24	28	30
White oak	80	100	130	150	170	180	190	200
Yellow pine............	70	90	120	140	150	160	180	190
White pine.............	50	70	90	100	120	140	150	160

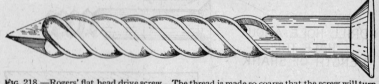

FIG. 218.—Rogers' flat head drive screw. The thread is made so coarse that the screw will turn as it is driven in by a hammer.

The values are in lbs. per linear inch of the threaded portion. For wood screws inserted *with the grain* use 60% of the table values.

NOTE.—*Force required to draw wood screws out of dry wood.* Tests made by Mr. Bevan. The screws were about two inches in length, .22 diameter at the exterior of the threads, .15 diameter at the bottom, the depth of the worm or thread being .035 and the number of threads in one inch equal 12. They were passed through pieces of wood half an inch in thickness and drawn out by the weights stated: Beech, 460 lbs.; ash, 790 lbs.; oak, 760 lbs.; mahogany, 770 lbs., elm, 665 lbs , sycamore, 830 lbs.

NOTE.—*Force required to draw screws out of Norway pine.*

½" diam. drive screw 4 in. in wood	Power required, average	2,424 lbs.
" " 4 threads per in. 5 in. in wood	" " "	2,743 "
" " d'ble thr'd, 3 per in 4 in in wood	" " "	2,730 "
" " lag-screw, 7 per in. 1½ in. in wood	" " "	1,465 "
" " lag-screw, 6 per in. 2½ in. in wood	" " "	2,026 "
" rail road spike 5 in in wood	" " "	2.191 "

The lateral or load at right angles to the screw is much greater than that of nails. For conservative designing assume a safe resistance of a No. 20 gauge screw at double that given for nails of the same length when the full length of the screw thread penetrates the supporting piece of the two pieces connected.

Lag Screws.—By definition, a lag screw is a *heavy duty wood screw provided with a square or hexagon head so that it may be turned by a wrench.*

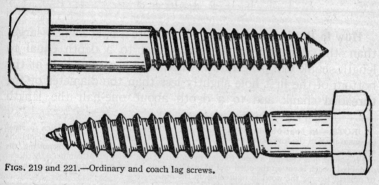

FIGS. 219 and 221.—Ordinary and coach lag screws.

The ordinary lag screw has a cone point as in fig. 219 but when provided with a gimlet point and hexagon head it is called a *coach screw*. These are large heavy screws used where great

NOTE.—*Tests of lag screws in various woods made by A. J. Cox, University of Iowa.*

Kind of Wood	Size Screw	Size hole Bored	Length in tie	Max. Resist. Lbs.	No. Tests
Seasoned white oak.............	⅝ in.	½ in.	4½ in.	8,037	3
" " "	¾₆ in.	⁷⁄₁₆ in.	3 in.	6,480	1
" " "	½ in.	⅜ in.	4½ in.	8,780	2
Yellow pine stick...............	⅝ in.	½ in.	4 in.	3,800	2
White cedar, unseasoned........	⅝ in.	½ in.	4 in.	3,405	2

strength is required as for fastening counter shafts, heavy timber work, etc. The following are the proportions of ordinary lag screws:

Lag Screws

Length	3	3½	4	4½	5	5½	6	6½	7	7½	8	9	10	11	12
Diameter........	5/16 to 7/8	5/16 to 1	5/16 to 1	5/16 to 1	5/16 to 1	5/16 to 1	5/16 to 1	7/16 to 1	7/16 to 1	7/16 to 1	7/16 to 1	7/16 to 1	1/2 to 1	1/2 to 1	1/2 to 1

How to Put in Lag Screws.—First bore a hole slightly larger than the diameter of the shank and to a depth equal to length shank will penetrate. Then bore a second hole at the bottom of the first hole slightly less than the diameter of the threaded shank and to a depth about one-half the length

NOTE.—*In boat building* long hand made bolts are generally used to fasten together the main parts of the frame such as stem, keel, dead wood, shaft log, etc. These special bolts are made from galvanized iron rods obtained in long lengths and cut to size. After cutting, the rod is placed in a vise and a head formed by upsetting the end with a hammer. A thread of desired length is cut on the other end to receive a nut. A washer is provided at each end to prevent tearing the wood in tightening up the nut.

NOTE.—*Resistance of drift bolts in timber.* The following tests by Rust and Coolidge give results of various drift bolts in white and Norway pine.

	White Pine	Norway Pine
1 in. square iron drove 30 in. in 15/16 in. hole......................	26,400 lbs.	19,200 lbs.
1 " round " " 34 " " 13/16 " "	16,800 "	18,720 "
1 " square " " 18 " " 15/16 " "	14,600 "	15,600 "
1 " round " " 22 " " 13/16 " "	13,200 "	14,400 "

NOTE.—*Holding power of bolts in white pine* (*Eng'g News*. Sept. 26, 1891).

	Round Lbs.	Square Lbs.
Average of all plain 1 in. bolts...........................	8,224	8,200
" " " " bolts 5/8 to 1⅛ in......................	7,805	8,110
" " " bolts...........................	8,383	8,598

Round drift bolts should be driven in holes 13/16 of their diameter. and square drift bolts in holes whose diameter is 11/16 of the side of the square

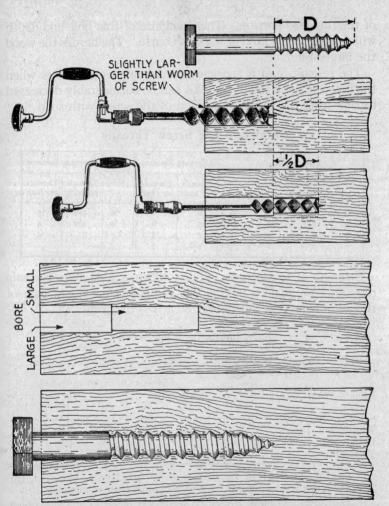

SLIGHTLY LARGER THAN WORM OF SCREW

BORE — SMALL — LARGE

FIGS. 222 to 225.—How to put in lag screws. *1*, bore hole slightly larger than shank to depth that shank will be inserted; *2*, continue boring with smaller bit (of size equal diameter of bottom of thread) to depth equal ½ length of thread. Fig. 224 shows completed hole, and fig. 225 lag screw screwed into hole. *If lag screw turn too hard cover thread with soap.*

of the threaded portion. The exact size of this hole and depth will depend on the kind of wood of course. The harder the wood the larger the hole.

The resistance of a lag screw to turning is enormous when the hole is a little small, but this can be considerably decreased by smearing the threaded portion of the screw with soap.

Standard Lag Screw Threads

Diameter	Alternate Systems		Diameter	Alternate Systems		Diameter	Alternate Systems	
	Threads per Inch	Threads per Inch		Threads per Inch	Threads per Inch		Threads per Inch	Threads per Inch
¼	10	10	½	6	6	¾	4½	5
⁵⁄₁₆	9½	9	⁹⁄₁₆	5	6	⅞	4½	4
⅜	7	8	⅝	5	5	1	3	4
⁷⁄₁₆	7	7	¹¹⁄₁₆	4½	5	.....	....	....

Strength of Lag Screws.—The following table gives the safe resistance or load to pulling out in pounds per linear inch of thread of lag screws when inserted across the grain:

Safe Loads for Lag Screws

(Inserted across the grain)

Kind of Wood...............	Diameter of Screw in Inches				
	½	⅝	¾	⅞	1
White Pine......................	590	620	730	790	900
Douglas Fir....................	310	330	390	450	570
Yellow Pine....................	310	330	390	450	570

Finish.—Steel screws are finished with blue, bronze, lacquered, galvanized, or tinned surface to match the cheaper class of trimmings.

The galvanized finish is used on boats and buildings at the seashore. Screws with blue surface called *blued screws* are generally used with japanned hardware and wherever a cheap round headed screw is desired. Nickel plated screws present a fine appearance.

CHAPTER 4

Bolts

By definition a bolt is *a pin or rod used for holding anything in its place, and often having a permanent head on one end*.

A bolt is generally regarded as a rod having a head at one end and threaded at the other to receive a nut; the nut is usually considered as forming a part of the bolt and prices quoted on bolts by dealers include the nuts.

Kinds of Bolts.—There is a multiplicity of forms of bolts to meet various requirements

The *common* or *machine bolt* has a head at one end and a short length of thread at the other end.

When a loop or "eye" is provided instead of a head it is called an *eye bolt*.

A *countersunk bolt* has a beveled head fitting into a countersunk hole.

A *key head bolt* has a head so shaped that, when inserted into a suitable groove or slot provided for it, it will not turn when the nut is screwed onto the other end.

Another method of preventing turning consists in forming a short portion of the bolt body square at the head end, the head itself being spherical in shape, such type being known as a *carriage bolt*.

A headless bolt threaded a certain distance at both ends is called a *stud bolt*.

In addition to the types just mentioned there are numerous others, such as milled coupling, railroad track, tire, stove, expansion bolts, etc

Early Methods.—The bolt and nut industry in America was started in a small way in Marion, Conn., in 1818.

In that year Micah Rugg, a country blacksmith, made bolts by the forging process. The first machine used for this purpose was a device known as a heading block, which was operated by a foot treadle and a connecting lever. The latter held the blank while it was being driven down into the impression in the heading block by a hammer. The square iron

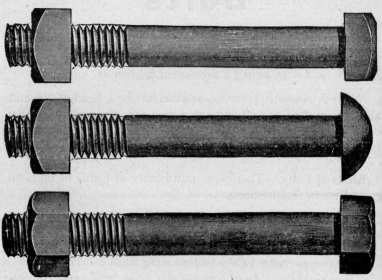

Figs. 226 to 228.—Common or machine bolts. Fig. 226, square head, square nut; fig. 227, button head, square nut; fig. 228, hexagon head, hexagon nut.

from which the bolt was made was first rounded, so that it could be admitted into the block.

At first Rugg only made bolts to order, and charged at the rate of 16 cts. apiece. This industry developed very slowly until 1839, when Rugg went into partnership with Martin Barnes. Together they built the first exclusive bolt and nut factory in the United States at Marion, Conn.

Bolts were first manufactured in England in 1838 by Thomas Oliver of

Darlston, Staffordshire. His machine was built on a somewhat different plan from that of Rugg's, but no doubt was a further development of the first machine. Oliver's machine was known as the "English Oliver."

The construction of the early machines was carefully kept secret. It is related that in 1842 a Mr. Clark had his bolt forging machine located in a room separated from the furnaces by a thick wall. The machine received the heated bars through a small hole cut in the wall; the forge man was not permitted to enter the room.

Modern Methods.—A plain bolt and rivet machine comprises two gripping dies, one movable and the other stationary, and a ram which carries the heading tool. The heated bar is placed

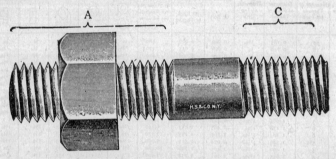

Fig. 229.—Stud bolt with U. S. chamfered and trimmed hexagon nuts. Regularly made in sizes ⅜ to 1¼, over all lengths 1½ to 6 ins. A, nut end; C, attachment end.

in the impression in the stationary gripping die, and against the gauge stop. The machine is then operated by pressing down a foot treadle. On this type of machine the stick is generally cut to the desired length before heading, especially when it is long enough to be conveniently gripped with the tongs, but it can be headed first and afterwards cut off to the desired length in the side shear. It is also possible in some makes of machine to insert a cutting tool to cut off the blank before heading, when the work is not greater in length than the capacity of the machine.

Proportions and Strength of Bolts.—Ordinarily bolts are manufactured in certain "stock sizes."

The table following gives these sizes for bolts ¼ up to 1¼ in., with length of thread.

Properties of U. S. Standard Bolts

(U. S. Standard Threads)

The tap drill diameters in the table provide for a slight clearance at the root of the thread, in order to facilitate tapping and reduce tap breakages. If full threads are required, use the diameters at the root of the threads for the tap drill diameters.

Diameter	Number of Threads per Inch	Diameter at Root of Thread	Diameter of Tap Drill	Area in Square Inches		Tensile Strength at Stress of 6000 Pounds per Square Inch	Dimensions of Nuts and Bolt Heads				
				Of Bolt	At Root of Thread						
1/4	20	0.185	13/64	0.049	0.026	160	1/2	0.578	0.707	1/4	1/4
5/16	18	0.240	1/4	0.076	0.045	270	19/32	0.686	0.840	5/16	19/64
3/8	16	0.294	5/16	0.110	0.068	410	11/16	0.794	0.972	3/8	11/32
7/16	14	0.345	23/64	0.150	0.093	560	25/32	0.902	1.105	7/16	25/64
1/2	13	0.400	27/64	0.196	0.126	760	7/8	1.011	1.237	1/2	7/16
9/16	12	0.454	15/32	0.248	0.162	1,000	31/32	1.119	1.370	9/16	31/64
5/8	11	0.507	17/32	0.307	0.202	1,210	1 1/16	1.227	1.502	5/8	17/32
3/4	10	0.620	41/64	0.442	0.302	1,810	1 1/4	1.444	1.768	3/4	5/8
7/8	9	0.731	3/4	0.601	0.419	2,520	1 7/16	1.660	2.033	7/8	23/32
1	8	0.838	55/64	0.785	0.551	3,300	1 5/8	1.877	2.298	1	13/16
1 1/8	7	0.939	31/32	0.994	0.694	4,160	1 13/16	2.093	2.563	1 1/8	29/32
1 1/4	7	1.064	1 3/32	1.227	0.893	5,350	2	2.310	2.828	1 1/4	1
1 3/8	6	1.158	1 7/32	1.485	1.057	6,340	2 3/16	2.527	3.093	1 3/8	1 3/32
1 1/2	6	1.283	1 11/32	1.767	1.295	7,770	2 3/8	2.743	3.358	1 1/2	1 3/16
1 5/8	5 1/2	1.389	1 27/64	2.074	1.515	9,090	2 9/16	2.960	3.623	1 5/8	1 9/32
1 3/4	5	1.490	1 17/32	2.405	1.746	10,470	2 3/4	3.176	3.889	1 3/4	1 3/8
1 7/8	5	1.615	1 21/32	2.761	2.051	12,300	2 15/16	3.393	4.154	1 7/8	1 15/32
2	4 1/2	1.711	1 49/64	3.142	2.302	13,800	3 1/8	3.609	4.419	2	1 9/16
2 1/4	4 1/2	1.961	2 1/64	3.976	3.023	18,100	3 1/2	4.043	4.949	2 1/4	1 3/4
2 1/2	4	2.175	2 15/64	4.909	3.719	22,300	3 7/8	4.476	5.479	2 1/2	1 15/16
2 3/4	4	2.425	2 31/64	5.940	4.620	27,700	4 1/4	4.909	6.010	2 3/4	2 1/8
3	3 1/2	2.629	2 11/16	7.069	5.428	32,500	4 5/8	5.342	6.540	3	2 5/16
3 1/4	3 1/2	2.879	2 15/16	8.296	6.510	39,000	5	5.775	7.070	3 1/4	2 1/2
3 1/2	3 1/4	3.100	3 11/64	9.621	7.548	45,300	5 3/8	6.208	7.600	3 1/2	2 11/16
3 3/4	3	3.317	3 3/8	11.045	8.641	51,800	5 3/4	6.641	8.131	3 3/4	2 7/8
4	3	3.567	3 5/8	12.566	9.963	59,700	6 1/8	7.074	8.661	4	3 1/16
4 1/4	2 7/8	3.798	3 27/32	14.186	11.340	68,000	6 1/2	7.508	9.191	4 1/4	3 1/4
4 1/2	2 3/4	4.028	4 3/32	15.904	12.750	76,500	6 7/8	7.941	9.721	4 1/2	3 7/16
4 3/4	2 5/8	4.255	4 5/16	17.721	14.215	85,500	7 1/4	8.374	10.252	4 3/4	3 5/8
5	2 1/2	4.480	4 9/16	19.635	15.760	94,000	7 5/8	8.807	10.782	5	3 13/16
5 1/4	2 1/2	4.730	4 13/16	21.648	17.570	105,500	8	9.240	11.312	5 1/4	4
5 1/2	2 3/8	4.953	5 1/32	23.758	19.260	116,000	8 3/8	9.673	11.842	5 1/2	4 3/16
5 3/4	2 3/8	5.203	5 9/32	25.967	21.250	127,000	8 3/4	10.106	12.373	5 3/4	4 3/8
6	2 1/4	5.423	5 1/2	28.274	23.090	138,000	9 1/8	10.539	12.903	6	4 9/16

Bolts larger in diameter and longer than given in the table are regularly threaded a length equal to three times their diameter.

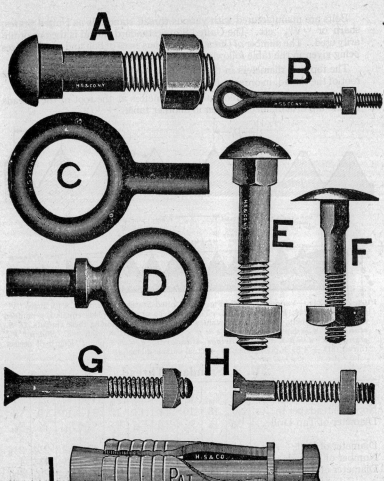

Figs. 230 to 238.—Various bolts. **A**, railroad track bolt; **B**, welded eye bolt; **C**, and **D**, plain and shouldered forged eye bolts; **E**, carriage bolt; **F**, step bolt; **G**, tire bolt; **H**, stove bolt; **I**, expansion bolt.

Bolts are manufactured with various thread standards as United States, sharp or "V", etc. The United States standard thread is the one ordinarily used. The number of threads for various sizes of bolt and tap drill sizes being given in the table following.

The tap drill diameters in the table provide for a slight clearance at the root of the thread, in order to facilitate tapping and reduce tape breakage.

If full threads be required, use the diameters at the root of the threads for the tap drill diameters, given in another table.

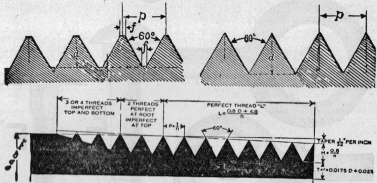

FIGS. 239 to 241.—Various threads. Fig. 239, United States standard; fig. 240, sharp "V" standard; fig. 241, Brigg's standard. The pitch (*p*) of these threads equals 1 ÷ number of threads per inch. The following values are used in proportioning these threads. *U. S. standard:* *d* = depth of thread; *e* = *p* × .64952; *f* = flat = pitch ÷ 8. *Sharp "V" standard:* *d* = *p* × .86603. *Briggs' standard:* *d* = .8 ÷ pitch; length of perfect thread (8D + 4.8) ÷ pitch, when D = actual outside diameter.

U. S. Standard Thread

Diameter of Bolt	$\frac{1}{4}$	$\frac{5}{16}$	$\frac{3}{8}$	$\frac{7}{16}$	$\frac{1}{2}$	$\frac{9}{16}$	$\frac{5}{8}$	$\frac{3}{4}$	$\frac{7}{8}$	1
No. of Threads per In	20	18	16	14	13	12	11	10	9	8
Diameter of Tap Drill	$\frac{13}{64}$	$\frac{1}{4}$	$\frac{5}{16}$	$\frac{23}{64}$	$\frac{27}{64}$	$\frac{15}{32}$	$\frac{17}{32}$	$\frac{41}{64}$	$\frac{3}{4}$	$\frac{55}{64}$
Diameter of Bolt	$1\frac{1}{8}$	$1\frac{1}{4}$	$1\frac{3}{8}$	$1\frac{1}{2}$	$1\frac{5}{8}$	$1\frac{3}{4}$	$1\frac{7}{8}$	2	$2\frac{1}{4}$	$2\frac{1}{2}$
Number of Threads	7	7	6	6	$5\frac{1}{2}$	5	5	$4\frac{1}{2}$	$4\frac{1}{2}$	4
Diameter of Tap Drill	$\frac{31}{32}$	$1\frac{3}{32}$	$1\frac{7}{32}$	$1\frac{11}{32}$	$1\frac{27}{64}$	$1\frac{17}{32}$	$1\frac{21}{32}$	$1\frac{40}{64}$	$2\frac{1}{64}$	$2\frac{15}{64}$
Diameter of Bolt	$2\frac{3}{4}$	3	$3\frac{1}{4}$	$3\frac{1}{2}$	$3\frac{3}{4}$	4	$4\frac{1}{4}$	$4\frac{1}{2}$	$4\frac{3}{4}$	5
Number of Threads	4	$3\frac{1}{2}$	$3\frac{1}{2}$	$3\frac{1}{4}$	3	3	$2\frac{7}{8}$	$2\frac{3}{4}$	$2\frac{5}{8}$	$2\frac{1}{2}$
Diameter of Tap Drill	$2\frac{31}{64}$	$2\frac{11}{16}$	$2\frac{15}{16}$	$3\frac{11}{64}$	$3\frac{3}{8}$	$3\frac{5}{8}$	$3\frac{27}{32}$	$4\frac{3}{32}$	$4\frac{5}{16}$	$4\frac{9}{16}$

The United States standard thread is also known as the Sellers thread and although it is the one most commonly used in the United States it should not be confused with the *sharp or V thread.* The sides of the U. S thread form an angle of 60 degrees with each other. The thread is flattened at the top and bottom as in fig. 239, whereas the top and bottom of the V thread are theoretically sharp, the sides being at 60 degrees as in fig. 240. The flattened portion of the U. S. thread equals ⅛ of the pitch. The number of threads for corresponding sizes of the two standards are the same with exception of the ½ and 1⅝ sizes, the U. S. thread for these sizes being 13 and 5½; V threads for same sizes being 12 and 5.

The Brigg's thread as shown in fig. 241 is the standard for wrought

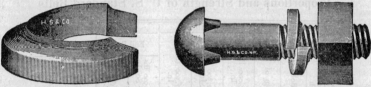

FIGS. 242 and 243.—National lock washer. When the nut is screwed upon the bolt, it first strikes the rib on the lock washer, which, being harder than the nut, progressively upsets and forces some of the metal of the nut into the thread of the bolt, thereby preventing the nut backing off or loosening.

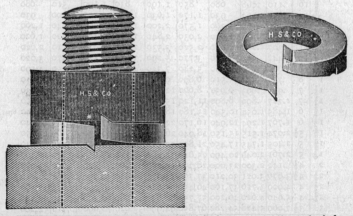

FIGS. 244 and 245.—Positive lock washer. The "body" of the washer carries the load of compression and the tapered ends are thus relieved, the spring being constant The barbs, being free to move when subjected to vibration, force themselves deeply into the nut and metal backing

pipe. Part of the thread is tapered as seen in the illustration, the taper principle being used to obtain a tight joint.

Evidently in computing the tensile strength of a bolt, allowance must be made for the metal cut away or reduction in diameter in forming the thread (except on special bolts having a "plus" thread). The table following giving cross areas at bottom of thread will aid in calculating the strength of bolts.

Proportions and Strength of U. S. Standard Bolts

Diameter of Bolt	No. of Threads per Inch	Areas		Tensile Strength			Shearing Strength			
		Full Bolt	Bottom of Thread	At 10,000 lbs. per Sq. In.	At 12,500 lbs. per Sq. In.	At 17,500 lbs. per Sq. In.	Full Bolt		Bottom of Thread	
							At 7,500 lbs. per Sq. In.	At 10,000 lbs. per Sq. In.	At 7,500 lbs. per Sq. In.	At 10,000 lbs. per Sq. In.
1/4	20	.049	.027	270	340	470	380	490	200	270
5/16	18	.077	.045	450	570	790	580	770	340	450
3/8	16	.110	.068	680	850	1,190	830	1,100	510	680
7/16	14	.150	.093	930	1,170	1,630	1,130	1,500	700	930
1/2	13	.196	.126	1,260	1,570	2,200	1,470	1,960	940	1,260
9/16	12	.248	.162	1,620	2,030	2,840	1,860	2,480	1,220	1,620
5/8	11	.307	.202	2,020	2,520	3,530	2,300	3,070	1,510	2,020
3/4	10	.442	.302	3,020	3,770	5,290	3,310	4,420	2,270	3,020
7/8	9	.601	.419	4,190	5,240	7,340	4,510	6,010	3,150	4,190
1	8	.785	.551	5,510	6,890	9,640	5,890	7,850	4,130	5,510
1 1/8	7	.994	.693	6,930	8,660	12,130	7,450	9,940	5,200	6,930
1 1/4	7	1.227	.890	8,890	11,120	15,570	9,200	12,270	6,670	8,900
1 3/8	6	1.485	1.054	10,540	13,180	18,450	11,140	14,850	7,910	10,540
1 1/2	6	1.767	1.294	12,940	16,170	22,640	13,250	17,670	9,700	12,940
1 5/8	5 1/2	2.074	1.515	15,150	18,940	26,510	15,550	20,740	11,360	15,150
1 3/4	5	2.405	1.745	17,450	21,800	30,520	18,040	24,050	13,080	17,440
1 7/8	5	2.761	2.049	20,490	25,610	35,860	20,710	27,610	15,370	20,490
2	4 1/2	.142	2.300	23,000	28,750	40,250	23,560	31,420	17,250	23,000
2 1/4	4 1/2	3.976	3.021	30,210	37,770	52,870	29,820	39,760	22,660	30,210
2 1/2	4	4.909	3.716	37,160	46,450	65,040	36,820	49,090	27,870	37,160
2 3/4	4	5.940	4.620	46,200	57,750	80,840	44,580	59,400	34,650	46,200
3	3 1/2	7.069	5.428	54,280	67,850	94,990	53,020	70,690	40,710	54,280

Example.—How much load may be put on a 1 in. bolt for a tensile stress of 6,000 lbs. per sq. in. ?

Referring to table (page 78) find in the line for 1 in bolt 3,300 lbs. corresponding to a stress on the bolt of 6,000 lbs. per sq. in.

Example.—What size bolt is required to support a load of 2,500 lbs for a stress of 6,000 lbs. per sq. in.?

$$\text{Area at root of thread} = \text{given load} \div 6,000$$
$$= 2,500 \div 6,000 = .417 \text{ sq. in.}$$

Referring to table (page 78 or 82) in the column headed area at root (or bottom) of thread, find .419 sq. in. nearest area; this corresponds to a ⅞ in. bolt.

Of course for the several given values of lbs. stress per sq. in., the result could be found directly from the tables, but the calculation above illustrates the method which would be employed for other stresses per sq. in. not given in the tables.

Example.—A butt joint with fish plates is fastened by six bolts through each timber. What size bolts should be used allowing a shearing stress of 5,000 lbs. per sq. in. in the bolts when the joint is subjected to a tensile load of 20,000 lbs.?

$$\text{Load carried per bolt} = 20,000 \div \text{number of bolts}$$
$$= 20,000 \div 6 = 3,333 \text{ lbs.}$$

Each bolt is in double shear, hence equivalent

$$\text{single shear load} = \tfrac{1}{2} \text{ of } 3,334 = 1,667 \text{ lbs., and}$$

$$\text{area per bolt} = \frac{1,667}{5,000} = .333 \text{ sq. in.}$$

Referring to table on page 82 the nearest area of bolt is .307 corresponding to a ⅝ in. bolt. In the case of a *dead* or "*quiescent*" load ⅝ bolts would be ample but for a *live* load take the next larger size or ¾ in. bolts.

The example does not give the size of the timbers but the assumption is they are large enough to safely carry the load. In practice *all parts should be calculated* as further instructed in the chapter on "The Strength of Timbers" in vol. 2.

The ideal joint is one so proportioned that the total shearing stress of the bolts equals the tensile strength of the timbers.

Material and Strength of Bolts.—The Navy Department specifications for steel bolts are, in part, as follows: Bolts must be made of a good quality of medium steel and conform to the United States standard for both heads and threads. Test bolts are to be bent cold on the unthreaded portion, through 180 degrees, around a diameter equal to one-half the bolt diameter, without breaking; only a slight fracture of the "skin" on one side will be allowed. When practicable, a tensile test of bolts and nuts combined shall be made. Bolts so tested must fracture at the threads and not at the juncture with the head; they must withstand a tensile stress of at least 58,000 pounds and have an elastic limit of not less than 30,000 pounds per square inch of sectional area.

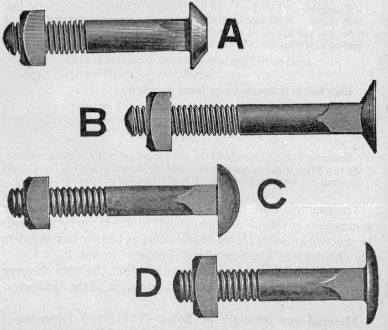

ғıgs. 246 to 249.—Various Philadelphia carriage bolts. **A.** bevel head: **B,** countersunk head; **C.** turned oval head: **D.** bastard head.

CHAPTER 5

Work Bench

In order to properly perform many of the numerous operations in carpentry a suitable work bench is essential. Broadly speaking, the bench may be regarded as a tool, especially when considered with its various attachments for holding and

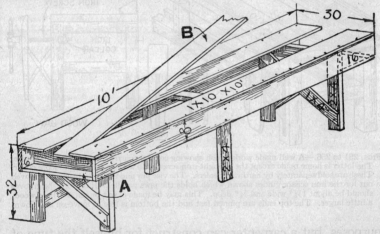

FIG. 250.—Quickly constructed work bench for temporary use showing construction. *Lumber required:* 5—2″×4″×8′; 1—1″×4″×16′; 3—1″×8″×10′; 3—1″×10″×10′ and one pound of 8d. and 10d. nails. It is 30 ins. wide on the top, 10 ft. long and 32 ins. high. For neatness all the ends are squared and the brace ends cut off flush with legs. The center legs add rigidity, though in a bench like this with only 8 feet distance between the end legs, it would not be generally necessary. The center cross piece and the wide sides all well nailed together makes the top very rigid. While this is the general construction, longitudinal diagonal braces give additional rigidity and are desirable where heavy work is to be done. The space at A, when partly enclosed by an outside board, provides a convenient receptacle for small articles.

clamping the material when undergoing the numerous operations known as bench work.

There is hardly a shop for any purpose but that requires a *work bench*, especially the carpenter's shop. Many of these shops have only a makeshift bench made of 2 × 4 and ⅞ in. boards, crudely put together, with no part of it strong enough and no place to attach vise; such benches temporarily knocked together on the job are not worthy to be called work benches. Substantial benches are manufactured and on sale, for all

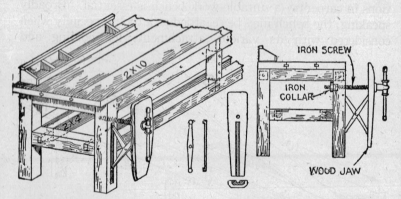

Figs. 251 to 256.—A well made work bench showing general construction with details of vise. The latter is home made except the wrought iron screw with wooden handle and loose collar. These are sold separately by hardware dealers. The vise jaw and the leg of bench are grooved out for the iron scissor guides shown which holds the jaws parallel. If of iron, the grooves should be about 1⅛″ wide and ⅝″ deep. This may be made of oak or suitable hard wood, a little larger. The top ends are pinned fast and the bottom is free to move up and down.

purposes, but a carpenter can construct for himself the type of bench best suited to his requirements.

Fig. 250 shows a quickly constructed bench such as would be used on a house job, and figs. 251 to 256, a bench constructed with more care for permanent installation in a shop.

The height of bench should be regulated by the character of the work to be done—high for light work and low for heavy work; also the height of the person who is to use it should be considered. In general, carpenter's benches are made 33 ins. high while those for cabinet and pattern makers are from two to four inches higher.

Work Bench Attachments.—Numerous devices are used with work benches to facilitate the operations to be performed. These devices or attachments are:

1. Vises

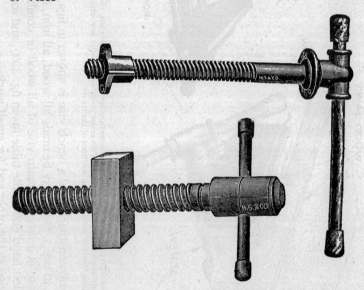

Figs. 257 and 258.—Iron and wooden bench screws as used for bench vises. *The iron screw* has a wooden handle with loose collar. Usual sizes: diam. 1 to 1¼ ins.; length of screw 15 to 20 ins. *The wooden screw* is made of some hard wood as hickory. *Usual sizes:* diam. 1¼ to 2⅜ ins.; length of screw 20 ins.

2. Support pegs
3. Stop
4. Hook
5. Support strips

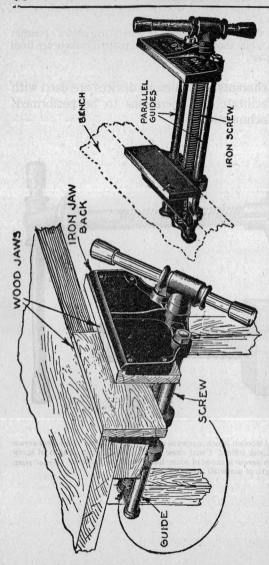

FIGS. 259 and 260.—Bench vise with guides for maintaining the jaws parallel. *In construction*, the inner jaw is fastened to the bench and causes a fixed nut in which the screw rotates. This screw controls the outer jaw which has attached to it two rods working in sleeves and keeping the jaws parallel for all positions of the travel.

Vises.—The general construction of a bench vise is shown in figs. 251 to 256. There are numerous types in use. They may be made all wood, all iron, or of wood with iron screw. Usually there is a large or main vise of all wood or combined wood and iron construction at the left hand end of the table (as in fig. 259), and sometimes a smaller or supplemental iron vise at the other end for small work.

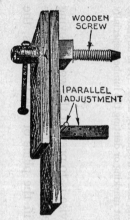

The accompanying cuts show construction of the various bench vises. An important requirement is that the construction be such that the vise jaws will remain parallel in any position. One method of obtaining parallelism is by scissors arrangement shown in fig. 256. Another method is by means of guides as in fig. 260.

In addition to these methods there is an adjustable peg arrangement for securing approximate parallelism as shown in fig. 261. Evidently this method requires frequent adjustment and parallelism cannot be obtained for all positions of the jaws without an undue multiplicity of peg holes.

FIG. 261.—All wood bench vise with adjustable peg arrangement for keeping the jaws *approximately* parallel. The vise here shown is for light duty such as wood carver's use and is usually made of maple with hickory screw. A size generally used is 42 ins. long, having 6 in. jaws and 12 in. opening.

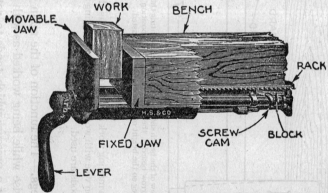

FIG. 262.—Quick-acting bench vise; a form used for general pattern making. *In operation,* the jaws are controlled by a lever which operates a cam, the latter controlling the engagement with, and release of the block from the rack. When the lever is brought to one position, the block drops out of contact with the rack and the jaw can be moved to the approximate desired position. Then turning the lever causes the block to engage with the rack and draw the movable jaw toward the fixed jaw. This type of vise is suitable for light and medium duty but not heavy duty unless very substantially constructed because of bending stress brought on the guides which tend to twist the jaws out of parallelism.

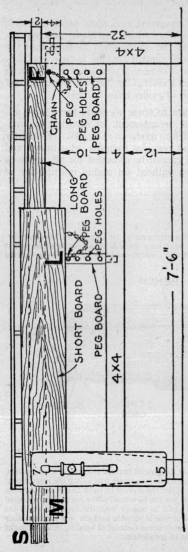

Fig. 263.—Front view of the bench shown in fig. 251, illustrating the use of supporting pins. In the vise is seen a short wide board M, and a long narrow board S, their ends being held in position by pegs L and F. A number of holes are provided in the peg boards for each peg so the height of support may be adjusted.

For pattern making work a quick closing vise as shown in fig. 262 is frequently used. It is advisable to face an iron vise with wooden or leather covering to prevent marking or denting the lumber especially when soft woods are used.

Support Pegs.—The function of the main bench vise is to prevent the wood moving side- or endwise while being worked as with a plane or chisel. In these operations the wood receives a pressure which tends to rotate it in the plane of the vise jaws, the latter acting as a pivot.

Evidently in the case of a long board this turning force or torque would become very great when a downward pressure is applied at the far end of the board, requiring the vise to be screwed up very firmly to prevent turning. To avoid this, the bench is provided with supporting pegs which carry the weight of the board and prevent it turning when a downward pressure is applied in tooling.

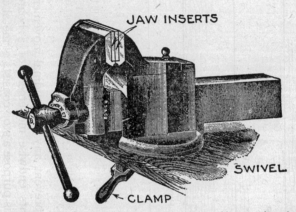

FIG. 264.—Parker's wood working vise with swivel back jaws and bottom. A good type of vise for use at the right end of the bench to supplement the main vise, being very useful for small work.

FIGS. 265 and 266.—Round and square forms of bench stop. These adjust by a center screw from flush to as high as required for the work being planed. The round one is fitted by boring a hole the diameter of top with extension bit and the deeper center with size of bit it requires. The other is shallow and mortised in flush.

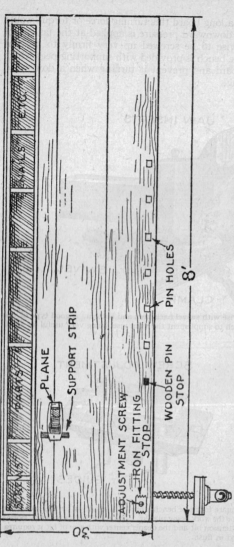

FIG. 267.—Plan of work bench (shown in fig. 263), showing iron stop and wooden peg stop, also the series of peg holes for peg stop.

A good arrangement of supporting pegs is shown in fig. 263, being adapted to short and long boards.

Stop.—This device is intended to prevent any longitudinal movement of the work while being tooled, that is, it prevents endwise movement of a board while being planed. As usually constructed for this purpose a stop consists of metal casing designed to set in flush with the bench and having a horizontal toothed plate working in vertical guides and having screw adjustment so that the plate may be set flush with

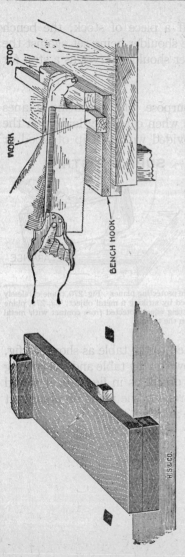

FIG. 268.—Bench hook secured in position by wooden pin stop. The bench hook is useful for a variety of operations such as odd sawing and chiseling, and serves also to prevent the bench being marred by such operations.

FIG. 269.—Method of using the bench hook in sawing with the back saw.

the top of the table (when out of use) or a little above so as to engage the end of the work and thus prevent endwise movement.

Figs. 265 and 266 show round and square forms of stop. A stop may be simply of a piece of wood about 2″ × 2 in. projecting through a mortise in the top of the bench. This kind of stop is suitable for use with the bench hook; for the main stop it is better to have some form of iron fitting such as shown in figs. 265 and 266.

Bench Hook.—This is virtually a movable stop that can be used at right angles to the front of the bench. It serves many purposes for holding and putting work together.

When it is desired to saw off a piece of stock, the bench hook is placed on the bench, one shoulder being set against the edge of the bench while the upper shoulder serves as a stop for the work while sawing.

Support Strips.—For the purpose of preventing planes resting upon their cutting edges when carelessly laid upon the bench, the latter should be provided with a strip of wood or

FIGS. 270 and 271.—Application of *support strip* in protecting planes. Fig. 270, plane carelessly thrown down on table with cutting edge dented by striking a metal object; fig. 271, plane properly placed on support strip showing cutting edge protected from contact with metal object or any water or moisture that may be on the table.

leather about ⅜ in. thick attached to the table as shown in fig. 270. Evidently if a plane be thrown on the table and the cutting edge strike a nail or other metal object as in fig. 270, it would likely result in a dent, whereas resting the plane on a support strip as in fig. 271, this would be avoided.

CHAPTER 6

Carpenters' Tools

A carpenter should possess a full set of tools, and in the selection of these *it is **important** to buy only the **best** regardless of cost.* Select carefully from standard makes, examining them carefully to be sure there are no visible defects. The temper of steel may be discovered only by use and any defect in the best grades of tools is made good upon complaint to the dealer, hence *buy only the best*.

In the classification of the multiplicity of carpenters' tools they should be classed according to some particular point of view which will divide them into well defined groups. Hence, *with respect to use,* tools may be classified as:

1. Guiding and Testing Tools.

Straight edge

Square
  - try square
  - mitre square
  - combined try and mitre square
  - framing or so-called "steel" square
  - combination square

Sliding T bevel
Shooting board
Mitre box
Mitre shooting board
Level
Plumb bob
Plumb rule

2. Marking Tools.

Chalk line
Carpenters' pencil
Ordinary pencil
Scratch awl
Scriber
Compasses and dividers

3. Measuring Tools.

Carpenters' two foot rule
Various folding rules
Rules with attachments
Lumber scales
Marking gauges

4. Holding Tools

Horses or trestles
Clamps
Vises

5. Toothed Cutting Tools.

Saws $\begin{cases} \text{hand} \\ \text{circular} \\ \text{band} \end{cases}$

Files and rasps
Sand paper

6. Sharp Edge Cutting Tools.

Chisels $\begin{cases} \text{paring} \\ \text{firmer} \\ \text{framing} \\ \text{slick} \\ \text{corner} \\ \text{gouge} \\ \text{tang and socket} \\ \text{butt pocket and mill} \end{cases}$

Draw knife

7. Rough Facing Tools.

Hatchet
Axe
Adze

8. Smooth Facing Tools.

Spoke shave

Planes
{
jack
fore
trying
jointer
smooth
block
moulding and special
}

9. Boring Tools.

Brad awl
Gimlets
Augers
Drills
Hollow augers
Spoke pointers
Counter sinks
Reamers

10. Fastening Tools.

Hammers
Screw drivers
Wrenches

11. Sharpening Tools.

Grind stones

Abrasives
Grinding Wheels
Oil stones $\begin{cases} \text{natural} \\ \text{artificial} \end{cases}$

CHAPTER 7

Guiding and Testing Tools

In good carpentry much depends on accuracy in measurement and in fitting parts together at the required angle. In order to insure this accuracy, various tools of guidance and direction

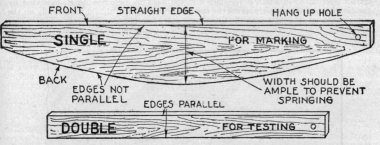

FIG. 272.—Ordinary single wooden straight edge for marking. When well made it is sufficiently accurate for ordinary use. *In making* a straight edge of this kind, clear, straight grained wood should be used. The back edge should not be parallel with the front because there should be greater width at the center than at the ends for stiffness, the width at the center depending upon the thickness. The length may range from a few inches to several feet, depending upon the intended use.

FIG. 273.—Ordinary double wooden straight edge for testing. This differs from the single straight edge in that both front and back edges are parallel so that it may be used for special tests such as for winding surfaces.

are used, otherwise joints, etc., could not be made with precision.

Straight Edge.—This tool is used to guide the pencil or

scriber in marking a straight line, and in testing a faced surface as the edge of a board to determine if it be straight. Anything having an edge known to be straight, as the edge of a steel

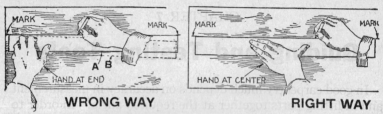

WRONG WAY   **RIGHT WAY**

Figs. 274 and 275.—The straight edge as a guiding tool. When held in position, as in fig. 274, with the hand at the end, the lateral pressure of the pencil as it nears the other end (especially when the pencil is held incorrectly as in fig. 279) will tend to push the straight edge from its correct position A, in which it registers with the mark to some positon B, indicated by the dotted lines. To properly secure the straight edge, the hand should press firmly on the straight edge at its center with the thumb and other fingers stretched wide apart. This will hold it firmly in position against any turning pressure due to the pencil.

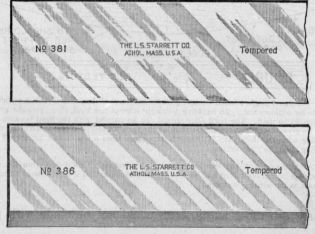

Figs. 276 and 277.—Starrett steel straight edges. Fig. 276, plain; fig. 277, beveled. These straight edges are nickel plated and while they are intended especially for draughtmen's work, they can be used to advantage by carpenters on work of precision. Made in lengths ranging from 12 to 72 ins.; width 1⅜ to 2½; thickness ⁵⁄₆₄ to ⅛.

RIGHT WAY

WRONG WAY

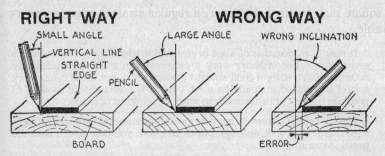

FIGS. 278 to 280.—*Right and wrong inclinations* of the pencil in marking with the straight edge. In fig. 278, the pencil should not be inclined from the vertical more than is necessary to bring the pencil lead in contact with the guiding surface of the straight edge. When inclined more as in fig. 279, and the pencil pressed firmly, considerable pressure is brought against the straight edge, tending to push it out of position. If the inclination be in the opposite direction, as in fig. 280, the lead recedes from the guiding surface introducing an error which is magnified when a wooden straight edge is used because of the excess thickness of the straight edge.

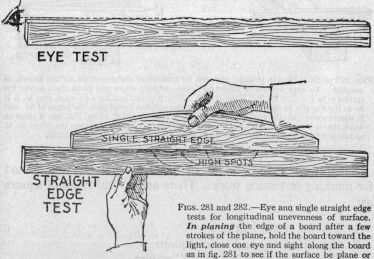

FIGS. 281 and 282.—Eye and single straight edge tests for longitudinal unevenness of surface. *In planing* the edge of a board after a few strokes of the plane, hold the board toward the light, close one eye and sight along the board as in fig. 281 to see if the surface be plane or uneven. With practice a good straight surface can be obtained. For precision used in addition to the eye test the straight edge test as in fig. 282. Hold board with straight edge between the eye and light and any unevenness will show plainly.

square may be used, however, a regular straight edge is prefer-able.

It may be made either of wood or steel and in length from a few inches to several feet. For ordinary work a carpenter can make one sufficiently accurate from a strip of good straight grained wood, but for accurate work a steel straight edge should be used. Wood is objectionable in work of precision because of its tendency to warp or spring out of shape.

Figs. 274 and 275 show correct and incorrect methods of holding a straight edge as a guiding tool, and figs. 278 to 280, how, and how not to hold the pencil in marking.

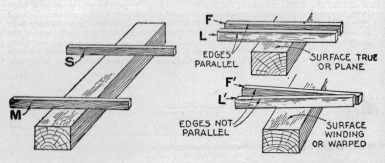

Figs. 283 to 285.—Double straight edge test for transverse unevenness of surface known as winding. *To test for wind,* take two double straight edges and place them across the surface to be tested as M, and S, in fig. 283. Now if the surface have no wind, that is, if it be at right angles to the side of the board at the sections tested then the edges of M and S, when viewed from the end of the board will be parallel as LF, in fig. 284, but if there be wind, that is if the sections tested be not at 90° to the side of the board, then the edges of M and S, will be inclined to each other when viewed at the end as L',F', in fig. 285.

Square.—This tool is *a 90° or right angle standard* and is used for marking or testing work. There are several types of square as:

1. Try (or trying) square
2. Combined try and mitre square
3. Framing or so called "steel" square
4. Combination square

Try Square.—In England this is called the *trying square* but here simply *try square*. It is so called probably because of its frequent use as a testing tool when squaring up mill planed stock. The ordinary try square used by carpenters consists of a steel *blade* set at right angles to the inside face of the *stock* in which it is held. The stock is made of some hard wood and is

FIG. 286.—Stanley try square with rose wood stock brass lined. 7½-inch scale divided into 8ths.

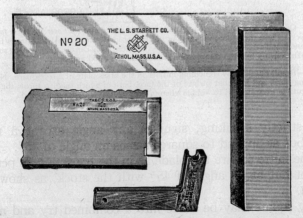

FIGS. 287 to 289.—Starrett hardened solid steel try square. A tool of precision for the discriminating worker and one that can be used as a standard. Fig. 288 shows stock support, and fig. 289. case.

always faced with brass in order to preserve the wood from injury.

The usual sizes of try squares have blades ranging from 3 to 15 inches long. The stock is about ½ inch thick with blade inserted midway between the sides of the stock. The stock is made thicker than the blade so that its face may be applied to the edge of the wood and the steel blade laid on the surface to be marked. Usually the blade is provided with a scale of inches divided into 8ths.

Mitre, and Combined Try and Mitre Squares.—The term

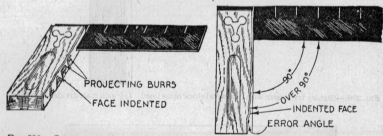

Fig. 290.—One way to ruin a good try square: *stamp your initials all over the brass face plate of the stock.* Place the square in a vise or preferably lay it on an anvil with brass face up. With stencils and a heavy hammer stamp the letters deep so all can see them—using sufficient force to thoroughly test the compression strength of the wood and brass.

Fig. 291.—Result obtained by stencilling initials on the brass plate of a try square. Note the projecting burrs and indented surface of the face, both of which tend to throw the square out of truth or even cause it to wobble when pressed against the edge of a board.

mitre, strictly speaking, signifies any angle except a right angle, but as applied to squares means an angle of 45°.

In the mitre square the blade as in the try square is permanent set but at an angle of 45° with the stock, as shown in fig. 292.

A try square may be made into a combined try and mitre square, when the end of the stock to which the blade is fastened is faced off at 45° as along the line MS in fig. 293. In use when

the 45° face MS, of the stock is placed against the edge of a
board, the blade will be at an angle of 45° with the edge of the
board as in fig. 295.

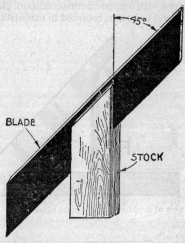

FIG. 292.—Mitre square. It differs from the ordinary try square in that the blade is set at an
angle of 45° with the stock and the latter is attached to the blade midway between its ends.

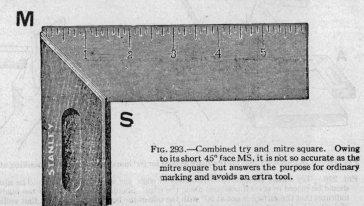

FIG. 293.—Combined try and mitre square. **Owing
to its short 45° face MS, it is not so accurate as the
mitre square but answers the purpose for ordinary
marking and avoids an extra tool.**

An improved form of combined try and mitre square is shown in fig. 294. Owing to the longer face LF as compared with MS, the blade describes an angle of 45° with greater precision. A square having a blade not exactly at the intended angle is said to be out of truth or simply "out," and good work cannot be done with a square in this condition. Hence a square should be tested and if found to be out, returned to manufacturer.

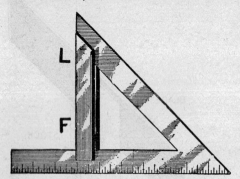

Fig. 294.—Improved form of combined try and mitre square.

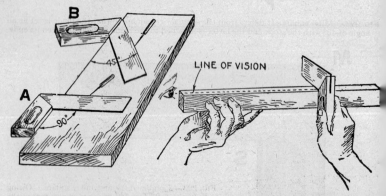

Fig. 295.—Combined try and mitre square as used for 90° marking at A, and 45° marking at B.

Fig. 296.—Try square used to test squareness of edge ace with side of board. The square should be placed in several positions along the edge. Should light show under the blade it indicates that the surface is not at 90° with the side of the board or "square" at that section, and all such places should be trued up with a plane.

The method of testing is shown in figs. 300 to 303, and this test should be made not only at the time of purchase but frequently afterwards as the tool may become imperfect from a fall or rough handling.

Under no circumstances should initials or other marking be stamped on the brass face of the ordinary try square as the burrs which project or bending of the brass face will throw the square out of truth and for this reason manufacturers will not take back a square with any marks stamped on the brass face. Figs. 290 and 291 show the result of stamping initials on the brass face.

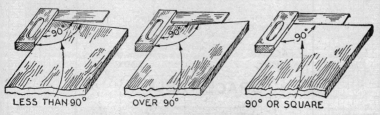

LESS THAN 90°   OVER 90°   90° OR SQUARE

FIGS. 297 to 299.—Application of try square for testing end of board to determine if the cross cut be "square" with longitudinal edge of board. Figs. 297 and 298 show end edge at angles less and greater than 90° and fig. 299, end edge at 90° or "square."

Framing or So-called "Steel" Square.—The ridiculousness of calling this type of square a *steel* square, must be evident from the fact that all types of square may be obtained made entirely of steel; see fig. 287. It is properly called a *framing* square because with its framing table and various other scales it is

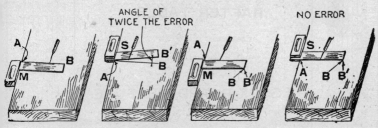

ANGLE OF TWICE THE ERROR   NO ERROR

FIGS. 300 to 303.—Method of testing a try square. If square be "out" (angle not 90°) scribed lines AB, and AB', for positions M, and S, of square (figs. 300 and 301) will not coincide. Angle BAB', is twice the angle of error. *Why?* If square be correct, AB and AB', for positions M and S, will coincide as in figs. 302 and 303.

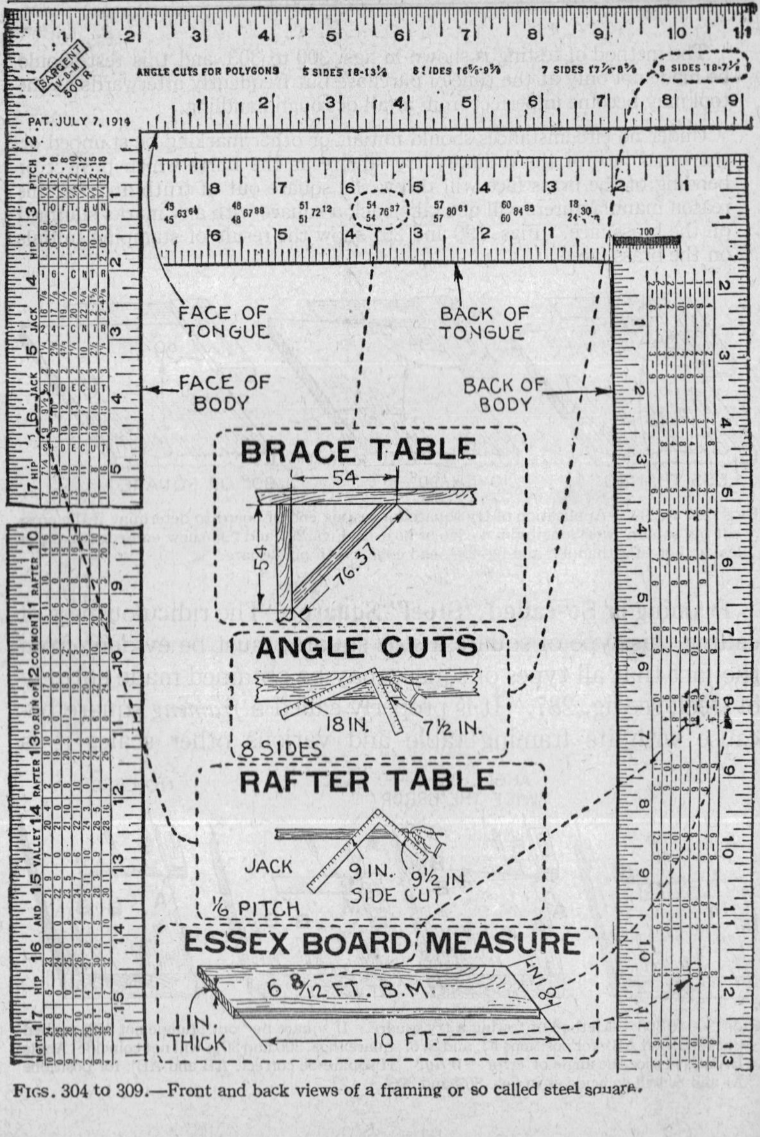
SARGENT
V-8-M
500 R
ANGLE CUTS FOR POLYGONS
5 SIDES 18-13⅛
6 SIDES 16⅝-9⅝
7 SIDES 17⅞-8⅝
8 SIDES 18-7½
PAT. JULY 7, 1914
FACE OF TONGUE
BACK OF TONGUE
FACE OF BODY
BACK OF BODY
BRACE TABLE
54
54
76.37
ANGLE CUTS
18 IN.
7½ IN.
8 SIDES
RAFTER TABLE
JACK
9 IN.
9½ IN
SIDE CUT
⅙ PITCH
ESSEX BOARD MEASURE
6 8/12 FT. B.M.
8 IN.
1 IN. THICK
10 FT.

FIGS. 304 to 309.—Front and back views of a framing or so called steel square.

adapted especially for use in house framing, although its range of usefulness makes it valuable to any wood worker. Its general appearance is shown in figs. 304 and 305.

The framing square consists of two essential parts: the **tongue** *and the* **body** *or blade.* *The* **tongue** *is the* **shorter** *narrower part and the* **body,** *the* **longer** *and wider part.* *The point at which the tongue and body meet on the outside edge is called the* **heel.**

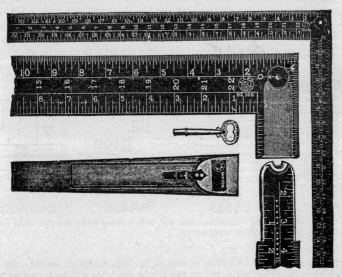

Figs. 310 to 314.—PS, and W, take down framing square showing face of square entire, **locking** device, key and waterproof carrying case. *In construction,* the body of the square has a shoulder against which the tongue bears when the two parts are fitted together. When assembled it can be locked tight. The locking cam is located at the center as shown. Evidently where compactness is required this is a desirable type of square is a handy **tool to** transport. With careful use a good take down square should not get out of truth.

There are several grades of square known as: polished, nickeled, blued and royal copper. The blued square with figures and scales in white is perhaps the most desirable. A size largely used has an 18 in. body and a 12 in. tongue, but there are many uses which require the largest size whose body measures 24 × 2 in. and tongue 16 or 18 × 1½ in

The feature which makes the square so valuable a tool is its numerous scales and tables. These are:

1. Rafter or framing table 4. Octagon scale
2. Essex table 5. Hundredths scale
3. Brace table 6. Inch scale
7. Diagonal scale

Rafter or Framing Table.—This is always found on the body of the square. It is used for determining the length of common valley hip and jack rafters and the angles at which they must be cut to fit at the ridge and plate.

The appearance of this table is a column six lines deep under each inch

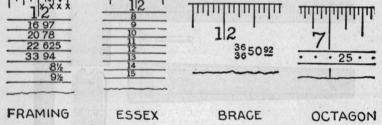

FRAMING   ESSEX   BRACE   OCTAGON

Figs. 315 to 318.—Framing square markings: Fig. 315, framing table; fig. 316, essex table fig; 317, brace table; fig. 318, octagon scale.

graduation from 2 to 18 inches as seen in fig. 315, which shows only the 12 inch section of this table, but at the left of the table will be found letters indicating the application of the figures given. The symbols × and ∧ are applied to this table to prevent errors in laying out angles for cuts.

Essex Table.—This is always found on the body of the square as shown in fig. 316. This table gives the board measure in feet and 12ths of feet of boards one inch thick of usual length and widths. On Stanley squares it consists of a table 8 lines deep under each graduation, as seen in the figures which represent this 12 inch section of this table.

Brace Table.—This table is found on the tongue of the square, a section of which is shown in fig. 317. The table gives the length of the brace to be used where the rise and run are from 24 to 60 ins. and are equal.

Octagon Scale.—This is located on the tongue of the square, as shown in fig. 318, and is used for laying out a figure with eight sides on a square piece of timber. It is a scale of which the graduations are represented by 65 dots located $5/24$ of an inch apart. On some squares a table of angle cuts for various polygons is given.

Hundredths Scale.—This scale is found on the tongue of the square and by means of a divider, decimals of an inch may be obtained. It is used particularly in reference to brace measure.

Inch Scales.—On both body and tongue there are along the edges scales

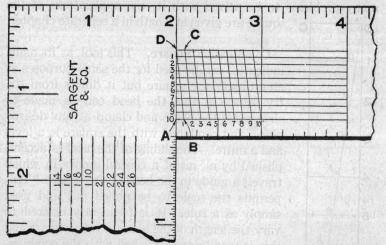

Fig. 319.—Diagonal scale as stamped on early Sargent framing squares intended for picking off hundredths of an inch with dividers.

of inches as seen in figs. 304 and 305, graduated to $1/32$, $1/16$, $1/12$, $1/10$, $1/8$ and $1/4$. Various combinations of the graduations can be obtained according to the type of square. These scales are used in measuring and laying out work to dimension.

Diagonal Scale.—Sargent framing squares are provided with what is known as a diagonal scale, as shown in fig. 319; one division ABCD, of this scale being shown enlarged for clearness in fig. 320.

The object of the diagonal scale is to give minute measurements without having the graduations close together where they would be hard to read. In construction of the scale (fig. 320), the short distance AB, is $1/10$ of an inch.

Evidently to divide AB, into ten equal parts would bring the divisions so close together that the scale would be difficult to read. Hence, if AB be divided into 10 parts and the diagonal BD, be drawn, the intercepts 1*a*, 2*b*, 3*c*, etc., drawn through 1, 2, 3, etc., parallel to AB, will divide AB into $^1/_{10}$, $^2/_{10}$, $^3/_{10}$, etc., Thus if a distance say $^3/_{10}$ of AB is required, it may be picked off by placing one leg of the dividers at 3 and the other leg at *c*, giving 3*c* = $^3/_{10}$ of AB.

Because of the importance of the framing square and the many problems to be solved with it, the applications of the square are given at length in a separate chapter.

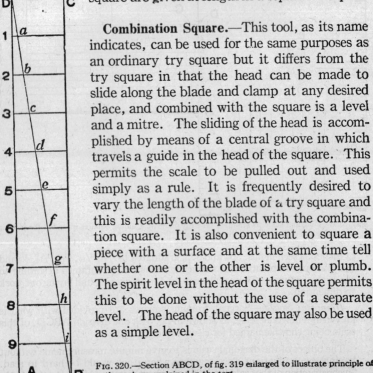

Combination Square.—This tool, as its name indicates, can be used for the same purposes as an ordinary try square but it differs from the try square in that the head can be made to slide along the blade and clamp at any desired place, and combined with the square is a level and a mitre. The sliding of the head is accomplished by means of a central groove in which travels a guide in the head of the square. This permits the scale to be pulled out and used simply as a rule. It is frequently desired to vary the length of the blade of a try square and this is readily accomplished with the combination square. It is also convenient to square a piece with a surface and at the same time tell whether one or the other is level or plumb. The spirit level in the head of the square permits this to be done without the use of a separate level. The head of the square may also be used as a simple level.

Fig. 320.—Section ABCD, of fig. 319 enlarged to illustrate principle of the scale as explained in the text.

Because the scale may be moved in the head, the combination square makes a good marking gauge, by setting the scale at the proper position and clamping it there. The whole combination square may then be slid along as with an ordinary gauge. As a further convenience, a scriber is held frictionally in the head by a small brass bushing. The scriber head projects from the bottom of the square stock in a convenient place to take out quickly.

In laying out, the combination square may be used to scribe lines at mitre angles as well as at right angles, for one edge of the square head is at 45°. Where micrometer accuracy is not essential, the blade of the combination

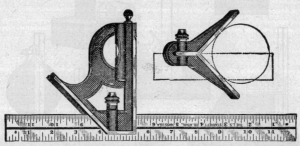

FIGS. 321 and 322.—Starrett combination square with hardened blade, level and centering attachment.

square may be set at any desired position and the square used as a depth gauge to measure in mortises, or the end of the scale may be set flush with the edge of the square and used as a height gauge.

The head may be unclamped and entirely removed from the scale and a center head substituted so that the same tool can quickly be used to find the centers of shafting and other cylindrical pieces. In best construction, the blade is hardened to prevent the corners wearing round and destroying the graduations, thus keeping the scale at all times accurate. This combination square combining as it does a rule, square, mitre, depth gauge, height gauge, level, and center head permits of more rapid work on the part of the mechanic, saves littering the bench with a number of tools each of which is necessary but which may be used only rarely, and tends toward the goal for which all mechanics are striving—greater efficiency.

Figs. 321 and 322 show a combination square and centering attachment; figs. 323 to 333 some of the uses of the square.

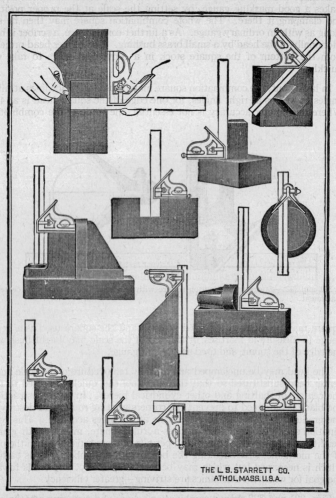

THE L. S. STARRETT CO.
ATHOL, MASS. U.S.A.

FIGS. 323 to 333.—Views showing range of work that can be performed with Starrett combination square.

Sliding "T" Bevel.—A bevel is virtually a try square having a sliding adjustable blade that can be set at any angle with the stock. In construction the stock may be of wood or steel; when of wood it has brass mountings at each end and is sometimes concaved along its length. The blade is of steel with parallel sides and its end at 45° with the sides as shown in fig. 334. The blade is slotted allowing linear adjustment and the insertion of

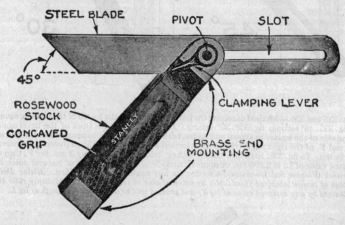

STEEL BLADE   PIVOT   SLOT

45°

ROSEWOOD STOCK

CONCAVED GRIP

STANLEY

CLAMPING LEVER

BRASS END MOUNTING

Fig. 334.—Sliding T bevel with steel blade, rosewood stock and brass end mountings. Incorrectly called the bevel square. It is used in marking and testing any angle. As the size of a bevel may be expressed by the length of either its stock or blade, care should be taken to specify which dimension is given in ordering to avoid mistakes.

a pivot or screw pin located at the end of the stock. When the blade has been adjusted to any particular angle, it is secured in position by tightening the screw lever on the pivot which

NOTE.—The bevel is often incorrectly called the bevel square. Strictly speaking the word square should never be applied to any tool except those which measure 90° as try or framing squares.

compresses the sides of the slotted stock together thus firmly gripping the blade.

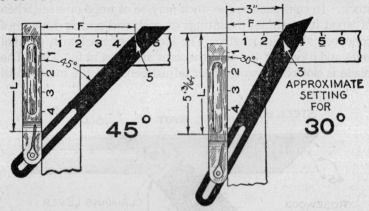

FIGS. 335 and 336.—Method of setting the bevel to various angles by aid of the framing square. Fig. 335, 45° setting; fig. 336, 30° setting. In fig. 335, place the stock of the bevel against one side of the square and adjust both stock and blade to square until the two legs L and F, of the right angle triangle thus formed are of equal length; as shown both measure 5 inches. In fig. 336, to obtain the 30° setting, taking a value of say 3 ins. for F, then the exact value of L, is 5.196 ins. or approximately $5^{13}/_{64}$. With a table of natural *sines* and *cosines* (F=*sine* and L=*cosine*), a setting for any angle may be obtained. *Rule: Divide value of cosine (obtained from table) by value of sine of required angle. Multiply ratio thus obtained by any assigned value of leg F, and product will be corresponding length of leg L.*

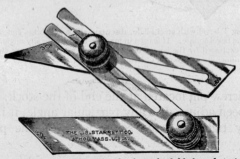

FIG. 337.—Starrett double-slot steel bevel. As shown both blade and stock are slotted, thus adapting it to adjustments that cannot be obtained with a common bevel. The clamping screw head which the cut does not show is let into a rabbet flush with the surface of the stock allowing it to lie flat on the work.

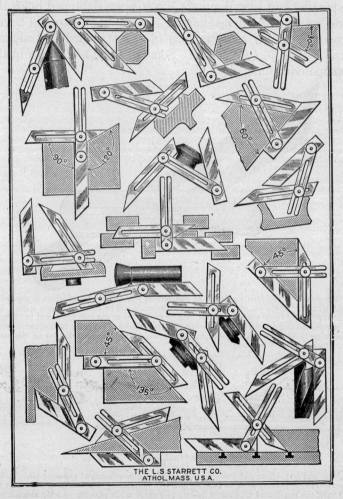

FIGS. 338 to 357.—Some of the various uses of Starrett combination bevel.

In selecting a bevel, care should be taken to see that the edges are parallel and that the pivot screw when tightened holds the blade firmly without bending it. In the line of special bevels there are various modifications of the standard or ordinary form of bevel just described. Some of these are shown in the accompanying cuts.

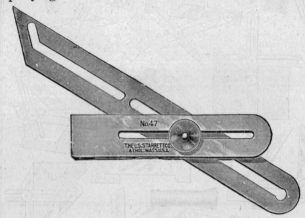

FIG. 358.—Starrett combination bevel. *It consists of* a bevel, one leg of which is pivoted to a straight edge as shown, so as to swing over the stock and be clamped at any angle. The slotted auxiliary blade with clamp bolt may be slipped on to the split blade and be clamped at any desired angle and used in combination with the stock of the other for laying out work, measuring or showing any angle desired and when so combined will lie flat on the work. The stock is about 4 ins. long.

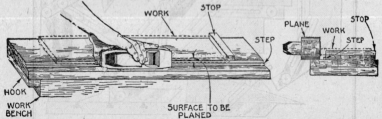

FIGS. 359 and 360.—Side and end views of a simple (non-adjustable) shooting board. The dotted rectangle shows work in position ready to be planed. By providing a hook at the left end, the board may be secured against movement while planing. In the absence of a hook the board may be pressed against the work bench stop pins.

Shooting Board.—In its simplest form a shooting board consists of two dressed boards, one fastened on the face of the other so that the lower board projects a few inches in advance of the upper board, the projection of the lower board forming a bed or alignment guide for the shooting plane, as in figs. 359 and 360. The object of this device is to hold the plane at 90° to the side of the board so that the edge of the board after planing will be square or at right angles with the side of the board

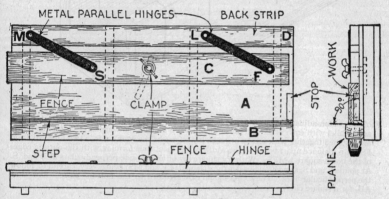

FIGS. 361 to 363.—Improved form of shooting board with adjustable fence and transverse ribs to prevent warping. *In construction,* the upper and lower boards A and B, are fastened together with the lower projecting so that the upper board forms a step. A movable fence is pivoted to the stationary back strip D, by the parallel hinges MS and LF. By means of the clamp which works in a curved groove through upper board A, the fence may be secured in any position. Hence, a plank may be planed so that the edge will be both at right angles with the sides of the board but both edges will be parallel. It is better to take more time and make a serviceable board as here shown than a makeshift as in figs. 359 and 360.

In "shooting an edge" the piece to be planed is held by the left hand against a stop with his edge projecting a little over the stop. Then the shooting plane, laid on its side, is moved steadily along its bed by the right hand, thus obtaining a planed edge at right angles with the side of the board being planed. An improved form of board has provision to prevent warping and

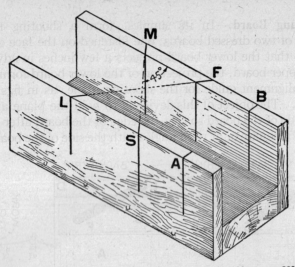

Fig. 364.—Non-adjustable or 45° mitre box. The three pieces should have true 90° edges that are parallel with each other and all surfaces should be true (no warping). After the pieces are fastened together with screws or nails, lay off across the working face two lines ML and FS, at a distance apart equal to the width of the face, thus forming with the outside edges of the box a square LMFS. With try square lay off on the side perpendiculars at L and S. At points L and S, saw through sides the diagonals LF and MS, being very careful to follow the perpendicular lines. These cuts should extend down to the bottom piece. Saw slots AB, for a square cut.

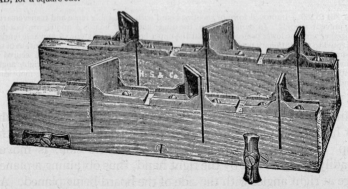

Fig. 365.—Wooden mitre box with iron mountings or guides adjustable to any thickness of saw.

has a fence with parallel motion which may be adjusted to width of the board to be planed as shown in figs. 361 to 363.

Mitre Box.—This device used to guide the saw in cutting work to form mitres consists of a trough formed of a bottom

FIG. 366.—Stanley mitre box. *In construction,* the saw guide uprights are securely clamped in tapered sockets in the swivel arm and can be adjusted to hold the saw without play, and also to counteract a saw that runs out of true, due to improper setting or filing. *The second socket* in the swivel arm permits the use of a short saw or allows a much longer stroke with a standard or regular saw. *The swivel arm* is provided with a tapered index pin which engages in holes placed on the under side of the base. These holes are made at the commonly used angles as designated on top of the base allowing 3, 4, 5, 6, 8, 12 and 24 sided pieces to be cut. The edge of the base is graduated in degrees and the swivel arm can be set and automatically fastened at any degree desired. This automatic fastening device holds the swivel arm firmly to the base in all positions. *The uprights,* front and back, are graduated in sixteenths of inches, and movable stops can be set by means of thumb screws to the depth of the cut desired. *Stock guides* hold all kinds of ordinary work, as well as irregular forms, and can be used as length gauges for duplicating short pieces. *Automatic catches* on the uprights hold the saw up, which allows the use of both hands in placing the work. The adjustable stop on top of the saw, coming in contact with the lever trip, releases the front catch, and the saw in falling pitches slightly forward automatically releasing the rear catch, without any necessity of taking the hand from the saw or touching the lever trip. Two cone pointed leveling screws on the rear feet prevent the box sliding when in use. The clamp extension at right of cut is to hold long pieces of wood.

and two side pieces of wood screwed together and having saw cut through the sides at angles of 45° and 90° as shown in fig. 364. It will be noted that there are two 45° cuts MS and LF; these are for cutting right and left mitres.

Mitre Shooting Board.—For fine work it is necessary to accurately dress the ends of the pieces cut by the saw in a mitre box. This is done with the aid of a mitre shooting board as shown in fig. 367. It is virtually a plain shooting board with two 45° stops fastened on top of the upper board.

Level.—This tool is used for both guiding and testing; to

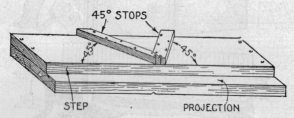

Fɪɢ. 367.—Mitre shooting board for dressing mitres after sawing in mitre box. The size of the board should be about 2 feet long.

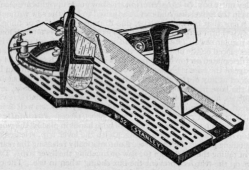

Fɪɢ. 368.—Stanley mitre shoot board and plane, designed for pattern makers, cabinet makers, picture framers and electrotypers. *In construction,* the board is ribbed and has an adjustable runway accurately machined for the plane. The swivel can be locked at any angle between zero and 90°, the quadrant being graduated between these points. The swivel is also fitted with a sliding back supporting the work to the edge. It is further provided with a sliding back clamp to hold any shaped work in position. The plane is especially constructed for the board, and its cutter has adjustment for depth of cut, also a lateral adjustment so that a cut giving any ordinary draught to a pattern can be made. Being set on a skew it will make a smooth clean cut.

guide in bringing the work to a horizontal or vertical position, and to test the accuracy of completed construction. It consists of a long rectangular body of wood or metal cut away on its side and near the end to receive glass tubes which are almost entirely filled with a non-freezing liquid which leaves a small bubble free to move as the level is moved.

LEVEL GLASS   PLUMB GLASS

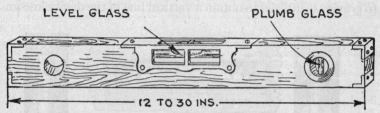

Fig. 369.—Wooden spirit level having horizontal and vertical tubes. The body of the level is made of some hard wood, as rose wood, and is preferably provided with brass mountings as shown.

The side and end tubes are at right angles, so that when the bubble of the side tube is at the center of the tube, the level is horizontal; when the bubble of the end tube is at the center the level is vertical. Accordingly by holding the level on a surface

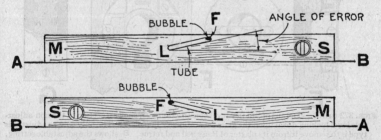

FIGS. 370 and 371.—How to test a spirit level. Lay level on a horizontal surface as AB, in fig. 370. If one end of tube as F, be high, the bubble will run to that end. Reverse level from position MS, fig. 370, to position SM, fig. 371, and it will be found that the bubble will remain at the high end. That is, in fig. 370 the bubble is seen at the right, and in fig. 371, at the left. In *adjustable* levels this error is easily corrected. When the adjustment has been correctly made, the bubble will remain at the center of the tube for both positions of the level when placed on a horizontal surface.

supposed to be horizontal or vertical, it may be ascertained if such surfaces be horizontal or vertical.

Plumb Bob.—The word *plumb* means *perpendicular to the plane of the horizon*, and since plane of the horizon is perpendicular to the direction of gravity at any given point, the force due to gravity is utilized to obtain a vertical line in the device known

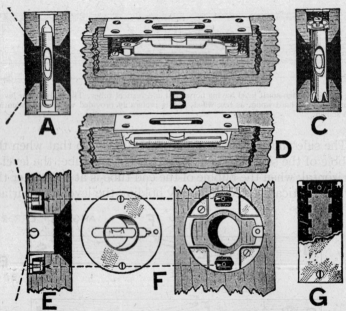

Figs. 372 to 378.—Details of Stanley level construction. **A**, shows a section of the non-adjustable level looking down upon the glass set stationary in plaster. The only way to adjust this type is to remove it from its plaster of Paris bed and retrue. **B**, shows the adjustable setting, having a set screw accessible by removing the plate. Figs. **E** and **F**, show the method of setting a duplex plumb glass close to the face or surface of level, giving the increased angle of vision shown at **E**, and the brass cylinder **F**, with the bulb in place ready for setting. The dotted lines cross the two adjusting screws show the slots for adjusting. **G**, is a cross end section showing how it is built up in three sections to hold against warping, and how end plate is screwed on. The easiest handled wood stocks are those grooved on the sides for finger grip

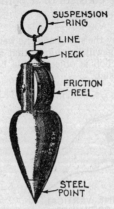

FIG. 379.—Adjustable plumb bob. A reel is placed between two arms at the upper end, upon which the line is wound, the end of the line being threaded through a small hole in the neck. *In using,* by dropping the bob with a slight jerk while the ring is held in the hand, any desired length of line may be reeled off.

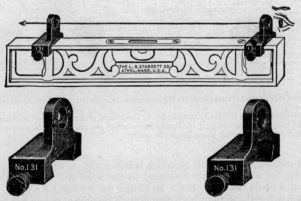

FIGS. 380 to 382.—Starrett metal level with level sight attachments. These attachments (figs. 381 and 382) are made to slip on and off the top side of the level and are held in place by set screws. They have sight holes, one with a cross wire to line accurately from top of and parallel with level. By sighting through the holes the level may be used for leveling the ground from a fixed point at long range preliminary to building foundations.

as a *plumb bob*. It consists of a pointed weight attached to a string.

When suspended by the string and the weight allowed to come to rest, as in fig. 383, the string will be plumb, that is, vertical. The ordinary top shaped solid plumb bob is objectionable because of 1, too blunt point, and 2, not heavy enough.

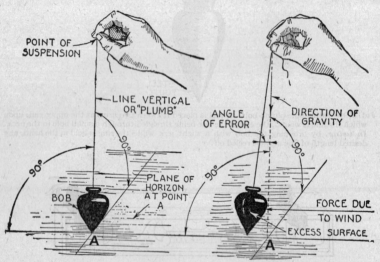

FIG. 383.—Ordinary solid iron plumb bob graphically defining a vertical or plumb line.

FIG. 384.—Error due to wind. In outside work, the lateral pressure due to the wind tends to push the bob to one side causing the line to move out of plumb. Hence to reduce this error a mercury bob of approved shape should be used.

For outside work the last objection is important, as when used with wind blowing the excess surface presented to the wind will magnify the error from this cause, as in fig. 384. To reduce the surface for a given weight, the bob is bored and filled with mercury. This type of plumb bob is shown in fig. 389.

An adjustable bob with self-contained reel on which the string is wound is shown in fig. 379. The convenience of this arrangement is apparent.

Plumb Rule.—This tool utilizes the principle of the plumb bob for vertical testing or guiding, instead of the spirit tube,

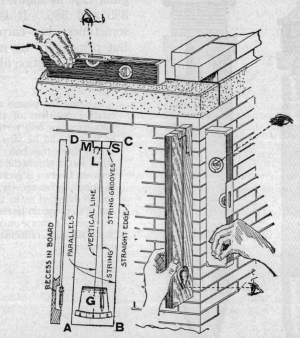

FIGS. 385 and 386.—Plumb rule of approved construction. *To construct,* select preferably some hard wood and make a double straight edge ABCD, say four or five feet long and four to six ins. wide to suit the conditions of use. At the middle point L, scribe a line parallel to the straight edge sides. Cut grooves M, L, and S, in which to fasten the suspension string. The lower portion of the board should be recessed as shown sufficiently for the bob to swing without interference. To make a nice job, a brass plate should be fitted across the lower side of the recess with its edge curved to an arc of radius LG. This plate should be graduated in degrees of fractions of a degree according to the range of the instrument in testing surfaces out of plumb. If the distance LG, from point of suspension to tip of bob be 60 ins., then the length of 1 degree on the scale—1.047 ins. *Rule: To obtain length of 1 degree on scale multiply distance LG, from point of suspension to tip of bob by factor .01745.* Each degree may be divided as closely as desired. By dividing the degrees into 12ths, each division will represent 5 minutes.

FIG. 387.—Brick walls of building in construction showing method of using wood level for making horizontal and vertical tests and application of plumb rule for vertical test.

and it is virtually a plumb bob working in a rectangular case as shown in figs. 385 and 386. It is used sometimes by carpenters but principally by masons in the construction of brick walls.

In using the plumb rule the relative positions of the suspension string and vertical line or axis should be viewed at a point near the bob because when out of plumb the distance between the two is greater than at points higher up. When the tool is designed as in figs. 385 and 386, it should be read from the scale. Of course on ordinary work no such refinements are necessary.

FIG. 388.—Starrett stolid steel plumb bob with improved device for fastening the string without a knot.

FIG. 389.—Starrett mercury plumb bob. *It is made* from solid steel, bored and filled with mercury. The features of this design are: great weight in proportion to size, low center of gravity, small diameter, hardened and ground point, knurled body, and fastening device. By drawing the line into the peculiarly slotted neck at the top, after unwinding the required length, the bob will hang true.

CHAPTER 8

Marking Tools

In good carpentry and joinery much depends upon the accuracy in laying out the work. The term *laying out* means *the operation of marking the work with pencil or scriber so that the various centers and working lines will be set off in their proper relation*. These lines are followed by the carpenter in cutting and other tooling operations necessary to bring the work to its final form.

In laying out, the guiding tools just described in Chapter 7 are used to guide the pencil or scriber, the measurements being made by aid of measuring devices described in Chapter 9.

According to the *degree of precision* desired in laying out, the proper marker to use is

1. $\begin{cases} \text{Chalk line and reel} \\ \text{Carpenter's pencil with rectangular lead} \end{cases}$

For very rough work.

2. Lead pencil with round lead

For rough work.

3. Scratch awl.

For semi-rough work.

4. Scriber.

For work of precision as fine joinery

For efficiency the carpenter should use judgment **to work** with proper *degree of precision*.

Thus, it would be ridiculous to use a machinist hardened steel scriber with a needle point to mark out rafters, or to use a carpenter's pencil with "an acre of soft lead" on the point to lay out a fine dove tail joint. Simply exercise common sense.

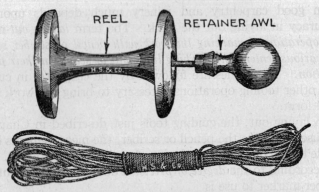

REEL   RETAINER AWL

FIG. 390.—Chalk line reel bored to receive the line retaining awl. The chalk line is wound on the reel when not in use and the awl inserted into reel as shown.

FIG. 391.—Chalk line. It can usually be obtained as follows: braided, 84 ft. hanks; cotton, light or heavy, 20 ft. hanks; Mason's linen, light, 84 ft. and heavy 50 ft. hanks; Mason's cotton, 450 to 600 ft. per lb. hank.

Chalk Line and Reel.—The special use of this device is to mark a long straight line between two points too far distant to permit the use of a square or straight edge as for instance in marking a long plank for the rip saw.

The line consists of a light string or cord.

It is rubbed with chalk and then stretched between the two points.

When the string is taut, it is pulled up and let spring back, thus marking a white line on the surface of the work. Boat builders use the chalk line to mark a "base line" and "station lines" is "fairing up" a design. In using a chalk line, note the right and wrong way to use the line as shown in figs. 392 and 393.

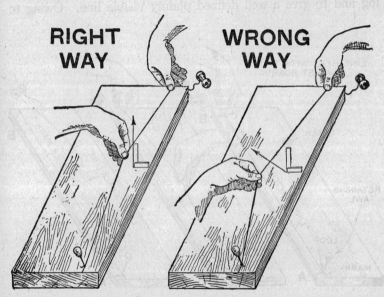

FIGS. 392 and 393.—Right and wrong way to use the chalk line. *In pulling up the line always pull it up in a direction at right angles with the board—not to one side.*

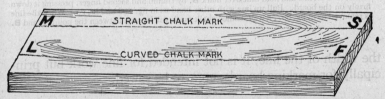

FIG. 394.—Chalk marks obtained by right and wrong methods of using the chalk line. When the line is pulled straight up, as in fig. 392, a straight chalk mark **MS**, will be obtained, but when pulled up to one side (as in fig. 393) a curved line **LF**, will be obtained.

Carpenter's Pencil.—The regulation carpenter's pencil has a lead of rectangular cross section considerably larger than an ordinary pencil. The object of making the lead in this shape is to permit its use on rough lumber without too frequent sharpening and to give a well defined plainly visible line. Owing to

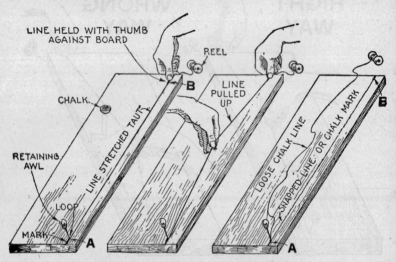

Figs. 395 to 397.—Method of using the chalk line. Mark the ends of the board as at **A** and **B,** the points between which it is desired to obtain a straight line. Insert retaining awl through loop at end of chalk line (after rubbing the chalk line with chalk), and into board through mark **A**. Pull line and hold taut over mark **B**, by thumb and second finger, pressing it down firmly on the board. Pull up line with other hand as in fig. 396 and let go. When the line is removed as in fig. 397, a well-defined chalk mark will be seen between the points **A** and **B**.

the width of the line, it is not intended for fine work but principally for marking boards, etc., to be sawed.

Fig. 398 shows clearly the general appearance of the pencil and shape of the lead. In marking with the carpenter's pencil the mark must be made in the direction of the long axis of the lead as shown in fig. 401—not as in fig. 402. The proper method of sharpening the pencil as shown in fig. 399 and 400 should be noted.

FIG. 398.—Ordinary carpenter's pencil showing shape of the large lead.

Ordinary Pencil.—This form of pencil with its cylindrical lead is familiar to all and needs no description. Since the lead is smaller than that of the carpenter's pencil it produces a finer lead. It is used on smooth surfaces where more accurate marking is required than with the carpenter's pencil. In using, the best results are obtained by twisting the pencil while

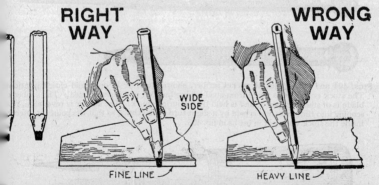

FIGS. 399 and 400.—Side and end views of carpenter's pencil showing proper method of sharpening.

FIGS. 401 and 402.—Right and wrong way of marking with the carpenter's pencil. Evidently when turned as in fig. 401 with the long side of the lead in the direction of the straight edge, a fine line will be obtained and considerable marking may be done before resharpening is necessary. When the pencil is turned around as in fig. 402 the great width of line gives no well defined guide for the cut and moreover the lead is quickly used, requiring frequent sharpening.

drawing the lines so as to retain the conical shape given the lead in sharpening.

Marking or "Scratch" Awl.—This consists of a short piece of round steel, pointed at one end and the other end fixed in a convenient handle. A scratch awl is a *cheap form of scriber* and is used in laying out fine work where a lead pencil mark would be too coarse for the required degree of precision.

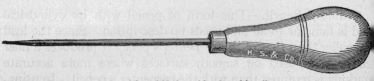

Fɪɢ. 403.—Ordinary scratch awl forged blade and hardwood handle.

Fɪɢs. 404 and 405.—Starrett pocket scriber, showing scriber in open and closed positions. The stock or handle is made from steel tubing knurled and nickel plated. The scriber o blade is of steel, tempered, and is held by a knurled chuck. The scriber is reversible, tele scoping into the stock, and is held by a slight turn of the chuck so that the point is protecte inside the stock when not in use as in fig. 405.

Fɪɢ. 406.—Timber scribe used for marking timber. It has a point for scratching and a knife fo cutting the marks.

Scriber.—This is a tool of extreme precision and while intended especially for machinists, it should be in the tool kit of carpenters and all mechanics who make any claim to being skilled in their occupation.

A scriber is *a hardened steel tool with a sharp point designed to mark very fine lines.*

The most convenient form of scriber is the pocket or telescoping type shown in figs. 404 and 405, the construction rendering it safe to carry in the pocket.

Compasses and Dividers.—The tool called *compasses* is *an*

FIG. 407.—Compasses. This tool should be used simply for describing arcs or circles and not for *dividing*, especially where a given arc or line is to be divided into many parts because an extremely small error in the setting will make a big error in the last division.

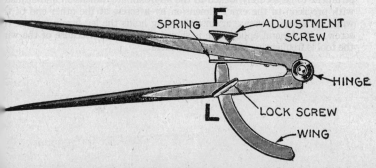

FIG. 408.—Winged dividers for describing and dividing arcs and circles. Evidently when the dividers are locked to the approximate setting by lock screw **L**, the tool can be set with precision to the exact dimension by turning adjustment screw **F**, against which the leg is always firmly held by the spring which prevents any lost motion.

NOTE.—The *inertia method of setting dividers* as employed by machinists, of hitting the leg of the dividers against the work, cannot be practiced in carpentry because of the soft and yielding nature of wood.

instrument used for describing circles or arcs by scribing. It consists of two pointed legs hinged firmly by a rivet so as to remain set in any position by the friction of the hinged joint. The usual form of carpenter's compasses is shown in fig. 407 and it should not be used instead of dividers for dividing an arc or line into a number of equal divisions because it is not a tool of precision.

FIGS. 409 to 412.—Starrett ball points for dividers. When it is necessary to use a hole as center for dividers or trammels it is, of course, impossible to use an ordinary divider point. In such cases a ball point of proper size placed in the hole forms a seat for the divider leg in scribing arcs or circles around the hole as center. For very accurate work however the ball point not recommended because it is impossible to keep the ball exactly in the center.

The difference between *dividers* and compasses is that the dividers provided with a quadrantal wing projecting from one of the two hinged legs through a slot in the other. A set screw on the slotted leg enables the instrument to be securely locked to the approximate dimension and adjusted with precision to the exact dimension by a screw at the other end of the wing. A spring pressing against the wing holds the leg firmly against the screw. Its general appearance is shown in fig. 408. Because of the wing the tool is frequently called *winged* dividers.

CHAPTER 9

Measuring Tools

In laying out work, after having scribed a line with one of the marking tools just described, aided by a guiding tool, the next step is usually to measure off on the scribed line some given distance. This is done with a suitable *measuring tool*. There are many kinds of measuring tools, known as *rules*, of which the following are of interest:

Carpenter's Two Foot Rule.—This is the most familiar form

FIG. 413.—Stanley two foot four fold box wood rule with round joints and middle plates. Graduated into 8ths and 16ths.

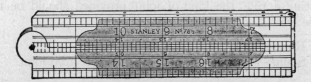

FIG. 414.—Stanley two foot four fold box wood rule with double arch joints, full bound Drafting scales and graduated into 8ths, 10ths and 16ths inches.

of rule and is usually made *four fold*, that is with three hinges spaced 6 inches apart and so arranged that it can be folded up as in fig. 413. It is made of boxwood and in different grades as to metal mountings and graduations. The more expensive rules being divided into 16ths, 8ths, 10ths and 12ths. In

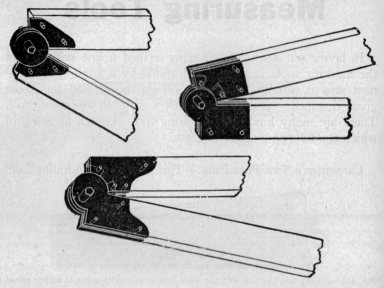

Figs 415 to 417.—Stanley two foot folding rule joints. Fig. 415. round joint; fig. 416, square joint; fig. 417, arch joint.

selecting a rule, the kind of joint provided should be noted. These are:

1. Round joint
2. Square joint
3. Arch joint
4. Double arch joint

The **round joint** is the cheapest (and weakest) as it has only one flange or wing embedded in each leg of the rule, the leg and wing being pinned together.

A better construction is the **square joint** which has two wings to each leg one on each outside face of the wood. The two wings are held together by rivets which go through all three, giving unusual strength.

The **arch joint** is a still better construction as the wings are larger and covering as they do more surface of the wood, add to the life of the rule.

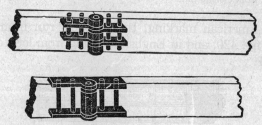

FIGS. 418 and 419.—Stanley two foot folding rule plates. Fig. 418, middle plates; fig. 419, edge plates.

The best construction is the **double arch joint;** this is substantially the same as the arch joint but is repeated at the folding point which again adds to the strength of the rule.

The **folding joint** is made in two styles: 1, with middle plates, and 2, with edge plates. The *middle plate* construction is that in which the plates are let in near the center of the wood and pinned. The *edge plate* construction is that in which the plates are fastened to the outer edges of the wood by rivets which go through both wood and plates and hold the three firmly together. Edge plate joints are stronger than middle plate joints. The construction of joints and plates is shown in the accompanying cuts.

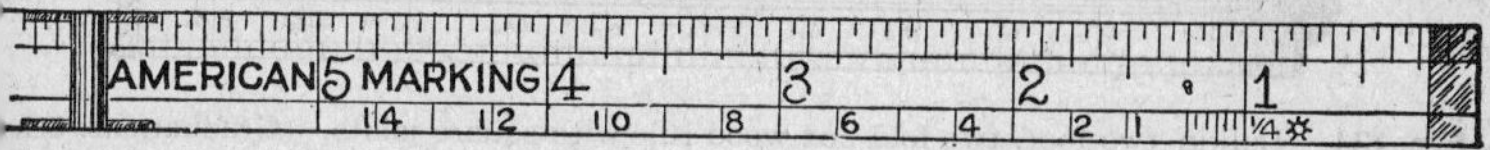

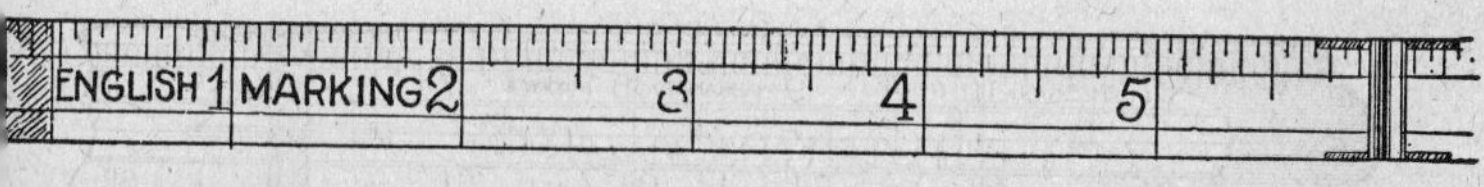

FIG. 420.—Right end of carpenter's two foot rule showing *American* system of marking—*from right to left.*

FIG. 421.—Left end of carpenter's two foot rule showing *English* system of marking—*from left to right.*

A full bound rule is one having a brass binding extending along both inside and outside edges of each leg.

A half bound rule is one having a brass binding extending only along the outside edges of the legs.

Bitted rules have a brass plate inserted on the edge of the rule to protect the wood from closing pin.

In the American marking, the numbers run from right to left as in fig. 420, and in English marking from left to right as in fig. 421.

FIG. 422.—Lufkin one foot four fold box wood rule, with arch joint full bound. Graduations 8ths and 16ths.

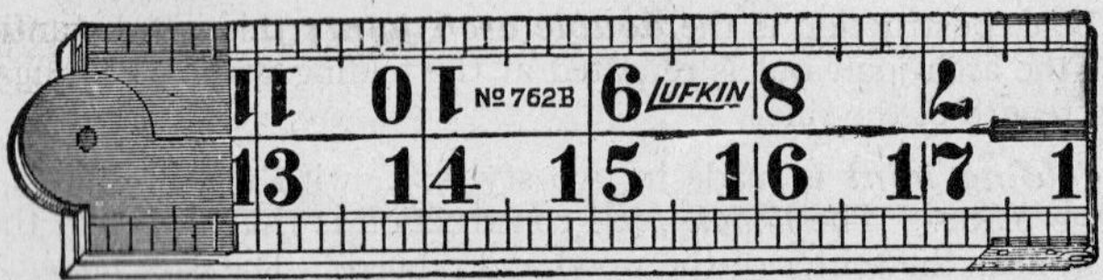

FIG. 423.—Lufkin two foot four fold box wood *blind man's* rule with square joint, edge plates unbound. Graduations: 8ths and 16ths. The large and distinct figures are especially adapted for use in poorly lighted places, or by persons with poor eye sight.

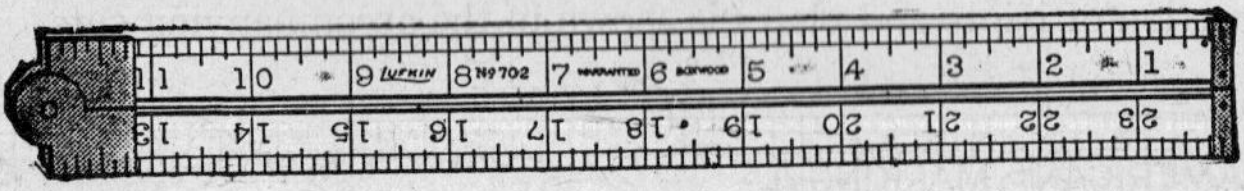

FIG. 424.—Lufkin two foot, two fold box wood rule with square joints. Graduations: 8ths and 16ths

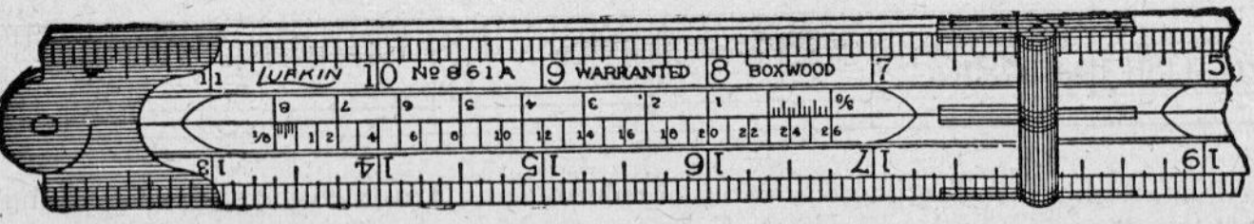

FIG. 425.—Lufkin two foot, four fold box wood *architect's* rule with arch joints, edge plates and having inside edges beveled for architects' scales. Graduations: 8ths, 10ths, 12ths, 16ths.

The two foot rule may be used as a protractor by aid of the following table:

Angles and Openings

Ang.	Dis.	Ang.	Dis.	Ang.	Dis.	Ang.	Dis.	Ang.	Dis.	Ang.	Dis.
°	In.	°	In.	°	In.	°	In.	°	In.	°	In.
1	.2	16	3.34	31	6.41	46	9.38	61	12.18	76	14.78
2	.42	17	3.55	32	6.62	47	9.57	62	12.36	77	14.94
3	.63	18	3.75	33	6.82	48	9.76	63	12.54	78	15.11
4	.84	19	3.96	34	7.02	49	9.95	64	12.72	79	15.27
5	1.05	20	4.17	35	7.22	50	10.14	65	12.9	80	15.43
6	1.26	21	4.37	36	7.42	51	10.33	66	13.07	81	15.59
7	1.47	22	4.58	37	7.61	52	10.52	67	13.25	82	15.75
8	1.67	23	4.78	38	7.81	53	10.71	68	13.42	83	15.9
9	1.88	24	4.99	39	8.01	54	10.9	69	13.59	84	16.06
10	2.09	25	5.19	40	8.2	55	11.08	70	13.77	85	16.21
11	2.3	26	5.4	41	8.4	56	11.27	71	13.94	86	16.37
12	2.51	27	5.6	42	8.6	57	11.45	72	14.11	87	16.52
13	2.72	28	5.81	43	8.8	58	11.64	73	14.28	88	16.67
14	2.92	29	6.01	44	8.99	59	11.82	74	14.44	89	16.82
15	3.13	30	6.21	45	9.18	60	12.	75	14.61	90	16.97

Angles and distances corresponding to the opening of the 2-foot rule should prove of value to students.

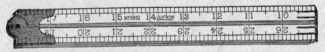

Fig. 426.—Lufkin three foot four fold box wood rule with arch joint, middle plates, unbound. Graduations: 8ths and 16ths.

Since rules are easily lost ("borrowed") or broken, many workmen provide themselves with a good rule of the quality shown in fig. 414 for scaling, and a cheap one such as shown in fig. 413 for general work. Fine quality rules are provided with

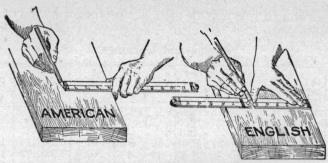

Figs. 427 and 428.—Methods of using carpenter's rule with American and English systems of marking. In fig. 427 the scale reads backwards so that when held in the left hand, as it should be, the right hand is free to use the marking instrument. In using the English system, fig. 428, the rule cannot be grasped firmly in the left hand but must first be placed in position on the board and then held by pressing it against the board with the fingers of the left hand, which necessarily cover up some of the figures on the rule.

Fig. 429.—Lufkin extension rule designed for quickly and accurately measuring the distance between fixed points (floor and ceiling, window frames, etc.), made in maple from 2 to 16 ft. having either two or three sections.

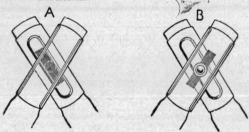

Figs. 430 and 431.—Types of joint of Stanley zig zag rules. A, concealed joint; B, rivet joint. The concealed joint has no hole through the wood, but in the rivet joint, the rivet is carried through both wood and joint. Both styles of joint contain a stiff spring which holds the rule rigid when open.

architect's scales such as ¼ in. = 1 ft.; ½ in. = 1 ft., etc., for measuring directly actual distances on a drawing of small size.

Various Folding Rules.—In addition to the standard rule just described, rules are regularly made of similar construction in lengths from six inches to four feet, as follows:

Two fold, six ins., two ft.

Four fold, one ft., three ft.; four ft. long.

For bench mechanics where compactness is not so important as for outdoor work, the length between the joints may be longer so that in many cases, the two fold two foot rule and

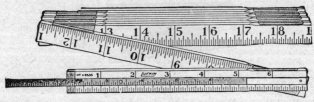

Fig. 432.—Lufkin boxwood extension rule particularly designed for taking inside measurements of openings, such as door and window frames, for boilers, etc., and such measurements as are difficult to take with the ordinary folding rule, but serves also as a common rule in ordinary measuring

Fig. 433.—Method of using Lufkin extension rule for inside measurements. To obtain inside measurements, open rule to within six inches or less of distance between points to be measured. Extend brass slide by push button to point of measurement. Add measurement on brass slide to that shown at extreme end of rule, which will give you exact distance between points measured.

---

*NOTE.—In combination with the framing square the carpenter's rule may be used to obtain directly the lengths by applying it as the hypothenuse (or long side) of a right angle triangle, and when provided with architect's scales the length of rafter may be read directly.

the four fold rules of three and four foot lengths are more desirable than with a greater number of joints.

Rules with Attachments.—To increase the utility of carpenters' rules they may be obtained with various devices such as calipers, level and protractor. Caliper rules are regularly made with the caliper left hand as shown in fig. 434, but may be obtained right hand.

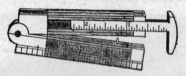

FIG. 434.—Stanley six inch two fold box wood caliper rule with square joints. Graduations 8ths, 10ths, 12ths and 16ths.

The level device is fitted as shown in fig. 435, being attached to the center section of a three fold rule, each outer section being hollowed to fit the level tube leaving the glass visible when closed.

Board Measure.—Lumber is estimated according to a system of arbitrary surface measure known as *board measure* (B.M.). Any board less than 1 in. in thickness is considered as being 1 in. thick; any board over 1 in. in thickness is

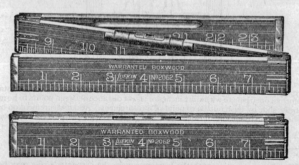

FIG. 435 and 436.—Lufkin two foot, three fold box wood combination rule and *level*. Graduations: 8ths and 16ths.

measured in inches and fractions of an inch. Thus a ½ in. board is considered as being 1 in. thick, and a 1½ in. board as being 1½ ins. thick.

Board Measure Rule.—*Multiply length in ft. by width in ft. of the board and multiply this product by 1 for boards an inch or less than an inch thick and by thickness in inches and fractions of an inch for boards over 1 inch thick.*

Example.—How many feet board measure in a board 12 ft. long by 18 ins. wide by 1¾ in. thick?

$$18 \text{ ins. width} = (18 \div 12) \text{ ft.} = 1.5 \text{ ft.}$$
$$12 \times 1.5 \times 1\frac{3}{4} = 31.5 \text{ feet board measure}$$

Fig. 437.—Lufkin two foot, four fold box wood rule filled with *level* and *protractor*. With the aid of the protractor an angle of any degree may be obtained. Graduations: 8ths and 16ths; architects' scales.

Example.—How many feet board measure in the board of the previous example if board were only ½ in. thick?

$$(12 \times 1.5) \times 1 = 18 \text{ ft. B. M.}$$

Lumber Scales.—In estimating lumber, much time is saved by using a lumber scale by means of which the feet board measure may be read off direct. This gives an approximate result. In using the scale it is customary to read to the nearest figure and when there is no difference to alternate between the lower and higher figures upon different boards. Fig. 439 shows a board scale graduated for boards of 12, 14 and 16 ft. lengths and method of using.

Decimal Log Scale.—The following information to users of

Fig. 438.—Lufkin hickory log rule with plain head and burnt figures. Figured 48 ins. with 8 in. handle. Full length 4 ft. 8 in.

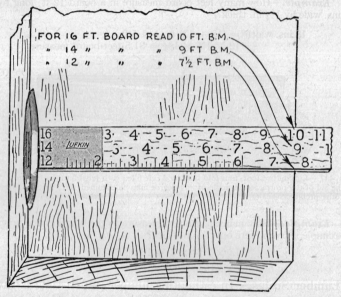

Fig. 439.—Hickory board rule for measuring lumber in board measure. The rule shown is for boards 12, 14 and 16 ft. long, these figures being seen at the left hand end of the rule. There is, as shown, a line of figures for each of these lengths. *To use the rule,* place the head against one edge of the board and read the figure nearest the other edge (width) of the board in the same line of figures upon which the length is found. *Thus,* in the lower line for a 12 ft. board, the edge, comes half way between 7 and 8 hence for a plank 1 in. thick there are 7½ ft. board measure. If the board were 14, or 16 ft. long there would be 9 or 10 ft. B. M., respectively reading to the usual figure. Note that the scale in the 12 ft. line measures inches and can be used for measuring the thickness of the board. The reason for this scale being in inches is apparent: *thus,* a board say $12' \times 6'' \times 1' = 12 \times \frac{6}{12} \times 1 = 6$ ft. B. M., hence if the rule were placed on a 12 ft. board 6 in. wide, the reading 6 which gives the width of the board would indicate the number of feet board measure.

decimal log scale is furnished by the Lufkin Rule Co.:

The decimal scale is based on Scribner's. It drops the units and takes the nearest tens; thus Scribner's scale gives a log 12 inches in diameter, 16 ft. long = 79 feet. Decimal scale makes it 80 ft. and is expressed with the figure 8 only.

There never were any authentic computations for Scribner's scale below 12 inches in diameter, Mr. Scribner at the time considering a log smaller than 12 inches unworthy of cutting.

Therefore, for logs below 12 inches, a number of independent computations have been made applying to decimal rules, and great trouble has arisen from this fact, we being at a loss to know what figures we should use. We

Decimal Scale Table

DECIMAL A.							DECIMAL B.							DECIMAL C.						
Inches,	6	7	8	9	10	11	Inches,	6	7	8	9	10	11	Inches,	6	7	8	9	10	11
12 ft.	1	1	2	3	4	5	12 ft.	1	2	2	3	4	4	12 ft	1	2	2	3	3	4
14 "	1	1	2	3	4	6	14 "	1	2	3	3	4	6	14 "	1	2	2	3	4	5
16 "	1	2	3	4	5	6	16 "	2	3	3	4	5	7	16 "	2	3	3	4	6	7
18 "	1	2	3	4	5	7	18 "	2	3	4	5	6	8	18 "	2	3	3	4	6	8
20 "	1	2	3	4	6	8	20 "	2	3	4	6	7	8	20 "	2	3	3	4	7	8
22 "	1	2	3	5	7	9	22 "	3	4	5	7	8	9	22 "	3	4	4	5	8	9
24 "	1	3	4	5	7	10	24 "	4	5	6	7	9	10	24 "	3	4	4	6	9	10

Miscellaneous Scales

NOTE.—*Biltmore or Forest cruiser sticks.* This stick gives the diameter and height of standing trees and was designed for the U. S. Forest Service in reconnaissance estimates of timber tracts. In addition to diameter and height scales it bears a table of decimal C log scale values for 16 foot logs and a tier of regular inch markings; 37 13/16 ins. long, ½ in. thick, 1 in. wide with one sloping face. Both ends are fitted with heavy cast brass ferrule.

NOTE.—*Spring Steel Board Rule.* It is made of tempered spring steel so that it will bend to the board and when released will return exactly straight. It is provided with a wood handle and leather slide for handling the rule at any part of the blade. *Types:* 3 tier, 3½ ft. inspectors' rule; 3 tier, 3 ft. board rule; 3 tier, 2½ ft. sorting rule. *Markings:* All three types are marked one side to measure 8, 10 and 18 ft., opposite side 12, 14, 16 ft., or 18, 20, and 22 ft.

NOTE.—*Gauging Rod.* Made of maple with brass point 3 to 4 ft. lengths. *In using,* the capacity of a barrel is ascertained by inserting the gauge rod through the bung hole into each end, reading the rod across the center of the bung hole for both insertions, and then taking the average of the two readings. If, for example, one reading show 50 gallons, and the other 48 gallons, the average, viz., 49 gallons, would be the correct measurement of the barrel when filled to the bung hole.

COMPARISON OF LOG TABLES.

A table comparing the measurements of a 16 ft. log, as given by the principal log scales used in different sections of the United States and Canada, showing wherein they differ.

Diameter in Inches.	Doyle's Scale.	Scribner Scale.	Favorite Scale.	Baxter Scale	Two-third Scale.	Dusenberry Scale.	Cumberland River Scale.	St. Louis Hardwo'd Scale.	Northwestern Scale.	Decimal Scale.	Spaulding's Pacific Coast Scale.	Combined Doyle and Scribner Scale.	
8	16	25	22	34	36			33	33	3		16	
9	25	36	29	44	48			46	45	4		25	
10	36	49	37	56	58	40	47	59	61	6	50	36	
11	49	64	48	69	70	54	57	72	70	7	63	49	
12	64	79	64	84	85	68	68	85	77	8	77	64	
13	81	97	82	100	100	80	80	100	97	10	94	81	
14	100	114	98	117	116	100	93	116	117	11	114	100	
15	121	142	120	136	133	117	107	133	144	14	137	121	
16	144	159	142	156	151	136	121	150	170	16	161	144	Doyle Scale.
17	169	185	166	177	171	157	137	172	188	18	188	169	
18	196	213	197	200	192	180	153	192	206	21	216	196	
19	225	240	226	224	213	204	171	213	226	24	245	225	
20	256	280	248	250	237	229	190	237	248	28	276	256	
21	289	304	285	277	261	256	209	261	285	30	308	289	
22	324	334	324	305	286	285	229	284	324	33	341	324	
23	359	377	357	335	313	315	250	312	357	38	376	359	
24	400	404	392	366	341	346	281	341	392	40	412	400	
25	441	459	434	399	370	379	296	369	421	46	449	441	
26	484	500	476	432	400	414	320	400	450	50	488	484	
27	530	548	520	468	432	450	345	432	520	55	528	530	
28	576	582	562	504	464	487	372	464	536	58	569	576	
29	625	609	596	543	498	526	399	498	584	61	612	609	
30	676	657	632	582	533	567	427	533	632	66	656	657	
31	729	710	678	623	569	609	456	568	678	71	701	710	
32	784	736	725	665	606	652	485	608	725	74	748	736	
33	841	784	785	709	648	697	516	645	785	78	796	784	
34	900	800	845	754	685	744	548	685	845	80	845	800	
35	961	876	882	800	725	792	581	725	882	88	897	876	
36	1024	923	920	848	768	841	614	768	920	92	950	923	Scribner Scale.
37	1089	1029	978	897	811	892	649	810	978	103	1006	1029	
38	1156	1068	1037	946	855	945	685	856	1037	107	1064	1068	
39	1225	1120	1098	999	901	999	721	901	1090	112	1124	1120	
40	1296	1204	1160	1052	944	1054	759	947	1160	120	1185	1204	
41	1369	1272	1213	1107	995	1111	798	996	1213	127	1248	1272	
42	1444	1343	1266	1.63	1045	1170	835	1045	1266	134	1312	1343	
43	1521	1396	1334	1221	1095	1227	877		1334	140	1377	1396	
44	1600	1480	1402	1280	1147	1300	918		1402	148	1448	1480	
45	1681	1518	1474	1340	1200	1350	960		1474	152	1512	1518	
46	1764	1587	1546	1401	1253	1410	1003		1546	159	1581	1587	
47	1849	1656	1621	1464	1309	1470	1048		1621	166	1652	1656	
48	1936	1728	1696	1529	1365	1580	1092		1696	173	1724	1728	

have recently carefully noted from our customers' orders these differences, and find that about three different computations are being used in different sections. We have therefore named them Decimal A, Decimal B and Decimal C, and shall hereafter mark our rules in this way. Below we give the figures. The difference being only for logs below 12 inches, we do not consider it necessary to tabulate the whole rule. In ordering rules, please state which is wanted, A, B or C.

As stated above, the difference in figures occurs only below 12 inches. From 12 inches upwards the figures are authentic, according to Scribner.

We would consider it a wise plan for the lumbermen of the Northwest, wherever this scale is used, to get together and decide on one standard rule."

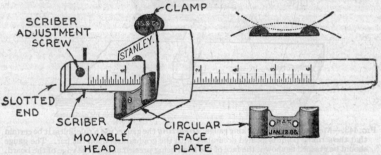

FIGS. 440 to 442.—Simple one point marking gauge fitted with circular face plate for marking on convex and concave surfaces. For straight marking the plate may be removed so in setting, measurements may be taken from the head direct.

Marking Gauges.—Tools of this class are used to mark a piece of wood that is to be sawed or otherwise tooled. There are several types of marking gauge, as

1. Single bar.   2. Double bar.   3. Single bar with slide.

Single Bar Gauge.—This is for making a single mark as for sawing. It consists of a bar having a scriber at one end and provided with a scale graduated in inches and sixteenths. The bar passes through a movable head that may be clamped at any distance from scriber point as in fig. 440.

NOTE.—*Wantage Rod.* Made of maple or boxwood 8 to 12 lines. *In using,* the rod is slowly inserted into a barrel until the brass angle rests under the staves at the bung hole. If, for instance, the rod be wet as far as 10, it shows a shortage of 10 gallons.

NOTE.—*Freight rule* designed especially for measuring packages for export and import shipments. It has a brass right angle hook on the end. First end is graduated on side and edge in inches and quarters. *Sizes:* 5 or 6 ft. × 1″ × ⅝″.

Double Bar Gauge.—In this type, designed especially for mortise marking, there are two independent bars working in the same head. One pin is affixed to each bar. After setting the bars for the proper marking of the mortise, one side is marked with one bar and the gauge then turned over for marking the other side. The construction is shown in fig. 446.

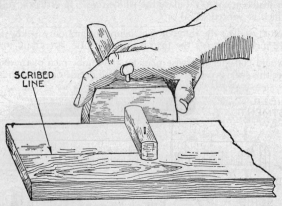

SCRIBED
LINE

Fig. 443.—Method of using a marking gauge. *In setting* the gauge, use a rule unless it be **certain** that the scribing point is located accurately with the graduations upon the bar. The gauge should be grasped as shown, the face of the head being pressed against the edge of the board, care being taken to keep it true with the edge so that the bar will be at right angles with the edge and the line scribed at the correct distance from the edge. The line is scribed usually by pushing the gauge though it may be pulled toward the worker as shown. Always work from the face side of the piece.

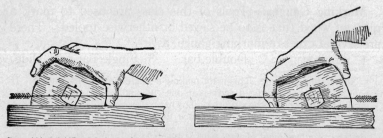

Figs. 444 and 445.—Methods of using marking gauge when the scriber is too long. If the point enter the wood too deeply when the tool is used as in fig. 443, the depth of cut may be regulated by slightly turning the bar so that it rests on one edge instead of its side. Turn the bar in the direction in which the tool is moved in making the cut as shown in the figures. It is better, however, to adjust the scriber, than turn the bar, and in selecting a gauge get one with a slotted end and adjustment screw as shown in fig. 446, rather than a cheap tool.

Slide Gauge.—An objection to the double bar gauge is that two operations are required which can be performed with a slide gauge in one operation. As shown in fig. 447, the under side of the bar is provided with a flush slide having a scriber B, at the end of the slide and there is another scriber A, at the end of the bar. These two scribers when set to the required distances from the head mark both sides of the tenon or mortise to the size required by one stroke. On the upper side there is one scriber C, for single marking.

Butt Gauges.—In hanging doors, there are three measurements to be marked:

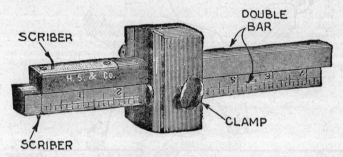

Fig. 446.—Double bar gauge for marking two parallel lines at any given distance apart and at a given distance from the edge of a board. Each bar has a set screw for clamping it in any desired position. This type of gauge is useful in making frames for panels and other work of this character.

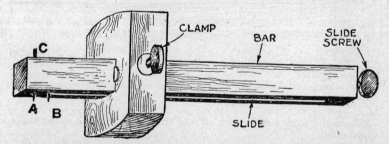

Fig. 447.—Slide gauge. *In construction,* the bar has a scriber C, on the upper side for single marking, and a scriber A, on the lower side, which with the scriber B, on the slide which works flush in the bar as shown, is used for double marking. A set screw in the head retains the bar in position. The distance between the scriber points A and B, is regulated by the slide screw at the end of the bar. The slide gauge is a more useful tool than either the single or double bar gauge.

1. The location of butt on the casing.
2. The location of butt on the door.
3. The thickness of butt on the casing.

A *butt gauge* is a type gauge having three cutters, purposely arranged so that no change of setting is necessary when hanging several doors. In reality these tools comprise rabbet gauges, marking gauges and mortise

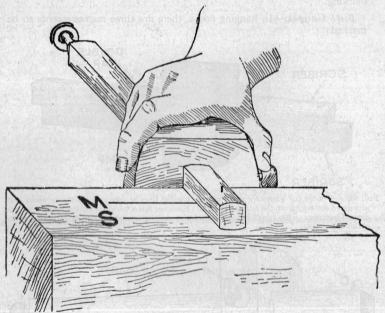

Fig. 448.—Method of using the slide gauge in marking a mortise—note the two lines M, S or marks for the sides of the mortise being scribed in one operation.

gauges of a scope sufficient for all door trim, including lock plates, strike plates, etc.

In the illustrations, figs. 449 to 452 for rabbeted jambs, cutter A, marks from the jamb in the rabbet; cutter B, from the edge of the door engaged in closing; cutter C, the thickness of the butt. Cutters A and B, are mounted on the same bar and set by one adjustment with proper allowance for clearance.

When casings have a nailed on strike instead of being rabbeted, a marking gauge which will work on a ledge as narrow as ⅛ inch is required; in this case the same distance is marked from the edge of the casing and from the edge of the door not engaged when closing. Gauges 94 and 93 can be used on such work, cutter "B" marking for the butt and cutter "C" for its thickness. Gauges 94 and 95 are made so that they can be used as inside or outside squares for squaring the edge of the butt on either door or jamb.

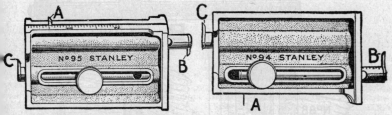

FIG. 449.—Stanley butt gauge for rabbeted jambs. It can also be used as a marking and mortise gauge, and as inside or outside square for squaring the edge of the butt on either door or jamb. Graduated in 16ths for two inches.

FIG. 450.—Stanley butt gauge for rabbeted jambs or nailed strikes. For rabbeted jamb, cutter A, marks from the jamb in the rabbet; cutter B, from the edge of the door engaged in closing; cutter C, the thickness of the butt.

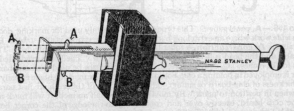

FIG. 451.—Stanley butt gauge for rabbetted jambs. It can also be used as a marking and mortise gauge. The dotted lines show gauge when set to be used as a mortise gauge. Graduated in 16ths for three inches.

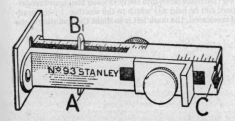

FIG. 452.—Stanley butt gauge for rabbeted jambs or nailed strikes. For nailed on strikes cutter B, when reversed, marks for the butt on both door and jamb; cutter C, the thickness of the butt.

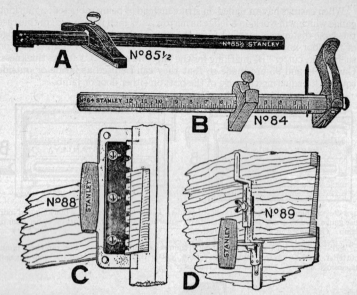

Figs. 453 to 456.—A, panel gauge. This type of gauge is mainly used for marking door panels and such *wide* work where an extra long bar is needed. The scriber is adjustable. **B**, handle slitting gauge. *In construction,* a roller bearing and large handle is provided. The cutter is adjustable and the head is held in position by a set screw. The bar is graduated in 8ths of inches for 12 inches. **C**, clap board siding marker tool can be used with one hand, while the other is employed in holding a clap board in position. The marking blade is easily adjusted to any thickness of clap board or siding. The sharp edges of the teeth are just parallel with the legs when in position to mark. By moving the tool half an inch, it will mark a full line across the clap board, exactly over and conforming to the edge of the corner board. **D**, clap board siding gauge. It is so constructed that two thin steel blades, which form a part of the base of the tool, will slide under the last clap board already laid. *In operation,* when the bottom of the gauge is held firmly to the lower edge of the clap board, press the handle over sidewise, and this will force another thin blade down into the next lower clap board rendering the tool immovable. The clap board can be held any width to the weather, by the graduated scale on the tool. After the tool is released, the mark left is so slight that painting alone will fill it.

CHAPTER 10

Holding Tools

An essential part of the shop equipment necessary for good carpentry, is the proper assortment of *holding tools*, for, as must be evident there are many tooling operations which require that the work be held rigid, even when considerable force is applied as in planing and chiseling.

The work bench considered broadly with its attachments may be called the main holding tool, and unless this important part of the equipment be constructed amply substantial and rigid it will be difficult to do good work.

The work bench and its attachments have already been described and in installing a bench it should be properly anchored or fastened to the wall of the building so as to be as near rigid as though it were a part of the building.

Holding tools may be classed as:
1. Supporting.
2. Retaining.

In marking or sawing, usually it is only necessary to support the work by placing it on the bench or on horses, but in planing, chiseling and some nailing operations, the work must not only be supported but held rigidly in position.

"Horses" or Trestles.—These are used in various ways simply to support the work, when it is of such large dimensions that the bench cannot conveniently be used, and especially for marking and sawing planks. *No shop equipment is complete without a pair of horses.*

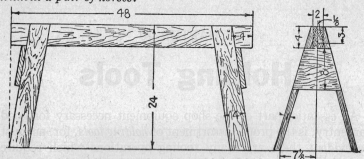

FIGS. 457 and 458.—Side and end views of horse with dimensions suitable for general use.

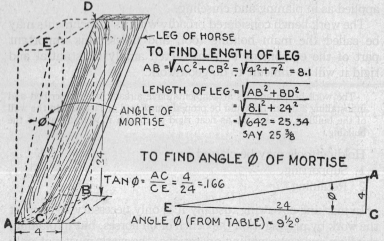

LEG OF HORSE

TO FIND LENGTH OF LEG

$$AB = \sqrt{AC^2 + CB^2} = \sqrt{4^2 + 7^2} = 8.1$$

$$\text{LENGTH OF LEG} = \sqrt{AB^2 + BD^2}$$
$$= \sqrt{8.1^2 + 24^2}$$
$$= \sqrt{642} = 25.34$$
$$\text{SAY } 25\tfrac{3}{8}$$

ANGLE OF MORTISE

TO FIND ANGLE ϕ OF MORTISE

$$\text{TAN } \phi = \frac{AC}{CE} = \frac{4}{24} = .166$$

ANGLE ϕ (FROM TABLE) = 9½°

FIGS. 459 and 460.—Method of finding length of horse leg, and angle ϕ or inclination of side of mortise for leg. To find ϕ by calculation, a table of *natural trigonometrical functions* is necessary. This table is found in any book on mathematics covering trigonometry, an elementary knowledge of which is of much value to the carpenter especially to fully understand the so called "steel square." The ordinary carpenter's method of setting bevel to 9½° is shown in fig. 461. In fig. 462, AE of angle ϕ is the projection of the horse leg AD, on the vertical plane.

A horse, as usually made, consists of a 3 or 4 ft. length of 2 × 4 or 2 × 6 stock for the cross beam, and having a pair of 1 × 3 or 1¼ × 4 legs at each end, depending upon the weight of the work.

The height of the horse is usually two feet. The general construction of

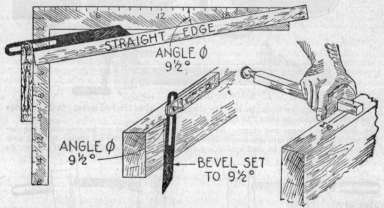

FIG. 461.—Method of setting bevel by aid of square and straight edge. Simply place straight edge on square so that one side of the right triangle thus formed will be 24 ins. (height of horse) and the other side 4 ins. (distance of edge of leg from end of beam of horse). Place blade of bevel against straight edge and stock against side of square and clamps to this angle which gives the proper slope (outward lengthwise) for side of mortise.

FIG. 462.—Bevel set to required angle and in position on beam for scribing line of side of mortise.

FIG. 463.—Scribing lines for top of mortises of horse legs with slide gauge—note the two lines M, S, being scribed in one operation.

horses is shown in figs. 457 and 458, and the method of using, as in sawing a plank, in figs. 501 and 502. Note that the legs are inclined outward both lengthwise and crosswise, and a problem arises to determine the length of the legs having this double inclination for a given height of horse; the solution is shown in figs. 459 and 460, and the method of obtaining the angular setting for the bevel to scribe mortise in fig. 461.

Clamps.—Frequently it is necessary to tightly press pieces of wood together that may have been mortised and tenoned, grooved and tongued, or simply glued. The bench vise is not always a convenient tool for this purpose, or its use may be

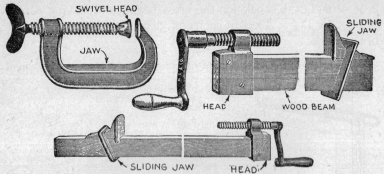

FIG. 464.—Single screw malleable iron jaw clamp with swivel head on screw. Ordinary range of sizes have openings from 2 to 10 ins.

FIG. 465.—Wood beam door clamp. By purchasing the iron fixtures for this clamp the carpenter can make the arm any length desired, most convenient for his work. It is not only a door clamp but may be used for holding any piece of glued work that will fit between its jaws.

FIGS. 466 and 467.—All wood clamps or hand screws showing *right and wrong way* to use them. *In using,* first set jaws to nearly the size of the material to be clamped. In placing the hand screws upon the work, the outside screw should be turned back so that it will not prevent the jaws being slightly closer at the outside screw than at the points. This will allow the strain which is applied in setting up the outside screw *to bring the jaws parallel, which is the only position in which they should be when clamping the work.* Since the screws are made of wood instead of iron *use some judgment and not apply too much pressure.*

required for other work. In such cases clamps are used and there is quite a variety, to meet the needs of the various kinds of work to be clamped.

Clamps may be classed as:

1. Single screw jaw.
2. Double screw.
3. Beam.

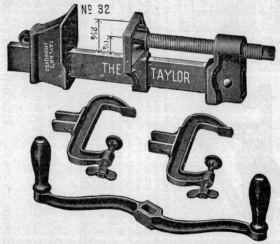

FIGS. 468 to 471.—Taylor steel beam heavy door clamp. This is an extra powerful clamp designed for the heaviest class of hard wood work. The supports shown (figs. 469 and 470) are for fastening the clamp to a trestle or "horse." Capacity: 40,000 lbs. safe clamping strain.

4. Mitre.
5. Chain.

The single screw type comprises the iron jaw clamps of small and moderate opening as shown in fig. 464. A form of double screw clamps sometimes called "hand screws" is shown in 466. It is all wood and if properly used will be found satisfactory,

NOTE.—Before using new hand screws, the screws should be treated with bees wax and beef tallow to make them work easy. The screws should be heated and the lubricant applied hot.

FIGS. 472 to 476.—Stanley bench bracket clamp and its applications. To adapt it to the bench bore one or more 1-inch holes are bored in the front of the bench. The shape of the tool is such that when the jaw or nose s put through the hole, it is automatically held in place, and by means of the screw clamp, the board being worked upon is quickly and firmly secured. The illustrations show clearly a few of the many ways in which this bracket may be used. For instance: fig. **B**, for holding a short board or box end—clamping same sufficiently rigid so that it can be sawed at any angle—as for mitreing, dovetailing, etc.; fig. **C**, for holding a long board (two brackets being used); fig. **D**, for use in connection with a bench vise; fig. **E**, for holding a door or window firmly in place while same is being fitted with lock or butts. The nail shown simply holds the bracket in a horizontal position.

however, a greenhorn or careless workman can easily destroy this type of clamp by abusing it as in fig. 467.

Hand screws may be quickly opened or closed by grasping the screw handles and revolving the clamp counter clockwise or clockwise respectively (as viewed from the right hand).

For large openings beam clamps are used. Attached to one end of the beam is a head in which the screw works. A jaw arranged to slide on the beam is quickly adjusted and secured in any position. The chain type of clamp is used for clamping built up column work.

Vises.—The essential features of a vise are rigidity, weight, strength, and accurately fitting and smoothly working parts. The vises here considered are iron vises.

Rigidity and weight are required to make effective the effort expended on the work held in the vise. The "anvil quality," or inertia sufficient to

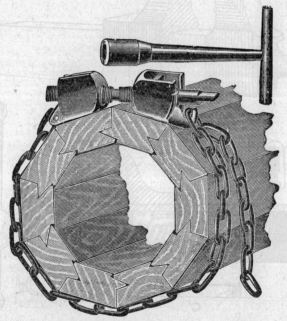

Figs. 477 and 478.—Taylor chain or column clamp. The ¾ in. steel screw is threaded right and left doubling the speed of opening and closing. The cylindrical bearing surface of blocks and heads permit the heads to adjust themselves to the inclination of the sides of the column as shown.

effectively hold a piece of work solidly against a blow, is a most important qualification in a vise, and a suitable mass of iron is just as necessary to supply this inertia as to supply strength against rupture. It is, of course, essential that a vise be strong enough to withstand any strain that may be legitimately put upon it.

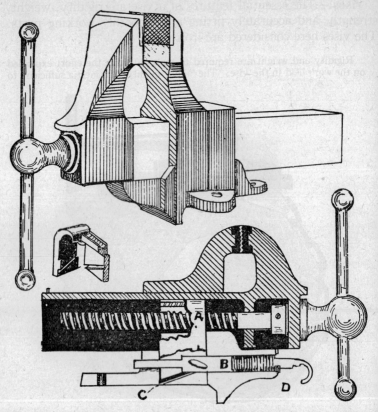

Fig. 479.—Prentiss "Bull dog" coach makers solid jaw, parallel, stationary bottom vise. Very high jaws and long arm. The deep throat and wide opening allow operator the maximum amount of room for holding work.

Figs. 480 and 481.—Prentiss quick-acting vise. Can be opened or closed full length with a single movement, and nut will engage screw at any point. Can also be operated from any position as an ordinary screw vise. **A**, half of nut in place, disengaged from screw; **B**, operating bar carrying two *inclines* or *ledges* (all in one piece) by which the nut is both opened and closed and locked by same movement. **C**, groove in which *incline* travels, thereby forcing one-half nut up and the other down simultaneously, on moving the *bar* to front or rear one-half inch. Grooves shown plainly in fig. 481. **D**, *ratchet catch* on operating bar, which, when engaged, holds nut open.

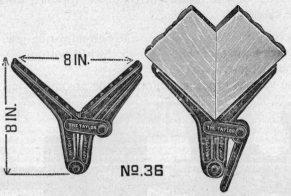

8 IN.

8 IN.

THE TAYLOR

THE TAYLOR

№. 36

FIGS. 482 and 483.—Taylor mitre clamp. *In construction,* the jaws are planed true and fitted to hold the work exactly square when closed. The pins are only large enough to give a grip that prevents slipping. The eccentric is so designed that the first part of the motion brings the jaw quickly into engagement and the latter part closes more slowly giving great holding power.

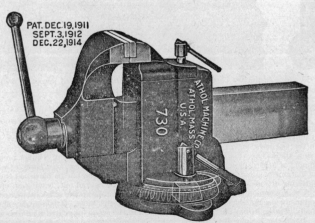

PAT. DEC.19,1911
SEPT. 3,1912
DEC. 22,1914

ATHOL MACHINE CO.
ATHOL.MASS.
U.S.A.

730

FIGS. 484 and 485.—Athol (Starrett's) vise with self-adjusting jaw and swivel bottom and adjustable handle.

The types of vise usually fitted to the top of a work bench may be classed as:

1. Screw.
2. Quick acting screw.
3. Parallel jaw.
4. Self-adjusting jaw.
5. Swivel bottom.

These various types are shown in the accompanying cuts.

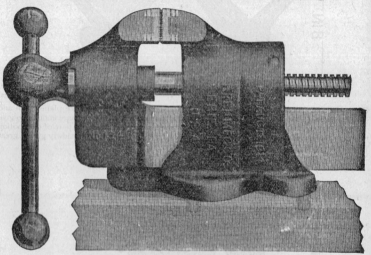

FIG. 486.—Reed stationary base steam fitters' vise. *Sizes:* Width of jaws 4 to 6 ins.; jaws open 5 to 9⅜ ins.; holds pipe ⅛ to 8 ins.— weight 52 to 155 lbs.

NOTE.—*Vise abuse.* There is probably no tool in a shop subjected to more abuse than a vise. A fruitful cause of breakage is the clamping near one end of a long piece of work which may thus have considerable overhang. Many times the operator, instead of hunting up a stick or other support to keep the free end from dropping, will attempt to hold it by excessive pressure between the vise jaws; and if in that condition the operation may involve any considerable hammering, the service exacted of that vise is most severe. One cause of a minor breakage is the clamping of a hard piece of metal so that the pressure is concentrated upon a small area near the margins or corners of the hardened jaw face; and if the jaw be hardened enough to resist battering or indentation, a piece is almost sure to be broken out, leaving an unsightly notch. A very common fault with vise users is the failure to keep the screw lubricated. The thread on many vise nuts has practically disappeared from this cause. The front jaw should be occasionally detached from the vise, turned over, and the screw lubricated its entire working length. When this is done at reasonable intervals, the screw and nut will wear indefinitely. The use of vises having smooth faces for their gripping jaws is not nearly as extensive as it would be with a better comprehension of their capabilities.

CHAPTER 11

Toothed Cutting Tools

In almost any carpentry job, after the work has been laid out by aid of the guiding, marking and measuring tools, and supported or held in position by a holding tool, the first cutting operation will in most cases be performed by a *toothed cutting tool*. The most important of this class of tool is the saw. As sawing is hard work, the carpenter should not only know how to saw properly but how to keep the saw in prime condition. The importance of this is emphasized by the amount of space here given to the saw.

Saws.—There are many different kinds of saws, but the types of interest to the carpenter may be classed

1. With respect to the kind of cut, as:

   a. Cross cut
   b. Rip
   c. Combined cross and rip (interrupted tooth)

2. With respect to shape of blade, as:

   a. Straight back
   b. Skew back
   c. Thin back
   d. Narrowed

3. With respect to reinforcement of back, as:

   a. Half back
   b. (Full) back

4. With respect to service, as:

a. Cabinet

b. Joiner

c. Mitre

d. Stair

e. Floor

f. Buck or wood (so-called)

g. Compass

h. Key hole

i. Coping

j. Hack

Etc.

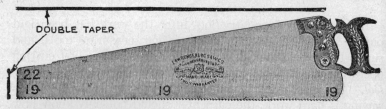

FIGS. 487 to 489.—Thin back saw. The plan and section show the taper and the figures show the gauge of blade to be 19 at the teeth and shoulder, graduated to 22 at the toe, increasing the strength of the blade as it approaches the driving end and diminishing to the toe where the least strength is required.

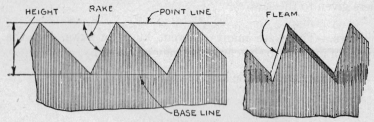

FIG. 490.—Section of saw blade illustrating the term, *base line, point line, height* and *rake of teeth.* The height of a tooth is fixed or determined by the number of points or teeth to one inch and the rake. The height is the distance between the base line and point line. The rake of the tooth which is its pitch, is the angle of the cutting edge of the tooth to the line of the points.

FIG. 491.—Section of saw blade illustrating the term *fleam.* This is the beveled edge of the tooth, which creates the knife or cutting edge.

The common hand saw consists of a thin, flat blade of crucible steel having a row of teeth along one edge. A wooden handle is fastened to the large end by screws. A saw of this kind of small size is called a panel saw.

The size of a saw is the length of the blade in inches. Hand saws range in size from 14 to 30 inches, thus:

Saw Sizes

Size Inches	Panel						Hand	Rip	
	14	16	18	20	22	24	26	28	30

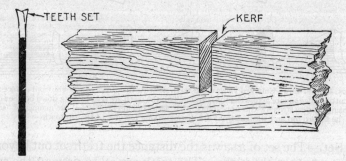

FIGS. 492 and 493.—Set of teeth, and *kerf*. The kerf is the channel cut by the saw to the width of its set.

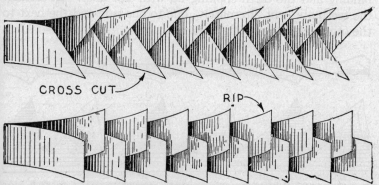

FIGS. 494 and 495.—Teeth of cross cut and rip saws. Views looking toward toe over the cutting edges, enlarged about 7 times.

Saw Teeth.—The cutting edge of a hand saw is a series of little notches all of the same size. On a cross-cut saw each side of the tooth is filed to a cutting edge like a little knife. On a rip saw, each tooth is filed straight across to a sharp square edge like a little chisel.

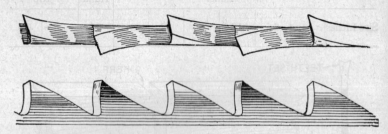

FIGS. 496 and 497.—Enlarged views of rip teeth showing their form of straight front or face and cutting edge square across the top. In fig. 496, the teeth are seen looking down on the edge, bringing out strongly the appearance of a series of chisel edges and the manner of "set." The square top and straight front are distinguishing features of the rip tooth.

Set.—The set of a saw is the distance the teeth set out beyond the surface of the blade. The teeth are *set* to prevent the saw binding and the teeth choking up with saw dust. In setting, the teeth are bent alternately, one to one side and the next to the other, as shown in fig. 496.

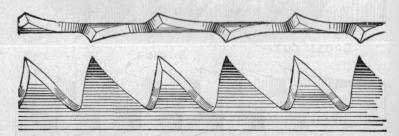

FIGS. 498 and 499.—Enlarged views of cross cut teeth showing their shape. In fig. 498 the teeth are seen looking on the cutting edge, which brings out in pronounced manner the "set" of the points on each side.

Action of the Cross-Cut Saw.—While each cross cut tooth is a little two edged knife, it cuts very differently.

In early times it was discovered that a knife blade must be free from nicks and notches to cut well. Then it could be pushed against a piece of wood and a shaving whittled off. At about the same time it was noticed

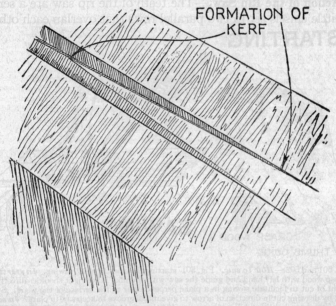

FORMATION OF KERF

Fig. 500.—Formation of *kerf* by cross cut saw as the saw severs the grain or fibre at right angles, rasping out the center by thrust, the saw progressively cutting deeper and deeper into the wood on both sides of the kerf. Accordingly a saw cuts wood by each of its many teeth making an incision one after the other in rapid succession. When sharp, the labor required is very little compared to that when dull.

that if the nicked knife were drawn back and forth across the wood, it would tear the fibers apart, making saw dust.

The set of cross-cut teeth makes them lie in two parallel rows.

A needle will slide between them from one end of the saw to the other. When the saw is moved back and forth, the points, especially their forward edges, sever the fibers in two places, leaving a little triangular elevation that is crumbled off by friction as the saw passes through. New fibers are then attacked and the saw drops deeper into the cut.

Action of the Rip Saw.—The teeth of the rip saw are a series of little chisels set in two parallel rows that overlap each other.

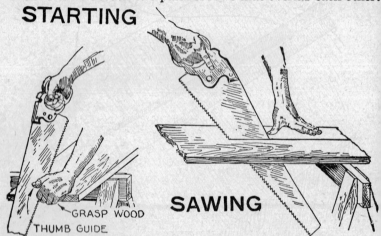

FIGS. 501 and 502.—*How to saw.* Fig. 501 starting the saw; fig. 502 sawing. *In starting,* grasp wood with left hand and guide the saw with thumb. Have right shoulder directly in front of cut to facilitate sawing in a plane perpendicular to the surface of the wood. Start cut by drawing cut in direction of arrow to give initial groove to keep saw in place. *In sawing,* grasp saw lightly and do not press saw into the wood but simply move it back and forth, using a long stroke. If the saw tend to run off the line, or cut may not be perpendicular to the work, slightly twist, or bend blade to one side. Occasionally test portion of blade with a try square.

At each stroke the sharp edge chisels off a little from the end of the wood fibers. The teeth are made strong with an acute cutting angle, but the steel is softer than that of a chisel to enable the teeth to be filed and set readily.

Angles of Saw Teeth.—The "face" of each cross-cut tooth

is slightly steeper than the back, making an angle with the line
of the teeth of about 66°. The compass teeth lean still further
with an angle of 75°. The rip saw face is at right angles (90°)
to the line of the teeth. Its cutting edge is at right angles to
the side of the blade. The angle of each tooth covers 60°.

Files and Rasps.—By definition a file is a steel instrument,
having its surface covered with sharp edged furrows or teeth,

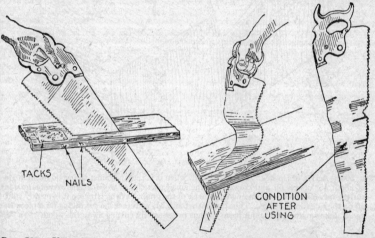

TACKS

NAILS

CONDITION
AFTER
USING

FIGS. 503 to 505.— *How not to saw,* or method of sawing as indulged in by most amateurs and
view of amateur's saws, showing result of using saw by jambing it into the wood as in fig. 504.
The presence of nails, tacks, etc., as in fig. 503, across the path of the saw is of no consequence to such sawyers except that they retard the progress of the saw.

used for abrading or smoothing other substances as metal
and wood.

A rasp is a very coarse file and differs from the ordinary file
in that its teeth consists of projecting points instead of V-shaped
projections extending across the face of the file.

Files are used for many purposes by wood workers. Figs. 526
to 535 show a variety of files.

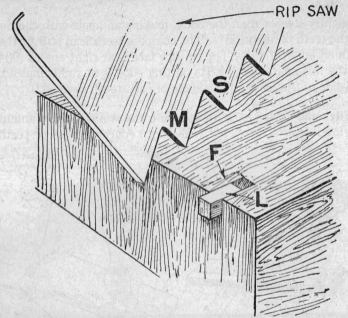

F̶ɪɢ. 506.—Action of rip saw. The first tooth, when it is thrust against the wood at an angle of about 45° chisels off and crowds out the small particles of wood. This requires no side cutting because the saw is running lengthwise of the grain, for which reason it is readily split off on the sides and bottom. Thus evidently tooth M, will start the cut taking off a piece L, and S, following will take off a piece F, thus progressively cutting away the wood.

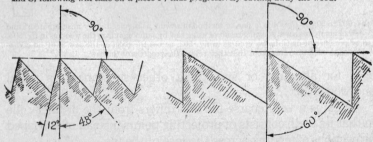

Fɪɢs. 507 and 508.—Proportions for cross cut and rip teeth. Fig. 507 cross cut teeth, fig. 508 rip teeth. The angles for the teeth remain the same as here shown for all sizes of teeth. It will be noted that the rip saw tooth is made with a straight front and the cross cut, with a slight pitch or rake.

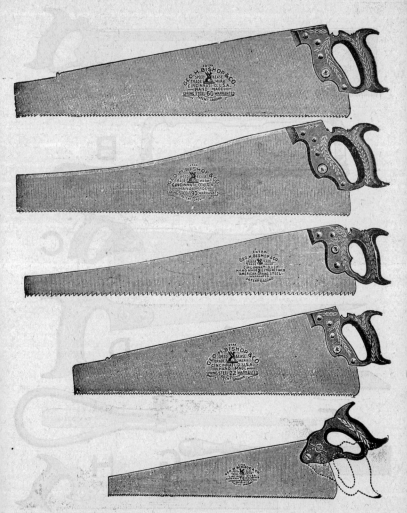

FIGS. 509 to 513.—*Various saws I:* Fig. 509, straight back rip; fig. 510, skew back rip; fig. 511, "narrowed" rip; fig. 512, hand; fig. 513, panel with adjustable handle.

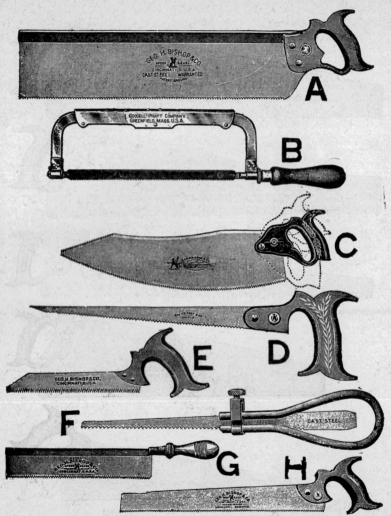

FIGS. 514 to 521.—*Various saws II:* **A**, back; **B**, hack; **C**, flooring; **D**, compass; **E**, pattern makers'; **F**, keyhole pad and blade (form of keyhole saw); **G**, dovetail; **H**, joiner or bench.

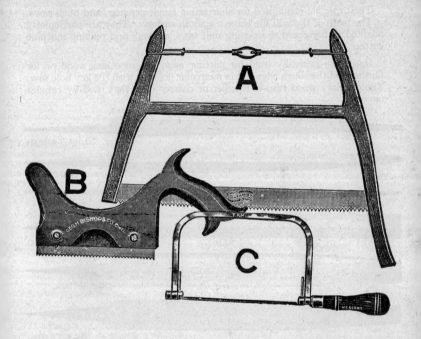

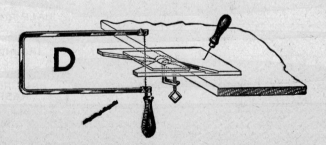

Figs. 522 to 525.—*Various saws III:* Fig. 522, wood or "buck;" fig. 523, stair builders'; fig. 524, coping; fig. 525, fret saw outfit.

The taper file is adapted for sharpening hand, pruning, and buck saws. The teeth of the mill file leave a smooth surface. They are particularly adapted to filing and sharpening mill saws, mowing and reaping machine cutters.

Rasps are generally used for cutting away or smoothing wood or for finishing off the rough edge left in a circular hole cut with the key hole saw. The ordinary wood rasp is rougher or coarser than that used by cabinet makers.

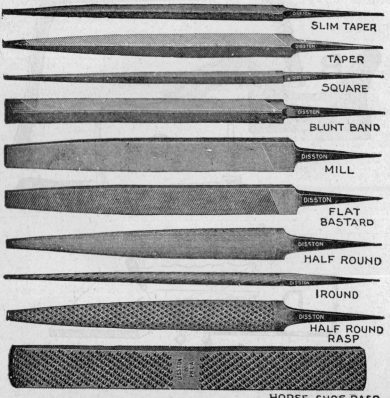

SLIM TAPER

TAPER

SQUARE

BLUNT BAND

MILL

FLAT BASTARD

HALF ROUND

ROUND

HALF ROUND RASP

HORSE SHOE RASP

Figs. 526 to 535.—Various files and rasps.

Wood files are usually tempered to stand lead or soft brass and should never be used on anything harder.

In drawing a file back between the cuts, do not allow it to drag, as it is injured thereby about as much as when it is cutting. In using large rasps or files whether for wood or metal, the work should be held in the vise or otherwise firmly fixed, as it is desirable to use both hands when possible. The handle of the tool should be grasped by one hand while the other is pressed, but not too heavily, on the end or near the end of the blade so as to lend weight to the tool and additional effect to its powers of abrasion.

Sand Paper.—This consists of *tough paper covered with finely crushed abrading material.*

Sand paper is manufactured in rolls of about 1,000 yards in length and widths of from 24 to 48 inches. It is cut in sheets 9 × 11 inches and sold in reams of 480 sheets, or furnished in rolls of various widths such as 6, 8, 14, 24, 30, 36, 40, 42 and 48 inches containing 50 yards. It is made on paper made especially for the purpose from old manila rope which produces paper of the very greatest strength.

The weights of paper used are 60 to 80 lbs. per ream—480 sheets 24 × 36 inches for sheet paper and 130 lbs. for roll paper, which is used on drum and belt sanding machine.

The cloth used is a special cotton cloth ordinarily in two weights: jeans 3½ to 4 yds. to the pound, 30 inches in width and drills 2½ to 3 yds. to the pound, 30 inches in width. There is also used a combination of paper and cloth.

The glue used in sand paper manufacturing is practically all hide glue of the best quality, as it is necessary to have the grains of sand not only firmly but rigidly anchored to the sheet.

The ordinary sand paper of commerce is made with crushed quartz rock, which is hard and sharp. Sea sand is never used as the sharp edges have been worn dull.

For sanding machine use and particularly for hard woods, garnet rather than flint is used, as it is harder, and lasts longer. Most of the garnet which is brown to red in color depending on the size of grit, comes from the Adirondack Mountains in New York, where it occurs in pockets in the rock. The rock and garnet are crushed together to a small size and the garnet separated on ore separating tables.

Practically all emery comes from Turkey in Asia or Greece.

Within the last few years several abrasives have been produced in electric furnaces under great heat and have been largely used by sand paper manufacturers on paper and cloth for the metal trades, for buffing leather, in sheets, rolls and special shapes for various buffing wheels. The two best known abrasives of this kind are first carbide of silicon, and second oxide of aluminum. The first has been designated by various trade names, such as carborundum, crystolon, carbolon, durite, etc., and the second by such names as aloxite, alundum, metalite and durundum. The grits of these artificial abrasive products instead of being known by the usual sand paper designations for size of grit such as Nos. 3/0, 2/0, 0, 1/2, 1, 1½, 2, 2½, 3 and 3½ (from fine to coarse) are known by the numbers 180, 150, 120, 100, 90, 80, 70, etc., representing the number of meshes per inch of screens through which the grains will just pass.

CHAPTER 12

Circular Saws

General.—The circular saw is one of the most popular machines in any woodworking shop or plant. Plants of any size usually have one or more power feed saws used exclusively for ripping and one or more for cross cutting. Beveling and mitering can be done with circular saws of the tilting arbor type, while grooving and dadoing can also be done by means of special cutters.

Circular saws are made in a large variety of types and sizes, among which are the *universal* and *variety saw*. The universal type is equipped with two arbors to permit mounting of both rip and cross-cut blades, either of which is brought into use by simply turning a hand wheel controlling the position of the arbor. The variety saw employs a single arbor and is generally fitted with mortising and boring attachments.

The main structural features of either machine are similar, however, and include the arbor, saw blades, table, ripping fence, cross-cutting and mitering fence or gauge, and a substantial base.

In recent years circular saws, mounted on a radial arm above the work have come into wide use. These are usually equipped for variable angle cutting and can also be used for dadoing or other cutting operations with special attachment.

Construction.—The circular saw, fig. 536 consists generally of a cast-iron base or frame, on which a table is mounted and an arbor or shaft which carries the saw blade or other cutter. The arbor or shaft revolves in two bearings bolted to the frame. It is driven by a belt which passes over a pulley, and this pulley is fastened to the shaft between two bearings.

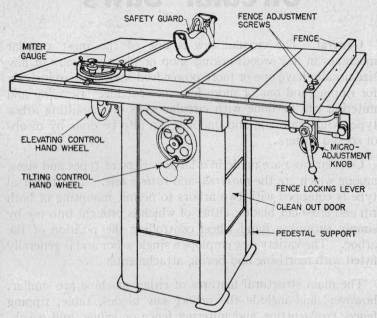

SAFETY GUARD

FENCE ADJUSTMENT SCREWS

FENCE

MITER GAUGE

ELEVATING CONTROL HAND WHEEL

TILTING CONTROL HAND WHEEL

MICRO-ADJUSTMENT KNOB

FENCE LOCKING LEVER

CLEAN OUT DOOR

PEDESTAL SUPPORT

FIG. 536.—Showing typical 10 inch tilting arbor saw. A circular saw of this type has a capacity of 3⅛ inch deep cuts with 10 inch blade; 2⅛ inch material at a 45 degree angle. Dado head cuts 1⅛ inch deep. The drive is by means of a 3,450 r.p.m. self contained electric motor, transferring power to the saw by means of a triple V-belt. The speed of the saw is 3,800 r.p.m. It is equipped with a cast iron table, having both front and side extensions, in addition to safety guard, fence and miter gauge. By means of an easily accessible hand wheel the entire arbor and drive unit may be tilted to any desirable angle for angle cutting.

In the conventional design the saw table can be tilted to an angle of 45 degrees, whereas on the tilting arbor type the table is fixed in a stationary, level position, tilt positions being obtained by tilting the saw blade.

This latter design is not only of great convenience to the operator, but also supplies a factor of safety since he does not have to work in an awkward position.

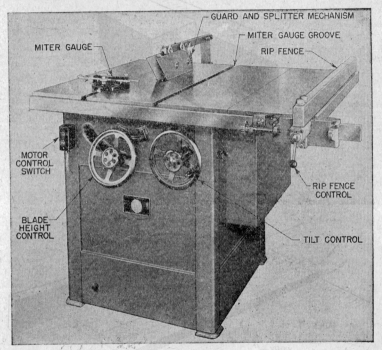

Fig. 537.—Photographic view of typical 12 inch tilting arbor saw. *Courtesy Walker-Turner, Division, Kearney & Trecker Corporation.*

When wood is cut on a circular saw it must be firmly held against a metal guide or fence, which can be set at any convenient distance from the saw blade. When the fence is used as a guide when cutting boards lengthwise, the operation is known as *ripping*. Some saw tables are equipped with two slots or grooves to accommodate a miter gauge which is used as a guide when sawing across a board the operation of which is known as *cross-cutting*.

Fig. 538.—Showing ripping operation on square stock.

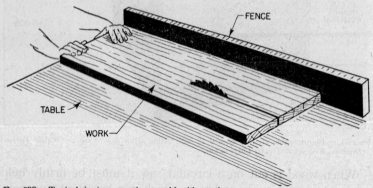

Fig. 539.—Typical ripping operation on wide thin stock.

Ripping Operation.—One of the most useful operations of the circular saw is that of ripping stock to its required width. This operation is generally accomplished as follows:

a. The fence is set to the graduated scale at the front of the table to cut the required width.

b. The saw is adjusted (raised or lowered) to project approximately ¼ inch above the stock to be ripped.

c. Observe that splitter and saw guard are in position to insure safe operation.

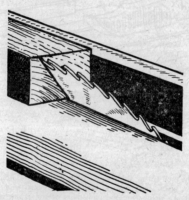

FIG. 540,—Illustrating bevel ripping on tilting arbor saw. Bevel cuts on the tilting table saw are made in the same manner as that on tilting arbor saw. Here the table is tilted and set at the required angle by means of a graduated scale located beside the tilting mechanism hand wheel.

d. Start the operation by holding the work close to the fence and push it toward the rotating saw with a firm even motion. A smooth uniform speed of feed should be used, avoiding jerky movements and jamming the work through too quickly. The operator should not stand directly behind the saw blade, but should take a position a little to either side and hold the stock near its end so that one hand will pass to the right and the other to the left of the saw.

Cross-cutting Operation.—Square cross-cutting work on the circular saw is performed by placing the work against the miter gauge and then advancing both the gauge and the work toward the rotating saw blade. The gauge may be used in either table groove, although most operators prefer the left-hand groove for average work.

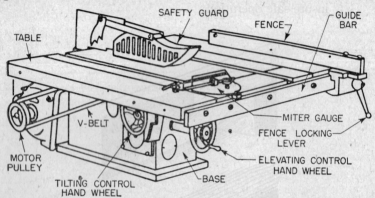

Fig. 541.—Typical eight inch tilting table saw having a speed of 3,450 *r.p.m.* It is equipped with a cast iron table, fence, miter gauge, and a safety guard which include two anti-kick-back pawls and splitter. Elevating mechanism is of the crank and link type. Tilting mechanism consists of hand wheel which tilts table by screw and nut action.

It is highly essential that the miter gauge be set correctly in order to obtain a square cut, therefore, it is customary to test the work by means of a try square before proceeding.

Mitering Operations.—Most miters are cut to an angle of 45 degrees because of the fact that four pieces cut at this angle when assembled will make a square or a rectangle. Miters are cut by setting the miter gauge at the required degrees. The angle of the miter for any regular polygon is obtained by dividing 180 degrees by the number of sides, and subtracting the quotient from 90 degrees. Thus, for example, to find the angle of pentagon (5 sides) we have $90 - 180/5 = 54$ degrees. Similarly to the angle for the miter of an octagon (8 sides) will be $90 - 180/8 = 67.5$ degrees, etc.

The gauge may be used in either one of the table grooves and may also be set on either side of the center position. Where great accuracy is required on miter cuts special miter clamp attachments are used.

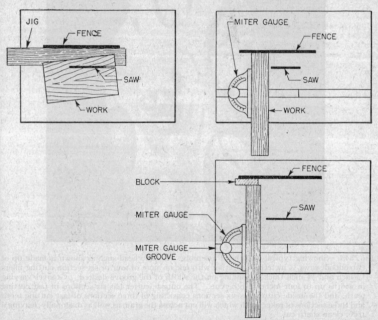

FIGS. 542 to 544.—Showing typical sawing operations on circular saw. In taper ripping such as that shown in fig. 542, work which is to be ripped on a taper cannot be guided against the fence but must be held in a tapering jig, and the same idea can be applied to a number of other forms. In cutting shoulders, the stock should first be squared on one end and cut to length, the miter gauge is used in connection with the fence to bring the shoulder cut the correct distance from the end as shown in fig. 543. In cross-cutting wide pieces to length; one end should first be squared and the gauge adjusted to the required length. Narrow pieces may be sawed to length by placing a block against the fence as shown in fig. 544, the distance from the saw to the block being the required length.

Grooving Operations.—These consist in making grooves that are wider than that cut by ordinary saws. Grooves of varying width are commonly performed on a circular saw by

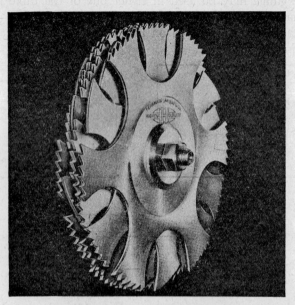

Fig. 545.—Showing typical dado head assembly. A dado head such as shown is made up of two outside saws ⅛ inch thick together with one or more of four or six section cutting fillers ¹⁄₁₆ inch and ⅛ inch thick depending on the width of the groove desired. Grooves varying in widths up to four inches can be cut. The outside cutter has six sections of fast cutting teeth, and the inside cutter has six sections consisting of three sections of fast cutting teeth and three sections of raker teeth which will cut across the grain as well as diagonally, leaving a true, clean sharp cut.

employing a special attachment known as a *dado head*. This is made up of two outside cutters and three or four inside cutters, as shown in fig. 545 by means of which grooves varying in width of from ⅛ to ¹³⁄₁₆ or larger can be made by using

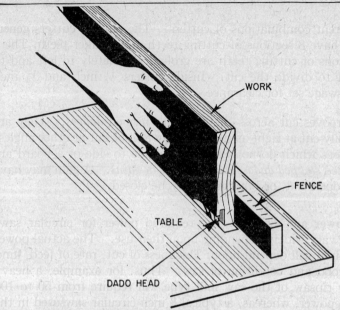

FIG. 546.—Illustrating method of cutting a rabbeted joint with dado head. Joints of this type are used extensively in drawer construction.

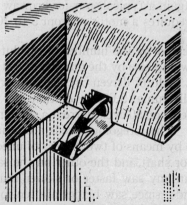

FIG. 547.—Showing method of cutting wide grooves by the application of dado head.

different combinations of cutters. The outside cutters generally have 8 sections of cutting teeth and 4 raker teeth. The 8 sections of cutting teeth are ground alternately to left and to right to divide the cut. Inside cutters ⅛ inch and ¼ inch are swage set for clearance.

Grooves cut across the grain are termed *dadoes*. They are usually cut at right angles, but may also be cut at other angles. Dadoes which do not extend from side to side of a board are termed *stopped dadoes*, *blind dadoes* or *gains*. A gain may have one open end, or both ends may be closed.

Power and Speed.—The required power for circular saws may vary widely depending upon their use. The actual power required will depend upon: Thickness of cut, rate of feed, kind of wood and condition of saw. Thus, for example, a heavy duty ripsaw of the saw mill type will require from 50 to 100 horsepower, whereas, a typical 8 inch circular saw used in the average home workshop will require a motor of from ⅓ to ½ horsepower. Again a typical spur-feed ripsaw used in a wood working plant requires a motor of from 5 to 10 horsepower.

Speed is indicated by the number of revolutions per minute made by the saw and also by the number of feet traveled by the rim per minute. Motor driven circular saws with motor direct on spindle usually run at 3,600 revolutions per minute (*r.p.m.*) on 60 cycle current, on 50 cycle current a similar motor operates at 3,000 *r.p.m.* The foregoing speeds are usually adjusted to a suitable value by means of two pulleys of unequal diameter— one on the motor shaft and the other on the saw arbor. It is a mistake to run any saw faster or slower than the manufacturer recommends, since saw blades are tensioned to run at a certain speed, and give best results at this speed.

Rules for Calculating the Speed of Saws and Pulleys

Problem 1.—The diameter of the driver being given, to find its number of revolutions.

Rule.—Multiply the diameter of the driven by its number of revolutions, and divide the product by the diameter of the driver; the quotient will be the number of revolutions of the driver.

Problem 2.—The diameter and revolutions of the driver being given, to find the diameter of the driven, that shall make any number of revolutions in the same time.

Rule.—Multiply the diameter of the driver by its number of revolutions, and divide the product by the revolutions of the driven; the quotient will be its diameter.

Problem 3.—To ascertain the size of the driver.

Rule.—Multiply the diameter of the driven by the number of revolutions you wish it to make and divide the product by the revolutions of the driver; the quotient will be the size of the driver.

Table of Speed of Circular Saws

Size of Saw	Rev. per min.	Size of Saw	Rev. per min.
8 in.	4,500	42 in.	870
10 in.	3,600	44 in.	840
12 in.	3,000	46 in.	800
14 in.	2,585	48 in.	750
16 in.	2,222	50 in.	725
18 in.	2,000	52 in.	700
20 in.	1,800	54 in.	675
22 in.	1,636	56 in.	650
24 in.	1,500	58 in.	625
26 in.	1,384	60 in.	600
28 in.	1,285	62 in.	575
30 in.	1,200	64 in.	550
32 in.	1,125	66 in.	545
34 in.	1,058	68 in.	529
36 in.	1,000	70 in.	514
38 in.	950	72 in.	500
40 in.	900	74 in.	485
Shingle Machine Saws			1,400

The foregoing table values applies to solid tooth saws. Inserted tooth saws should be run slower, say not over 55 *r.p.m.* as a large mill saw at a high speed will naturally stretch at the rim, thus having a tendency to loosen the holders and bits. With gasoline or diesel power units, a speed of between 450 and 500 will be found most suitable.

Rim Speed.—Nine thousand feet per minute, that is nearly two miles per minute, for the rim of a circular saw to travel, may be laid down as a rule. For example, a saw 12 inches in diameter, three feet around the rim, 3,000 revolutions; 24 inches in diameter, or six feet around the rim, 1,500 revolutions; three feet in diameter, or nine feet around the rim, 1,000 revolutions, etc. Of course it is understood that the rim of the saw will run a little faster than this calculation, on account of the circumference being more than three times as large as the diameter. Shingle and some other saws, either riveted to a cast iron collar, or very thick at the center and thin at the rim, may be run with safety at a greater speed.

CHAPTER 13

Band Saws

These are manufactured for a large variety of uses. For ripping and resawing, large machines with blades three to five inches wide are generally used. The type most adaptable to the general wood shop is the band scroll saw, which has blades from ¼ to 1 inch wide and is used particularly for cutting curved outlines and lines not parallel to an edge of the piece being cut.

Essentially, a band saw consists of a table, wheels, guides, saw blade, and suitable guards. On most of the larger machines, the table can be tilted, usually 45 degrees one way and 10 degrees the other. Some, however, are built to permit bevel cutting by varying the blade angle. The band saw is generally used for resawing because of its thinner kerf.

Construction.—A band saw, fig. 548 such as is used in woodworking shops, consists generally of an endless band of steel with saw teeth upon one edge, passing over two vertical wheels and through a slot in a table, the blade being held in position against the thrust of the wood against the teeth by two guides.

The two vertical wheels over which the blade is fitted are usually made of cast iron, and their rims are equipped with rubber tires and provided with adjustments for centering the saw upon the rims and for giving the saw blade the proper tension.

The table supporting the work is fastened to a casting directly above the lower wheel. It is slotted for the saw blade from the center of one edge. To prevent the blade from twisting sideways in the slot and to give it support when cutting, the band saw is provided with guides, the design of which

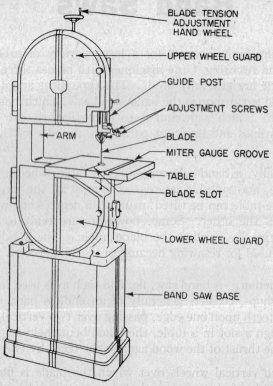

BLADE TENSION
ADJUSTMENT
HAND WHEEL

UPPER WHEEL GUARD

GUIDE POST

ADJUSTMENT SCREWS

ARM

BLADE

MITER GAUGE GROOVE

TABLE

BLADE SLOT

LOWER WHEEL GUARD

BAND SAW BASE

Fig. 548.—Showing a typical 14 inch band saw suitable for the small and medium sized wood-working shop. Tension and tilt regulated by convenient hand wheel and knob. The blade guides are designed to provide maximum support close to work, with blade fully shielded for safety. The saw band wheels are dynamically balanced and the upper wheel unit rides on two heavy ground steel rods, with spring cushion to absorb blade shock. The blade speed of the saw illustrated is 2,535 surface feet per minute (680 *r.p.m.*) with a 1,740 *r.p.m.* motor.

varies for different types of saws. Band saw tables are also usually equipped with a ripping fence and some are also provided with a groove for a miter gauge.

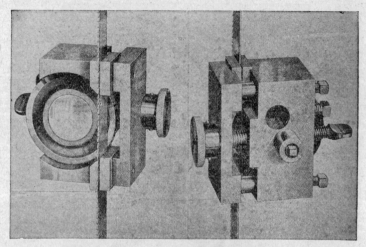

FIGS. 549 and 550.—Views of guide on typical band saw. Guide wheel revolves freely on ball bearings and thorough lubrication is assured by means of a self-feed oil cup. Upper and lower jaws are made of hardened tool steel and are constructed in such a way that they may be reversed and will thus deliver double wear before they are worn out. Adjusting the guide is accomplished by a knurled hand knob that can be locked in any position by tightening two small screws on the rear side of the guide.

The size of the band saw depends upon the diameter of the wheels, which may vary in size from 10 to 40 inches approximately. Thus, a saw having 10 inches diameter wheels would be called a 10 inch saw, and one with 30 inch wheels would be called a 30 inch saw, etc. Of course, the larger the wheels, the larger in proportion are all the other parts of the saw, and consequently larger size stock can be sawed on it. Other important dimensions of the band saw are the table size and the height between the table and the upper blade guide.

Straight Cutting Operation.—Although a band saw is essential for curved cutting, it may also be used for making straight cuts both cross cutting and ripping, where a circular saw is not

Fig. 551.—Showing construction of saw suspension wheels in typical band saw.

available. For all straight cuts it is advisable to use the widest blade possible since it is easier to follow a straight line with a wide blade.

The use of the miter gauge in cross cutting wide stock follows the same general procedure as used for similar work on the circular saw. In the absence of a miter gauge a wide board with square ends and sides may be used in its place.

The use of an auxiliary wood fence screw fastened to the gauge will facilitate the handling of large boards and will result in more accurate work. Unlike the auxiliary circular saw fence, the wood fence for the band saw should be kept low, so that it will work under the guides.

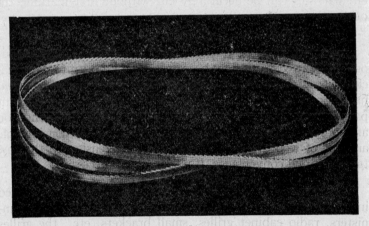

Fig. 552.—Illustrating typical band saw blade.

Ripping and re-sawing may be performed on a band saw by the use of the ripping fence furnished with most saws. When the stock is worked flat on the table the operation is known as *ripping*, and when the board is worked on edge the operation is usually known as *re-sawing*.

Another type of guide frequently used in these operations is known as the *pivot block*, which consists of a specially formed wood block, clamped to the table to hold it in the desired position. Here, the guide is set opposite the blade and at the proper distance from it to cut the required thickness.

Cutting Circular Arcs and Segments.—In cutting circular arcs the usual procedure is to make an outline by means of a compass or divider after ascertaining the correct radius or diameter. If several pieces all having the same curvature are to be sawed, a jig may preferably be made, in which case the circular arcs can be accurately cut without first marking the outline.

Multiple Sawing Operation.—To secure maximum output on band-sawed work, it is necessary to use an up-to-date machine, securely mounted on a substantial foundation to eliminate danger of vibration. The blades are the next important part of the equipment and need to be kept in prime condition and properly adjusted on the wheels. When a considerable amount of wood is to be processed, an extension to the saw table is a real convenience, if not an actual necessity.

The numerous furniture parts which are frequently sawed in multiple include ornate chair and table stretchers, chair bannisters, radio cabinet grilles, small brackets, etc., the grilles and similar items being usually scrolled out on a jig saw. Dependable machines are usually provided with accurate tension devices which assist the operator in securing volume production as well as turning out high class work.

Some present day jig saws are constructed with the table and saw guides set at such an angle with reference to the machine column that extreme lengthy material may be readily sawed.

Fig. 553.—Method of cutting circular disk on band saw.

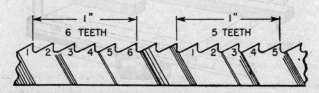

Fig. 554.—Showing method of designating number of teeth to the inch.

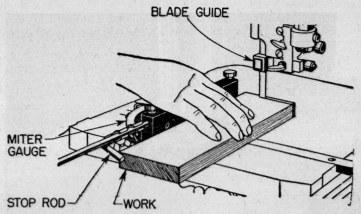

Fig. 555.—Illustrating cutting to length by the use of mitre gauge and stop rod. The rod should be carried on the outer end of the miter gauge.

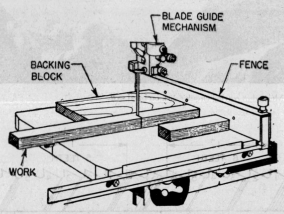

Fig. 556.—Showing method of cutting short pieces to length using square board or fence, when miter gauge is not available

When milling certain classes of thick material, best results may be obtained by sawing one piece at a time, particularly where there are pitch spots and checks and knots to be dodged.

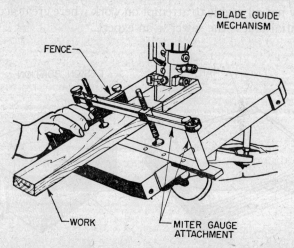

FIG. 557.—Illustrating use of miter gauge clamp attachment. An attachment of this type is useful in many cross-cutting operations and particularly when cutting at an angle with the table tilted.

On the other hand, anywhere from 8 to 18 pieces of veneer or thin plywood can often be scrolled out simultaneously, depending on the thickness of the stock. Some favor the idea of tacking pieces together lightly before sawing, but a more satisfactory system is to cut two or more ¾ inch slits in their edges after stacking them up evenly on the saw table. A hardwood wedge driven into each of these slits will serve to hold the stock together while being processed.

When the job consists in cutting openings in radio cabinet backs to accommodate wires to connect with aerials and bat-

teries, it is customary to do the work on a band or jig saw.
It is not unusual to find workmen scrolling eight or more pieces
of ¼ inch plywood at one time without fastening plies together
in any manner. This calls for considerable dexterity and it
is really not advisable to attempt on work where great accuracy
is essential unless the sawer is an expert.

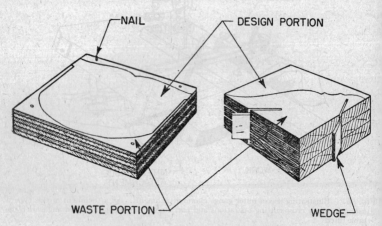

FIGS. 558 and 559.—Showing method of assembly in multiple sawing operations. In fig. 558
nails are driven into the waste portions of the design, their function being to hold the parts
together while being sawed. Fig. 559 shows multiple sawing operations with the stock
wedged together.

Pointers on Band Saw Operation.—In order to obtain the
maximum quantity as well as the best possible quality from
the band saw it is necessary that the operator understand its
operation and is able to adjust it properly.

Prior to the actual sawing it is necessary that the operator
be carefully instructed in the various safety features with which
the band saw is equipped. He should be familiar with the

emoval of the wheel guards and before operating the band aw should make certain that they are securely fastened. Some band saws are equipped with a braking device whereby he drive wheel may be stopped quickly for blade changes. One type is provided with an automatic brake which instantly tops the wheels should the blade break.

Emphasis should be placed on the fact that the widest blade possible should be used, giving consideration to the minimum adius to be cut on a particular class of work. A rule of thumb sed by many is that the width of the blade should be one-ighth the minimum radius to be cut. Thus if the part on and has a 4 inch radius the operator would select a ½ inch lade. This rule should not be construed to mean that the inimum radius which can be cut is eight times the width of he blade, but rather that such a ratio indicates the practical mit for high speed band saw work.

Probably the most frequent cause of difficulty in obtaining ood results at the band saw is the misalignment of the blade uides. There are several styles of guides available, each of hich has certain advantages. Most have a hardened steel isc mounted on a ball bearing which serves as a support to he back of the blade. The purpose of the back guide is to old the blade as the work is being cut and prevent it from eing pushed from the wheels.

When the saw blade is properly tracked on the wheels the ack guide will not be in contact with the blade. Where it is constant contact with the back support the resulting friction ill in time cause the back edge of the blade to become case ardened. Such a blade with unequal tension throughout its idth is susceptible to fractures and breakage. A blade in ntact with the back guide wheel when it is not cutting also indicates that there is excessive tilt in the upper wheel which will cause too much wheel bearing wear.

In addition to the back support wheel the band saw guide is equipped with two side pressure guides which prevent the blade from twisting as the work is cut. These are either square pieces of hardened tool steel or rollers, depending on the type of guide.

The square tool steel type is most common and should be set so that the teeth are slightly forward from the guide pins so the blade will not be dulled and the set removed from the teeth by contact with the guides. The proper clearance between side guides and blade can be measured by placing a piece of paper between them when adjusting. When the guides are properly set up the blade will not touch them while the saw is running under no load. This requires perfect alignment between upper and lower guide sets. When correctly adjusted there should be $1/64$ inch clearance between the blade and all guides.

Another type of band saw guide which has come into limited use during the past few years is pivoted on a yoke arrangement so that it allows the blade to twist in following curves. Such an arrangement it is felt, allows more rapid and accurate cutting of curved sections with less effort than required where the conventional type of guide is used.

The problem of obtaining correct blade tension is difficult for inexpereinced operators on band saws not equipped with tension gauge. Several band saws have tension scales which are calibrated to show correct tension for each of the various width saw blades. Where the saw is not so equipped the operator must learn to adjust the blade tension by "feel". One method of testing blades $1/2$ inch and narrower is to raise the upper guide and place the first and fourth fingers on one side of the blade and push the blade with the thumb on the opposite side. If the blade can be deflected slightly the tension is about right, but if the blade cannot be flexed it is tensioned too tightly.

On blades wider than ½ inch with the upper guide raised 12 inches above the lower guide, the blade should flex about ⅛ inch for proper tensioning. The inexperienced operator should consult with his foreman to make certain the blade is correctly tensioned before proceeding with his work, because improper tensioning is often the cause of breakage.

Where the band saw is operated continuously the tension may have to be increased gradually during the day, because the heat of the blade will cause it to expand and stretch. As the blade expands tension will decrease and cutting will become more difficult. At the end of the day's work, the blade tension should be relieved since the blade will contract as it cools, and may fracture if the tension be too great.

Since smooth band saw operation depends on proper adjustment of guides and proper tensioning and tracking of the blade, the operator who does not understand how to adjust the band saw cannot be expected to turn out first-class work. The operator should also be able to select the correct blade for the class of work at hand.

As previously mentioned, the widest blade possible should be used, taking into consideration the radius of the curves to be cut. The reason is that on straight or gently curving portions of the work it is much easier to follow the contour with a wide blade, since narrow ones often have a tendency to wander in straight cutting.

Band saw blades are commonly classified as 4, 5, 6 or 7 tooth blades. This designation refers to the number of teeth per inch of blade length. Where smooth cuts are desired the 6 or 7 tooth variety should be used. Where speed is of more importance than the smoothness of a cut, a four tooth blade should be employed, because its larger teeth will cut more rapidly.

Another point upon which the foreman should instruct the beginner is the proper folding of blades. While the novice's antics in attempting to fold a blade may prove amusing to others in the shop, they certainly will add nothing to the productive output.

The foreman would be wise to show the operator several of the tricks of the trade in multiple sawing through the use of box jigs, or by lightly brading several parts together. In the band sawing of Cabriole legs the operator should be cautioned to save the waste from the first cut and braid it into the waste of the second to provide a base upon which to rebuild the stock while making the second cut.

CHAPTER 14

Jig Saws

The jig saw differs radically in construction from the band saw although the type of work for which it is designed is very similar. The jig saw is more adaptable than the band saw for cutting small, sharp curves because much smaller and finer blades may be used. Inside cutting is also better accomplished on the jig saw, since the blade is easily removed and inserted through the entrance hole bored in the stock.

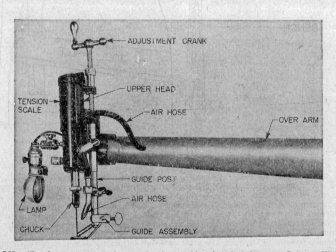

FIG. 560.—Showing over arm and upper head assembly of typical jig saw. *Courtesy Walker-Turner, Division, Kearney & Trecker Corp.*

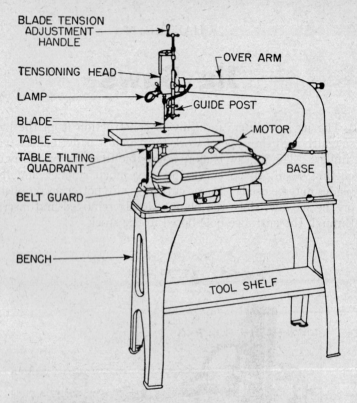

BLADE TENSION ADJUSTMENT HANDLE

TENSIONING HEAD

LAMP

BLADE

TABLE

TABLE TILTING QUADRANT

BELT GUARD

BENCH

OVER ARM

GUIDE POST

MOTOR

BASE

TOOL SHELF

FIG. 561.—Illustrating component parts of typical jig saw. A saw of this type uses standard six inch blade, but can accommodate any blade five to 15 inches because of hollow vises and shafts. The cast iron table can be tilted to 45 degrees both ways, and is equipped with a graduated quadrant showing the exact number of degrees of tilt. The upper head adjusts on dovetail ways by means of hand crank and knurled lock nut. Blade tension is shown on scale, and may be regulated to minimum amount of vibration while machine is running. The drive mechanism is of the reciprocating type with link and counter balanced crank. The air pump is powered by the main drive shaft and keeps cutting line clear at all speeds of the saw. The guides are completely adjustable for front and side sawing and are equipped with a soft refaceable blade support and a ring type hold-down device.

FIG. 562.—Showing principal parts of completely assembled jig saw. *Courtesy Walker-Turner Division, Kearney Trecker Corp.*

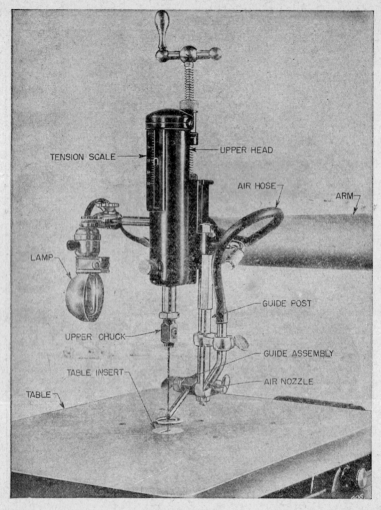

TENSION SCALE

UPPER HEAD

AIR HOSE

ARM

LAMP

GUIDE POST

UPPER CHUCK

GUIDE ASSEMBLY

TABLE INSERT

AIR NOZZLE

TABLE

FIG. 563.—Illustrating upper head and guide assembly of typical jig saw. *Courtesy Walker-Turner Division, Kearney & Trecker Corp.*

Construction.—The jig saw consists essentially of a *base* or *frame, driving mechanism, table, tension mechanism, guides* and *saw blade.* The driving mechanism has a motor driven wheel which is connected by a steel rod to a bar, termed the "cross head", which moves up and down between two vertical slides. This arrangement converts the *rotative motion* of the motor into a *reciprocating* (up and down) movement of the blade.

Fig. 564.—Showing driving gears and table assembly of typical jig saw, the over arm and upper head of which is illustrated in fig. 560. *Courtesy Walker-Turner Division, Kearney & Trecker Corp.*

The table built around the blade is usually designed for tilting at an angle of up to 45 degrees. The size of the saw is generally expressed in terms of the throat opening, that is, the distance from the blade to the edge of the supporting arm.

The distinguishing feature of saws of this type, as previously noted, is that the blade moves with a *reciprocating motion* instead of continuously in one direction as in the case of circular and band saws. Accordingly *only half of the distance traveled by the saw is effective in cutting.*

With the jig saw and its numerous attachments, there are comparatively few cutting operations which may not readily

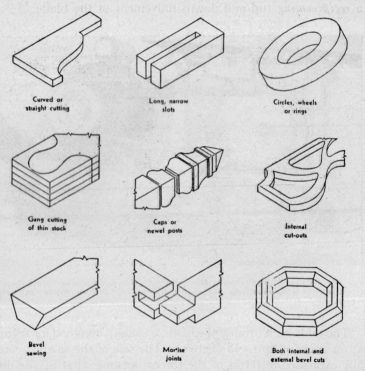

Curved or straight cutting	Long, narrow slots	Circles, wheels or rings
Gang cutting of thin stock	Caps or newel posts	Internal cut-outs
Bevel sawing	Mortise joints	Both internal and external bevel cuts

FIGS. 565 to 574.—Illustrating various items produced by means of jig saw cutting. One of the most important steps in cutting any shape from wood is that of marking pattern shapes on the wood stock to be cut. This is usually done by drawing the pattern by the aid of suitable squares or by the use of a projector. The paper pattern so produced can sometimes be mounted directly on the wood as a cutting guide, or else the pattern may be produced directly on the work by means of carbon paper.

be accomplished. Its primary uses are for cutting out intricate curves, corners, etc., as in wall shelves, brackets and novelties of wood, metal and plastics.

Jig Saw Operation.—As previously pointed out the jig saw is used primarily for making various types of intricate cuttings on work which cannot readily be made on the band saw.

The chucks are generally made to accommodate various blade sizes, which are inserted with the teeth pointed in a downward direction. In operation the front edge of the guide block should be in line with the gullets of the teeth and should be

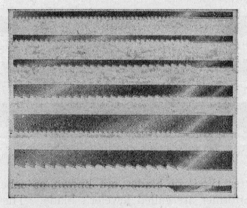

Figs. 575 to 581.—Illustrating various types of jig saw blades varying in size of from 20 to seven teeth per inch.

fastened in that position. The guide post is then brought down until the hold-down foot rests lightly on the work to be sawed. For most work the operation of the jig saw does not differ in any important respect from that of the band saw.

The speed of the saw is generally determined by the material to be cut, as well as the type of blade used in addition to the skill of the operator. Various speeds of from 650 to 1,700 cutting strokes per minute, may be selected by the use of the proper step on the cone pulley.

Jig saw blades vary a great deal in length, thickness, width and fineness of the teeth. All blades, however, may be grouped under two general classifications, namely:

1. Blades which are gripped in both upper and lower chuck, and

2. Blades which are held in the lower chuck only.

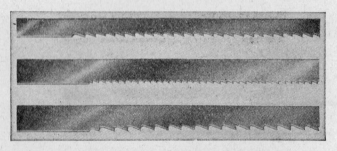

Figs. 582 to 584.—Various sizes of saber saw blades suitable for use on the jig saw.

These latter types of blades are known as saber blades, whereas the former are called jeweler's blade. The jeweler's blades are useful for all fine work where short curves predominate, while saber blades are faster cutting tools for heavier materials and medium curves. Where it is desirable to make inside cuts, a starting hole is drilled at a suitable location.

CHAPTER 15

Saw Filing

The term "**sharpen**" is here used in its broad sense to include all the operations necessary to put a used saw in first class condition. There are five steps in the sharpening of a saw, they are:

1. Jointing.   4. Filing.

2. Shaping.   5. Dressing.

3. Setting.

Sharpening Handsaws.—Handsaws are of two main types, namely: the *crosscut* and *ripsaw*. The crosscut saw as the name implies is used to cut across the grain, and to cut wet or soft woods. Ripsaws, on the other hand, are used to cut wood along the grain. They are similar in construction, but ripsaws are slightly heavier, and differ also in the rake of the teeth. Other types of handsaws are: Back saws, Miter saws, Dovetail saws, Compass saws, Keyhole saws, Coping saws, Butcher saws, etc.

In sharpening handsaws, the first thing to do is to place the saw in a suitable clamp or saw vise. In the absence of a good saw vise, a home made clamp may easily be made in which the saw is supported. In this clamp the saw should be held so tight that there shall be no vibration. The saw is then ready to be jointed.

Jointing.—Jointing is done only when the teeth are uneven or incorrectly shaped, or when the tooth edges are not straight. If the teeth be irregular in size and shape jointing must precede setting and filing. To joint a saw, place it in a clamp with

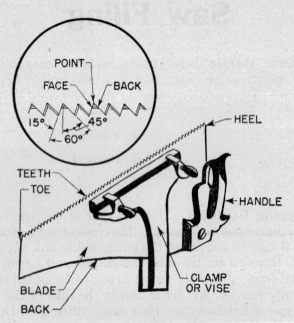

Fig. 585.—Showing method of fastening handsaw in saw clamp or vise.

handle to the right. Lay a flat file lengthwise on the teeth and pass it lightly back and forth the length of the blade and on top of the teeth until the file touches the top of every tooth. The teeth will then be of equal height, as shown in fig. 586. Hold the file flat; do not allow it to tip to one side of the other. The jointing tool or hand saw jointer will aid in holding the file flat.

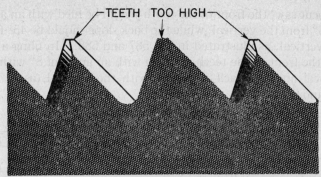

FIG. 586.—Illustrating method of jointing teeth. In the absence of a handsaw jointer proceed as follows: Place the saw in a clamp handle to the right. Lay a mill file lengthwise flat upon the teeth. Pass it lightly back and forth the length of the teeth until the file touches the top of every tooth. In case the teeth are very uneven, it is best not to make the teeth of equal height the first time they are jointed, but to joint the highest teeth first, then shape the teeth that have been jointed and joint the teeth a second time. The teeth will then be of the same height. Do not allow the file to tip to one side or the other, but hold it flat.

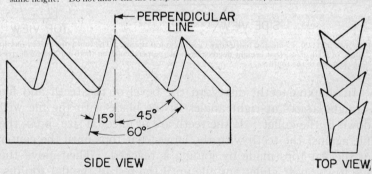

FIGS. 587 and 588.—Showing side and tooth edge view of crosscut saw. The angle of a crosscut saw tooth is 60 degrees, the same as that of a ripsaw. The angle on front of the tooth is 15 degrees from the perpendicular, while the angle on the back is 45 degrees.

Shaping.—Shaping consists in making the teeth of uniform width. This is done after the saw has been jointed. The teeth are filed with a regular hand saw file to the correct uniform size and shape. The gullets must be of equal depth. For the crosscut saw, the front of the tooth should be filed with an angle of 15° from the vertical, while the back slope should be 45° from the vertical, as illustrated in figs 587 and 588. In filing a rip-saw the front of the teeth are filed with an angle of 8° with the vertical and the back slope 52° with the vertical, as in figs. 589 and 590.

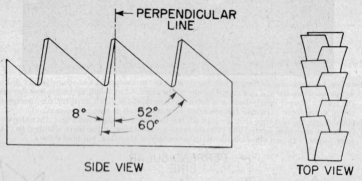

FIGS. 589 and 590.—Side and tooth edge view of typical ripsaw. The tooth of a ripsaw has an angle of 60 degrees, that is eight degrees from the perpendicular on the front and 52 degrees on the back of the tooth.

In shaping teeth, disregard the bevel of the teeth and file straight across at right angles to the blade with the file well down in the gullet. If the teeth are of unequal size, press the file against the teeth with the largest flat tops until the center of the flat tops made by joining is reached. Then move the file to the next gullet and file until the rest of the flat top disappears and the tooth has been brought to a point. Do not bevel the teeth while shaping. The teeth, now shaped and of even height, are ready to be set.

Setting.—After the teeth are made even and of uniform width they need to be set. Setting is a process by which the points of the teeth are bent outward by pressing with a tool called a saw set. Setting is done only when the set is not sufficient for the saw to clear itself in the kerf. It is always necessary to set the saw after the teeth have been jointed and shaped. The teeth of a hand saw should be set before the final filing to avoid injury to the cutting edges. Whether the saw be fine or coarse, the depth of the set should not be more than half that of the tooth. If the set be made deeper than this, it is likely to spring, crimp, crack the blade or break out the teeth.

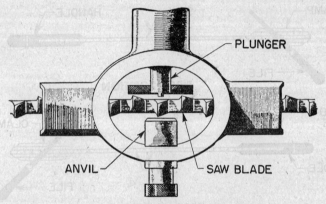

FIG. 591.—Showing position of saw set on saw for setting of teeth.

In setting teeth, particular care must be taken to see that the set is regular. It must be the same width the entire length of the blade and the same width on both sides of the blade. The saw set should be placed on the saw so that the guides are over the teeth with the anvil behind the tooth to be set, as shown in fig. 591. The anvil should be correctly set in the frame, the handles pressed together. This causes the plunger to press the tooth against the anvil and bends it to the angle of the bevel of the anvil. Each tooth is set in the manner described.

Filing.—Filing a saw consists in sharpening the cutting edges. Place the saw in a filing clamp with the handle to the left. The bottom of the gullets should not be more than ¼ inch above the jaws of the clamp. If more of the blade projects, the file will chatter or screech. This dulls the file quickly. If the teeth of the saw have been shaped, it will aid the saw filer to pass a file over the teeth as described in jointing to form a very small flat top. This acts as a guide to the filer; it also evens the teeth.

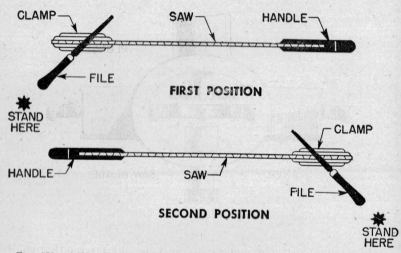

FIGS 592 and 593.—Showing standing positions for filing of crosscutting saw. *Note:* Saw clamp should be moved along blade as filing progresses.

To file a crosscutting handsaw, stand at the *first position* as shown in fig. 592. Begin at the point of the saw, pick out the first tooth that is set toward you, place the file in the gullet to the left of this tooth, and hold the handle in the right hand with the thumb and three fingers on the handle, the forefinger on top of the file or handle; hold the other end with the left hand, the thumb on top, and the forefinger underneath. The file may be held in the file holder guide as shown in fig. 594. The guide holds the file at a fixed angle throughout while each tooth is sharpened.

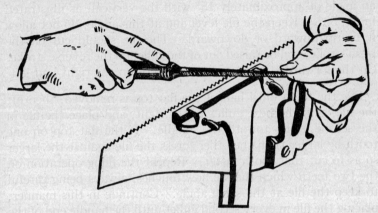

FIG. 594.—Showing method of holding file when filing typical handsaw.

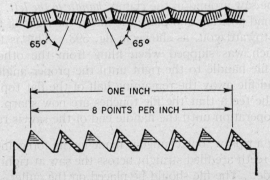

FIGS. 595 and 596.—Showing side angle at which to hold file when filing crosscutting saw having eight points per inch. Points to the inch is a term used to designate the size of teeth in a saw. The saw with a smaller number of tooth points to the inch, seven points for example, will make a rougher cut, although it will cut somewhat faster.

Hold the file directly across the blade then swing the file to the left to the desired angle. The correct angle is approximately 65° as shown in fig. 595. Tilt the file so that the breast (the front side of the tooth) side of the tooth may be filed at an angle of approximately 15° with the vertical, as illustrated in fig. 587. Keep the file level and at this angle, do not allow it to tip upward or downward. The file should cut on the push stroke, and be raised out of the gullet on the reverse stroke. On the forward stroke, it cuts the teeth on the right and left.

File the teeth until half of the flat top is removed, then lift the file, skip the next gullet to the right, and place the file in the second gullet toward the handle. If the flat top on one tooth be larger than the other, press the file against the larger so as to cut that tooth faster. Repeat the filing operation on the two teeth which the file now touches, always being careful to keep the file at the same angle. Continue in this manner, placing the file in every second gullet until the handle end of the saw is reached.

Turn the saw around in the clamp, *handle to the left*. Stand in the second position and place the file to the right of the first tooth set toward you, as shown in fig. 593. This is the first gullet which was skipped when filing from the other side. Turn the file handle to the right until the proper angle is obtained, and file away the remaining half of the flat top on the tooth. The teeth that the file touches are now sharp. Continue the operation until the handle end of the saw is reached.

In filing a ripsaw, one change is made in the foregoing operation; the teeth are filed straight across the saw at right angles to the blade. The file should be placed on the gullet so as to file the breast of the tooth at an angle of 8° with the vertical as shown in fig. 589. Stand in positions as shown in fig. 597.

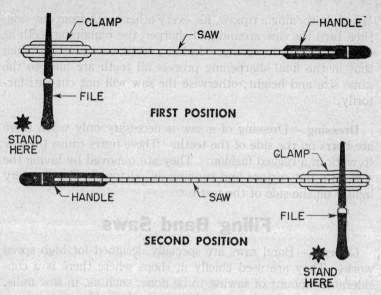

FIGS. 597 and 598.—Showing standing positions when filing typical ripsaw.

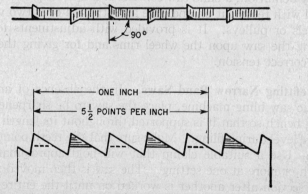

FIGS. 599 and 600.—Showing side angle at which to hold the file and points per inch of typical ripsaw.

When sharpening a ripsaw, file every other tooth from one side, then turn the saw around and sharpen the remaining teeth as described in the foregoing. In filing teeth, care must be taken that in the final sharpening process all teeth are filed to the same size and height, otherwise the saw will not cut satisfactorily.

Dressing.—Dressing of a saw is necessary only when there are burrs on the side of the teeth. These burrs cause the saw to work in a ragged fashion. They are removed by laying the saw on a flat surface and running an oilstone or flat file very lightly on the side of the teeth.

Filing Band Saws

General.—Band saws are specially designed for high speed work. They are used chiefly in shops where there is a considerable amount of sawing to be done, such as, in saw mills, furniture factories, home work shops and the like.

By definition, a band saw consists of a thin strip of tempered steel with teeth cut on one edge and strained over two vertical wheels or pulleys. It is provided with adjustments for centering the saw upon the wheel rims and for giving the blade the correct tension.

Refitting Narrow Band Saws.—In the absence of an automatic saw filing machine, place the saw to be sharpened on a long bench so that it is supported throughout its length on the same level during filing. Make sure that the teeth point to the left. Use a suitable clamp that will hold approximately 50 teeth or more at one setting. The saw is then moved so that one section after another is worked on until the entire length of the saw has been sharpened.

A good enough emergency vise for occasional use is made by simply clamping two boards about 10 inches wide in the woodworkers vise, the boards being high enough to bring the saw to a comfortable height for filing. The bottom of the gullets of the teeth should be about ⅛ inch above the jaws of the clamp to prevent chattering.

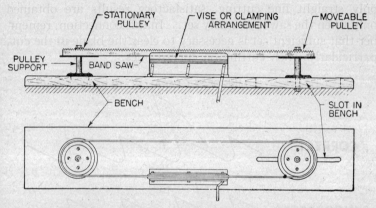

FIG. 601.—Showing home made band saw filing stand. This arrangement consists essentially of two equal size pulleys or wheels mounted horizontally to receive the band saw. The right hand pulley is moveable along the center in a suitable slot to fit various saw sizes.

It is customary to joint the section slightly before commencing to file the teeth. This is done with a saw jointer or by running a mill file lightly over the teeth to make them all of uniform height. The best guide in shaping of the teeth is a new saw, or to follow the shape of the teeth in the saw being sharpened provided the latter are not too much worn.

In filing hold the file in a horizontal position. File each tooth straight across the saw at right angles to the blade raising the file on the back stroke. If the point of any tooth is not brought up sharp after the stroke of the file, do not do extra filing to sharpen this particular tooth. Instead, continue until the section being worked on is filed. By this method, each section may require two or three goings over before the filing job is completed.

When setting is necessary, it should be done before the teeth are filed. It should be remembered that if the saw is to do only straight line cutting, satisfactory results are obtained only when the saw is correctly set. In this connection, remember that sufficient set is necessary to clear the blade in the cut, particularly when cutting on curved lines.

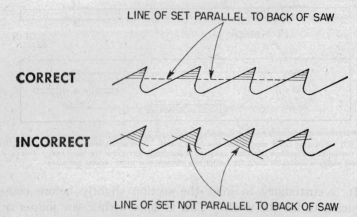

FIGS. 602 and 603.—Illustrating outline of correctly and incorrectly set band saw teeth. When setting, do not set the tooth more than half-way down, otherwise the whole body of the tooth will be distorted. It is important to remember when setting a band saw that the line of the set should be kept parallel to the back of the blade and not at an angle to the back.

When setting, do not set the teeth more than half-way down, because if set too deeply the body of the teeth will become distorted. Also remember to keep the line of the set parallel to the back of the blade as shown in fig. 602 and not at an angle to the back.

Brazing.—When the band saw breaks, regardless of the cause, it may be joined together again either by brazing or silver-soldering. Blades as obtained from the manufacturer are often welded electrically but this requires special equipment not readily available in the average saw filing or refitting shop.

The brazing and silver-soldering method also requires certain special equipment and because of the complexity of the process the average user is advised to return the broken blade to the manufacturer or else take it to a reliable saw filing shop properly equipped for brazing or welding.

Filing Circular Saws

Jointing.—The first step in refitting circular saws is that of jointing it. This consists in making all points of the saw exactly the same distance from the center. This may be done by running the saw slowly backward by hand on the mandrel, while holding a piece of emery stone or a mill file lightly against the top of the teeth. Continue until the tops of all the teeth show that they have been touched by the emery stone or file.

Shaping. Saws of large diameter may be filed while in place if their blades are sufficiently rigid to prevent chattering. Small circular saws should be removed from their arbors for filing and may be held in a clamp in the same way as hand saws.

After jointing, put the saw in a filing clamp and shape the teeth as near to the original shape as possible. Have all the teeth of the same shape with gullets of even depth and width. A slim taper file will be found satisfactory for circular crosscut and circular combination saws. For filing the teeth of circular ripsaws, the mill bastard file with one round edge will be found satisfactory. The round edge permits the filer to shape the gullets and teeth with the same file.

Setting.—After the teeth have been shaped they should be set. The setting operation (sometimes called swaging) is most commonly accomplished by a saw set which makes the setting of any saw comparatively easy.

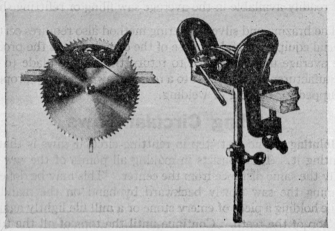

Figs. 604 and 605.—Illustrating circular saw filing clamp. Tools of this type are very handy for filing small and medium size circular saws. They are readily fastened to work bench with thumb screws and are designed to permit tilting at any convenient angle.

The purpose of setting the teeth of saws, that is, springing over the upper part of each tooth (not more than the half of the tooth nearest the point), one to the right, the next to the left and so on alternately throughout the entire tooth edge, is to make the saw cut a kerf slightly wider than the thickness of the blade. This gives clearance and prevents friction which would cause the saw to bind and push hard in the cut.

Whether the saw be fine or coarse, the depth of the set should not go lower than half the tooth. This is important. If deeper than this it is likely to spring, crimp or crack the blade, if it does not break out a tooth.

A taper ground saw requires very little set, for the blade, being of uniform thickness along the entire tooth edge, tapers thinner to the back and also tapers from butt to point along the back which provides the measure of clearance necessary for easy running.

Soft, wet woods require more set and coarser teeth than dry, hard woods. For fine work on either hard or soft dry woods, it is best to have a saw with fine teeth and only a slight set.

In setting the teeth of a circular saw the saw should project fairly well above the clamp jaws. Place the die and anvil of the saw set on the tooth to be set, taking care not to carry the set down too far on the tooth. If this be done the body of blade (below the gullets) will be distorted. Be sure every other tooth is set in the same direction it was when the saw was new. After setting, any teeth which are not in alignment with the others, should be corrected.

The raker teeth of flat ground combination saws should not be set. The teeth and rakers of hollow ground combination saws should not be set. Saws for electric hand saws should have more set than bench saws, about .018 to .025 on each side.

Filing.—After setting, file the teeth as nearly as possible to the same shape as when the saw was new. In filing, do not reduce the length of the teeth; simply bring them up to a sharp point. If the teeth be uneven, the saw cannot cut properly. Have all teeth of the same shape, with gullets of even depth. Do not file sharp corners or nicks in the bottom of the gullets. This usually results in cracks in the gullets. Bevel the teeth in crosscut saws on both the face and back edges. More bevel, however, is filed on the face than on the back of the teeth.

File ripsaw teeth straight across to a chisel-like edge. Then give the teeth a very slight bevel on the back of the teeth. In filing any saw, take care that the bevel does not run down into the gullets. The bevel on both the face and back should be about one-third the length of the teeth.

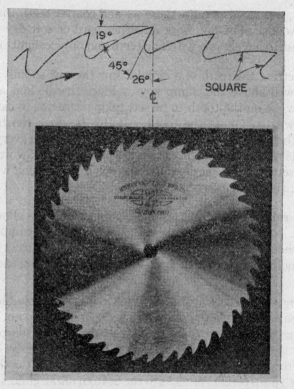

FIGS. 606 and 607.—Circular ripsaw and tooth details. Ripsaw teeth are filed to many different patterns. The face of the tooth is on a line tangent to a circle one-third to one-fourth the diameter of the saw. The teeth are filed square across to give a true chisel point. Due to the rough work for which this saw is intended the point of the teeth must be strong and are therefore cut to an angle of 40 degrees or more depending upon the type of saw.

In filing a flat ground combination saw, which cross-cuts, rips and mitres, use the same method for beveling the scoring teeth as is used in sharpening a cutoff saw. Some combination saws have rakers, or cleaner teeth, to remove the material left in the cut by the beveled cutting teeth, hence the points of

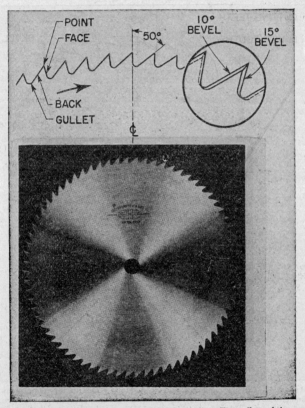

Figs. 608 and 609.—Circular crosscut saw and tooth details. The gullets of the crosscut saw are quite sharp, yet they should be slightly rounded to prevent cracking. The front face of the tooth is on line with the center of the saw and is filed to a 15 degree bevel. The back of the tooth is filed to a 10 degree bevel.

these rakers or cleaner teeth should be filed $\frac{1}{64}$ inch shorter for hardwood, $\frac{1}{32}$ inch for soft wood, than the points of the beveled cutting teeth. After filing these teeth shorter, square the face of each raker tooth and bring it to a chisel-like edge by filing on the back of the tooth only.

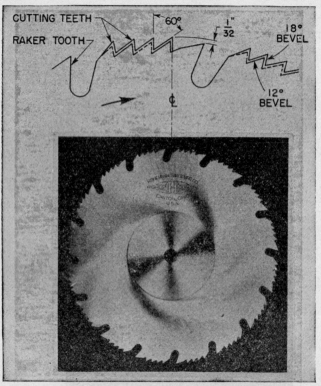

FIGS. 610 and 611.—Circular planer saw and tooth details. This is a very popular saw, for rip, miter and crosscut work. The planer saw is a hollow ground blade, the cutting edge of which is shaped as shown. This same tooth pattern is also used for flat ground saws. The planer saw has two kinds of teeth namely: *Cutting* teeth and *raker* teeth. The cutting teeth sever the wood fibers on either side of the cut while the raker teeth clean out the wood fibers. Raker teeth are therefore cut approximately $\frac{1}{32}$ shorter than the cutting teeth.

In sharpening a hollow ground combination saw, follow the method used with a flat ground combination saw, but do not set the teeth, as the hollow grinding provides ample clearance.

Setting.—The teeth of circular saws may be set in two ways, known as 1. *Swage set* and 2. *Spring set.* Some factories use one method of setting, some use the other. There is the advantage in the swage, however, that all teeth cut entirely across the work, whereas the spring set teeth cut alternately.

Swage set.—Since swaged teeth cut entirely across the face, this method of setting will produce smoother work than spring set teeth. A good many plants do not use swaged saws and many mill men are under the impression that it is harder to keep them in order. With a few inexpensive tools and a little care, any ordinary filer who can keep up a spring set blade properly can soon master the technique of swaging. To swage set a saw:

1. Make it round by holding a piece of grind stone or soft emery against the rim as the saw revolves.

2. File all the teeth to a keen point.

3. Swage from under or top side according to the swage used, $\frac{1}{16}$ inch on each side of the tooth.

4. Joint again and file square across or grind to a keen edge without changing the hook.

5. Side file to bring all teeth to a uniform width. Sharpen saws from two to four times in a full day's sawing.

Spring Set.—In handling spring set blades it is important that the saw blade is at all times put on the spindle in the same position. A good plan is to have a mark on the spindle, turn the mark up and put the saw on with the etched trade mark directly over the mark. When jointed in this position, and put back the same way, it will run true.

For spring set follow the same steps as outlined under "swage set" but instead of swaging, bend teeth alternately, first one to the right, then one to the left. File front of teeth square to the side of the saw, beveling each tooth slightly on the back. Cut off teeth are given more bevel at the points where the cutting takes place. All saws are left stiffer for spring set than for swaging.

Gumming.—Saws running at present day speeds must have plenty of throat room to take care of the saw dust. Insufficient throat room is an aid to cracks. After repeated filings, it may be necessary to lengthen the teeth by gumming. Use a thin, free cutting round nose wheel. Grind lightly, going around several times. To grind heavily on one tooth will heat the rim and destroy the tension. If this occurs, the saw will not run true until re-hammered. Fast grinding also causes case-hardening which results in cracks. Do not use a thick wheel making wide gullets at the base of tooth. A narrow tooth does not have the proper strength and is liable to vibrate in the cut.

Small Circular Rip Saws.—These saws should be kept perfectly round and true on edge and the gullets round at the bottom, of equal depth and width. They should never be filed to sharp corners at the bottom of the teeth for this will cause them to crack at this point.

The best result can only be obtained by keeping the points of the teeth sharp and in proper shape to cut. They should be set or swaged for clearance and this work should be carefully done. If swaged the corners should be of uniform depth, and sufficiently stout so they will not crumble off in the cut.

Saws are frequently complained of as being either too hard or too soft, when in reality the trouble is entirely due to the manner in which they are filed. For instance, if the teeth be lacking in hook and are extremely stout at the points, they will cut hard even when sharp. When they become slightly dull, which they will in a very short time, on account of the blunt shape of the points, they will not cut at all and are very liable to crack when in this condition. An emery wheel or round file is indispensable to the proper care of these saws, for it is impossible to maintain the desired shape with the use of a common flat file only. Machines are now made to keep these teeth in perfect shape.

In order to maintain the original pitch and back line of the tooth, it is necessary that about the same amount of filing be done on the back as on the front of the tooth. For if there be more filing done on the face of the tooth than on the back, the original shape is soon destroyed and it is almost impossible to restore it to the proper shape without retoothing the saw. Sharp corners at the bottom of the teeth will cause cracking at the rim.

No matter whether rip saws be fitted with swage or spring set, they should be filed straight across in front and back of the teeth. It is a mistake to think that rip saws will do better if beveled than if dressed square across. A beveled tooth has a tendency to split the fiber instead of cutting it off squarely across. The bevel also produces a lateral motion which causes the teeth to chatter and vibrate in the cut. Many saws are cracked from this cause.

Small Circular Cut Off Saws.—In filing small circular cut off saws, as in the filing of small ripsaws, it is essential in all cases that they be kept pefectly round and true on the edge. The teeth should be of uniform width and shape and the gullets of equal width and depth. Every tooth should have the proper amount of bevel and this bevel should be alike on both sides of the tooth when a "V" tooth is used.

The amount of set should be the least that will clear the plate sufficiently to prevent friction. The set should never extend too far into the body of the tooth, neither should the tooth be set too close to the point.

Fine Tooth Cut Off Saw.—For smooth work these saws require no pitch or hook to the teeth. If rapid work be desired a pitch to the center will give speed, but the work will not be quite so smoothly done.

Large Circular Saws.—The points of teeth in large circular ripsaws, as in small saws, are the only portion of the saw which should come in contact with the timber. They must be kept sharp by the use of a file or emery wheel, and set by springing or spread by swaging. They should be swaged and side dressed so the extreme point of the tooth should be widest and diminish back from the point.

A saw fitted full swage will stand up better in fast feed than if fitted spring set, but as there is more friction on the edge on account of the points of the teeth being wider, it takes more power to drive the saw. However, for log sawing this style is most reliable. As the swage wears faster on the log side, and thus makes an unequal strain on the saw, it is a mistake to try to run a saw without swaging nearly every time it is filed. Where the timber is clean and free from grit, a saw may sometimes be run two or three times after being swaged before needing to be swaged again, and if carefully filed, will do very good work.

The sharpening of crosscut saws differs from that of ripsaws only in the shape of the teeth and the manner of filing them. Large crosscut saws for cutting off large logs where power feed and rapid work is required, should have the pitch line from four to eight inches in front of the center of the saw for soft wood. For hard wood a trifle more hook is preferable.

In heavy sawing where a very smooth cut is required, as in cutting off logs for pulp there is more bevel required than for ordinary work, and the bevel should be about equally divided between the back and front of the tooth. It is a mistake to try and run a large crosscut saw for heavy work, where a large amount of bevel is required, with all the bevel on the front of the teeth. A very great bevel on the face of the tooth creates a severe lateral strain. The teeth are thus spread apart as it were, and forced out of line into the sides of the cut.

With extremely stout teeth, the strain is transmitted to the bottom of the gullets, usually resulting in cracks at the rim. Remedy, gum out teeth deeper. When a crack starts, drill a hole at the bottom of crack to prevent it extending further into the plate. Bevel only the point of the tooth for ordinary work, but in special cases, as cutting up cedar logs into shingle bolts, a larger and wider bevel is necessary. For heavy work, where a smooth cut is not necessary, a crosscut saw should be filed with the front of the tooth slightly beveled.

Inserted Tooth Saws.—The teeth of these saws are drop forgings made separate from the disc and arranged to be inserted and locked firmly in place on the rim of the disc.

Inserted tooth circular saws have the following advantages over solid:

The teeth being drop forged from bar steel are regular in size and shape and of better material than possible to use for the whole saw.

The teeth are capable of having more and better shaped throat—a special advantage for coarse feeds and for soft, wet or fibrous woods.

They effect a great saving in time, files and blades over gumming and sharpening.

The diameter of saw is not reduced as by constant filing of solid saws. One file will go as far toward keeping a good inserted tooth in order as ten with a solid saw.

Fɪɢ. 612.—Disston Goulding bit with inserted teeth.

The particular size or style of tooth that will operate to best advantage in a mill is determined by the work to be done. Manufacturers have a variety of teeth to meet all working conditions.

Inserting New Points.—Before inserting new points, the grooves in the plate and shanks should be wiped perfectly clean and well oiled, so that the points will draw easily into the plate. When inserting a point, pick it up with the left hand. After dipping the grooved part in oil, place it in position, holding it even with the sides of the shank. Great care must be taken to have the point seat clean and free from particles of fine dust or gum which may have collected there in the use of the saw, as this is often the cause of saws being out of round.

CHAPTER 16

Sharp Edge Cutting Tools

The reason so many amateurs fail in carpentry is that they *do not keep their sharp edge cutting tools sharp*. Not only should the edge be whetted as soon as any sign of dullness is observable, but the tools should always be kept perfectly clean and free from rust. The tools to be considered here are what may be called *hand guided* sharp edge cutting tools, such as chisels, draw knives, etc., as distinguished from *striking* tools (as hatchets) and *self-guided* tools (as planes), etc.

Chisels—In carpentry, tne chisel is an indispensable tool. It is one of the tools most abused, being often used for prying open cases, and even as a screw driver, although adapted solely for cutting wood surfaces.

A chisel consists of *a flat thick piece of steel one end being ground to an acute bevel to form a cutting edge, and the other end provided with a wooden handle*.

Chisels may be classed:

1. With respect to duty or service, as

    a. Paring.
    b. Firmer.
    c. Framing or mortise.

2. With respect to length of blade, as:

    a. Butt
    b. Pocket
    c. Mill

3. With respect to abnormal width of blade, as

    a. Slick

4. With respect to edges of blade, as:

    a. Plain
    b. Bevel

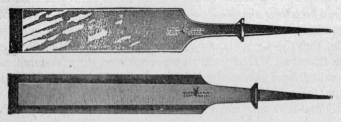

Figs. 653 and 654.—Various chisels classified *with respect to sides of blades*. Fig. 653, Buck firmer tang chisel *with plain edges;* fig. 654, Buck, paring firmer chisel *with beveled edges*

5. With respect to the method of attaching the handle, as:

    a. Tang
    b. Socket

6. With respect to shape of the blade, as:

    a. Flat
    b. Round (gouge)
    c. L (corner)

Paring Chisel.—This is a *light* duty tool for shaping and preparing the relatively long plane surfaces, especially in the direction of the grain of the wood. It is manipulated by a steady sustained pressure by the hand. It must not be driven by blows

Firmer Chisel.—The term firmer here implies a more substantial tool than the paring chisel, adapting it to *medium* duty. The firmer chisel is a tool for general work and may be used either for paring or light mortising, being driven by hand pressure in paring, and by blows from a mallet in mortising.

FIG. 655.—White socket firmer chisel. Laid crucible steel blade, hickory handle with iron ring. Sizes ¼ to 2 in.

Let it be said here, that *a hammer or other metal tool should* **not** *be used to drive a chisel—use only a mallet.* Wood to wood in driving. An exception to this rule is the framing chisel with special handle.

Framing or Mortise Chisel.—This is a *heavy* duty tool adapted to withstand severe strain, as in framing, where deep cuts are necessary. In best construction an iron ring is fitted

FIG. 656.—White framing or mortise chisel. Made of crucible steel, hickory handle, with iron ring. Sizes ⅛ to ⅝ in. blade 4 in. long.

to the end of the handle to protect it from splitting, thus permitting the use of a heavy hammer in driving the tool into the wood. The framing chisel may be used as a deck chisel in ship construction work.

Slick.—Any chisel having a blade wider than 2 ins. is called a *slick*. The regular sizes are 2½, 3, 3½ and 4 ins. Slicks are adapted for use on large surfaces where there is a great deal of material to be taken off, or where unusual power is required. They may be used to advantage in ship work in cutting down to a curve or bevel. They may be used either with a mallet or simply with the hands.

Gouge.—By definition this is a chisel with a hollow shaped

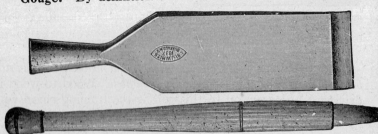

Figs. 657 and 658.—L. and I. J. White carpenters' slick and handle. Made of solid crucible steel; apple wood socket handle. Sizes 2½, 3, 3½ and 4 ins. wide; length of blade 8, 10, or 12 ins.

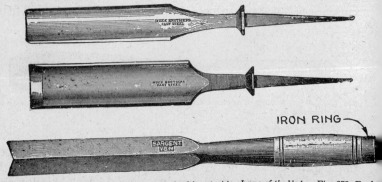

Figs. 659 to 661.—Various chisels classified *with respect to shape of the blade*. Fig. 659, Buck firmer *gouge with outside bevel*; fig. 660, Buck firmer gouge *with inside bevel*; fig. 661, Sargent socket corner c……

blade for scooping or cutting round holes. There are two kinds of gouge: outside bevel and inside bevel as shown in figs. 659 and 660. The outside bevel is the more common of the two.

Corner Chisel.—This type of chisel having an L-shaped blade may be used to advantage in clearing out corners and angles (90° and over), in squaring holes and in general for a V-cut as in pulley stiles or in hand rail mouldings.

Tang and Socket Chisels.—According to the method by which the blade and handle are joined chisels are called *tang* or *socket*. The distinction is shown in fig. 662 and 663.

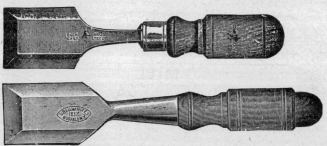

FIGS. 662 and 663.—Various chisels classified *with respect to the method of attaching the handles.* Fig. 662, Buck beveled butt chisel *with tang handle;* fig. 663, L. and I. J. White beveled butt chisel *with socket handle.*

The tang chisel has a projecting part or *tang* on the end of the blade which is inserted into a hole in the handle. The reverse method is employed in the socket chisel, that is, the end of the handle is inserted into a socket on the end of the blade. The term "socket firmer" as applied to a firmer chisel having a socket end does not mean (as generally supposed by some carpenters) "hit it firmer," although that is what actually happens in operation, the blows tending to drive the handle firmer into the tapered socket.

Butt, Pocket, and Mill Chisels.—This classification relates simply to the relative lengths of the blades. The regular lengths are about as follows: butt, 2½ to 3¼′, pocket 4 to 5; mill, 8 to 10 ins.

How to Select Chisels.—A chisel should be absolutely **flat** on the back (the side not beveled). An inferior chisel is ground off on the back near the cutting edge, with the result that, in use, it tends to follow the grain of the wood, splitting it off unevenly, as the user cannot properly control his tool. The flat back allows the chisel to take off the very finest shaving,

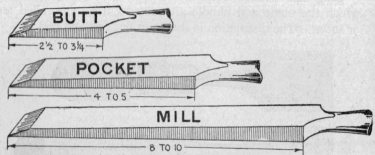

Figs. 664 to 666.—Various chisels classified *with respect to length of blade.* Figs. 664, butt; fig. 665, pocket; fig. 666, mill, or millwright.

and where a thick cut is desired, it will not strike too deep. This is a point to be found in good chisels.

The best chisels are made of selected steel with the blade almost imperceptibly widening toward the cutting edge. The blades are oil tempered and carefully tested. The ferrule and blade of the socket chisel are so carefully welded together that they practically form a single piece. The highly finished hickory handles are all of selected and thoroughly seasoned wood. Socket chisels are preferred to the tang type by most carpenters because they are stronger and the handles are less apt to split.

In the foreign market the tang chisel is still very largely used, although the American socket is making inroads. The tang chisel being the shorter of the two, permits the user to get closer to his work. In order to avoid somewhat the tendency to split, the handles of the tang chisels are not driven into place, which allows for expansion before the tool is put into service.

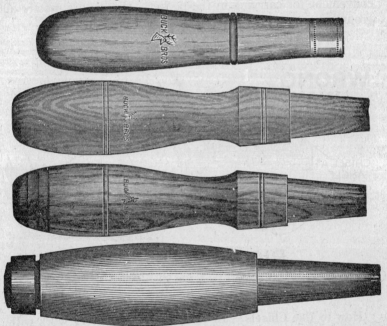

FIGS. 667 to 670.—Various chisel handles. Fig. 667, tang; fig. 668, socket; fig. 669, socket with leather tip; fig. 670, socket framing with iron ring tip.

Beveled edges are preferable to plain blades as they tend to drive the tool forward and also have greater clearance. The leather heads furnished on the handles serve to protect them from splitting.

The butt chisel, owing to its short blade, is adapted for close accurate work, where not much power is required. It is particularly suited for putting on small hardware, which does not necessarily require the use of a hammer. It may be used almost like a jack knife with the hand placed well down the blade toward the cutting edge. The short blade and handle make it convenient for carrying in the pocket. Chisels are mostly all ground sharp and hand honed, ready for use when sold.

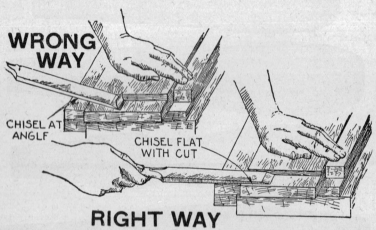

WRONG WAY

CHISEL AT ANGLE

CHISEL FLAT WITH CUT

RIGHT WAY

FIGS. 671 and 672.—Wrong and right way to use a paring chisel. Have flat side of the chisel facing the cut and parallel with the cut as in fig. 672—*not at an angle* as in fig. 671.

How to Use Chisels.—In order to do satisfactory work with chisels the following instructions should be carefully noted and followed:

1. Don't drive the chisel too deep into the work, requiring extra pressure to throw the chips.

2. Don't use a firmer chisel for mortising heavy timber.

3. Keep the tool bright and sharp at all times.

4. Protect the cutting edge when not in use.

5. Never use a chisel to open boxes, to cut metal, or as a screw driver or putty knife.

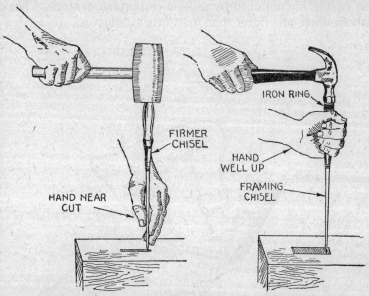

FIG. 673.—Method of using a firmer chisel for light mortise work. Note chisel held close to end of blade. By holding it thus, it may be guided more accurately at the beginning of the cut than if held as in fig. 674 After starting a chisel accurately in a small mortise, the hand will naturally slip up toward the handle. The back of the chisel should be kept toward the end of the mortise toward which the chisel is approaching. Under no conditions should chisel cuts be made parallel with the grain until after the wood in the center of the mortise has all been cut out, as the wood at the side may be split.

FIG. 674.—Method of using a framing chisel for cutting a large mortise. Note chisel held by hand near the handle end of the chisel. Here the chisel is shown driven by a hammer instead of a mallet. This is permissible with a framing chisel when the handle is properly reinforced by an iron ring as shown.

A skilled mechanic does not need the advice here given. It is intended for those users of tools who learn through experience that the unsatisfactory results frequently obtained are due to the fact that the user and not the tool is defective.

How to Sharpen Chisels.—In honing a chisel, use a good grade oil stone. Pour a few drops of machine oil on the stone or if you have no machine oil, use lard oil, or sperm oil. The best results are obtained by using a carborundum stone. The carborundum cuts faster than most other abrasives.

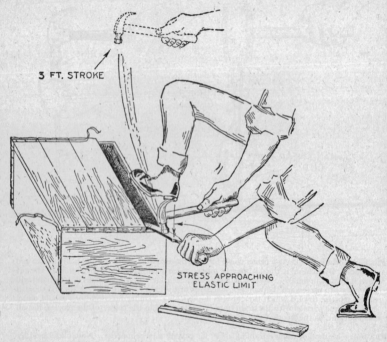

3 FT. STROKE

STRESS APPROACHING ELASTIC LIMIT

FIG. 675.— *How not to use a chisel.*

Hold the chisel in the right hand and grasp the edges of the stone with the fingers of the left hand to keep from slipping; or better, place the stone on a bench and block it so it cannot move. Both hands will thus be free to use in honing.

In this case grasp the chisel in the right hand where the shoulder joins the socket; place the middle and fore finger on the blade near the cutting edge; rub the chisel on the stone away from you, being careful to keep the original bevel.

Never sharpen the chisel on the back or flat side; this should be kept perfectly flat. For paring, the taper should be long and thin about 15°. The longer the bevel on the cutting edge, the easier the chisel will work, and the easier it is to hone it.

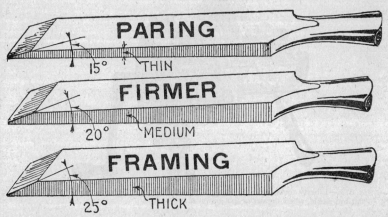

FIGS. 676 to 678.—Various chisels classified *with respect to duty.* Fig. 676, paring or light duty; fig. 677, firmer, medium duty; fig. 678, framing, heavy duty.

In sharpening a firmer chisel, it should be ground at an angle of not less than 20°, and 25° for a framing chisel. See figs. 676 to 678. In honing a chisel the taper should be carefully maintained and unless the back be kept flat it will be impossible to work to a line. Bevel edge chisels are more easily sharpened than the plain edge, as there is not so much steel to be removed.

In case the chisel be badly "nicked" it will have to be ground on a grindstone before honing. Never use a file. Be sure to use plenty of water or the stone, so as not to injure the temper of the chisel, and be particular to keep the original taper of the bevel. After grinding, hone on an oil stone as instructed.

Draw Knife.—This tool consists of a large sharp edge blade having at each end a handle at right angles to the blade. It is

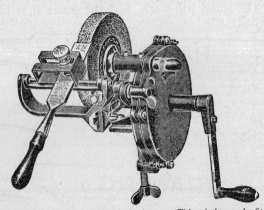

Fig. 679.—Liberty tool grinder with chisel attachment. This grinder can be fitted with chisel, flat bit, sickle, wheel dresser or foot-power attachments.

Fig. 680.—Swan shingle heavy draw knife with steel caps and ferrules. Sizes of blade: 8, 10, 12, and 14 ins.

used for trimming wood by drawing toward the user. When sharp and some degree of force is applied, it does its work quickly and effectually.

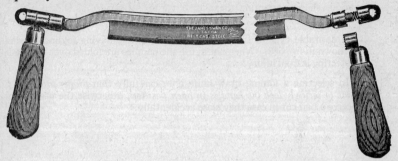

FIGS. 681 and 682.—Swan carpenter's razor blade draw knife with adjustable handles, showing one handle detached in fig. 682.

FIG. 683.—Swan folding draw knife showing handles in closed position. The handles are grooved so as to set over blades and protect the edge. Each handle can be adjusted to four different angles.

FIGS. 684 to 691.—Cross sections of various draw knife blades. Fig. 684, carpenters' razor blade; fig. 685, carpenters' light blade; fig. 686, carriage makers' narrow blade; fig. 687, coach makers' razor blade; fig. 688, wagon makers' heavy blade; fig. 689, shingle shave heavy blade; fig. 690, saddle tree shave heavy blade; fig. 691, spar shave heavy blade.

This tool was formerly much used for the rapid reduction of stuff to gauge, an operation that is now generally performed by sawing or planing machines. The draw knife is very effective on narrow surfaces that must be considerably reduced. Draw knives are made with cross section of various shapes, adapting them for a variety of service as shown in figs. 684 to 691.

A desirable type of knife for general use is one having folding handles as shown in fig. 683. When not in use the handles are folded over the blade protecting it from injury.

In selecting a folding draw knife note carefully that *proper provision is made to securely lock the handles in open position*, otherwise the user might receive a bad cut in case they close accidentally.

CHAPTER 17

Rough Facing Tools

The tools described in this section are classed by some writers as striking tools because the work is done by a series

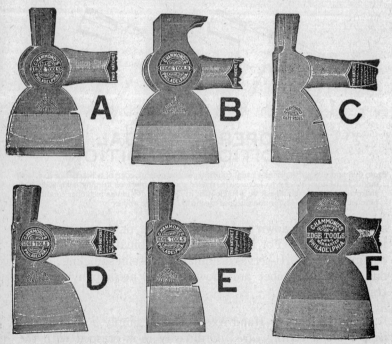

Figs. 692 to 697.—Various hatchets. **A**, shingling; **B**, claw; **C**, barrel; **D**, half; **E**, lath; **F**, broad.

of blows. They might also be classed as *inertia* tools because when the rapidly moving tool strikes the wood its *inertia*, or property of matter that causes it to resist a change from motion to rest drives the tool into the wood. Evidently the cut produced by this method is rough as compared with that made by other tools, hence the classification *rough* facing tools.

Hatchet.—This is a general utility tool familiar to all. In framing timber it can be used as a hammer and for sharpening

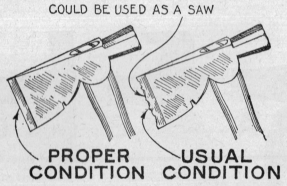

COULD BE USED AS A SAW

PROPER
CONDITION

USUAL
CONDITION

Figs. 698 and 699.—Proper and usual condition of the cutting edge of a hatchet or axe. It ought to be unnecessary to lecture the reader on the subject of keeping such tools well sharpened. There should not be a single nick in the edge, for unless in proper condition, a hatchet or axe is useless for any purpose except to "cut" fire wood.

stakes or cutting down timber to rough size, or for splitting wood it is invaluable. For lathing it is a combination hammer and cutting off tool. It serves a similar purpose in shingling. Various types of hatchet are shown in the accompanying illustrations.

Broad Hatchet or Hand Axe.—This is simply *a large hatchet with a broad cutting edge*. Ordinarily it is grasped with the right hand at a distance of about one-third from the end of the handle, but the position of the hand will be regulated in a great measure by the material to be cut, that is, by the intensity of

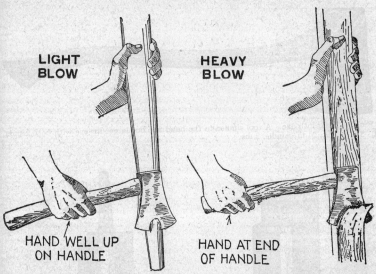

FIGS. 700 and 701.—How to use the hand axe. Fig. 700 shows hand grasping handle about half way between ends for light blow, and fig. 701, hand at end of handle to obtain the necessary swing for a heavy blow.

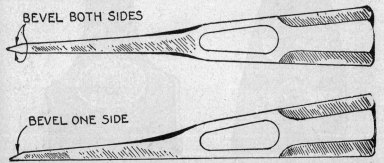

FIGS. 702 and 703.—Methods of sharpening hatchets and axes. *For general use* bevel both sides of the cutting edge as in fig. 702; *for hewing to a line,* bevel only one side as in fig. 703.

the blow. Thus to deliver a heavy blow, the handle is grasped close to the end, and for a light blow, nearer the head.

Fig. 704.—Griffith axe. A tool similar to the hand axe but larger for use with both hands. 3½-in. cut, 24-in. handle, 2 lbs.

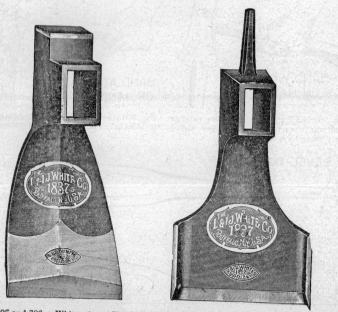

Figs. 705 and 706 —White adzes. Fig 705, house carpenter's adze, cut 4 to 5 ins, weight, 3½ to 4 lbs ; fig. 706, ship adze (lipped), cut 4 to 6 ins , weight 2¾ to 3½ lbs.

Axe.—This tool is similar to the hand axe but of larger size and longer handle intended for heavy cutting using both hands. A typical axe is shown in fig. 704.

Fɪɢ. 707.—Method of using the adze illustrating its dangerous character. Evidently since the work is usually held by the foot there is danger of a misdirected blow cutting the foot, especially as the tool to be of any use must have a very keen edge.

Adze.—Briefly, an adze is a form of hatchet in which *the edge of the blade is at* **right angles** *to the handle*. The blade is curved or arched (toward the end of the handle), thus permitting an advantageous stroke of the tool while the operator is standing over the work. The edge is beveled on the inside only, the handle being removed when necessary to grind the tool.

In house carpentry the adze is not so much used as when more timber was hand hewn, it has its many uses for rough dressing and shaping preparatory to finishing tools as in log cabin work, etc. An important use for the adze is in ship carpentry. The method of using the adze is shown in fig. 707.

Amateurs are advised *to give the adze a wide berth* as it is a dangerous tool, even ship carpenter's often inflict severe wounds on their feet with this tool, the edge of which to be of any use must be very sharp and in perfect condition—no nicks.

In sharpening an adze (or an axe) the tool should be traversed across the face of the grindstone, holding it at the proper angle until all the nicks have been taken out. Then to secure a keen edge rub with a slip of stone. It is important in sharpening an adze to bevel only on the inside.

CHAPTER 18

Smooth Facing Tools

The kind of tools the author has in mind under this classification are those sharp edge cutting tools in which the cutting

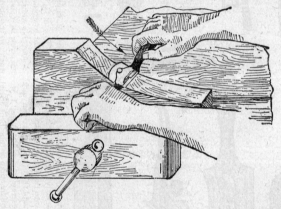

FIG. 708.—Method of using the spoke shave. The spoke shave cuts when being drawn toward the user as indicated by the arrow. In using the spoke shave be careful to work in the direction in which the tool cuts without tearing the grain—the same precaution as is taken in using a jack knife.

edge is guided by contact of the body of the tool with the work instead of by hand.

For example, a plane as distinguished from a chisel. The former, being positively guided gives a smooth cut in contrast with the rough cut obtained by the hand guided chisel, hence the term *smooth* facing tools. These tools

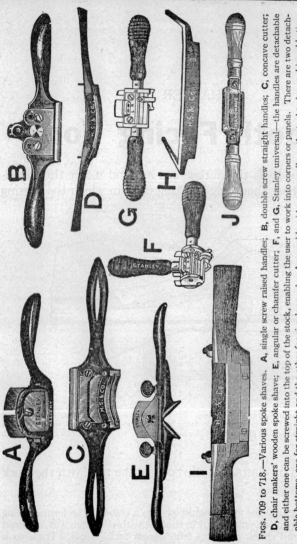

FIGS. 709 to 718.—Various spoke shaves. **A,** single screw raised handles; **B,** double screw straight handles; **C,** concave cutter; **D,** chair makers' wooden spoke shave; **E,** angular or chamfer cutter; **F,** and **G,** Stanley universal—the handles are detachable and either one can be screwed into the top of the stock, enabling the user to work into corners or panels. There are two detachable bottoms, one for straight and the other for circular work. A movable widge gauge allows the tool to be used in rabbeting; **H,** cast steel blade for wooden screw iron spoke shave; **I,** wooden screw iron spoke shave showing the blade of fig. **H,** in place. At each end of the blade is a square spike or tang bent at right angles to the blade. These spikes pass through the holes in the stock and retain the blade securely in position parallel to the length of the tool. The space between the sole and the blade may be regulated by lightly tapping the end of each tang so as to drive the blade farther from the sole, or when provided with screws, the blade may be drawn toward the frame by tightening the screws; **J,** Hargrave circular spoke shave. It is designed solely for circle work, and will cut in any circle from 1¼ ins. diam. up. The knife is adjustable by two screws for thin or thick cuts.

are virtually chisels set in appropriate frames, so that the contact of the frame with the work during the movement of the tool will give a positive guide to the cutting edge thus resulting in a smooth cut.

Spoke Shave.—This tool is a kind of modified draw knife, whose blade is set in a boxlike frame which forms a positive guide. The blade is adjustable the same as a plane to govern the thickness of the cut.

Spoke shaves may be of wood or metal and they have obtained their name from the fact that they were used in the making of wagon spokes before the invention of the automatic spoke making machines. They may be used to smooth curved edges and to round irregular surfaces.

There are a multiplicity of types as shown in the accompanying cuts. With respect to the cutter, spoke shaves are made with cutters of various shape, as straight, hollow, round, angular, etc.

Spoke shave cutters may be sharpened by removing the blade from the stock and rubbing it on the inside with a flat slip of oil stone and lightly rubbing the outside on an ordinary oil stone.

To more firmly hold the small blade, place it into a saw kerf made across the end of a small, flat piece of wood with the edge of the blade projecting beyond the wood. The latter should be beveled to allow the blade to lie on the stone at the proper angle. It may then be sharpened like a plane iron.

Planes.—Briefly a plane is a tool for smoothing boards or other surfaces of wood forming mouldings and the like, consisting of a stock, of wood, or iron, or a combination of the two, from the under side or face of which projects slightly the cutting edge of the "iron," which inclines backwards and has an aperture in front of the escape of shavings.

The plane is essentially a finishing tool and while it is adapted for use in bringing down wood surfaces to a desired thickness, owing to its construction it will produce this result gradually as compared with a hatchet or mattock. For this reason it is the *last tool* to be used in finishing a wood surface.

There are a multiplicity of planes to meet the varied requirements and a classification to be comprehensive should be taken from several points of view, as:

1. With respect to the material of construction, as

    a. Wood
    b. Iron
    c. Combined wood and iron

2. With respect to direction of the cut, as:

    a. Bench (with the grain)
    b. Block (cross grain)

3. With respect to size and service (bench plane), as:

    a. Jointer (28 to 30 ins.)
    b. Trying (22 to 24 ins.)
    c. Fore (18 ins.)
    d. Jack (14 to 16 ins.)
    e. Smooth (5½ to 12 ins.)

4. With respect to the "iron," as:

    a. Single
    b. Double

5. With respect to the bottom or *face*, as:

    a. Iron $\begin{cases} \text{plain} \\ \text{corrugated} \end{cases}$
    b. Wood

6. With respect to unusual features, as:

    a. Moulding
    b. Special

Jack Plane.—As its name implies, this plane is intended for heavy rough work. It is the first plane used in preparing stuff, its purpose being to remove irregularities left by the saw and to produce a fairly smooth surface. It is long and heavy enough to make it a powerful tool so that it will remove considerable

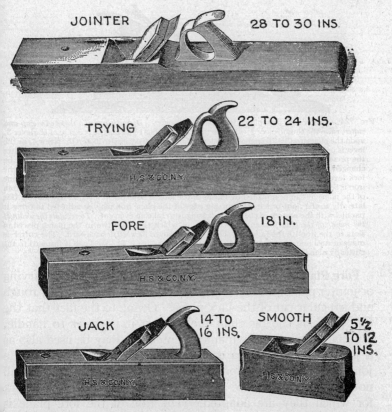

FIGS. 719 to 723.—Various bench planes illustrated in order from longest to shortest. Note in fig. 719 the recessed portion of the stock permitting the handle to be placed lower down. Planes having this feature are called *razee* planes. Any size plane may be obtained razee type.

chip on each cut. The cutting edge of the "iron" is ground rounding (later described), this form being best adapted for roughing. If properly sharpened the jack plane may be used as a smooth plane, or as a jointer on small work, as it is capable of doing as good work as any plane.

FIG. 724.—Union iron jack plane, with parts numbered. *Directions:* *To remove the cap and cutter,* raise the thumb piece 2, which acts as a cam, thus releasing the pressure of the lever 3, upon the plane iron 1. To remove this lever 3, it is not necessary to loosen the screw 4, as the lever is provided with a slot, which allows of its being easily removed. This screw 4, regulates the pressure of the lever upon the plane iron, and when properly adjusted, should not be changed. *To regulate the depth of cut* revolve the adjusting screw 5, which operates upon the fork lever 6, to the right or left, thus lowering or raising the plane iron. After the plane iron is set to cut a shaving of the thickness required, if it is not exactly true with the bottom of the plane, it can be adjusted by means of the lateral adjustment lever 9. By moving this laterally to the right or left, the cutting edge of the plane iron may be adjusted to bring it parallel with the bottom of the plane, causing it to take an even cut. *To regulate the width of the mouth of the plane* loosen the screws 8, of which there are two in the plane, placed in slots in the frog 10, thus allowing the frog to be moved forward or backward. The cutter is made of steel tempered and ground to a keen cutting edge. The steel cap is fastened to the cutter by a small screw which operates in a slot in the cutter same as in a wooden plane.

Fore Plane.—This plane is for the same purpose as the trying or jointer plane, that is, *to straighten and smooth the* rather rough and irregular cut of the jack plane. Owing to the fact that the fore plane is shorter than the jointer, it is easier to handle, especially for a journeyman carpenter. It may be used also as a jack plane. Where a carpenter has not both a jack and a jointer he can make a fore plane serve for both although it will not give as good service as either of the other two in the work for which they are adapted. The iron of the fore plane is sharpened to a straight line and is set for a finer cut than that of the jack plane.

Trying and Jointer Planes.—The great length and weight of these planes keep the cutter from tearing the wood and with

FIGS. 725 and 726.—Stanley *iron*, and combined wood and iron or *wood bottom* planes. Fig. 725, jack iron plane with corrugated bottom; fig. 726, jack wood bottom plane.

FIG. 727.—Stanley scrub plane for planing down to a rough dimension any board that is too wide to conveniently rip with a hand saw, an operation that is sometimes called "hogging." This is made possible by reason of the peculiar shape of the extra heavy cutter, the cutting edge of which is round instead of square.

the cutter set fine it is the plane for obtaining the smoothest finishes. These planes will true up better than other types of planes, two wood surfaces that are to be brought together where a very close fit is required. A *trying* plane is *simply a small jointer*.

in this country the word jointer is applied to both planes—that is all sizes from 22 to 30 ins. The term *trying plane* is used in England. The choice between a trying or jointer plane depends upon the degree of precision required in bringing a surface to a true plane.

Evidently the **length** *of the plane determines the* **straightness** *of the cut.*

Thus a smooth plane, owing to its short length, will if used on an uneven surface follow the irregularities of the surface, taking its shaving without interruption, whereas, a fore, trying, or jointer plane similarly applied will first touch only the high spots, progressively lengthening the cuts until upon reaching the lowest spots a continuous shaving will be taken. The final cut will approach a true plane surface in degree depending upon length of the tool and length of irregularities or undulations of surface originally present.

The cutting edge for a tying or jointer plane is ground straight and set for a fine cut.

Smooth Plane.—Evidently the small length of this plane adapts it for finishing off uneven surfaces, as owing to its small

FIGS. 729 and 730.—Union combined wood and iron smooth planes. Fig. 729, plain plane 8 or 9 ins., 2 or 2⅜ in. cutter; fig. 730, handle plane, 9 in. long, 2 in. cutter, 10 ins. long, 2⅜ in. cutter; "Jenny smooth" 13 ins. long, 2⅝ in. cutter

FIG. 728.—Coopers' or very long jointer plane. Made in lengths from 3 to 5½ feet, 2½ inch irons.

size it will find its way into minor depressions of the wood without taking off much material. In this it differs from the trying and jointer planes as all three are finishing planes, the trying and jointer being, however, for finer work.

Block Plane.—This type of plane which is the smallest made (length 3½ to 7½ ins.) was designed to meet the demand for a

Figs. 731 and 732.—Stanley block planes. Fig. 731, plane for soft woods with iron at 20°; fig. 732, low angle plane for hard woods with iron at 12°.

plane which could be easily held in one hand while planing *across* the grain, particularly the ends of boards, etc. This latter work many carpenters call "*blocking in*," hence the name *block* plane. Since the block plane is for planing across the grain, no cap iron is necessary to break the shavings as there are no shavings.

The bevel of the iron is turned up instead of down. Owing to the small size of the block plane it is usually operated with one hand, the work being

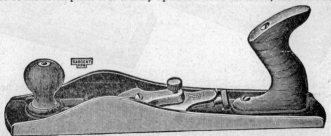

Fig. 733.—Sargent low-angle adjustable iron block plane. This plane is especially intended for cutting across the grain, the cutter being set very low. It is a heavy plane, making it desirable for use on knurly cross grained wood where the ordinary block plane would be too light. The bearing surface for the cutter is arranged so that the cutter may be swung easily from side to side, in case the cutting edge is not ground exactly true with the bottom.

held by the other hand, hence, as distinguished from this method of using, other planes are called *bench* planes.

The angle of the iron for block planes is much smaller than for bench planes. This angle is 20° for soft woods and 12° for hard woods; planes having the iron at 12° are called "low angle" block planes.

Block Plane.—This type of plane which is the smallest made

Moulding and Special Planes.—There is a multiplicity of

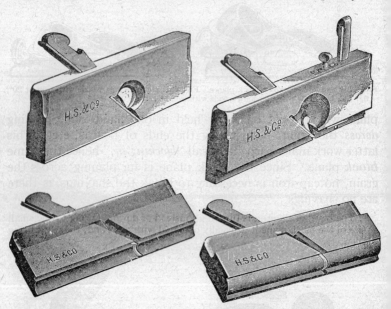

Figs. 734 to 737.—Various wooden *moulding* planes. Fig. 734, rabbet; fig. 735, dado; fig. 736, quarter round; fig. 737, cove.

planes designed to make cuts of various shape, some performing one operation and some a variety of operations. The following brief description will, together with the accompanying cuts, give a clear understanding of these various planes.

Rabbet or Rebate Plane.—In this plane, as shown in fig. 734, the iron projects slightly from the side as well as from the bottom of the plane. There are various forms of rabbet planes, the one here shown being a simple wooden plane. With the tool

FIG. 738.—Stanley bull nose rabbet plane for working close up into corners or other difficult places. Adjustable mouth.

FIG. 739.—Stanley edge trimming block for trimming or smoothing the edge of boards for a square or close fit. The cutter works on a skew. Wood blocks of various bevels may be attached enabling the user to make a slanting cut.

the edge of a board can be cut away so as to leave a rebate or "sinking" like a step along its length to fit over and into a similar indentation cut in the edge of another board. Rabbet planes are adapted to cut *with*, or *across* the grain according as the iron is respectively set at *right angles* or *obliquely* across the sole or face of the plane.

FIG. 740.—Sargent adjustable iron dado and rabbet plane for use in cutting grooves away from the edge of a surface. As the cutter is at an angle, the plane in use gets a shearing cut; spurs directly in front of the cutter serve to cut across the grain of the wood and insure a clean cut for that reason. The depth gauge is regulated by the forward thumb screw.

FIG. 741.—Stanley dovetail plane. It will cut any size grooves and tongues to fit with sides at flare of 20° where the width of the neck is more than ¼ in. and the depth of groove not over ¾ in. The tongue and groove are cut separately and can be made with parallel or tapering sides.

Filletster Plane.—On account of the difficulty of using a rabbet plane with accuracy, it is usual to use a plane with an adjustable fence or guide that may be attached to the side of the plane, and regulated according to the width of the rebate to be made. A screw stop is also placed on the side of the plane farthest from the operator to regulate the depth of cut.

FIG. 742.—Stanley skew cutter fillester and rabbet plane. It has an extra wide skew cutter and an adjustable spur on each side. The fence and depth gauge can be attached to either side the fence sliding under the bottom. Remove arms and fence, and a skew cutter rabbet plane is obtained.

FIG. 743.—Stanley special dado plane for blind wire grooving as well as for many other purposes. Fitted with a double spur which prevents splintering and a depth gauge allowing a groove to be cut up to the limit of the plane—½ in.

Grooving Plane.—This plane (sometimes called a *trenching* plane) is used for cutting grooves *across* the grain. It has a rebated or stepped sole, the cutters being in the tongue portion which is usually ½ in. deep and varies from ¼ to 1⅛ ins. A screw stop adjusts the depth of cut and a double toothed cutter separates the fibres in front of the iron.

NOTE.—*The word filletster,* or *fillister,* is defined in carpentry as a kind of moulding plane designed for making grooves or forming rabbets, as in window sashes, the rabbet on the sash bar for receiving the edge of the glass and the putty.

Router.—Planes of this type are for surfacing the bottom of grooves or other depressions parallel with the general surface of the wood.

The *closed throat* type is the ordinary form of router; the *open throat* is an

FIG. 744.—Sargent adjustable iron fillester and rabbet plane with two seats for cutter. When cutter is placed in the forward seat the plane can be used as a bull nose rabbet. The arm and "fence" can be placed on either side of the plane making a right, or left hand fillester.

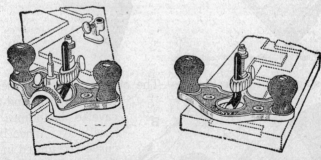

FIGS. 745 and 746.—Stanley router planes. Fig. 745, open throat; fig. 746, closed throat. These planes are used for surfacing the bottom of grooves or other depressions parallel with the surface of the work. A wooden bottom of any size can be attached enabling the user to rout on large openings. The cutters are adjustable and can be held as shown for regular work or on the back of the cutter post for bull nose work.

improved design giving more freedom for chips and a better view of the work and cutter. The latter has an attachment for regulating the thickness of the chip and a second attachment for closing the throat for use on narrow surfaces. The bottoms of both styles are designed so that an extra wooden bottom of any size desired can be screwed on, enabling the user to rout large openings.

Rounds and Hollows.—These moulding planes are used to produce convex and concave surfaces. They may be obtained in pairs of opposite but similar curvature for various sizes, and both square and skew mouthed. The latter work the cleaner but are more liable to choke than the former.

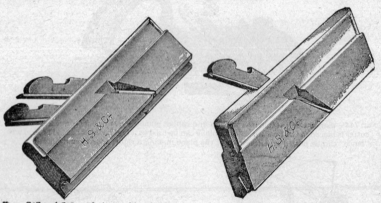

Figs. 747 and 748.—Nosing and bead planes.

Nosing and Scotia Planes.—The object of these planes is to work half round and cavetto mouldings respectively. When both curves are united in the same stick it is termed a *stair tread moulder.*

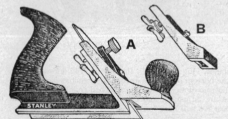

Figs. 749 and 750.—Stanley adjustable chamfer plane for chamfer or stop chamfer work. It has a 90° V bottom which acts as a mitre guide. To this is attached an adjustable front A, having a flat bottom which carries the cutter. This front can be set for different sizes of chamfer. Front A, may be detached and B, substituted, permitting the plane to be worked close up into corners.

Chamfer Plane.—This plane produces a regular chamfer upon the salient angle of a board. An adjustable stop sliding in the mouth of the plane regulates the width of the chamfer, which, however, is limited to an angle of 45° with the sides. An ordinary plane can be arranged to cut a chamfer by glueing

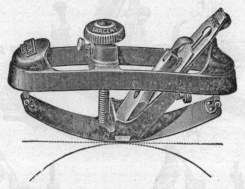

FIG. 751.—Sargent adjustable iron circular or *compass* plane. The flexible steel face may be adjusted to the required arc, either convex or concave, for planing curved surfaces and is accurately set and firmly held in position by the knob and set screw.

strips of hard wood to its sole. A chamfer at any angle can be cut by giving the strips the desired angle.

Plane "Irons" or Cutters.—The so-called "iron" which does the cutting is similar to a chisel but differs in that its sides are parallel and the thickness is less. Plane irons are classed:

1. With respect to thickness, as:

    a. Heavy
    b. Thin

2. With respect to the shape of the cutting edge, as:

a. Curved
b. Straight (square)
c. Skew (oblique)
d. Toothed

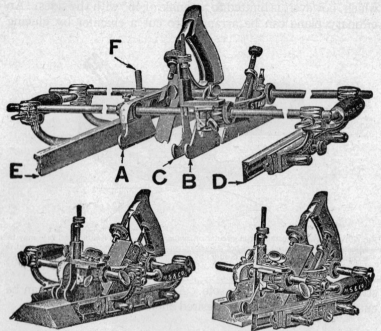

Figs. 752 to 754.—Stanley *universal* plane comprising a plow, dado, rabbet, beading, reeding, fluting, round, hollow, sash, match, fillester, slitting chamfer, and general moulding plane in one tool. By means of an adjustable bottom and the auxiliary center bottom it is possible to use a cutter of practically any shape with the plane. Fig. 752 shows plane used as a champer plane, and fig. 753, as a moulding plane. *The plane consists of: a main stock* **A**, with two sets of transverse sliding arms, a depth gauge, **F**, adjusted by a screw, and a slitting cutter with stop; a sliding section, **B**, with vertically adjustable bottom; an auxiliary center bottom, **C**, which is to be placed in front of the cutter as an extra support, or stop, when needed. This bottom is adjustable both vertically and laterally; *fences* **D**, and **E**, fence **D**, has a lateral adjustment by means of a screw, for extra fine work. The fences can be used on either side of the plane, and the rosewood guides can be tilted to any desired angle, up to 45°, by loosening the screws on the face. Fence **E**, can be reversed for center beading wide boards; *an adjustable stop*, to be used in beading the edges of matched boards is inserted on the left hand side of slicing section **B**. By means of the adjustable bottom and the auxiliary center bottom it is possible to use a cutter of practically any shape with this plane.

3. With respect to provision for breaking the chips, as:

   a. Single
   b. Double

Heavy cutters are usually No. 12 gauge, and thin cutters No. 14 gauge. The heavy cutter offsets the tendency found in spring cap planes to vibrate when used on cross grained wood, the additional weight helps to avoid chattering.

The thin cutter is satisfactory when the plane is properly constructed

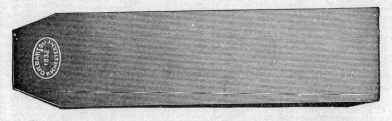

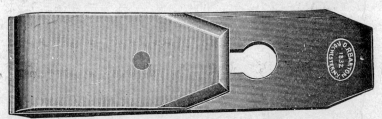

FIGS. 755 and 756.—Barton single and double plane irons.

NOTE.—*Instructions for using Stanley universal plane* (figs. 752 to 754). *Moulding plane.* Insert a cutter and adjust bottom of sliding section B, to conform to the shape of the cutter; then, by means of the two check nuts on the transverse arms, fasten this section firmly—*before tightening* the thumb screws which secure the sliding section to the arms. When needed, adjust auxiliary center bottom C, for an additional support in front of the cutter. By tilting the rose wood guides on fences D, and E, mouldings of various angles may be formed. *Match, sash, beading, reeding, fluting, hollow, round, plow, rabbet and fillester plane.*—Use in same manner as for mouldings. In working match and sash cutters, the auxiliary center bottom C, may be used as a stop. *Dado.*—Remove the fences D, and E, and set the spurs parallel with the edges of cutter. Insert long adjustable stop on left hand side of sliding section. *Slitting Plane.*—Insert the cutter and stop on right hand side of the plane, and use fence D, or E, for guide. *Chamfer.*—Insert the desired cutter; fasten a fence on each side of the plane, and tilt the rosewood guides to required angle. For chamfer beading use in the same form as above, and feed the cutter down, gradually, by use of thumb nut for adjustment

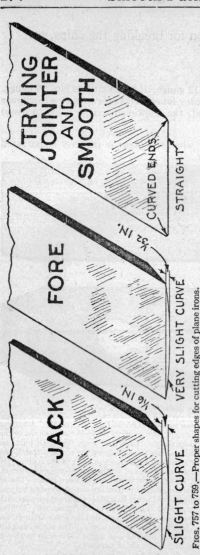

FIGS. 757 to 759.—Proper shapes for cutting edges of plane irons.

so that firm support is given the cutter over a considerable portion of its length. It has the slight advantage of quicker grinding.

For the first or roughing cut with the jack plane the cutting edge is ground slightly curved (convex) as in fig. 757, because being used for heavy work it removes thick shavings and if the cutter were ground straight. the plane would cut a rectangular channel from which the wood must be torn as well as cut as in fig. 760.

Moreover such a shaving would probably stick fast in the throat or require undue force to push the plane. Compare this with the shaving made with fully curved cutting edge of the jack plane as shown in fig. 761.

When a full set of planes is on hand the fore plane should have some curvature to the cutting edge as in fig. 758, in this case the process of transforming the grooved surface produced by the jack plane to a flat surface is accomplished in three operations using jack, fore, and trying or jointer plane as shown in figs. 762 to 764.

The cutting edge of the trying jointer and smooth plane irons are made straight with rounded corners as in fig. 759, because it makes a very fine cut, the groove caused by the removal of so delicate a shaving is sufficiently blended with the general work by the rounded corners of the iron.

Bevel of the Cutting Edge.—Many of the complaints about

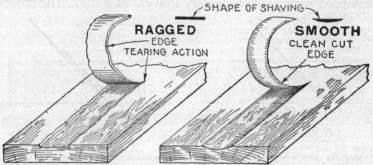

Figs. 760 and 761.—Action of jack plane with straight and curved cutter.

poorly cutting plane irons are due to improper grinding of the cutters. The bevel should always be at an angle of 25°, which means that it must be twice as long as the cutter is thick. If

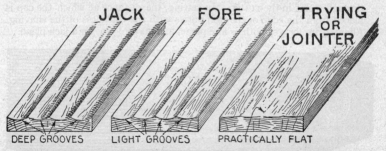

Figs. 762 to 764.—Appearance of surface of board when planed with the jack, fore, and trying or jointer planes having cutters as shown in figs. 757 to 759. Note transformation of the deep grooved surfaces in fig. 762 to the approximately flat surface in fig. 764.

the bevel be too long, the plane will jump and chatter; if too short, it will not cut.

It is a good rule perhaps to have a thin long bevel for soft wood, and a 25° bevel for the hard woods, although cross grained timber will require a short bevel.

Double Irons.—The term double iron means a plane iron equipped with a supplementary iron called a *cap*. The object

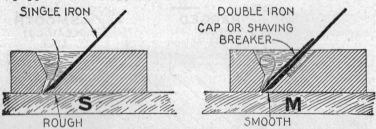

Figs. 765 and 766.—Action of single and double irons. The single iron cuts satisfactory only when the grain is favorable as at M, fig. 766, but when it varies from the line of the cut, as at S, the shaving by running up on the iron acquires a leverage which causes it to split in advance of the cutting edge, below the reach of which it breaks, leaving a very rough surface.

of the cap is *to break the shaving as soon as possible after it is cut*. The action of the cap is shown in fig. 766.

The cap is attached to the cutting iron by tightening a screw which passes through a slot in the cutter. In setting, the distance at which the cap is placed from the edge of the iron varies with the thickness of the shaving. Allow 1/32 in. for a smooth or fore plane, and about 1/8 in. for a jack plane.

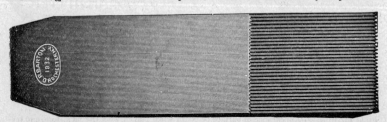

Fig. 767.—Barton tooth plane iron

Plane Mouth.—This is the rectangular opening in the face of the plane through which the cutter projects and in operation, through which the shavings pass. The width of the mouth has an important bearing upon the proper working of the plane. That portion of the plane face forward of the mouth prevents the wood rising in the form of a shaving before it reaches the mouth.

If there were no face in front of the cutter as in the case of a bull nose plane there would be nothing to hold down the wood in advance of the cutter and the shaving would not be broken.

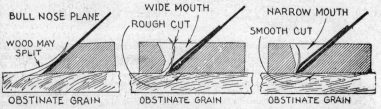

BULL NOSE PLANE

WOOD MAY SPLIT

OBSTINATE GRAIN

WIDE MOUTH

ROUGH CUT

OBSTINATE GRAIN

NARROW MOUTH

SMOOTH CUT

OBSTINATE GRAIN

Figs. 768 to 770.—Influence of width of mouth. The bull nose plane may be regarded as an ordinary plane with a mouth of infinite width; there being nothing in front of the cutter to hold down the wood, a splitting action, as shown, is possible in extreme case with obstinate grain. Figs. 769 and 770 show results obtained with wide and narrow mouth.

Evidently in obstinate grain the rougher will be the work and a splitting, instead of cutting action may result. Accordingly, *the wider the mouth, the less frequently the shaving will be broken,* and, in obstinate grain, *the rougher the work.*

How to Use a Plane.—In order to obtain satisfactory results with planes, it is necessary to know not only the proper method of handling the tool in planing but also how to put it in good working condition. Accordingly the user must know:

1. How to sharpen the cutter.
2. How to adjust the cutter.

3. How to plane.

4. How to joint a plane.

Sharpening Planes.—This involves two operations, *grinding* and *whetting*. Before sharpening, the iron must be released as shown in figs. 773 and 774.

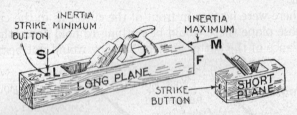

FIGS. 771 and 772.—Location of "strike buttons" on planes for releasing the iron and the reason. Evidently in the case of a long plane, the effect of a hammer blow at the end in the direction of arrow M, would be much less than if struck on top in the direction of arrow S. This is because the blow is opposed by the entire weight of the plane in the first instance and only by part of it in the second instance. Accordingly, a blow struck at L, will be much more effective in "jarring" the iron loose than if struck at F. On small planes, where the weight is much less, the strike button is located at the end as shown in fig. 772. The strike button consists of a cylindrical piece of very hard wood inserted in the plane and which projects a little to receive the blow and thus prevents the plane being battered by the hammer. A mallet should be used but in practice the careless workman uses anything within reach, even though it be a lathing hatched with corrugated head.

RELEASING

FIGS. 773 and 774.—Method of *releasing* iron in long and short planes. *Never try to release the iron by knocking the wedge on one side and then the other—this will ruin the plane.*

In grinding, the cutter must be ground perfectly square, that is, the cutting edge must be at right angles to the side. Enough metal must be removed to take out any nicks in the cutting edge. Before grinding unloosen the cap and set it back about ⅛ in. from the edge and it will serve as a guide by which to square up the edge.

The cutter should be held firmly on the grind stone at the proper angle and moved continually from side to side of the stone to prevent wearing

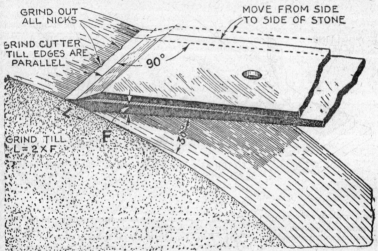

GRIND OUT ALL NICKS

MOVE FROM SIDE TO SIDE OF STONE

GRIND CUTTER TILL EDGES ARE PARALLEL

90°

GRIND TILL L = 2 × F

F

30°

Fig. 775.—Proper position of plane cutter on grind stone. Note the conditions which must be fulfilled to grind properly.

the stone out of true. Grind on the bevel side only. The bevel angle should be about 30° as before stated and this angle is attained when the length of the bevel is twice the thickness of the cutter. Fig. 775 shows proper position of the cutter on the grind stone.

In grinding, the edge should be shaped to one of the forms shown in figs. 757 to 759, depending on the type of plane and requirements.

After grinding, the cutter will be found to have a *wire edge*, which is to say that the coarse grit of the grinder has left and will always leave the edge comparatively coarse or rough in its fibre, and the edge is not *keen* as it should be to cut smoothly.

This wire edge is removed by the aid of an oil stone as shown in figs. 776 and 777.

In the case of a "double" iron, the cap should be kept with a fine, but not a cutting edge which must be made to fit the face of the cutter accurately, for if it do not, the plane will quickly "choke" with shavings, because of the shavings driving between the two irons. *This is important* and it

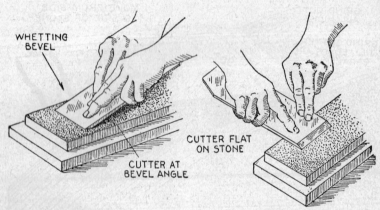

WHETTING BEVEL

CUTTER FLAT ON STONE

CUTTER AT BEVEL ANGLE

Figs. 776 and 777.—Method of whetting plane iron on oil stone after grinding. In fig. 776, grasp iron firmly in the right hand with palm downward, pressing down with left hand near cutting end to give rubbing pressure. Rub to and fro nearly the length of the stone. Never use an undulating motion as this will produce a round edge, necessitating frequent grinding. After whetting the bevel side turn iron over and hold perfectly flat on the stone as in fig. 777; give it two or three strokes to remove any wire edge.

should be noted that a very minute opening between the irons will let the shavings drive in and choke the plane.

Adjusting the Cutter.—After sharpening the cap of a double iron, enter the screw in the slot and tighten screw lightly with cap up to within ¼ in. of the cutting edge, then tighten screw. Finish the setting by driving cap up to its final position, striking lightly on the set screw.

The "set" of the iron is the amount of cutter face exposed below the edge of the cap and the iron is said to be set *coarse* or *fine* according to the amount exposed. The set, as before explained regulates the thickness of the shavings and is varied

TIGHTENING

FIGS. 778 and 779.—Method of *tightening* the wedge or to make the cutter project a little more for a deeper cut. The same method is adopted for both long and short planes. It would be more effective to strike the long plane on its face but this is of course not permissible. As a rule neither the wedge nor the iron should be struck in adjusting, though occasionally a very light tap may be given to the wedge in tightening or the iron in adjusting.

according to the nature and kind of wood to be planed. For soft woods the set should be: ½ in. for jack; ¹⁄₁₆ for trying and jointer; ¹⁄₃₂ for smooth plane. If the wood be hard or cross grained allow about one-half of the settings just given.

The accompanying cuts show method of releasing, tightening and adjusting. To adjust cutter put in place, allowing its cutting edge to rest on the fore-

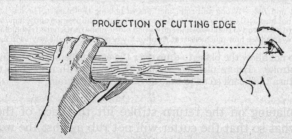

PROJECTION OF CUTTING EDGE

FIG. 780.—Method of gauging adjustment of cutting edge by sighting along the face of plane.

finger to keep it from projecting beyond the face. Insert wedge, tap gently
and adjust cutter to final position by the method shown in figs. 778 and 779.

How to Plane.—Satisfactory results in the use of a plane
depend largely on the plane being in perfect condition and
properly adjusted as to "set" and depth of cut to suit the kind
of wood to be planed.

The first thing to learn is the correct way of holding the
plane as shown in fig. 782.

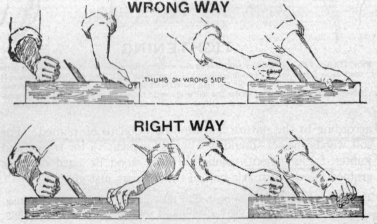

Figs. 781 and 782.—Wrong and right methods of holding the plane. The left hand **thumb**
should not be placed on the right side of the plane because the position of the hand will **become**
awkward at the end of the stroke and the motion of the plane restricted—try holding the **plane**
both ways and see how much easier it is to work when held the right way as in fig. 782.

Do not allow the plane to drop over the end of the board at either end of
the stroke. Before planing examine the board with respect to the grain
and turn the board so as to take advantage of the grain.

In planing on the return stroke lift the back of the plane
somewhat so that the cutter will not rub against the wood and
thus prevent it being quickly dulled.

This refers to large surfaces especially when they are rough, but on small work it is not necessary.

In planing a narrow surface let the fingers project below the plane and press against the side of the board as a guide to keep the plane on the work.

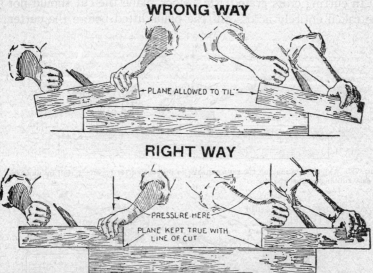

WRONG WAY

← PLANE ALLOWED TO TILT

RIGHT WAY

PRESSURE HERE

PLANE KEPT TRUE WITH LINE OF CUT

Figs. 783 and 784.—Wrong and right methods of beginning and ending the stroke. When the plane is allowed to tilt as in fig. 783, too much wood will be taken off at the ends so that the cut will not be true. To prevent this, press down with the left hand in beginning the stroke and with the right in ending the stroke as in fig. 784, the object being to keep the face of the plane in contact with the wood during the entire cut.

Should the plane choke with shavings look for the cause instead of just removing them.

Remove the iron and examine carefully the edge of the cap. This must as before stated be a perfect fit otherwise there will be continual trouble.

In planing a long surface as a long board, begin at the right hand end. Take a few strokes, then step forward and take the same number of strokes, progressing this way until the entire surface is passed over.

To preserve the face of the plane, apply occasionally a few drops of oil.

In cutting cross grain with a block plane the cut should not be taken entirely across but the plane lifted before the cutter

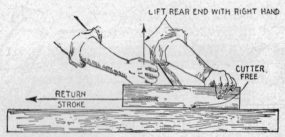

FIG. 785.—Method of making the return stroke to prevent cutter becoming dull by unnecessary rubbing against the wood.

FIG. 786.—Method of using the fingers to guide the plane. It is better not to depend on this method because the hand must be placed in the wrong position, and the probability of getting splinters in the fingers.

FIGS. 787 and 788.—Method of using the block plane across grain. Evidently the cut must not be taken entirely across the board because it would split. In planing lift the plane before the cutter runs off the edge. Take a few strokes as in fig. 787, with board in position MS, then reverse board to position SM, fig. 788, and continue planing as before.

reaches the edge of the board, otherwise the wood will be split at the edge. After taking a few strokes reverse the board and continue as just directed as in figs. 787 and 788.

Jointing.—The term *jointing* means *the operation of truing up the face of a wooden plane so that all points in the face lie in a plane at right angles to the sides of the plane.* This is done by planing the face with a jointer plane until the desired surface is

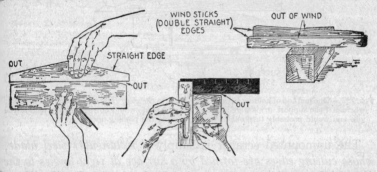

Figs. 789 to 791.—Tests for truth of surface of plane preliminary to jointing. Longitudinal truth of surface is determined by applying a straight edge as in fig. 789 In the try square test for transverse truth note first the shape of the sides whether straight, or (as in the case of some smooth planes) slightly curved. Of course unless the sides be straight, the try square cannot be applied. Fig. 791 shows application of wind sticks in testing for wind.

obtained. It is a job for an expert carpenter and not for an amateur.

The face of the plane after continued use and especially rough handling will wear out of true and become battered, hence occasionally the face should be tested as in figs. 789 to 791 to determine if it should be jointed. Use the fore plane or jointer and plane off the high spots as indicated by the tests until a true surface is obtained. In doing this make frequent tests with straight edges by square to determine if the surface is approaching the true form.

After the face has been brought to the proper surface, the sharp edges between the face and two sides should be eased with a slight chamfer to prevent splinters. After jointing, a few drops of lubricating oil rubbed on the face will improve the operation of the plane.

Scrapers.—The term scraper usually signifies a piece of steel plate of about the thickness and hardness of a saw. There are several types of scrapers, as:

1. Unmounted.
2. Handle scraper.
3. Scraper plane.

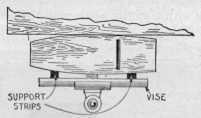

FIG. 792.—One method of holding a curved side-plane in the vise. This will give a rigid support, whereas if the support strips were not inserted, the plane would not be securely held in the vise and would probably turn out of position during the planing operation.

The unmounted scraper is simply *a rectangular steel blade, whose cutting edges are formed by a surface at right angles to the sides.* Quicker cutting is secured by having the cutting edge more acute, but more labor is required to keep it sharp.

The cutting edge is sharpened by filing or grinding.

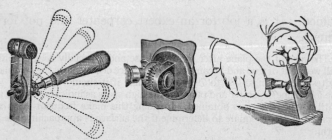

FIGS. 793 to 795.—Union adjustable handle scraper. Fig. 793, shows some of the settings to enable the blade to reach any desired place. *To adjust*, loosen thumb nut at the back, releasing the teeth. Further adjustment is made by loosening the nut at the front of the blade, permitting rotation in either direction. Fig. 794 shows interlocking teeth at back of blade, and fig. 795, position of hands in using the scraper.

For smooth work the roughness of the edge may be removed by an oil stone but the rougher edge will cut faster.

In cutting, the scraper is inclined slightly forward and is more conveniently held when provided with a handle or mounted as a plane. The accompanying cuts show various scrapers.

FIG. 796.—Union adjustable veneer scraper for veneers and cabinet work. It can also be used as a tooth plane.

FIG. 797.—Stanley cabinet makers scraper, plane. *In working*, the blade springs backward opening the mouth and allowing the shaving to pass through. As soon as the working pressure is released, the blade springs back to its normal position.

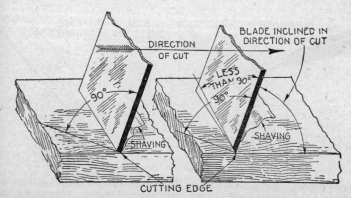

FIGS. 798 and 799.—Scraper with normal (90°) cutting edge and acute (less than 90°) cutting edge showing position of scraper in cutting.

To Sharpen Scraper Blade for Heavy Work.—A good method of sharpening the scraper so as to avoid too frequent use of the oil stone is as follows:

1. File cutter to a keen edge, removing wire edge with a coarse, medium oil stone.

FIGS. 800 and 801.—Scraper steels or *burnishers*. Fig. 800, oval form fig. 801, round form. This tool is used to turn the cutting edge of a scraper after filing and honing. By *turning* is meant pushing the particles of steel which form the corner over so that they will form a wire edge which will stand at an angle with the sides of the scraper.

2. Holding burnisher in both hands, turn the edge.

3. Begin with light pressure and hold the steel at nearly the same angle as the file was held in filing.

4. Bear on harder for each successive stroke, and let the tool come a little

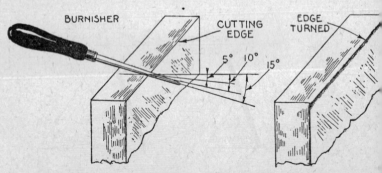

FIGS. 802 and 803.—Application of burnisher in turning the edge of a scraper after filing and honing. Fig. 802 shows angles at which burnisher should be held. The edge is usually turned in two or three strokes with burnisher at 5°, 10° and finally at 15° as shown. Fig. 803 shows appearance of turned edge (greatly enlarged).

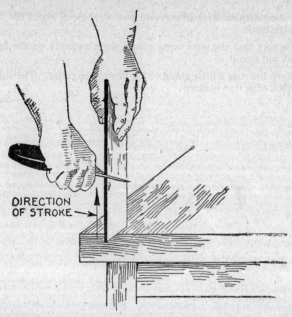

DIRECTION
OF STROKE →

Fig. 804.—Turning edge with burnisher. Note angle at which the tool is held. The stroke is made from bottom up as indicated by the arrow. Slightly lubricate burnisher to assist it in sliding over the edge of the scraper without scratching.

Fig. 805.—Union adjustable veneer scraper with wood bottom. *It is used* for scraping veneers and cabinet work and because of its peculiar form it is well adapted to fine work. The wood bottom reduces friction. This scraper can also be used as a tooth plane.

nearer level each time, finishing with tool at angle of about 60° from the face of the blade.

5. Be sure that the steel never comes down squarely on the fine edge, for that will ruin it.

6. Keep the edge a little ahead of the face of the cutter. The object is to get a hook edge that is sharp.

—*Sargent.*

CHAPTER 19

Boring Tools

There are several kinds of boring tools, each class adapted to meet special working conditions, such as:

1. Punching
2. Boring
3. Drilling
4. External boring (turning)
5. Counter sinking
6. Enlarging

The various kinds of tools used for these operations are respectively: brad awls, gimlets and augers, drills, hollow augers and spoke pointers, counter-sinks, reamers. These various tools are called *bits* when provided with a *shank* instead of a *handle* for use with a *brace*.

FIG. 806.—Brad awl. Sizes ¹⁄₁₆ to ³⁄₁₆ diameter. Smaller sizes are made, called *sprig* tools.

INITIAL POSITION CROSS GRAIN

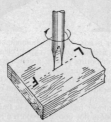

FIGS. 807 to 809.—Method of using the brad awl. *Always start with the edge of the tool across the grain of the wood* as in fig. 807. *In forcing* the tool into the wood do not turn the tool completely around but give only sufficient turning movement in alternate directions to cut and crush the fibres, extreme positions LF, and the arrows indicating this movement.

Brad Awls.—An awl is *a pointed tool for piercing small holes.* The blade is shaped and pointed to suit the conditions of use. Brad awls have an edge like a screw driver and can be used as such on small screws. Its principal use is in quickly making

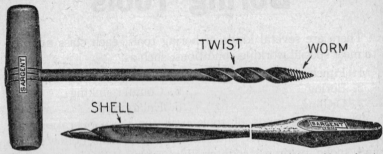

TWIST WORM SHELL

FIGS. 810 and 811.—Gimlet and gimlet bit showing two constructions of the working end, *twist* (fig. 810) and *shell* (fig. 811). *In using* the gimlet the handle is grasped in the right hand and pressed into the wood by the palm (in starting), the shaft of the tool projecting between the first and second fingers. It is driven into the wood by a series of half turns, being released and re-grasped at each half turn.

FIGS. 812 to 815.—Bit and auger heads. Fig. 812, single cutter, extension lip, coarse screw. Recommended for general all around boring; rapid, clean cutting and very easy boring. Particularly adapted for difficult boring in wet, green, very hard or knotty wood and boring with the grain. Fig. 813, double cutter, extension lip, fine screw. Recommended for furniture and cabinet work, or wherever a particularly smooth hole is essential: bores easily and clears readily. Fig. 814, ship head with single cutter and coarse screw. Note absence of lip. Recommended for deep boring or in woods with strong grain. Especially adapted for boring plug holes in making riveted copper fasteneo joints in fine boat construction (see page 56). Will stand many sharpenings: does not bore as smooth a hole as types with spur. Fig. 815, ship head single cutter without either screw or lip, sometimes called "bare foot." Especially recommended for deep boring in wet pitchy woods or when particularly straight boring is essential, *as in boring shaft og of boat for propeller shaft.* Having no screw it has little tendency to follow or drift with the grain of the wood.

a hole for starting a nail or screw into hard wood. Figs. 807 to 809 show method of using the awl.

Gimlets.—These are for boring small holes by hand pressure, though the bit form of gimlet is used in a brace being adapted to heavier and quicker boring than the gimlet which has a handle. There are two kinds of gimlet: 1, twist, and 2, plain

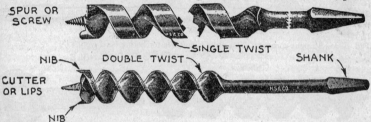

SPUR OR SCREW

SINGLE TWIST

NIB DOUBLE TWIST SHANK

CUTTER OR LIPS

NIB

Figs. 816 and 817.—Single and double twist auger bits. *In operation,* the screw on the end of the bit draws the tool into the wood, making a heavy pressure unnecessary. The nibs make an incision on the wood below the cut made by the cutters which take the shavings out and into the twist, this in turn lifting them out of the hole. In the single twist auger the cuttings are thrown into the center of the hole and delivered more easily than with the double twist auger, which crowds the cuttings to the walls of the hole where they are likely to become jammed between the tool and the work. The single twist type is thus adapted to boring deep holes.

or shell as shown in figs. 810 and 811. Extra large gimlets (¼ to ½ in. diam.) are called auger gimlets.

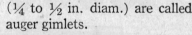

A gimlet serves many purposes when a brace and bit are not at hand or when only one hole is to be bored, saving the time of setting bit in driver.

Figs. 818 and 819.—Single and double thread. *The single thread* (fig. 818) is coarse pitch for quick boring. Especially adapted for hard or gummy woods, end grain boring, mortising doors, etc. *The double thread* (fig. 819) is unsurpassed for accurate work in seasoned wood not extremely gummy or hard and is preferred by cabinet makers. A bit with double thread can be used for practically all work but it bores more slowly than the coarse single thread bit.

NOTE.—If finish be looked for around the point the double thread will have a lead to each lip and has some advantages as a starting cut. The single thread has the advantage of an extra amount of wood that would be taken with the other lead, say a fine screw of 28 threads on point per inch with a lead of 14, would bore one inch with 14 turns. But, to take into consideration all kinds of wood on regular work 16 per inch is good, but for fast, rough work, six or eight turns single is used with good results.—*The James Swan Co.*

Augers.—These are used for boring holes from ½ up to two inches. The sizes are listed in 16ths, thus a 2 inch auger is listed 32. When made with a shank for use in a brace, this style of auger is commonly called a bit.

STRAIGHT CORE

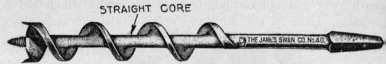

THE JAMES SWAN CO. No.40.

FIG. 820.—Straight core bit. This style is suitable for boring hard woods.

RING FOR HANDLE

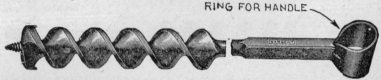

SARGENT

FIG. 821.—Ring auger, for heavy work, principally on hard woods. Augers of this type are adapted for heavy timbers, and for large, deep boring. *In using*, a handle, preferably of hard wood, is inserted in the ring for turning the auger. In this way a tremendous leverage is obtained. These augers, so far as the worm and twist are concerned, are similar in design to the nut augers and to the boring machine augers.

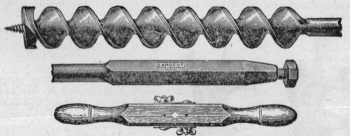

FIGS. 822 to 823.—Nut auger and handle for boring where greater dimensions or depths are required than can be secured with ordinary bits. They are used with wooden handles, giving the operator both hands for controlling the tool. In mill or bridge work in boring heavy timbers they are especially valuable. They are constructed with side lips, but without spurs, which make them bore easily, and give them lasting qualities.

NOTE.—*Boring speed. The pitch of the screw determines the speed of the bit.* It is impracticable to make a different pitch for every kind of boring but certain standards have been adopted for general work. The thread is made fine, coarse, or very coarse, according to speed of boring permitted by the nature of the wood to be bored. For instance, a very coarse (single thread) is used on electrician's bit, giving a speed of one inch per six turns—evidently such speed is only desirable in soft woods. Fine double thread, double lip bits have a speed of one inch per 18 turns.

Owing to the enormous variety of bits on the market, it is difficult to select the one best adapted for a given purpose. For accurate boring, for rapid boring for rough boring, the bit adapted for the purpose must be used to get the proper result.

It is not generally understood how important a part the thread of the screw plays in boring. The terms "coarse" and "fine" as applied to a screw are relative, and may be applied to either single thread or double thread. The bit having a given number of double threads to the inch, provided the cutters are pitched to correspond with those threads, will bore just as fast

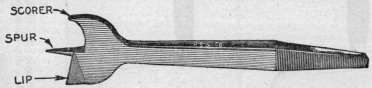

FIG. 824.—Center auger bit for boring through thin material which might split with bits of other types. The spur is set at the center of the hole to be bored and serves to guide the bit. The scorer makes a circular incision in the wood and the lip following removes the wood

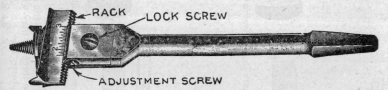

FIG. 825.—Wright expansive auger bit with screw adjustment and cap binder. Before the plate bind firmly the position of extension may be adjusted by the adjustment screw on the side, to its exact position and then the plate firmly locked by the lock screw. It is seen that they can bore up to a three inch hole. Shorter extensions come separately for boring smaller holes larger than 1 in.

FIG. 826—Foerstner auger bit. This bit unlike other auger bits, is guided by its circular rim instead of its center, hence it will bore any arc of a circle, and can be guided in any direction regardless of grain or knots, leaving a smooth surface. It is specially adapted to delicate pattern work core bores, veneers, screen scalloping, fancy scroll, twist columns, newels, ribbon moulding, mortising, etc. *Directions:* To bore an angle or to bore an arc, hold the bit near the flange firmly upon the wood with the thumb over the shank, and the fingers underneath the board or block, being careful not to crowd the bit too fast at first, until the whole flange is in the wood in its desired course. With practice many new uses will be found for the bit.

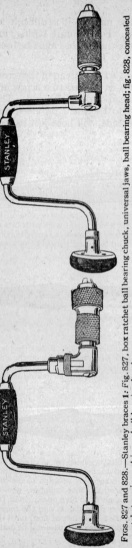

FIGS. 827 and 828.—Stanley braces 1: Fig. 827, box ratchet ball bearing chuck, universal jaws, ball bearing head; fig. 828, concealed ratchet, universal jaws, ball bearing head.

FIGS. 829 and 830.—Stanley braces 2: Fig. 829, concealed ratchet, ball bearing chuck, universal jaws, ball bearing head; fig. 830, concealed ratchet, alligator jaws, ball bearing head.

as a bit with half that number of single threads to the inch, provided the cutters are of the same pitch. If the cutters have less pitch than the threads, they will act as a stop gauge, not permitting the bit to bore as fast as it would without such obstruction.

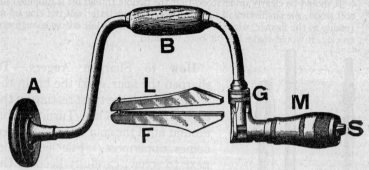

Figs. 831 and 832.—Ratchet brace for holding bit. The jaws LF, are held in the screw sleeve M, by means of which they are adjusted. The ends of the jaws which hold the bit are seen projecting from the sleeve at S. A, is a cap which turns loosely on the end of the brace. The auger is guided by holding the cap in the left hand, and turned by revolving the brace with handle B. The ring G, adjusts the ratchet for right or left release.

Fig. 833.—Goodell-Pratt angular brace for boring in close places. The brace can be fastened at any desired angle, the setting mechanism preventing slipping.

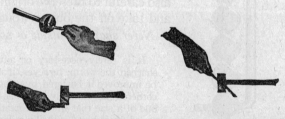

Figs. 834 to 836.—Sharpening a Foerstner bit. *To sharpen the bit,* take a hard three-cornered file, grind smooth at front end, thus making a three-cornered scraper (fig. 834); scrape inside of flange until sharp, and take off outside wire edge with oil stone (fig. 835). File the cutters with small fine cut file (fig. 836). For *very smooth work,* take the edge off, so as to form a very slight bevel on outside edge of flange, always being careful to have the flange project a little beyond the cutters. In case a bit be too hard, heat a pair of tongs, and take hold of the shank back of and close to the flange, and draw the temper to a light blue color, then cool in water. Then the bit can be easily filed and scraped.

It should be clearly understood that the double thread bit is intended for soft wood, the single thread for hard wood, as the latter will not clog up as readily as the former, while if the double thread were left coarse enough not to clog, it would make the bit bore too hard.

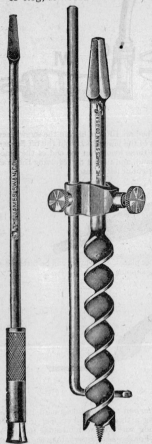

How to Sharpen Augers.—To

sharpen the spur, hold the bit in the left hand with the twist resting on the edge of the bench. Turn the bit around until the spur to be sharpened comes uppermost. File side spur, next to screw, carefully keeping the original bevel. File lightly until a fine burr shows upon the outside, which carefully remove by a slight brush with a file; result, a fine cutting edge.

To sharpen the cutter, hold bit firmly in left hand with the worn point down on edge of bench, slanted away from the hand with which you file and file from inside back, and be also careful to preserve original bevel and take off the burr or rough edge. *Never sharpen outside of spur.*

It is rarely necessary or advisable to sharpen the worm, however, it may often be improved if battered by using a three-cornered file, carefully manipulated, using one of a size that fits the thread. A half round file is best for the lip and with careful handling may be used for the spur

Fig. 837.—Swan extension bit holder (standard electricians' size). This holder will follow through a ⅝ in. hole.

Fig. 838.—Swan depth auger gauge. A convenient attachment where a number of holes are to be bored to a given depth. Easily adjusted to any depth.

Twist Drills.—In addition to augers and gimlets, a carpenter should possess a set of twist drills. These are for drilling small holes where the ordinary auger or gimlet would probably split

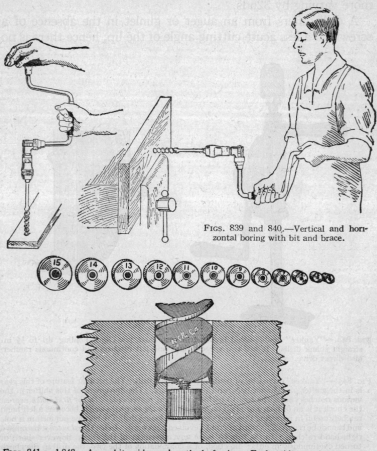

FIGS. 839 and 840.—Vertical and horizontal boring with bit and brace.

FIGS. 841 and 842.—Auger bit guider and method of using. Each guider consists of a brass disc with a soft metal center so as to accommodate itself to the screw point. It is used as shown to rebore or counter bore to a larger size any hole previously made.

the wood. They come either with square shanks for breast dull shocks or with round shanks for use with a brace as shown in figs. 845 and 846. These drills come in sizes from $\frac{1}{16}$ to $\frac{5}{8}$ or more varying by 32nds.

A drill differs from an auger or gimlet in the absence of a screw and a less acute cutting angle of the lip, hence there is no

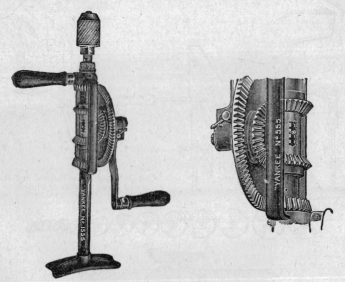

Fig. 843.—"Yankee" double-speed breast drill with three jaw chuck holding up to $\frac{1}{2}$ in. straight shank drills. It has two speeds, right and left ratchets and continuous ratchet; also direct drive.

Fig. 844.—"Yankee" drive gear of double-speed breast drill. The peculiar feature of this gear is in the shifter on cylinder between the small gears. The movement of this shifter in the various notches causes the tool to perform different movements. *In the first notch* nearest the chuck it is an ordinary or plain breast drill. *In the second notch* it becomes a left hand ratchet, useful in removing taps, but especially to loosen drill if it become jammed in a hole and cannot be removed forward or crank revolved backward. *In the third notch* it becomes a right hand ratchet. *In the fourth notch* any movement of the crank, however short, or turned continuously in either direction, or a combination of the two, the drill in the chuck will always turn to the right and drill continuously, hence no time is lost and double the work is done as compared with single or a right hand ratchet. It is especially convenient in corners etc., where crank cannot be turned.

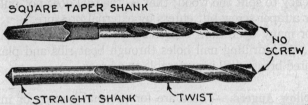

FIGS. 845 and 846.—Bit stock twist drill for use with brace and straight shank twist drill for use in breast drill chuck. Note absence of screw on cutting end which prevents splitting of the wood.

FIG. 847.—"Yankee" chain drill with automatic and ratchet feed. The taking up and releasing of chain is done with a friction feed, by simply turning brace or breast drill by which chain drill is operated. When the chain is tight, the automatic feed operates by turning of small lever to horizontal position as in illustration. When drill has reached desired depth the automatic feed is thrown off by turning lever to upright position. Reverse movement of brace and drill is withdrawn, chain slackened in moment. The automatic feed is positive, fixed and without adjustment for drills up to ½ inch, so that drills cannot be broken in use. There is no hand feed, nor any parts requiring attention, and nothing to catch or pinch the fingers in use.

tendency to split the wood, that is, the tool does not pull itself in by a taper screw but enters by external pressure.

For many operations especially where the smaller drills are used, as in drilling nail holes through boat ribs and planking, a geared breast drill is preferable to a brace.

Hollow Augers.—These are for external boring, or in other

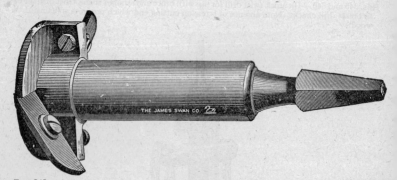

Fig. 848.—Ames hollow auger. Cuts from ⅜ to 1½. The two wing like projections seen at the left are the cutters; these are adjustable by the screws to the precise size wanted.

Fig. 849.—Swan spoke pointer or conical hollow auger. The illustration plainly shows the cutter, which is held in position by the central screw, and adjusted by the two upper screws.

words, turning. A frame centered and attached to a bit shank carries the cutters, there being provision for adjusting the cutters to various diameters within the range of the tool.

Spoke Pointers.—These are similar to hollow augers but cut a conical, instead of a cylindrical surface. The cutter is placed lengthwise.

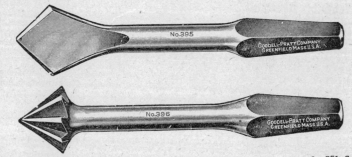

FIGS. 850 and 851.—Goodell-Pratt counter sinks. Fig. 850, flat, or two cutter; fig. 851, fluted or multi-cutter, sometimes called "Rose."

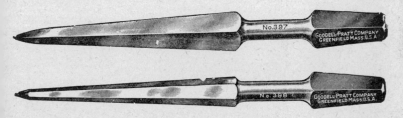

FIGS. 852 and 853.—Goodell-Pratt reamers. Fig. 852, square type; fig. 853, octagonal type.

Counter Sinks.—Sometimes it is necessary to make a conical shape enlargement of a hole at the surface of the wood. This is done by a bit tool called a counter sink which is worked in a hand brace.

Reamers.—A reamer is a long tapered cutting tool for enlarging holes. While used chiefly by machinists there are frequent occasions in carpentry when a reamer may be employed to advantage, as for instance, enlarging holes in hinges when too small for the screws on hand, etc. Fig. 852 shows a desirable type of reamer with square shank for use with brace.

CHAPTER 20

Fastening Tools

The term *"fastening"* for want of a better word, is here used to classify those tools employed in the operation of securing such parts of the work that must be fastened together with

FIG. 854.—Stanley bell face, octagonal neck and poll, nickel plated mahoganized handle nail hammer.

FIG. 855.—Goodell-Pratt nail set.

nails, tacks, screws, bolts, etc., the tools used comprising the various hammers, screw drivers and wrenches.

Hammers.—The hammer is an important tool in carpentry and there are numerous types to meet the varied conditions of use. All hammers worthy of the name are made of best steel carefully forged, hardened and tempered.

Don't expect to get a good hammer in the five and ten cent store, but buy only the best.

The variations of form in the different nail hammers lie in the shape of the claw, whether curved as C (fig. 856) or so-called straight as B (fig. 857). Also, referring to the two figures, the shape of the face, whether flat, A, or rounded D, (the latter

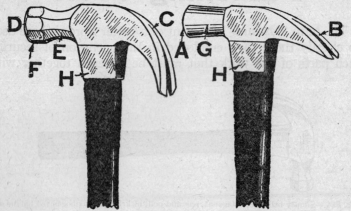

FIGS. 856 and 857.—Curved and so-called "straight" claw nail hammers.

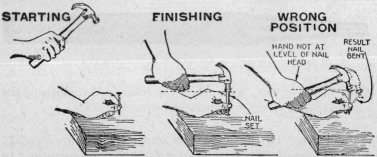

FIGS. 858 to 860.—Method of driving a nail. Fig. 858, guiding nail with left hand at start; fig. 859, using nail set to drive nail head below surface of the wood and to prevent hammer marks. Fig. 860 shows result of not hitting nail square due to wrong position of hand; dotted line shows nail knocked sidewise.

called Bell Face), style of neck E, poll F, and general
finish.

The bell face pattern D, differs from the plain face pattern A, in that the
face of the former is slightly rounded, rendering less liable the possibility
of the hammer head marring the wood. In the bell face pattern the neck E,
is of smaller diameter than the poll F, and either the neck or poll or both
are round or octagonal. In all flat or plain face hammers the neck G, forms
the poll and is either round or octagonal. These differences are clearly
shown in the cuts.

The handles are usually of hickory, mahoganized or ebonized

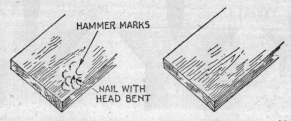

FIGS. 861 and 862.—Appearance of board after nail is driven by an amateur and by an experienced carpenter. Fig. 861 shows five misses—the usual average. These indentations, especially with soft wood, are quite marked and unsightly.

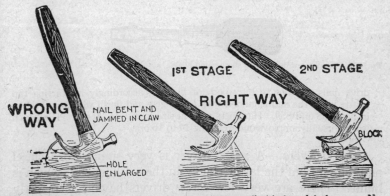

FIGS. 863 to 865.—Wrong and right methods of drawing a nail with claw of the hammer. No explanation necessary.

In using a hammer, the handle should be grasped at a short distance from the end and a few sharp blows rather than many light ones given. Keep the hand and wrist level with the nail head so that the hammer will hit the nail squarely on the head instead of at an angle. Failure to do this is the reason for the difficulty so often experienced in driving nails straight.

The face must be free from grease or dirt to drive a nail straight, hence frequently rub the face of the hammer on wood. Hammers are designed to

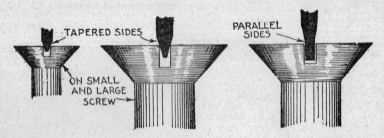

FIGS. 866 to 868.—Action of screw driver with ends having tapered and parallel sides. Figs. 866 and 867 show large range of work with tapered sides but considerable downward pressure must be exerted to prevent the screw driver rising out of the slot. Fig. 868 shows correct shape. Evidently with parallel sides there will be no tendency for the screw driver to rise, no matter how much turning force be exerted.

FIG. 869.—Small screw driver with short round blade.

drive nails and not to hit wood (or fingers), accordingly in starting tap gently while the nail is guided with the fingers and finish with a nail set as in figs. 858 and 859. Hammers vary in size from 5 to 20 ozs. The bench worker usually employs one weighing 14 to 16 ozs.

Screw Drivers.—A screw driver is very similar to a chisel and differs from the latter chiefly in the working end, which is blunt. There are very few screw drivers having a correctly shaped end. Usually the sides which enter the slot in the screw are tapered. This is done so that the end will fit into screws of widely varying sizes.

In using a screw driver having a tapered end a force is set up due to the taper which tends to push the end of the tool out of the slot. Accordingly it is better to have several sizes with properly shaped parallel sides than to depend on one with

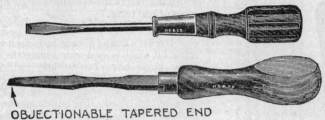

OBJECTIONABLE TAPERED END

FIGS. 870 and 871.—Plain screw drivers. Fig. 870, round pattern; fig. 871, flat pattern. In fig. 871, note the objectionable tapered sides at the ends. The reason manufacturers shape the ends this way is to adapt the tool to a large range of work, because most workmen make the mistake of false economy and buy only one screw driver, whereas they should have several different sizes with properly shaped ends as explained in the text.

FIG. 872.—Swan screw driver bit for use with brace.

FIG. 873.—"Yankee" ratchet screw driver, right and left hand. At the blade end there are two spring jaws fastened together as shown and kept in place by ring surrounding them, which ring is fastened to fork on end of blade. A spring between fork and lower end of jaws keeps latter in position to hold screw eye, as shown. Pushing up the jaws with thumb of hand holding driver, the point of jaws readily open to insert screw eye, which should be pushed down into holder so it rests solidly in V-shaped groove. The jaws are then released and grasp screw eye. The ratchet works either right or left hand, for driving or taking out screws. *In operation*, the jaws are pushed over screw eye and driver turned, the spring jaws holding screw eye when loosed, so it does not fall to floor. The knurled washer on blade is to start screw eye with thumb and forefinger, while the hand holds the tool. Especially adapted to places where only one hand can be used.

FIGS. 874 to 876.—"Yankee" quick return spiral ratchet screw driver with springs. *In operation*, it drives or draws screws by pushing on handle, or by a ratchet movement, or it can be made rigid, as an ordinary screw driver. The spindle has two spirals, one right and one left hand with corresponding nuts. To drive screws in, the shifter is moved to end of slot toward bit, to drive screws out, it is moved to end of slot toward handle. Screws can be ratcheted in or out by turning the handle as in a ratchet screw driver (setting shifter same as for pushing screws in or out), with the tool closed up and locked by turning the milled collar in front of shifter case a quarter turn to the left. When closed and locked (with shifter midway between ends of slot), the tool becomes rigid or as an ordinary screw driver. It can also be made rigid with spindle fully extended and shifter midway between ends of slot. In this position it becomes especially effective as a long screw driver to reach out of the way places.

tapered sides for all sizes of screws. There are two general classes of screw drivers, the *plain*, and the so-called *automatic*.

Figs. 870 and 871 show typical plain screw drivers. The operation of driving a screw with a plain screw driver consists of giving it a series of half turns.

Where a number of screws are to be tightened there is a saving in time by using a screw driver bit which is used with a brace the same as an auger bit. The quickest method of driving a screw is by means of the so-called automatic screw driver shown in fig. 874 (there being various types). The advantage over the plain screw driver is that instead of grasping and releasing the handle from 25 to 30 times in turning a screw home, it is grasped once and with two or three strokes back and forth the screw is driven home, thus saving labor and time.

NOTE.—Special screw drivers may be obtained with spirals of different angles to suit working conditions, Goodell Pratt's practice is: 40° spiral for rapidly driving small screws; 30° spiral for general work; 20° spiral for driving large screws in hard wood.

NOTE.—"Yankee" *push brace.* This tool is so named because it will hold all the small tools used in a bit brace, but is operated by pushing the handle to revolve the tools, in same manner as a Yankee spiral ratchet screw driver. It is adapted especially to the lighter work ordinarily done by a brace. It will, with little effort, bore $\frac{3}{16}$ holes in metal, drive $\frac{3}{8}$ inch auger bit in hard woods or will drill holes, drive screws in our out; can be used for tapping holes, and with socket bit drive in small lag screws, run burrs, or nuts, on bolts, etc. The tool being straight and cylindrical and operated by pushing, can reach into many places, in corners, holes back of obstructions where a brace cannot be operated. The ratchet movements enable this push brace to be used for occasional extra heavy work than can be conveniently done by the push movement. The spiral rod is of steel, grooved for both right and left hand, with extra long ($1\frac{1}{2}$ in.) nuts of hard bronze, to secure extra durability. All the working parts are protected by sleeves, so no parts are exposed to dirt and grit. This push brace is especially useful in car shops, for fitting up either wood or steel cars, bridge or structural work templates, pattern makers, in garages.

Wrenches.—There has been placed on the market an undue multiplicity of wrenches—of many kinds and patterns for every

FIG. 877.—Goodell-Pratt double end type plain wrench. The feature of this wrench is that it will fit two sizes of nuts and the sides of the jaws being at an angle to the body of the wrench, admits of turning a hexagon nut with a smaller swing than would be possible with the straight type. This permits working in close places.

conceivable use. The wrench, though it may not be so considered, is a somewhat dangerous tool, when very great force is

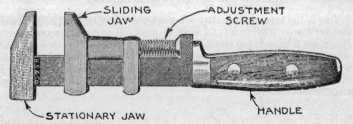

SLIDING JAW ADJUSTMENT SCREW

STATIONARY JAW HANDLE

FIG. 878.—P, S, and W, "monkey" wrench.

applied to start an obstinate nut. Often under such conditions the jaws slip off the nut, resulting in injury to the workman by

NOTE.—*How to use a "monkey" wrench.* Fit the jaws of the wrench squarely on the nut, with the screw toward the user so as to bring the strain on the screw and bolster. Turn the screw up tight, so as to be sure the jaws grip perfectly. Keep the screw oiled to prevent rust. Don't use too small a wrench where a large one is needed. Don't try to turn with the tips of the jaws. Don't get the habit of using a wrench for hammer. Don't increase the leverage of a wrench by attaching a length of pipe to the handle, unless perfectly willing to take the risk of disabling the wrench.

violent contact with some metal part. There are three general classes of wrench:

1. Plain.
2. Adjustable.
3. Socket.

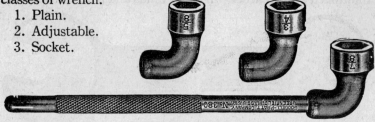

FIGS. 879 to 881.—Goodell-Pratt socket wrench and sockets. Evidently such type of wrench is adapted to working in close places and since the socket surrounds the wrench there is no danger of it slipping off the nut as in the case of the two jaw wrench.

Plain wrenches are made in a variety of patterns, the jaws being fixed with opening to suit a certain size nut.

The principal adjustable wrench is the Screw or so-called "monkey" wrench of which everyone is familiar.

This is the type wrench that will meet the carpenter's occasional needs and he should possess several sizes to meet his particular requirements. Never use a wrench too small for the job, and it is well to remember that wrenches should not be used as hammers. A late development in wrenches is the socket type. These wrenhces are designed especially for working in close places and are intended more for machinists and automobile repair men than for carpenters.

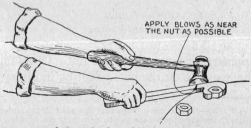

APPLY BLOWS AS NEAR THE NUT AS POSSIBLE

FIG. 882.—Starting an obstinate nut or bolt. Rusty, or large nuts or bolt heads often require more than a straight pull. A sharp blow with a hammer often starts an obstinate hold, where a straight pull would not. It is not advisable only in extreme cases to use the hammer on wrench, but a hard wood block will do as well. In extreme cases a steady pull aided with blows will do the work. *The blow should be delivered as near the nut as possible*, as shown in the figure, *instead of at the other end of the wrench as is usually and erroneously done*, thus avoiding the spring and inertia of the wrench, and delivering the full energy direct to the nut.

CHAPTER 21

Sharpening Tools

Especially for the amateur too much cannot be written on the subject of sharpening tools and methods of sharpening. In fact if an expert carpenter cannot turn out good work with dull tools, how can an amateur expect to work at all with dull tools. This section should accordingly be carefully read by all. The tools used for sharpening by the carpenter (in addition to files already described) are:

1. Grind stone.
2. Oil stone.

Grind Stones.—A grind stone consists of a large flat disc mounted on a shaft between bearings and arranged to turn either by foot or belt power. Grind stones are selected with reference to their "grit." They are natural sand stones, and their cutting material is oxide of silicon, or quartz sand, as it is commonly called.

A coarse soft grit stone will remove material more rapidly than one with finer grit, but the surface produced will be rough as compared with that produced by the other. Hence, a grind stone suitable for grinding carpenter's tools should be of fine grit; it should also be soft.

Most of the grind stones come from Huron, Mich., Berea, Ohio, and from Grind Stone Island, Nova Scotia. Berea stones are rather coarse, those from Nova Scotia are of all grades.

Grind stones are softer when wet than when dry, hence they should never be left standing with one side in the water, because when the stone is again used, the wet side will wear faster than the dry side.

The tangential speed of a grind stone for carpenter's tools should be from 500 to 600 ft. per minute. A rough rule for tool grinding is that the stone is at its maximum speed when, if run faster, it would throw water from its face.

Use of Water on Grind Stones.—Water is used as a medium

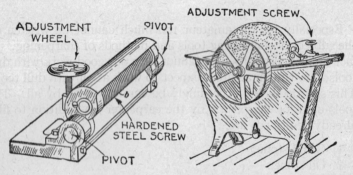

FIGS. 883 and 884.—Grind stone turning device and method of attaching. The hardened steel screw is free to revolve in its frame which is pivoted off center as shown. By turning the adjustment wheel the steel screw may be brought toward or away from the grind stone. When forced against the stone the screw at once begins to revolve. The effect of the sidewise advancement of the threads gives a shearing cut across the face of the stone thus grinding off the high spots. To sharpen the screw it is softened and recut.

for carrying off the heat produced in grinding and also for washing off the particles of stone and steel resulting from the grinding. These particles if allowed to remain would fill the interstices of the stone and make the surface too smooth to cut. Water is best supplied from an elevated tank with a stop cock so as to shut off the supply when the stone is not in use.

NOTE.—*In mounting a grind stone* never use wooden wedges because they are either driven in too tight or become wet and swell sometimes bringing so much pressure on the stone as to cause a crack. To properly mount, fill the space around the arbor with lead or cement after the stone is centered. Use wooden washers or double thickness of leather between the flanges and stone

To True a Grind Stone.—After considerable use, the face of the stone will wear out of true and must be brought back to its circular form concentric with the axle. While this may be done with hand tools it is best to use one of the various truing devices which do the work with lathe precision. These are shown in the accompanying cuts. Where these devices are not available,

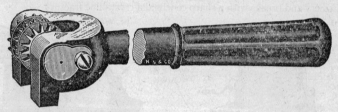

FIG. 885.—Emery wheel disc dresser. The disc cutter which revolves in the jaws is specially hardened.

a simple method of truing a stone is to wear it down against a bar of iron or large worn out file held firmly down across the trough or frame in such a position that the projecting parts of the cutting surface scrape against it as the stone revolves.

Tool Rests.—For general tool grinding, a rest is used. There

FIG. 886.—Emery wheel diamond point dresser. A small diamond (which is the hardest cutting material known) is inserted in the end of the rod. Diamond dressers are not guaranteed by the manufacturer and only experienced mechanics should use them.

are various kinds, but the ordinary wooden rest is preferred by many because should the tool catch, the rest would be thrown out and the danger of damage to the stone or operator minimized.

Abrasives.—Corundum, carborundum, alundum and emery

are the ordinary abrasive materials. These vary in hardness. The best cutting abrasive is not necessarily the hardest but its form of fracture has much to do with its cutting quality.

Corundum is oxide of aluminum and its fracture is conchoidal and generally crystalline. Carborundum is a silicide of carbon, being the product of the electric furnace. Its fracture is sharply crystalline.

Alundum consists of a fused oxide of alunimum. It has the thoughness of emery and breaks with a sharp conchoidal crystalline fracture.

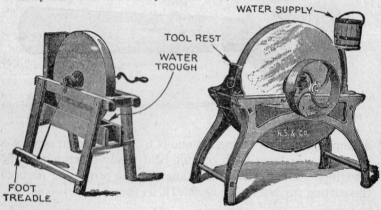

FIGS. 887 and 888.—Hand or foot power and engine-driven grind stones. In fig. 887, the water is contained in the trough underneath the wheel. It is important not to let the wheel stand in the water when not in use.

Grinding Wheels.—The composition of a grinding wheel consists of the cutting material or abrasive (usually called grit) and the bond. The cutting quality of a wheel depends chiefly on the grit and the hardness on the bonding material. The object of the bond is not only to hold the particles of grit together with proper factor cf safety, but to vary its tensile strength, the wheel being called hard or soft according to the tenacity with which the bond holds the particles together. A wheel is said to be too hard when the bond retains the surface or cutting particles until they become dull. and too soft when the particles are not held long enough to prevent undue wear of the wheel. Wheels are bonded by the vitrified, silicate, elastic and rubber processes.

Grinding wheels of corundum, carborundum, and emery are frequently used in place of grind stones because of the more rapid cutting. In using one of these wheels to grind a tool, it should be noted that on account of the high speed of revolution considerable heat is generated, hence the tool should be held lightly against the stone and frequently dipped in water, otherwise it will be burned. If an emery wheel burn badly it may be because it needs dressing.

ADJUSTABLE TOOL HOLDER →

FIG. 889.—Geared hand power emery wheel grinder with adjustable tool holder that may be set for any bevel.

Oil Stones.—These are used after the grinding operation to give the tool the highly keen edge necessary to cut wood smoothly. The oil stone is so called because oil is used on it for the same reason that water is used on a grind stone—that is, to carry off the heat resulting from friction between the stone

NOTE.—*Directions for installing and using emery wheels.* Before putting on a wheel, tap it lightly with a hammer to ascertain if it be sound. If it ring, it has not suffered from ill usage. To get the best results, the wheel should run at a surface speed of from 5,000 to 5,500 feet a minute, but for tool grinding, or when running the wheel in water, a slower speed is advisable. In grinding, avoid heavy pressure, as it causes the wheel to glaze and fill up more rapidly. Mount wheels on a strong, substantial stand, and see that they are kept true by using a diamond or dresser. Iron flanges, with rubber or leather washers, should be used on both sides of the wheel. Wheels should be run toward the operator, and constant care taken so that the rests are kept close to wheel. Do not run wheels on small spindles. The following rule is a good one to adopt: wheels 4 inches diameter and under, ½-inch spindle; 5 to 10 inches, ¾-inch spindle; 12 inches, 1-inch spindle; 14 to 16 inches, 1¼-inch spindle; 18 to 20 inches, 1½-inch spindle; 22 to 36 inches, 2-inch spindle.

and tool and to wash away the particles of stone and steel that are worn off by the rubbing. The process of rubbing the tool on the stone is called honing. There are two general classes of oil stones:

1. Natural.
2. Artificial.

Natural Oil Stones.—There are two general classes of natural

Fig. 890.—Goodell Pratt bench grinder with all gears enclosed. The wheel is 4 inches diameter with a 1-inch face. It is geared so that the wheel makes 22 revolutions to each revolution of the crank.

stones grouped according to locality where found, as 1, *Washita*, and 2, *Arkansas*.

Washita Oil Stone.—Washita stone is found in the Ozark Mountains of Arkansas, and is composed of nearly pure silica, very similar to the Arkansas, but much more porous. It is known throughout the world as the best natural stone for sharpening carpenter's and general wood worker's tools. Its sharpening qualities are due to small, sharp pointed grains or crystals, hexagonal in shape and much harder than steel. It is found in various grades, from perfectly crystallized and porous grit to vitreous flint and hard sandstone. The sharpness of grit depends entirely upon its crystallization. The best oil stones are made from very porous crystals.

Lily White Washita is the best selection or grading of natural Washita, perfectly white in color, uniform in texture and nicely finished.

Rosy Red Washita has an even porous grit somewhat coarser than the Lily White grading and is therefore faster cutting.

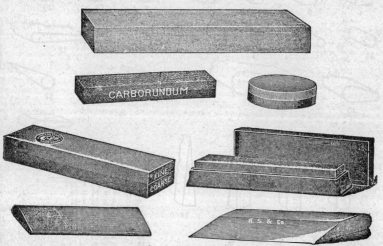

FIG. 891.—Natural oil stone. The different kinds of natural oil stone, their characteristics and care are described in the text.

FIG. 892.—Artificial carborundum oil stone. These stones are specially desirable for carpenters and mechanics. They are made with one face of coarse and one face of very fine grit. The coarse side can be used for sharpening dull tools; the fine side to bring the required keen, sharp edge.

FIG. 893.—Combination round-pattern carborundum oil stone. This shape is made to meet the sharpening needs of the carpenter and general mechanic. It is a novel as well as a decidedly practical addition to the tool box. The stone is made in the round form so as to allow for the circular motion required in sharpening chisels and similar tools. The stone is made with one side coarse grit for taking out nicks and bringing the tool to an edge and the other side of a very fine grit for giving the keen, finished edge.

FIG. 894.—India artificial oil stone with coarse and fine sides. These stones are in reality single stones, the two grits being vittrified together, so that no amount of throwing about or ill usage will cause them to come apart.

FIG. 895.—Iron oil stone box with stone in place. The box is fitted with four cork feet, which will to a great extent prevent it sliding on bench while in use. The stone rests on a piece of felt in bottom of box, which, absorbing a quantity of oil, keeps the stone moist. When top gets dry, reverse the stone.

FIGS. 896 and 897.—Round edge "slip" pattern oil stones. Fig. 896 regular Arkansas; fig. 897, soft Arkansas for carving tools.

Oil Stones
(Miscellaneous Shapes)

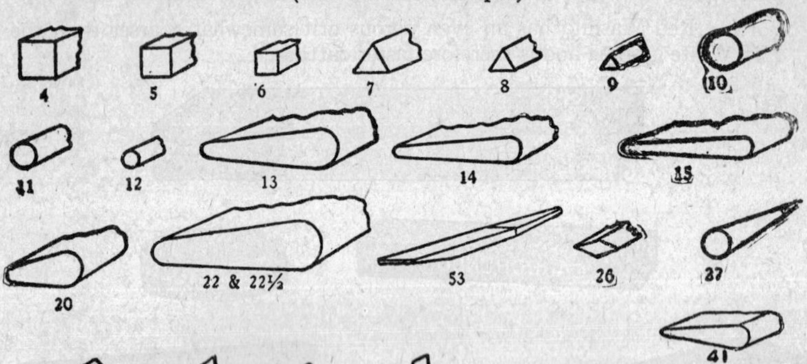

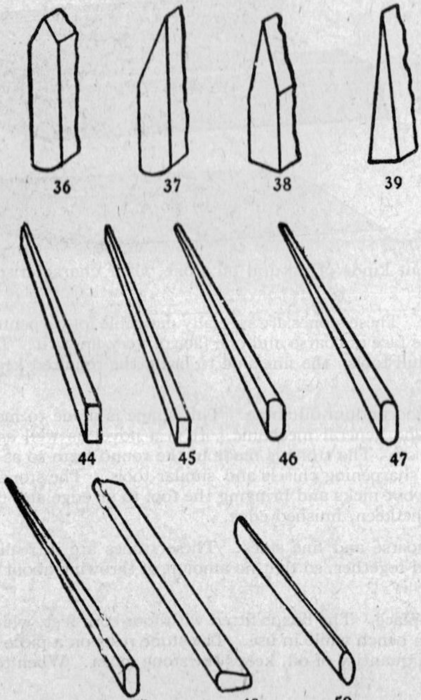

Medium or Fine

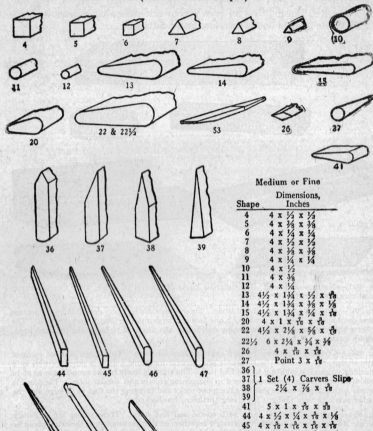

Shape	Dimensions, Inches
4	4 x ½ x ½
5	4 x ⅜ x ⅜
6	4 x ¼ x ¼
7	4 x ½ x ½
8	4 x ⅜ x ⅜
9	4 x ¼ x ¼
10	4 x ½
11	4 x ⅜
12	4 x ¼
13	4½ x 1¾ x ½ x 3/16
14	4½ x 1¾ x ⅜ x ⅛
15	4½ x 1¾ x ¼ x 1/16
20	4 x 1 x 7/16 x 3/16
22	4½ x 2⅛ x ⅝ x 3/16
22½	6 x 2¼ x ¾ x ⅜
26	4 x 9/16 x 3/16
27	Point 3 x 5/16
36, 37, 38, 39	1 Set (4) Carvers Slips 2¼ x ⅞ x 3/16
41	5 x 1 x 5/16 x 3/32
44	4 x ½ x ¼ x 5/16 x ⅛
45	4 x 5/16 x 3/16 x 5/16 x 1/16
46	4 x ½ x ¼ x 5/16 x ⅛
47	4 x ½ x 3/16 x 3/16 x 1/16
48	4 x ⅜ x 3/16 x ⅛ x 1/16
49	4 x 7/16 x 3/16 x ⅛
50	3½ x 7/16 x 3/16
53	Automobile Stone

FIGS. 898 to 92?.—Miscellaneous shapes of India oil stones

No. 1 Washita is a good oil stone for general use, where a medium-priced stone is wanted. It is far superior to the many cheap so-called "oil stones" on the market that are only sandstones with a polished face, but it is not as uniform as the Lily White.

Arkansas Oil Stone.—Genuine Arkansas stone is composed of pure silica crystals, microscopic in size, and silica is among the hardest of known minerals. So hard and perfectly crystallized is the Arkansas stone that is is nearly sixteen times harder to cut than marble, as the hardest of steel tools with the finest points or blades may be sharpened on the Arkansas stone without grooving. Arkansas stone is prepared for commercial purposes in two grades, hard and soft.

Hard Arkansas is much harder than steel and will therefore cut away and sharpen steel tools. The extreme fineness of texture makes it a slow cutter, but a perfect sharpener.

Soft Arkansas is not quite so fine grained and hard as the Hard Arkansas, but it cuts faster and is better for carvers, file makers, pattern makers and of all workers in hard wood.

Artificial Oil Stones.—These are made of carborundum, emery, corundum and other artificial abrasives, and are largely used in place of natural stones because they cut faster and may be made of any degree of fineness and of even texture.

Carborundum Oil Stones.—These are made from carborundum and may be used dry, or with water or oil; are quite porous, and may be tempered clean and bright, never fill or glaze, and are made in three grades as follows: Fine (FF). For procuring a very smooth, keen edge on tools of hard steel, etc. Medium (180). For sharpening tools quickly, where an extremely keen edge is not necessary. Coarse (120). To sharpen very dull and large tools, which may later be finished with a fine stone, or in cases where a fine finish is not required.

India Oil Stones. These are made from alundum. They possess the characteristics of hardness, sharpness and toughness, as well as uniformity. They cut rapidly, and are especially adaptable to the quick sharpening of all kinds of machinists' tools, made of modern tool steels, such as scrapers, taps, reamers, milling cutters, lathe and planer tools. All India stones are oil filled by a patented process. This feature insures a moist, oily sharpening surface with the use of only a small quantity of oil. It also insures a good cutting surface by preventing the stone filling with particles of steel.

India stones are made in three grades or grits as follows:

Coarse: For sharpening large and very dull or nicked tools, machine knives, and for general use where fast cutting is required without regard to fine finish.

Medium: For ordinary sharpening of mechanics' tools not requiring finishing edge. Especially recommended for tools used in working soft woods, cloth, leather, and rubber.

Fine: For machinists and engravers, die workers, instrument workers, cabinet makers and all users of tools requiring a very fine, keen edge.

CHAPTER 22

How to Sharpen Tools

It cannot be said too often that *edged tools must always be kept in perfect condition*, in order to do satisfactory work. This means that the cutting edge must be: 1, keen; 2, free from nicks; and 3, have the proper bevel. Sharpening is done by subjecting the tool to friction against an abrasive. The process includes:

1. Grinding.
2. Honing.

First the tool is placed on a grind stone (or grinding wheel in order to bring the bevel to the correct angle and to grind out any nicks that may be in the cutting edge.

Although this takes out the nicks and irregularities visible to the eye, the edge is still rough as may be seen under a microscope. This roughness is considerably reduced by honing on an oil stone although it is impossible to make the edge perfectly smooth because of the granular structure of the material. Although emery wheels are largely used in place of grind stones, they are objectionable for reasons already mentioned, hence the advice of a prominent manufacturer of chisels and other edged tools: *"Don't grind tools on dry emery wheels. Use a good grind stone and plenty of water."*

Plane cutters vary very much in their make, temper, quality of steel and uses, and must be ground and sharpened for the sort of work they are intended to execute. As already explained it is usual to grind a jack plane cutter slightly curved, a fore plane, almost flat, and a jointer, trying or smooth plane flat except at the corners (see figs. 927 to 929),

Before condemning any plane, therefore, carefully measure and compare the bevel of cut and thickness of cutter. If the bevel be too long, the plane will "jump and chatter." If too short, it will not cut, so it must be ground to a proper base or bevel.

Make the length of bevel twice the thickness of the iron as explained in fig. 930 (ordinarily but see figs. 676 to 678.)

When grinding tools on a stone without any guide or rest, the tool is pressed to and held at an angle of about 60° firmly on the face of the revolving stone, with both hands, the left in front. It is kept steady thus, the elbows being held closely to the person's sides and the whole body rigid and standing stiff on the floor or ground.

In order to avoid water running down from the stone on the operator's hands, the tool should be applied to the grind stone high enough up so that it may be held level while in contact with the stone at the proper bevel angle. Do not apply too much pressure, especially when grinding with the rapidly revolving emery wheels as the operator is liable to burn the temper out of the tool. Sparks may fly out but too much friction will burn, and the edge must be continuously watched especially with dry wheels. In the latter case the tool must be immersed in water very frequently to prevent over heating.

Hatchets, axes and adzes are ground to their proper bevels.

NOTE.—*General Instructions* (*Mack & Co.*, tool makers). Don't get your bevels too long; a ⅜-inch bevel on a new chisel is enough, with a short bevel on edge to strengthen it. In whetting a tool whet on bevel side only. Our own men in our wood shop where we make our planes and wood coopers' tools have an old piece of leather belting fastened to the top of the cover of the oil stone box on which to finish after using the oil stone. To keep tools clean and bright rub over with a little mercurial ointment which will form a slight coating resisting moisture, or take six parts lard and one part rosin and heat slowly together until rosin is all melted, then add benzine to thin it down, in about the proportion of one pint of benzine to one-half pound of lard. Rub Over tools lightly. This last preparation is what we have used in our own works for years. Tools treated with it will resist rust even when immersed in salt water and left for some time. We make the best leather capped handle that we know of. You can make just as good and perhaps better than any of the ready-made handles in which leather washer are used with top of handle cut away and coming through and showing in center of washer on top. It can be done thus: level off the top of a regular chisel handle, cut a piece of sole leather to fit, and glue it to top of handle, then put in five or six shoemaker's heel tacks, driving them well home. A leather-capped handle made in this way will last for years when the ordinary kind with end of wood coming through to surface will break out.

Some have double, and others single bevels (see figs. 931 and 932).

In grinding, the head is held to the stone surface with the right hand, the handle with the left, and on the left side, reversing the tool as the opposite side is being ground or sharpened.

Draw knives and spoke shave cutters are held with both hands and the blade kept horizontally flat on the stone as it revolves toward the person.

Some prefer to grind with the stone rotating *toward* the cutting edge, others with the stone rotating *away from* the cutting edge. The latter is the safer method, as with the stone advancing there is danger of injury to the operator in case the tool dig into the stone. Hence, with an advancing stone be careful not to use too much pressure.

In sharpening hatchets, axes and adzes, if it be desired to have a very keen edge, after grinding as just described, the tool should be honed on an oil stone.

Honing.—A tool after being ground on a grind stone or emery wheel will be found to have a wire edge, and this must be removed and the cutting edge made smooth by *honing* on an oil stone. The oil stone is constantly needed during all operations in carpentry in which the plane and chisel are used. It is needed more frequently than the grind stone, because the latter is only necessary when the tool becomes nicked, or the edge too dull to be sharpened on the oil stone without an undue amount of labor. A size of oil stone for general use is about 2 × 8 or 9 ins. long.

A very desirable stone is the double carborundum, that is, one made of carborundum having one side coarse and the other fine. With this type stone begin to hone on the coarse side and finish on the fine side. *It is absolutely necessary to keep the stone*

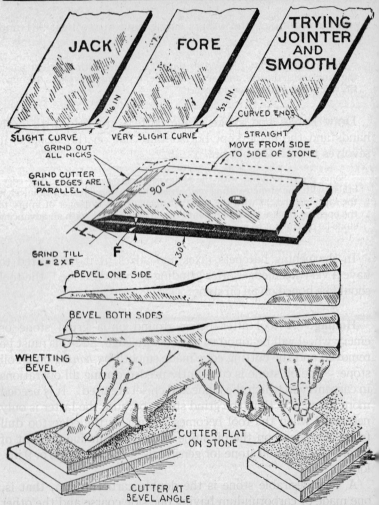

JACK

SLIGHT CURVE
GRIND OUT
ALL NICKS

¾₆ IN.

FORE

VERY SLIGHT CURVE

¹⁄₃₂ IN.

TRYING JOINTER AND SMOOTH

CURVED ENDS

STRAIGHT
MOVE FROM SIDE
TO SIDE OF STONE

GRIND CUTTER
TILL EDGES ARE
PARALLEL

90°

GRIND TILL
L = 2 × F

F

30°

BEVEL ONE SIDE

BEVEL BOTH SIDES

WHETTING
BEVEL

CUTTER FLAT
ON STONE

CUTTER AT
BEVEL ANGLE

Figs. 927 to 934.—How to sharpen tools. In figs. 927 to 929, the proper shape of cutting edge is shown for jack, fore, trying, jointer and smooth planes; fig. 930, ordinary bevel for chisels—for precision: make bevel angle 15° for paring; 20° for firmer, and 30° for framing chisel figs. 931 and 932, show single and double bevel hatchets; figs. 933 and 934, method of honing.

clean and in perfect condition. If no attention be paid to this advice, experience will soon compel the amateur to do as directed. * *Oil stones should always be kept in case when not in use.*

On oil stones use only a thin, clear oil and wipe the stone clean after using. Then moisten with clean oil.

In applying chisels and plane irons to an oil stone, the tool is held face up with both hands, the left in front, palm up, with thumb on top, the fingers grasping the tool from underneath. The right hand behind, palm down, thumb under and the fingers reaching across the face of the tool.

Held thus, the edge is rubbed back and forth with a sliding rotary motion on the face of the stone, which is first lubricated with oil or water, the angle generally being a little above 60°, say about 65, and after 10 or 12 rubs it is turned over and rubbed flat on the face side. It is then stropped, which may either be done by a slapping action, striking on the left hand or rubbed on a handy piece of old belting or leather set on top of the oil stone case or separate on a board. When this is done the keenness may be tested with the thumb or by drawing the edge across the left thumb nail, but this test must be done very carefully to avoid cutting.

Should the edge be not sharp, then the rubbing or *honing* must be repeated again and again, until it is so keen as to "bite," as mechanics say, and be fully fit for the duty intended.

Outside gouges are sharpened in a similar way as chisels.

The tool should be rolled forward and backward in grinding the bevel.

NOTE.—*To repair a broken oil stone,* heat the pieces thoroughly on a hot plate, so as to remove all oil, then clean in regular way. Dust the broken edges thickly with powdered shellac, which melt by reheating on the hot plate. Place the pieces together and clamp tightly until cold. If the joining be carefully done, the stone will give as good service as when new and may be used until worn out.

*NOTE.—*To clean an oil stone.* Wa shIndia or carborundum stones in kerosene, which will remove the gummed surface oil. This may be more easily and thoroughly done by heating on a hot plate, or sticking in the fire, which latter will not damage the stones. A natural stone may also be heated on a hot plate to remove the surplus or gummed oil, after which a good cleaning with gasolene or ammonia will usually restore its cutting qualities, but if it do not, then scour the stone with loose emery or sand paper fastened to a perfectly smooth board.

A *slip stone* is used to remove the wire edge by rubbing on the inside concave surface, and it is requisite that the curved edge of the slip stone fit to the arc of each gouge as closely as possible.

Inside gouges must be ground on a curved stone and whetted to keen edges with the oil and slip stones.

Hollows and rounds, beading and other special plane cutters are usually sharpened with slip stones and rarely require grinding. If nicked or injured on their edges they are utterly useless.

Cold chisels, punches and nail sets are best sharpened or pointed on grind stones. Carving tools are sharpened with small fine slip stones.

In honing or whetting fine bench chisels the burnished face side must be kept perfectly flat on the face of the oil stone by pressing firmly down with 2nd and 3rd fingers of the left hand, the handle being held in the right. The rubbing must be gentle and rapidly repeated turning the tool repeatedly over.

The edge may be sloping slightly to the side of the oil stone and the movement back and forward partially rotary on an oblong stone or entirely rotary on a circular oil stone. Care must be exercised not to raise the angle too high so as to dig into and cut the oil stone's surface and it should be wiped clean and re-oiled frequently if several or many tools are being sharpened.

CHAPTER 23

How to Use The Steel Square

On most construction work, especially in house framing the so-called "steel square" is invaluable for accurate measuring and for determining angles. The author seriously objects to the term "*steel* square." The proper name is *framing square*, because the square with its markings was designed especially for marking timber in framing. However, the wrong name has become so firmly rooted that it will have to be put up with.

The square as a tool with its various scales and tables has been explained in Chapter 7. The present treatment is to explain more in detail these markings and their application by examples showing actual use of the square. The following names used to identify the different portions of the square should be noted and remembered:

Parts of Framing Square

Body.—The longer and wider member.

Face.—The sides visible (both body and tongue) when the square is held by the tongue in the right hand, the body pointing to the left.

Tongue.—The shorter and narrower member.

Back.—The sides visible (both body and tongue) when the square is held by the tongue with the left hand, the body pointing to the right.

The size square most generally employed is that with a 12

in. tongue and an 18 in. body, but there are many purposes
which require a 16 to 18 in. tongue, and a 24 in. body.

The body of the larger is 2 in. wide and the tongue 1¾ ins.
wide, ³⁄₁₆ in. thick at the heel or corner for strength, diminishing, for lightness to the two extremities to about ³⁄₃₂ in.

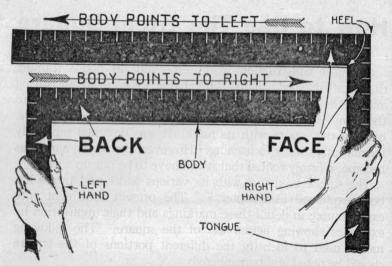

Figs. 935 and 936.—Face and back sides of square with names used to identify its different portions. These are defined in the text and should be firmly fixed in mind by aid of the illustrations. The body of the square is sometimes called the *blade*.

The various markings on squares are of two kinds:

1. Scales or graduations.
2. Tables.

In buying a square it is advisable to get one with all the markings rather than a cheap square with some of the scales and
tables omitted. Thus

Markings of Cheap Square

Tables	Graduations
Rafter—Essex—brace	$1/16$, $1/12$, $1/8$, $1/4$

Complete Markings

Rafter, Essex, brace, octagon, $1/100$, $1/32$, $1/16$, $1/12$, $1/10$, $1/8$, $1/4$
polygon cuts

The square with the complete markings will cost more, but in the purchase of tools make it a rule *to purchase only the finest made*. The general arrangement of the markings on squares differ somewhat with different makes, hence, it is advisable to examine the different makes before purchasing to select the one best suited to individual requirements.

Application of the Square.—As before stated the markings on squares of different makes sometimes vary both in their position on the square and the mode of application, but a thorough understanding of the application of the markings on any first class square will enable the student to easily acquire proficiency with any other square.

The various markings may be divided into two groups:

1. Scales.
2. Tables.

The application of the scales will be first considered, as before explaining the use of the tables, the student should understand the general arrangement of roof frame work, names of the different kinds of rafters, other parts, etc.

Scale Problems.—The term *scales* is used to denote the inch divisions of the tongue and body length found on the outer and inner edges, and the inch graduations into $1/4$, $1/8$, $1/10$, $1/12$, $1/16$, $1/32$, and $1/100$. As before stated all these graduations should be on a first class square (hence, look for them in purchasing a square)—but, on cheap squares will be found only a few of these graduations—as $\frac{1}{16}$, $\frac{1}{8}$, $\frac{1}{4}$.

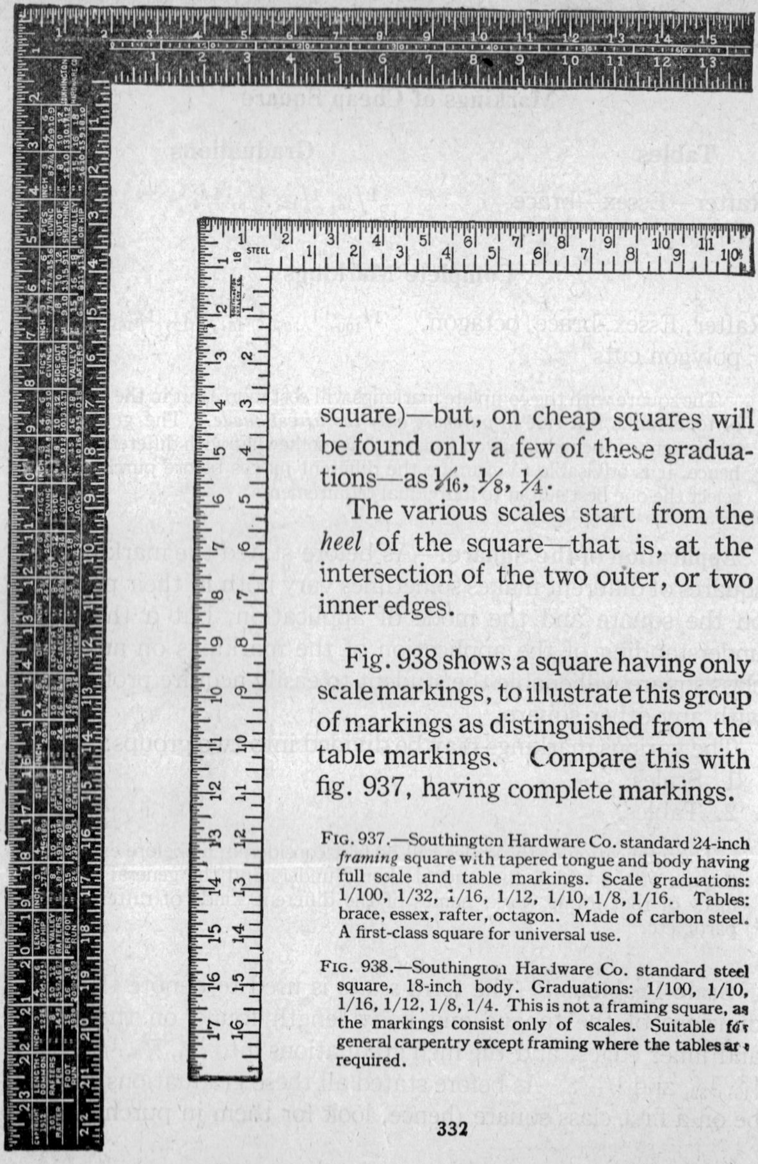

The various scales start from the *heel* of the square—that is, at the intersection of the two outer, or two inner edges.

Fig. 938 shows a square having only scale markings, to illustrate this group of markings as distinguished from the table markings. Compare this with fig. 937, having complete markings.

FIG. 937.—Southington Hardware Co. standard 24-inch *framing* square with tapered tongue and body having full scale and table markings. Scale graduations: 1/100, 1/32, 1/16, 1/12, 1/10, 1/8, 1/16. Tables: brace, essex, rafter, octagon. Made of carbon steel. A first-class square for universal use.

FIG. 938.—Southington Hardware Co. standard steel square, 18-inch body. Graduations: 1/100, 1/10, 1/16, 1/12, 1/8, 1/4. This is not a framing square, as the markings consist only of scales. Suitable for general carpentry except framing where the tables are required.

A square having only the scale markings as shown in fig. 938, is adequate to solve many problems in laying out carpentry work. An idea of its range of usefulness is shown in the following problems.

Problem 1.—*To describe a semi-circle with given diameter.*

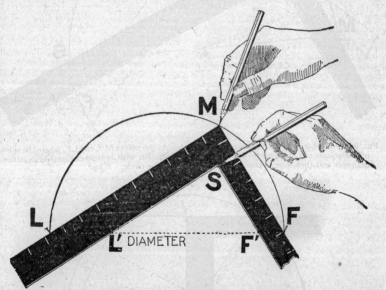

FIG. 939.—Problem 1: *To describe a semi-circle with given diameter.* **Outer heel method:** Drive brads at points L, F, extremities of the given diameter. With pencil held at the **outer heel M,** slide square around with its sides in contact with L, and F, then with the **pencil** held at M, describe a semi-circle. **Inner heel method:** Obviously if the pencil be held at **S,** it will be better guided, than at M. In this method, the distance L'F', should be taken **to** equal diameter, the inner edges of the square sliding on the tacks—the same edges (in either **case**) that guide the pencil.

At the ends of the diameter LF (fig. 939) drive brads. Place the **outer** edges of the square against the nails and hold a lead pencil at the outer **heel** M, any semi-circle can be described as indicated.

This is the *outer heel* method, but a better guide for the pencil is obtained by the *inner heel* method also shown in the figure.

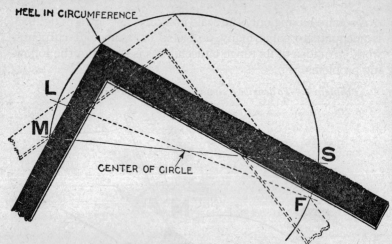

Fig. 940.—*Problem 2: To find the center of a circle.* At the points MS, and LF, where the sides of the square cut the circle when placed in any position with heel in circumference, draw diameter and then intersection will be the center of the circle. ***Why?***

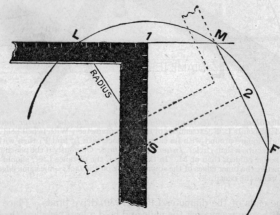

Fig. 941.—*Problem 3: To describe a circle through three points not in a straight line.* Let L, M, and F, be the given points. Join these points with lines LM, and MF, bisecting them at 1 and 2. Apply square with heel at 1 and. 2 as shown and the intersection of perpendiculars thus obtained at S. will be the center of circle which, with radius LS, may be described through LM and F

Problem 2.—*To find the center of a circle.*

Lay the square on the circle so that its outer heel lies in the circumference.

Mark the intersections of the body and tongue with the circumference. A line connecting these two points is a diameter and by drawing another diameter (obtained in the same way) the intersection of the two diameters is the center of the circle as shown in fig. 940.

Problem 3.—*To describe a circle through three points not in a straight line.*

Joint points with straight lines; bisect these lines and at the points of bisection erect perpendiculars with the square. The intersection of these

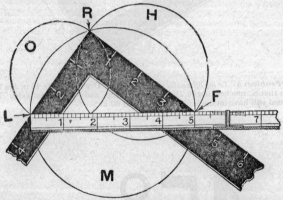

IG. 942.—*Problem 4: To find the diameter of a circle whose area is equal to the sum of the areas of two given circles.* Let O, and H, be the given circles (drawn with diameters LR, and RF, at right angles). Suppose diameter of O, be 3 inches, and diameter of H, 4 inches. Then points L, F, at these distances from the heel of the square will be 5 inches apart as conveniently measured with a two-foot rule as shown. This distance LF, or 5 inches, is diameter of the required circle. *Proof:* $LF^2 = LR^2 + RF^2$, that is $5^2 = 3^2 + 4^2$ or $25 = 9 + 16$.

perpendiculars is the center from which a circle may be described through the three points as in fig. 941.

Problem 4.—*To find the diameter of a circle whose area is equal to the sum of the areas of two given circles.*

Lay off on tongue of square diameter of one of the given circles, and on body diameter of the other. The distance between these points (measure across with a two foot rule) will be diameter of the required circle as in fig. 942.

Problem 5.—*To lay off angles of 30° and 60°.*

Mark off 15 ins. on a straight line and lay the square so that the body

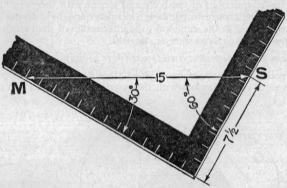

FIG. 943.—*Problem 5: To lay off angles of 30° and 60°.* Draw line MS, 15 inches long. Place square so that S, touches tongue 7½ inches from hip, and M, touches body. The triangle thus formed will have an angle of 30° at M, and 60 at S.

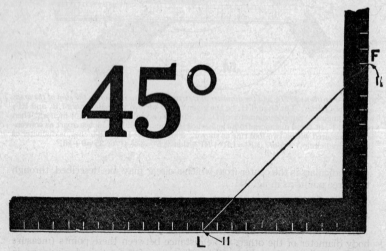

FIG. 944.—*Problem 6:* To lay off an angle of 45°. Take equal measurements **L, F,** on body and tongue of the square then with ∠ L = ∠ F = 45°.

touches one mark and 7½ ins. on the tongue is against the other mark as in fig. 943. The tongue will then form an angle of 60° with the line, and the body, 30°.

Problem 6.—*To lay off an angle of* 45°.

The diagonal line connecting equal measurements on either arm of the square forms angles of 45° with the blade and tongue as in fig. 944.

Problem 7.—*To lay off any angle*.

The accompanying table gives values for measurements on tongue and body of the square such that by joining the points corresponding to the measurements any angle may be laid out from 1 to 45° as explained in fig. 945.

Angle Table for Square

Angle	Tongue	Body	Angle	Tongue	Body	Angle	Tongue	Body
1	.35	20.	16	5.51	19.23	31	10.28	17.14
2	.7	19.99	17	5.85	19.13	32	10.6	16.96
3	1.05	19.97	18	6.18	19.02	33	10.89	16.77
4	1.4	19.95	19	6.51	18.91	34	11.18	16.58
5	1.74	19.92	20	6.84	18.79	35	11.47	16.38
6	2.09	19.89	21	7.17	18.67	36	11.76	16.18
7	2.44	19.85	22	7.49	18.54	37	12.04	15.98
8	2.78	19.81	23	7.8	18.4	38	12.31	15.76
9	3.13	19.75	24	8.13	18.27	39	12.59	15.54
10	3.47	19.7	25	8.45	18.13	40	12.87	15.32
11	3.82	19.63	26	8.77	17.98	41	13.12	15.09
12	4.16	19.56	27	9.08	17.82	42	13.38	14.89
13	4.5	19.49	28	9.39	17.66	43	13.64	14.63
14	4.84	19.41	29	9.7	17.49	44	13.89	14.39
15	5.18	19.32	30	10.	17.32	45	14.14	14.14

Problem 8.—*To find the octagon of any size square timber.*

Place the body of a 24 in. square diagonally across the timber so that both extremities (ends) of the 24″ body touch opposite edges. Make a mark at 7 ins. and 17 ins. as in fig. 946. Repeat the process at the other end and draw lines through the pairs of marks, these lines showing the portion of material necessary to come off the corners.

Square and Bevel Problems.—By the application of a large bevel to the framing square, it becomes a calculating machine, and by its means arithmetical processes are greatly simplified. This bevel is preferably made of steel blades, procurable from a tool maker; the following points being observed in its construction:

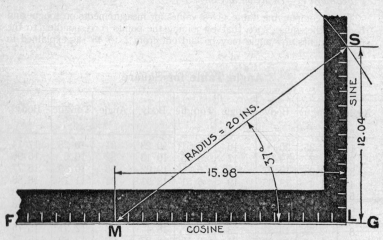

Fig. 945.—*Problem 7: To lay out any angle.* Let 37° be the required angle. Place body of square on the line FG, and from the table lay off on tongue LS = 12.04 inches, and LM, on body = 15.98 inches. Draw MS, then angle LMS = 37°. By measurement MS, will be found to be equal to 20 inches for any angle, because the values given in the table for LS. and MS, are *natural sines* and *natural cosines* multiplied by 20, hence MS = 1 × 20.

The edges of each blade must be true; the blade *e* in fig 948 must lie under the square so as not to hide the graduations; the

NOTE.—The side of an inscribed octagon can be obtained from the side of a given square, by multiplying the side of the square by five and dividing the product by twelve. The quotient will be the side of the octagon.

NOTE.—The side of a *hexagon* is equal to the radius of the circumscribing circle. If the side of a desired hexagon be given, arcs should be struck from each extremity of it at a radius equal to its length. The point where these arcs intersect is the center of the circumscribing circle, and having described it, it is sufficient to prick off chords on its circumference, equal to the given side, to complete the hexagon

two blades must be fastened together by a thumb screw to lock them; the blade *l* should have a hole near each end and one in the middle so that blade *e* may be shifted as required, with a

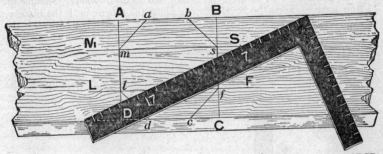

FIG. 946.—*Problem 8: To find the octagon of any size timber.* First lay out a square ABCD. Placing the body of a 24-inch square as shown parallel lines MS and LF, are drawn through points 7 and 17 as shown. These intercept sides *ml*, and *sf*, of the octagon. To lay off side *sb*, place square so that tongue touches *s*, and body touches *l*, with heel touching line AB. The remaining sides are obtained in a similar manner.

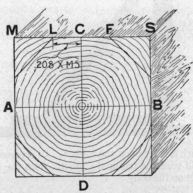

FIG. 947.—*Problem 8: To find the octagon of any size timber* (second method). Let AB, and CD, be center lines and MS, one side of the square timber. *Rule: Multiply length of side by .208 and product is half side of octagon.* Thus lay off CF and CL, each = .208 ×MS, then LF, is side of octagon. Set dividers to distance CL and lay off other sides from center A, B, D, and complete polygon.

large notch as shown, near each hole in order to observe the position of blade *e*.

Problem 9.—*To find the diagonal of a square.*

Set the blade *e* to 10⅜ on the tongue and 15 on the body. Assume an 8 in. square. Slide the bevel sidewise along the tongue until the blade *e*, is against 8, when the other edge will touch 11⁵⁄₁₆ on the body which is the required diagonal.

Problem 10.—*To find the circumference of a circle from its diameter.*

Set the bevel blade to 7 on the tongue of the square and to 22 on the body. The reading on the body will be the circumference corresponding to the

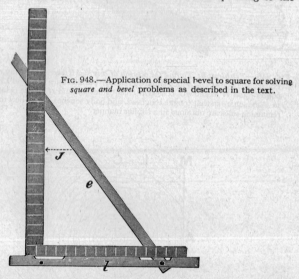

Fig. 948.—Application of special bevel to square for solving *square and bevel* problems as described in the text.

diameter to which *e*, is set upon the tongue. To reverse the process, use the same bevel, and read the required diameter from the tongue, the circumference being set on the body

Problem 11.—*Given the diameter of a circle, to find the side of a square of equal area.*

Set the bevel blade to 10⅝ on the tongue and 12 on the body, then the diameter of the circle, on the body, will give the side of the equal square upon the tongue. If the circumference be given instead of the diameter, set the bevel to 5½ on the tongue and 19½ on the body, finding the side of the square on the tongue as before.

Problem 12.—*Given the side of the square, to find the diameter of a circle of equal area.*

This, together with the preceding problem, is very useful in making calculations for spouts and pipes. Using the same bevel as in Problem 11, the blade *e*, is set to the given side upon the tongue of the square, the required diameter being read off the body.

Problem 13.—*Given the diameter of the pitch circle of a gear wheel, and the number of teeth; to find the pitch.*

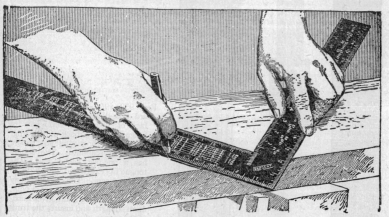

Fig. 949.—Framing square in use on board.

Take the number of teeth or a proportional part upon the body of the square, and the diameter or a similar proportional part upon the tongue, and set the bevel blade to those marks. Slide the bevel along to 3.14 on the body, and the number given on the tongue, multiplied by the proportional divisor will be the required pitch.

Problem 14.—*Given the pitch of teeth and diameter of pitch circle in a gear wheel, to find the number of teeth.*

Set the bevel blade to the pitch on the tongue, and 3.14 on the body of the square. Move the bevel along until it marks the diameter upon the tongue when the number of teeth can be read from the blade. If the

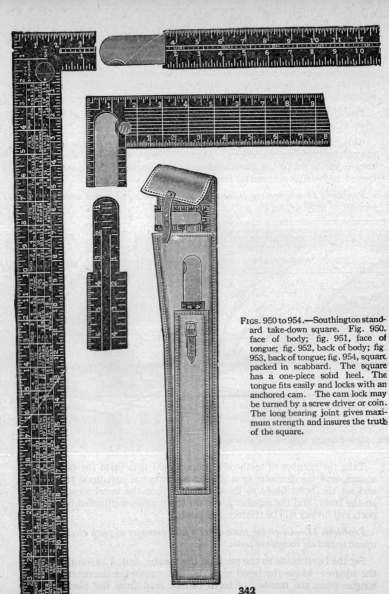

FIGS. 950 to 954.—Southington standard take-down square. Fig. 950. face of body; fig. 951, face of tongue; fig. 952, back of body; fig. 953, back of tongue; fig. 954, square packed in scabbard. The square has a one-piece solid heel. The tongue fits easily and locks with an anchored cam. The cam lock may be turned by a screw driver or coin. The long bearing joint gives maximum strength and insures the truth of the square.

diameter be too large for the tongue, divide it into proportional parts, also the pitch, multiplying the number found by the same figure.

Problem 15.—The side of a polygon being given to find the radius of the circumscribing circle.

Set bevel to the pairs of numbers in the table below taking one-eighth or one-tenth of an inch as a unit. The bevel, when locked, is slid along to the given length of side, and the required length of radius is read upon the other leg of the square.

TABLE FOR INSCRIBED POLYGONS.

Number of Sides	3	4	5	6	7	8	9	10	11	12
Radius	56	70	74	60	60	98	22	89	80	85
Side	97	99	87	60	52	75	15	95	45	44

Thus, having to set out a pentagon with a side of six inches, the bevel is set to the figures in column 5, the lesser number on the tongue. In this case $^{74}/_8 = 9\frac{1}{4}$ on the tongue, and $^{87}/_8 = 10^{7}/_8''$ on body of the square. Sliding the bevel to 6 upon the body, the length of the radius, $5^{3}/_{32}$ will be read upon the tongue.

Problem 16.—To divide the circumference of a circle into a given number of equal parts.

From the column marked Y in the following table, take the number opposite the given number of parts. Multiply it by the radius of the circle, the product will be the length of chord to set off upon the circumference.

TABLE OF CHORDS OR EQUAL PARTS.

No. of Parts		Y	Z	No. of Parts	Y	Z	No. of Parts	Y	Z
3	Triangle	1.732	.5773	15	.4158	2.4050	40	.1569	6.3728
4	Square	1.414	.7071	16	.3902	2.5628	45	.1395	7.1678
5	Pentagon	1.175	.8006	17	.3675	2.7210	50	.1256	7.9618
6	Hexagon	1.000	1.0000	18	.3473	2.8793	54	.1163	8.5984
7	Heptagon	.8677	1.1520	19	.3292	3.0376	60	.1047	9.5530
8	Octagon	.7653	1.3065	20	.3129	3.1962	72	.0872	11.462
9	Nonagon	.6840	1.4619	22	.2846	3.5137	80	.0785	12.738
10	Decagon	.6180	1.6184	24	.2610	3.8307	90	.0698	14.327
11	Undecagon	.5634	1.7747	25	.2506	3.9904	100	.0628	15.923
12	Duodecagon	.5176	1.9319	27	.2322	4.3066	108	.0582	17.182
13		.4782	2.0911	30	.2090	4.7834	120	.0523	19.101
14		.4451	2.2242	36	.1743	5.7368	150	.0419	23.866

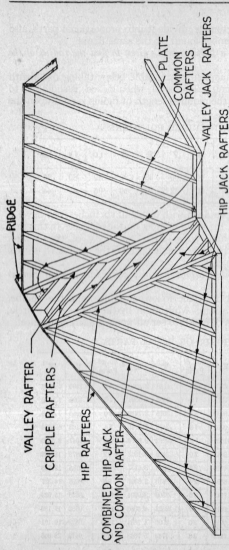

RIDGE

PLATE
COMMON RAFTERS

VALLEY JACK RAFTERS

HIP JACK RAFTERS

VALLEY RAFTER

CRIPPLE RAFTERS

HIP RAFTERS

COMBINED HIP JACK AND COMMON RAFTER

Fig. 495.—Roof frame showing ridge, plate, and different kind of rafters.

Problem 18.—Given the length of a chord, to find the radius of the circle.

This is the same as Problem 16, but the present form may be found more expeditious for calculations. The method is useful for ascertaining the diameter of gear wheels, the pitch and number of teeth having been given.

Multiply the length of the chord, width of side, or pitch of tooth by the figures found corresponding to the number of parts in column Z of the table page 343. The result is the radius of the desired circle.

Table Problems.—The term *table* is here used to denote the various markings on the framing square except the scales already described. As these tables relate mostly to problems encountered in cutting lumber for roof frame work it is necessary first to know something about roof construction so as to be familiar with the names of the various rafters and other parts.

Fig. 955 is a view of a roof frame showing the various members. In the figure it will be noticed that there is a *plate* at the

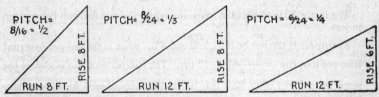

Figs. 956 to 958.—Sections of various roofs illustrating *pitch*. To obtain the pitch: **Rule**— *Divide the rise by twice the run.*

bottom and ridge timber at the top, these being the main members to which the rafters are fastened.

Main or Common Rafters.—The following definitions relating to rafters should be carefully noted:

The *rise* of a roof is *the distance found in following a plumb line from a point on the central line of the top of the ridge to the level of the top of the plate.*

The *run* of a common rafter is *the shortest horizontal distance from a plumb line through center of ridge to the outer edge of the plate.*

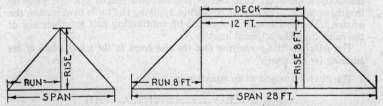

Fig. 959.—Section of roof illustrating the terms *run, rise,* and *span.*

Fig. 960.—Roof with *deck*. **Rule**—*Where rafters rise to a deck instead of a ridge, subtract the width of the deck from the span.* Here the span is 28 feet and deck 12 feet. The difference is 16 feet and the pitch is 8 ÷ (2×8). or 8 ÷ (28—12) = ½.

The **rise per foot run** *is the basis on which rafter tables on some squares are made.* The term is self-defining.

To obtain the rise per foot run, multiply the rise by 12 and divide by the run, thus:

$$\text{rise per foot run} = \frac{\text{rise} \times 12}{\text{run}}$$

The factor 12 is to obtain a value in inches, the rise and run being given in feet.

Example: If the rise be 8 ft., and run 8 ft., what is the rise per foot run?
Rise per foot run $= \dfrac{8 \times 12}{8} = 12$ ins. The rise per foot run is always the

same for a given pitch and can be readily remembered for all ordinary pitches, thus:

Pitch	½	⅓	¼	⅙
Rise per foot run (ins.)	12	8	6	4

In roof construction the rafter ends are cut to roof angles to rest respectively against ridge and plate as shown in figs. 961 and 962.

The **top** or **plumb cut** *is the cut at the rafter end which rests on the ridge.*

The **bottom** or **heel cut** *is the cut at the rafter end which rests against the plate.*

The **length** of a common rafter is *the shortest distance between the outer edge of the plate and the central line of the top of the ridge.* It should be distinctly understood that this is not the *real* length but the *artificial* length, or value, which must be used in applying the table markings on the square. The real length is obtained by subtracting half the thickness of the ridge from the artificial length.

The **pitch** is the *proportion that the rise bears to the whole width of the building (or the span).**

The pitch expressed as an equation is:

$$\text{pitch} = \frac{\text{rise}}{\text{span}} \quad \dotfill (1)$$

---

*NOTE.—Where rafters rise to a ridge instead of a ridge, it is necessary to subtract the width of the deck from the total spa·

Example.—A building 24 ft. wide has a roof with a rise of 8 ft. What is the pitch of the roof?

Substituting in (1)

$$\text{pitch} = {}^{8}/_{24} = \tfrac{1}{3}$$

The question is often asked, what constitutes full pitch? From an inspection of equation (1) this is easily answered. Since the pitch is full when the value of rise ÷ span = 1 then from the equation evidently the pitch is full when the rise is equal to the span that is, equal to twice the run. Accordingly

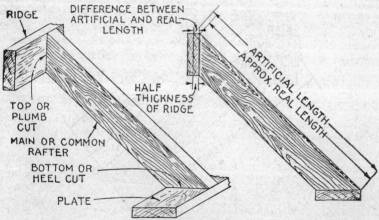

FIG. 961.—Portion of roof frame illustrating *top* or *plumb cut* and *bottom* or *heel cut.*

FIG. 962.—End view of portion of roof frame illustrating artificial and real length of rafter. Rafter-tables as given on framing squares are figured for an arbitrary length being the shortest distance from the outer edge of the plate to the center of the top of the rafter. This would be the actual length of the rafters if they rested at the upper end against each other instead of against the ridge. This arbitrary or artificial length must be assumed as a basis for the rafter table, otherwise separate values would be necessary for various thicknesses of the ridge member and it would be not only confusing but impossible to put all the figures in the limited space available on the square. Hence, to obtain approximate real length of rafter *subtract half thickness of ridge from the artificial length or value given on the square.* It should be understood that this is the *approximate real length,* or near enough for practical use. However, the enlightened carpenter will want to know what is the *actual real length* and why it is not used in practice as explained in fig. 963. Note in fig. 963, that the rafter, as cut, is too short.

for full pitch if the run be say 12 ft., the rise is 24 ft. With this as a basis a table of various pitches made thus:

Pitch Table

Pitch	1	$^{11}/_{12}$	$^5/_6$	$^3/_4$	$^2/_3$	$^7/_{12}$	$^1/_2$	$^5/_{12}$	$^1/_3$	$^1/_4$	$^1/_6$	$^1/_{12}$
Run	12	12	12	12	12	12	12	12	12	12	12	12
Rise	24	22	20	18	16	14	12	10	8	6	4	2

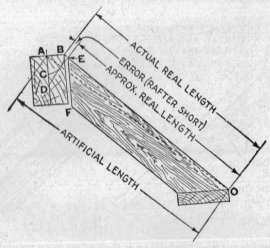

FIG. 963.—Detail of rafter and ridge illustrating why rafters are cut only to approximate real length. OA, is the length the rafter would be if there were no ridge board; this is the length found on the square. *In cutting* a rafter to fit against a ridge, an allowance must be made for the space taken up by the ridge each side of the center line, as AB. Hence OB, is the actual or real length of the rafter, *but this length cannot be conveniently found. In practice* therefore, an approximation is made by subtracting from the artificial real length OA, or value given on the square, an amount AB, equal to half the thickness of the ridge board. With A, as center and AB, as radius, describe arc BC, and with O, as center describe arc DE, tangent to BC. This gives the point E, such that OE, is the approximate rafter length, that is, the length OA, less half thickness of the ridge, the upper end of the rafter being indicated by the line EF, the rafter being actually too short by the distance BE. In the diagram, BE, appears large because a very thick ridge was selected to augment the error. *In practice* with a ridge of normal thickness, the error BE, is very small and when the rafter is in place is hardly noticeable.

Now with a 24 in. square diagonals connecting 12 on the tongue (corresponding to the run) and value from table for rise will give pitch angle for any combination or run and rise.

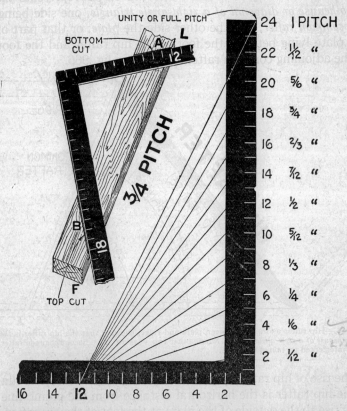

24	1 PITCH
22	11/12 "
20	5/6 "
18	3/4 "
16	2/3 "
14	7/12 "
12	1/2 "
10	5/12 "
8	1/3 "
6	1/4 "
4	1/6 "
2	1/12 "

FIG. 964 and 965.—Application of the framing square for obtaining various pitches as given in the accompanying table. In fig. 964 the square is seen applied to a rafter with the 12-inch mark on tongue and 18-inch mark on body at the edge of the rafter. The inclinations A, and B, of the tongue and body of the square with the edge LF, of the rafter give the correct angles for cutting so that edge F, will have ¾ pitch when placed in position, that is, when A, is horizontal and B, vertical or plumb.

Thus lay off 12 on tongue and 8 on body for $\frac{1}{3}$ pitch. The various pitches given in the table are shown in fig. 965.

Hip (and Valley) Rafters.—The hip rafter represents *the hypothenuse or diagonal of a right-angle triangle*, one side being the *common rafter*, and the other side the *plate*, or that part of the plate lying between the foot of the hip rafter and the foot of the adjoining common rafter as shown in fig. 966.

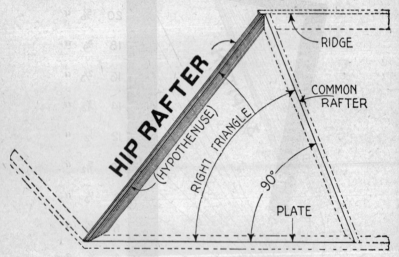

Fɪɢ. 966.—Hip rafter as framed between plate and ridge, showing that the hip rafter is *the hypothenuse of a right angle triangle*, whose other two sides are the adjacent common rafter and intercepted portion of the plate.

The rise of hip rafter is the same as common rafter. The run of the hip rafter is the horizontal distance from the plumb line of its rise to the outside of the plate at the foot of the hip rafter. This run of the hip rafter is to the run of the common rafter as 17 is to 12. Therefore, for $\frac{1}{6}$ pitch the common rafter run and rise are 12 and 4, while the hip rafter run and rise are 17 and 4.

For the top and bottom cuts of the common rafter, the figures are used that represent the common rafter run and rise, that is, 12 and 4 for ⅙ pitch, and 12 and 6 for ¼ pitch, etc., but for top and bottom cuts of hip rafter use the figures 17 and 4, and 17 and 6, etc., the run and rise of the hip rafter.

Valley Rafters.—The valley rafter is the hypothenuse of a

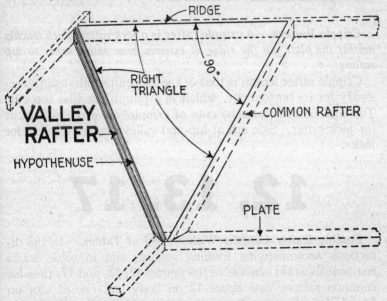

Fig. 967.—Valley rafter as framed between plate and ridge, showing that the valley rafter is the hypothenuse of a right triangle whose other two sides are the adjacent common rafter and intercepted portion of the ridge.

right angle triangle made by the common rafter with the ridge, corresponding with the right angle triangle made by the hip rafter with common rafter and plate; and, therefore, the rules for the lengths and cuts of valley rafters are the same as for hip rafter.

Jack Rafters.—These are usually spaced either 16 inches apart or 24 inches apart, and, as they lie against the hip or valley equally spaced, the second jack rafter must be twice as long as the first, the third three times as long as the first, and so on. The reason for 16 and 24 inch spacing on jack rafters is because laths are 48 inches long, therefore the rafter must be 16 or 24 inches so the lath may be nailed to it

Cripple Rafters.—A cripple rafter is *a jack rafter which touches neither the plate nor the ridge; it extends from valley rafter to hip rafters.*

Cripple rafter length is that of the jack rafter plus length necessary for its bottom cut, which is a plumb cut like top cut. Top and bottom (plumb) cuts of cripples are same as top cut for jack rafter. Side cut at hip and valley same as side cut for jacks.

12, 13, 17

Finding Rafter Lengths Without Aid of Tables.—In the directions accompanying framing squares and in some books frequent mention is made of the figures **12, 13,** and **17,** thus for common rafters "use figure **12** on body and rise of roof on tongue;" for hip or valley rafters, "use figure **17** on body and rise of roof on tongue"—and no explanation of how these fixed numbers are obtained. The intelligent workman should not be satisfied with knowing which number to use but he should

---

NOTE.—In the tables the common rafter length is given to the center of the ridge, and so with the hip rafter length. The jack rafter length is given to the center of its hip or valley rafter. In using the tables, make allowances indicated, depending upon the thickness of ridge, hip and valley rafters.

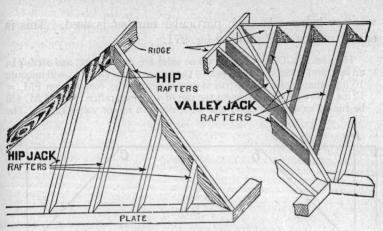

Fig. 968.—Hip jack rafters as framed *between the plate and hip rafters.*

Fig. 969.—Valley jack rafters as framed between the valley rafter and ridge.

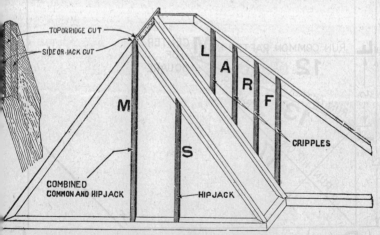

Fig. 970.—Combined common and hip jack rafter and cripple rafters. When a jack as rafter **M,** joins with the end of the ridge it forms a combination of common and hip jack rafters, because at the ridge end it has the common rafter plumb cut and the hip jack side cuts, these being plainly shown in the enlarged detail of end. **S,** is a hip jack rafter. **L,A,R,F,** are cripple rafters.

want to know *why* each particular number is used. This is easily understood by aid of fig. 971.

Here let ABCD be a square whose sides are 24 ins. long, and *abcdefg* L, an inscribed octagon. Each side of the octagon as *ab*, *bc*, etc., will measure 10 ins., that is, LF = one-half side = 5 ins. and by construction FM, = 12 ins. Now let FM, represent the run of a *common* rafter. Then LM, will be run of an *octagon* rafter, and DM, run of a hip or valley rafter. The

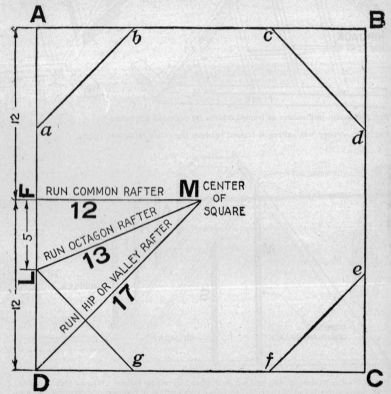

Fig. 971.—Square and inscribed octagon illustrating method of obtaining and use of points 12, 13, and 17 in application of square in obtaining length of rafters without aid of rafter tables.

values for run of octagon and hip or valley rafters (LM and DM) are obtained thus:

$$LM = \sqrt{FM^2 + LF^2} = \sqrt{12^2 + 5^2} = 13$$

$$DM = \sqrt{FM^2 + DF^2} = \sqrt{12^2 + 12^2} = 16.97, \text{ say } 17$$

Example.—What is the length of a *common* rafter having a 10 foot run and ⅜ pitch?

For a 10 ft. run the span = 2 × 10 = 20 ft. and with ⅜ pitch
rise = ⅜ of 20 = 7.5 ft.

$$\text{rise per foot run} = \frac{\text{rise} \times 12}{\text{run}} = \frac{7.5 \times 12}{10} = 9 \text{ ins.}$$

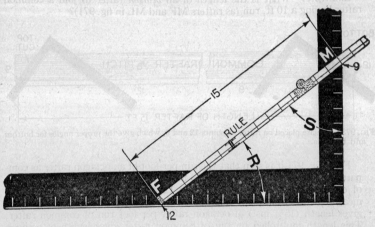

Fig. 972.—Rule placed on square at points 12 and 9, for obtaining length of common rafter per foot run with ⅜ pitch.

On the body of the square, fig. 972, take 12 ins. for 1 ft. of run, and on the tongue, 9 for rise per foot run. The diagonal or distance between the points thus obtained will be length of common rafter per foot run with ⅜ pitch. This distance FM, in fig. 971 measures 15 ins., or by calculation:

$$FM = \sqrt{12^2 + 9^2} = 15 \text{ ins.}$$

Since the length of run is 10 ft.,
length of rafter = 10 × length per foot = 10 × 15 = 150 ins., = 150 ÷ 12 = 12½ ft.

The combination of figures 12 and 9 on the square as in fig. 972 not only gives the length of rafter per foot run, but if the rule be considered as the rafter, the angles S and R, for top and bottom cuts are obtained. The points for making are accordingly found *by placing the square upon the rafter so that a portion of one arm of the square represents the run and a portion of the other arm, the rise.* For the common rafter with ⅜ pitch the points are 12 and 9, the square being placed on the rafter as in fig. 973.

Example.—What is the length of an *octagon* rafter to join a common rafter having a 10 ft. run (as rafters MF and ML in fig. 971)?

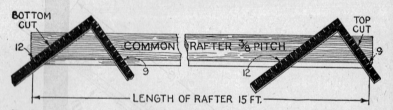

BOTTOM CUT 12 COMMON RAFTER ⅜ PITCH 9 TOP CUT 12 9

← LENGTH OF RAFTER 15 FT. →

Fig. 973.—Square placed on rafter at points 12 and 9, which give the proper angles for bottom and top cuts.

From fig. 971 it is seen that the run per foot of an octagon rafter as compared with a common rafter is as 13 to 12, and that the rise per 13 ins. run of octagon rafter is the same as per 12 ins. of common rafter. Hence measure across from point 13 and 9 on the square as MS in fig. 974, which gives length (15¾ ins.) of octagon rafter per foot run of common rafter. This length multiplied by run of common rafter gives length of octagon rafter, thus:

$$15\tfrac{3}{4} \times 10 = 157\tfrac{1}{2} \text{ ins.} = 13 \text{ ft. } 1\tfrac{1}{2} \text{ ins.}$$

Points 13 and 9 on the square (MS in fig. 974) give angles for top and bottom cuts.

Example.—What is the length of a hip or valley rafter to join a common rafter having a 10 ft. run (as rafters MF and MD in fig. 971)?

Fig. 971 shows that the run per foot of a hip or valley rafter as compared with a common rafter is as 17 to 12 and that the rise per 17 ins. run of hip or valley rafter is the same as per 12 ins. of common rafter. Hence measure across from points 17 and 9 on the square as LS in fig. 974 which gives length

(19¼ ins.) of hip or valley rafter per foot of common rafter. This length multiplied by run of common rafter gives length of hip or valley rafter, thus:

$$19¼ \times 10 = 192½ \text{ ins.} = 16 \text{ ft. } ½ \text{ in.}$$

Points 17 and 9 on the square (LS in fig. 974) give the angles for top and bottom cuts.

The following table gives the points on square for top and bottom cuts of various rafters.

Square Points for Top and Bottom Cuts

	PITCH	1	11/12	5/6	3/4	2/3	7/12	1/2	5/12	1/3	1/4	1/6	1/12
Tongue	Common						**12**						
	Octagon						**13**						
	Hip or Valley						**17**						
Body		24	22	20	18	16	14	12	10	8	6	4	2

Rafter Tables.—The arrangement of these tables varies considerably with different makes of square, not only in the way it is calculated but also in its position on the square. On some squares the rafter table is found on the face of the body, on others, on the back of the body. There are two general classes of rafter table, grouped according as the figures give:

1. Total length of rafter, or
2. Length of rafter per foot run.

Evidently where the total length is given there is no figuring to be done, but when the length is given per foot run, the reading must be multiplied by the length of run to obtain total length of rafter. To illustrate these differences directions for using several well known squares will now be given. These differences relate to the common and hip or valley rafter tables.

Class 1.—*Reading total length of rafter*

The Sargent square is selected as an example of **Class 1** reading rafter lengths direct without any figuring. The rafter tables occupy both sides of the body instead of being combined in one

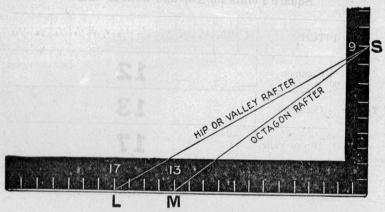

Fig. 974.—Measurements across square for octagon, and hip or valley rafters illustrating use of points **13** and **17**. MS, (**13**, 9) octagon rafter length per foot run of common rafter; LS, (**17**, 9) hip or valley rafter per foot run of common rafter ⅜ pitch.

table; that is, the common rafter table is found on the back side *and the hip, valley and jack* table on the face side.

Common rafter table.

The common rafter table, fig. 975, includes the outside edge graduations of the back of the square on both body and tongue and is in twelfths. The inch marks may represent inches or feet, and the twelfth marks, twelfths of an inch or twelfths of a

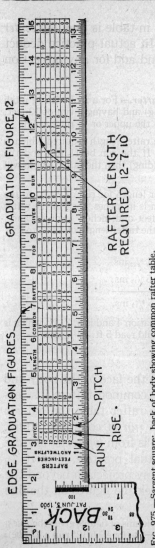

EDGE GRADUATION FIGURES

GRADUATION FIGURE 12

RAFTER LENGTH
REQUIRED 12-7-10

PITCH

RISE •

RUN

FIG. 975.—Sargent square; back of body showing common rafter table.

foot (that is inches), as a scale. The *edge graduation figures* above the table represent the *run* of the rafter and under the proper figure on the line representing the *pitch* will be found in the table, the rafter length required. The pitch is represented by the figures at the left of the table under the word PITCH thus:

12 feet run to	4 feet rise	is	1/6	pitch			
12	"	6	"	"	"	1/4	"
12	"	8	"	"	"	1/3	"
12	"	10	"	"	"	5/12	"
12	"	12	"	"	"	1/2	"
12	"	15	"	"	"	5/8	"
12	"	18	"	"	"	3/4	"

The length of common rafter given in table is *from top center of ridge board to outer edge of plate*. In actual practice deduct for one-half thickness of ridge board and add for any projection of eave beyond the plate.

To Find the Length of a Common Rafter.— For a roof with ⅙ pitch (that is, rise = ⅙ the width of the building) and having a run of 12 feet, follow in the common rafter table (fig. 975) the upper or ⅙ pitch ruling.

Find under the graduation figure 12, the rafter length required which is 12, 7, 10 which means 12 feet 7 $^{10}/_{12}$ ins. If the run be 11 feet and the pitch ½ (or the rise ½ the width of the building) then the rafter length will be 15, 6, 8, which means 15 feet 6 $^{8}/_{12}$ ins.

Again, if the run be 25 ft., add the rafter length for run of 20 ft. to the rafter length for run of 5 ft. When the run is in inches, then in the rafter table read inches and twelfths instead of feet and inches. For instance, if with ½ pitch the run be 12 ft. 4 ins., add the rafter length of 4 ins. to that of 12 ft. as follows:

For run of 12 ft. the rafter length is 16 ft. 11 $^{8}/_{12}$ ins.

For run of 4 ins. the rafter length is 5 $^{8}/_{12}$ ins.

Total 17 ft. 5 $^{4}/_{12}$ ins.

The run of 4 ins. is found under the graduation 4 and is 5, 7, 11, which is approximately 5 $^{8}/_{12}$ ins. If it were ft. it would read 5 ft. 7 $^{11}/_{12}$ ins.

Hip rafter table.

This table as shown in fig. 976 is on the face of the body and is used substantially as the table for common rafters just explained. In connection with the hip rafter table the outside edge graduation figures represent the *run* of common rafters. The length of rafter given in the table is from *top center of ridge board to outer edge of plate*. In actual practice, deduct ½ thickness of ridge board and add for any projection beyond the plate for eave. In using the table, seek the figures on the line with the required pitch of the roof.

Under heading "Pitch" the set of three columns of figures gives the *pitch*; the seven pitches in common use, as ⅙ — 12 — 4 (for each 12″ run a 4″ rise).

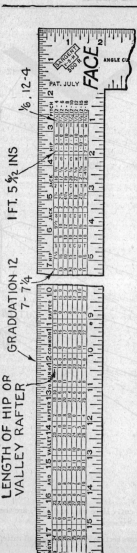

FIG. 976.—Sargent square; face of body showing hip rafter table and hip or valley readings referred to in the text.

Under heading "Hip" *the set of figures gives for each pitch the length of hip and valley rafter per foot* of run of common rafter, as 1 ft. 5⁵/₁₂ ins. for ⅙ pitch.

Under heading "Jack" *(16 ins. on center) the set of figures gives the length of the shortest jack rafter, spaced 16 ins. on center which is also the difference in length of succeeding jack rafters.

Example.—If the jack rafters be spaced 16 ins. on center for a ⅙ pitch roof, find lengths of jacks and cut bevels.

NOTE.—Home made *fence* for square. A *fence* may be defined in general as *a guide fitted to a tool.* As adapted to the steel square it is a long strip arranged to be clamped to the body and tongue in any angular position, being useful where a number of pieces such as rafters must be similarly marked. A good home made fence for the square may readily be made from a stick of hard wood about 2 ins. wide, 1¼ ins. thick and 2½ ft. long. Cut a saw kerf from both ends into which the saw will slide, leaving about 8 ins. solid wood near the middle. The fence is secured to the square in any desired position by means of clamp bolts. A series of holes may be bored through the fence to receive the bolts or in place of these narrow slots may be cut each side of the solid middle section, extending almost to the ends of the fence, and in which the bolts may slide to desired position and there clamped. Evidently where a number of pieces are to be similarly marked (as rafters) they may be uniformly marked by using a fence, whereas with independent setting each time no two would be marked exactly alike, owing to the difficulty of placing the setting numbers exactly over the edge of the timber, especially when hurriedly done.

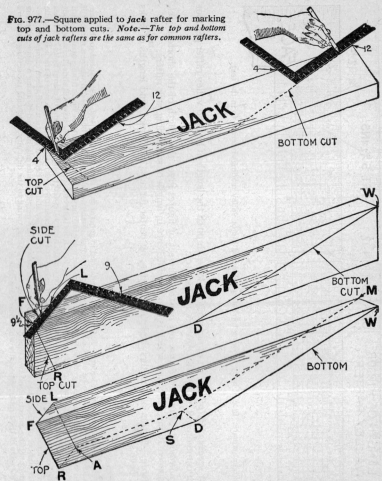

Fig. 977.—Square applied to *jack* rafter for marking top and bottom cuts. *Note.—The top and bottom cuts of jack rafters are the same as for common rafters.*

Fig. 978.—Square applied to *jack* rafter for marking side cut. Here FR, and DW, are the marks for top and bottom cuts previously marked in fig. 977.

Fig. 979.—*Jack* rafter cut as marked in fig. 978 LARF, shows section cut at top end of rafter and MSDW. section cut at bottom end

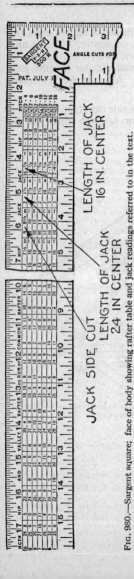

FIG. 980.—Sargent square; face of body showing rafter table and jack readings referred to in the text.

The jack top and bottom cuts (or plumb and heel cuts) are same as for common rafter. Take 12 on tongue of square (as before explained) and on the body take the figure which represents the rise per foot of the roof, or if the pitch be given take the figures in the table on page 357 corresponding to the given pitch. Thus for ⅙ pitch these points are 12, 4.

Fig. 977 shows square on jack in this position for marking top and bottom cuts.

Look along the line of ⅙ pitch (fig. 980) under *jack* (16 in. center) and find 16⅞ which is the length in *inches* of the shortest jack and is also the amount to be added for the second jack. Deduct for half the thickness of hip rafter because jack rafter lengths given in table are to centers. Also add for projection beyond outer edge of plate if any.

Look along the line of ⅙ pitch (fig. 980) under *Jack* (*side cut*) and find 9-9½ for ⅙ pitch. These figures refer to the graduated scale on the edge of the arm of the square.

To obtain the required bevel take 9 on one arm and 9½ on the other as shown in fig. 978.*

It should be carefully noted that the *last figure or figure to the right* gives the point on the marking side of the square, that is, mark on the 9½ side as shown in the figure.

---

*NOTE.—The figures for side cuts of jacks are also correct for cuts of the valley moulding at the junction of two gables, etc. In stair building as a rule the stringers rise on a rough floor, hence, allow for the thickness of finished floor in measuring for the first rise.

Under heading "Jack" (**24 ins. on center**) the set of figures gives the length of the shortest jack rafter spaced 24 ins. on center, which is also the difference in length of succeeding jack rafters, as 2 ft. 1¼ ins. for ⅙ pitch. Deduct for half the thickness of hip or valley rafter because jack rafter lengths given in the table are to centers. Also add for projection beyond the plate.

Under heading "Hip" the set of figures gives the side cut of hip and valley rafter against ridge board or deck, as 7—7¼ for ⅙ pitch (mark on the 7¼ side).

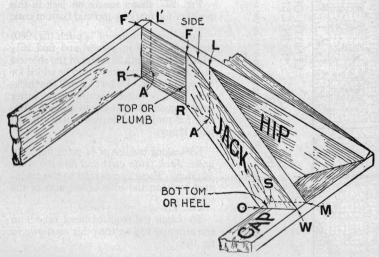

FIG. 981.—*Jack* rafter (as cut by method in figs. 977 to 979) in position on roof showing fit at ends with hip rafter and cap. Here as in fig. 979 LARF, shows section cut at top end of jack, and MSODW, section cut at bottom end.

To get the cut of the sheathing and shingles (whether hip or valley) reverse the figures under hip—as 7¼—7 instead of 7—7¼.

For (hip) top and bottom cuts take 17 on body of square and take on tongue the figure which represents the rise per foot of the roof.

Figs. 982 to 984 show marking and cut of hip rafter and fig. 981 rafter in position resting on cap and ridge. Here the section L'A'R'F' resting on ridge is the same as L'A'R'F' in fig. 984.

Under heading "Hip and Valley" the set of figures gives for each pitch the length of hip or valley rafter of run of common rafter. For instance, for roof having ⅙ pitch under the figure 12 (representing the run of common rafter or half the width of the building) along the ⅙ pitch line of figures find 17, 5, 3 which means 17 ft. 5 $\frac{3}{12}$ ins., length of hip or valley rafter. Deduct for half the thickness of the ridge board and add for eave overhang beyond the plate, which is the length of hip or valley rafter required for roof of ⅙ pitch and common rafter run of 12 ft.

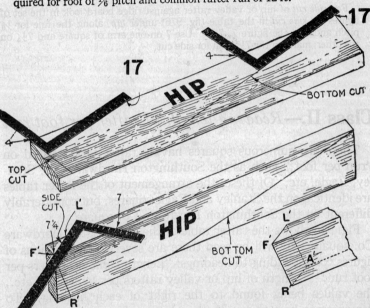

Fig. 982.—Square applied to *hip* rafter for marking top and bottom cuts. Note that the fixed number *17* is used for hip rafters.

Fig. 983.—Square applied to *hip* rafter for marking side cut. Here F'L' is the mark for side cut and F'R' the mark for top cut previously made in fig. 982.

Fig. 984.—Detail of upper end of *hip* rafter showing section L'A'R'F, cut to bevel required for ridge.

Example.—Find the length of hip rafter for a building 24 ft. span, ¼ pitch (4 ins. rise per ft.).

In the hip rafter table (fig. 976) along the line of figures for ⅙ pitch and under the graduation figure 12 (representing half the span or run of common rafter) find 17, 5, 3 which means 17 ft. 5 $\frac{3}{12}$ ins. the required length of hip or valley rafter. Deduct for half the thickness of the ridge board and add for any overhang required beyond the plate

For top and bottom cuts of hip or valley rafter take 17 on body and 4 (the rise of the roof per ft.). Mark on 17 side gives the bottom cut, on 4 side, the top cut.

For *side cut* of hip or valley rafter against ridge board look in the set of figures for *side cut* in the table (fig. 976) under *hip*, along the line for $\frac{1}{6}$ pitch and find the figure 7, 7¼. Use 7 on one arm of square and 7¼ on the other; mark on the 7¼ arm for side cut.

Class II.—*Reading length of rafter per foot run*

There are numerous squares having rafter tables based on "run per foot," such as the Southington Hardware Co., Stanley, Eagle, etc. Of these, the arrangement of the rafter tables are identical on the Stanley and Eagle squares, but considerably different on the Southington Hardware Co. square.

Fig. 985 shows the rafter table of the Southington Hardware Co. square. As will be seen there are several combinations of figures corresponding to headings: "Length common rafters per foot run," "Length of hip or valley rafters per foot run," etc., the values being found to the right of each heading. To demonstrate how to use these values or figures take the first combination of figures headed "Length of common rafter per foot run." To the right of this heading are several pairs of figures, the upper figure of each pair, as 3, 4, 6, 8, 10, 12, 15, 16, 18, means *rise (in ins.) per foot run*. Under each of these numbers is a number which means the *length of rafter per foot run*, corresponding to the rise given immediately above.

Example.—Find the length of a common rafter on a building 24 ft. wide and ½ pitch

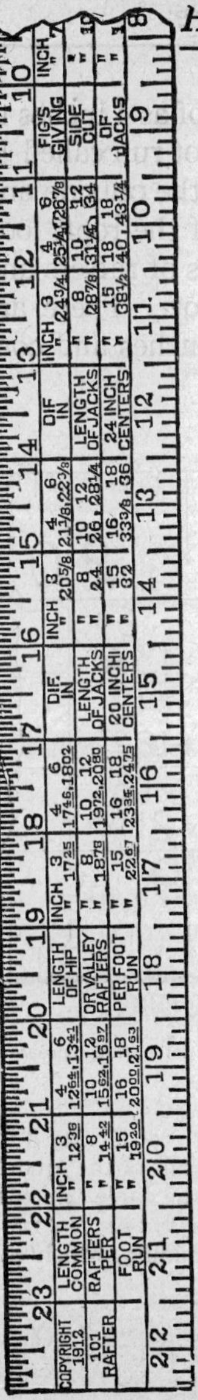

The rise per foot run = pitch × span ÷ run

= ½ × 24 ÷ 12 = 1 ft. or 12 ins.

In the combination of numbers headed "Length of common rafter per foot run" (fig. 985) look for 12, and under the number will be found 16.97, which is the length of a common rafter per foot run. Hence, since run is 12 ft.

length common rafter = 16.97 × 12 = 203.64 ins., or

203.64 ÷ 12 = 16.97 ft.

This reading is shown in detail in fig. 986.

The other combinations of figures for hip or valley rafters, jacks are read in a similar manner rendering further explanation unnecessary.

The Eagle rafter table, as shown in fig. 987, is located on the face of the body of the square and is composed of six rows of figures which are lettered at the left end of the body to show their use.

The figures found in these six rows refer to the outside edge graduations which in the case of the side cuts are clearly marked beyond all mistake.

The inch marks may represent inches or feet, and the twelfths may represent twelfths of an inch or twelfths of a foot that is regarded as a

FIG. 985.—Southington Hardware Co. square; back of tongue showing rafter table and illustrating *Class II* in which the reading gives *length of rafter per foot run*, and the grouping of rafter values, the latter feature being special with this square.

scale. The edge marks represent the rise of a roof as 4 inches to the foot run called 1/6 pitch, or 6 inches to the foot run called 1/4 pitch. After looking at the inch line figures on the outside and finding the figure that is the same as the rise of the roof, look underneath it and find a table giving the lengths of rafters and all side cuts. The run in every table is 1 foot. There are seventeen of these tables commencing at two inches and continuing to eighteen inches.

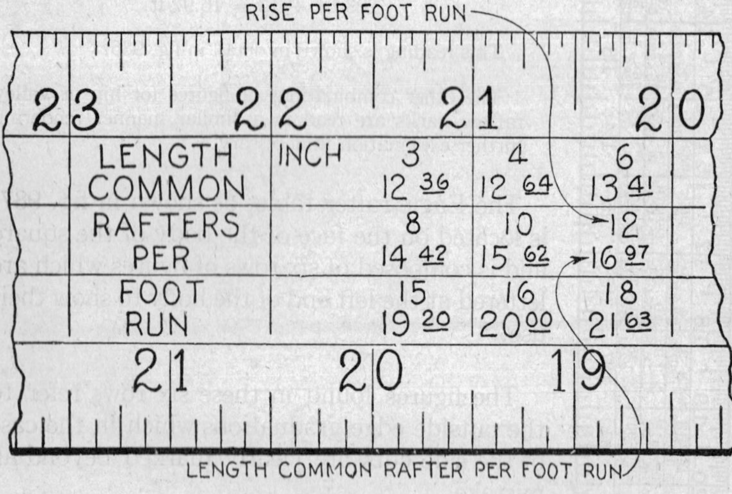

Fig. 986.—Southington Hardware Co. square; enlarged portion of rafter table showing reading referred to in the text.

Example.—Find the length of a common rafter for a roof having 8 in. rise or 1/3 pitch. 2C ft. span under 8 on the upper edge scale of the square, fig 987, will be found a table and the first figures of the table which is designated at the left end of the body, "*Length of main rafters per foot run*" are 14.42. Multiply this by half of the width of the building, which will give the whole length of the rafters, thus:

$$14.42 \times \tfrac{1}{2} \text{ of } 20 = 144.2 \text{ ins., or}$$
$$144.2 \div 12 = 12.02 \text{ ft.}$$

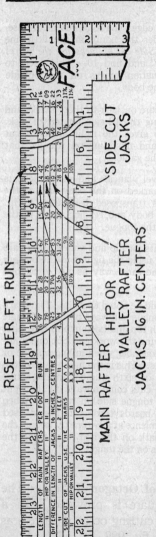

MAIN RAFTER   HIP OR
VALLEY RAFTER
JACKS 16 IN. CENTERS

SIDE CUT
JACKS

RISE PER FT. RUN

FIG. 987.—Back quare; face of body showing rafter tables and readings referred to in the text.

Example.—Find the length of a hip or valley rafter for a roof having 8 in. rise per foot run or ⅓ pitch 20 ft. span. On the outer edge scale, fig. 987, find 8. Look below this number on second line marked "*Length of hip or valley rafters per foot run*" and find 18.76, then

Length of hip or valley rafter = 18.76 × ½ of 20 = 187.6 ins. = 187.6 ÷ 12 = 15.63 ft.

Example.—Find the lengths of jack rafters for a roof with 8 in. rise per foot run ⅓ pitch 16 in. centers; 2 ft. centers.

In fig. 987 take 8 on the outer edge scale to represent the rise. Look under the figure in the third

line marked "*Difference in lengths of jacks 16 in. center*" and find 19.23 ins. This is the length of the first jack rafter when they are spaced 16 ins. between centers, and it is also the difference between the lengths of the others, each one being 19.23 ins. longer than the one nearer the first one. The figure immediately below in the fourth line, 28.84 ins. is the length of the first jack when they are spaced 24 ins. between centers and is also the difference in lengths of the others.

Example.—Find side cuts on jacks and hip and valley rafters for roof with 8 in. rise or ⅓ pitch.

The numbers 8 and 12 are points for top and bottom cuts as before explained. In fig. 987, take 8 on

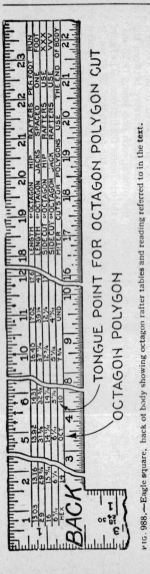

FIG. 988.—Eagle square, back of body showing octagon rafter tables and reading referred to in the text.

the upper edge scale to represent the rise Look under the figure in the fifth line marked *"Side cut of jacks use the marks* ∧ ∧ ∧ ∧*"* and find 10. This refers to the graduation marks on the outside edge of the body.

Set square on jack to these marks and mark along the 12 side for cut of jack. This also gives the right angle to cut plancier and moulding on the jet that runs up the gable.

The level plancier and moulding cuts can be marked on the body side or the references transposed using the 12 in. mark on body and reading given in the table on the tongue.

Side cuts for hip and valley rafters are found by using the figures in the bottom line in the same way as just explained for jacks.

It should be noted that the 12 in. mark on the tongue is always used in all angle cuts, both top and bottom and side cuts, thus leaving the workman but one number to remember when laying outside or angle cuts. This is the figure taken from the fifth or sixth number in the table. The side cuts come always on the right hand or tongue side on rafters. When marking boards these can be reversed for convenience at any time by taking the 12 in. mark on the body and using the references on the tongue.

Table of Octagon Rafters.—The Eagle square is provided with a table for cutting octagon rafters as shown in fig. 988.

In this table the first line of figures from the top gives the length of *octagon hip rafters* per foot of run.

The second line of figures gives length of *jack rafter* for one foot space from octagon hip.

The third line of figures gives the reference to the graduated edge that will give the side cut for octagon *hip rafters*.

The fourth line of figures gives the reference to the graduated edge that will give the side cuts for *jacks*.

The tables are used in a manner similar to that used for the

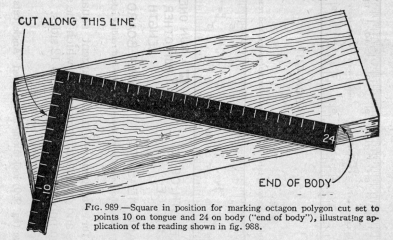

Fig. 989 —Square in position for marking octagon polygon cut set to points 10 on tongue and 24 on body ("end of body"), illustrating application of the reading shown in fig. 988.

regular rafter tables just described and need no further explanation except the last line or bottom row of figures which gives the bevel of intersecting lines of various regular polygons. It is used as follows: At the right end of body on the bottom line may be read *mitre cuts for polygons—use end of body*.

Example.—Find angle cut for an octagon.

For a figure of 8 sides to the right of the word *Oct.* in last line of figures find 10. This is the tongue reading, the end of the body being the other point as shown in fig. 989.

FIG. 990.—Sargent square; face of tongue showing table of *angle cuts for polygons,* and reading referred to in the text.

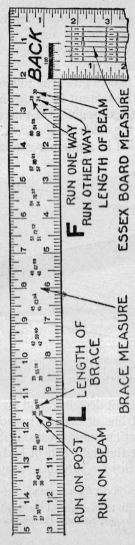

FIG. 991.—Sargent square; back of tongue showing table of *brace measure* and reading referred to in the text.

Table of Angle Cuts for Polygons.—On the Sargent square this table is found on the face of the tongue and gives setting points at which the square should be placed to mark cuts for common polygons having from 5 to 12 sides.

Example. Find bevel cuts for an octagon or 8 side.

On the face of the tongue (fig. 990) look along line marked "Angle cuts for polygons" and find the reading "8 sides 18—7½." This means that the square must be placed at 18 on one arm and 7½ on the other to obtain the octagon cut as in fig. 992.

Table of Brace Measure.—This table on the Sargent square as shown in fig. 991 is along the center of the back of the tongue and gives the length of common braces.

Example.—If the run be 36 ins. on the post and the same on the beam, what is the length of the brace?

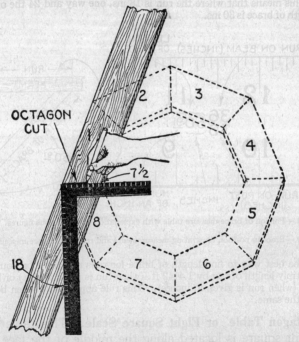

Fig. 992.—Application of square for angle cuts of polygons. The square is here shown set to points 18 and 7½ In constructing an 8-sided figure as an octagon cap for instance, mark the last figure in the reading is the setting for marking side: mark as shown Saw eight pieces of equal length, having this angle cut at each end of each piece, and the pieces will fit together to make an eight-sided figure, in size depending upon the length of the pieces. The dotted lines show figure as it would appear with the eight pieces in position

In the brace table or collection of figures, along the central portion of the back of the tongue (figs. 991 and 993) look (at L) for

$$\frac{36}{36} \; 50.91$$

This reading means that for a run of 36 ins. on post and 36 ins. on beam the length of beam is 50.91 ins. At the end of the table (at F near body) will be found the reading

$$\frac{18}{24} \; 30$$

This means that where the run is 18 ins. one way and 24 the other, the length of brace is 30 ins.

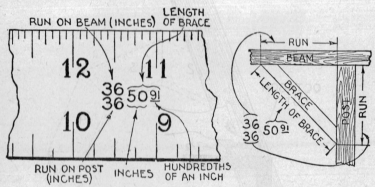

Fig. 993.—Portion of brace measure table with explanation of the various figures.

Fig. 994.—Brace in position illustrating measurements and reading of brace measure table.

The best way to find length of brace for runs not given on square is to multiply length of run by 1.4142 ft. (when run is given in feet) or by 16.97 ins. (when run is given in inches). This rule applies only when both runs are the same.

Octagon Table or Eight Square Scale.—This table on the Sargent square is located along the middle of the face of the

---

NOTE.—*Hundredth scale.* On most squares there is a scale of 1 inch length graduated into 100 parts, sub-divided into 20 parts, that will be found convenient when using the brace and rafter tables where decimal fractions occur. This is usually located in the corner near the brace measure table.

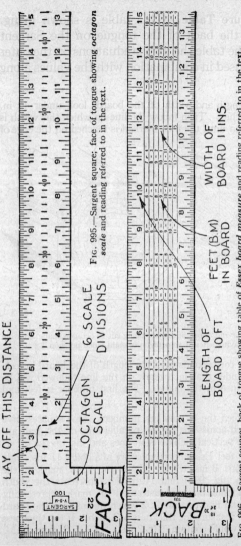

Fig. 996.—Sargent square; back of tongue showing table of *Essex board measure* and reading referred to in the text.

Fig. 995.—Sargent square; face of tongue showing *octagon scale* and reading referred to in the text.

tongue and is used for laying off lines to cut an *eight square* or *octagon* stick of timber from a square timber.

In fig. 997, let ABCD, represent the end section or butt of a square stick of timber 6 × 6 inches. Through the center draw the lines AB and CD, parallel with the sides and at right angles to each other. With dividers take as many spaces, 6, from the scale as there are inches in width of the stick, and lay off this space on either side of the point A. as A*a* and A*h*; lay off in the same way the same spaces from the point B, as B*d*. B*e*; also C*b*, C*c*, and D*f*. D*g*. Then draw the lines *ab*, *cd*, *ef*, and *gh*. Cut off at the edges to lines *ab*, *cd*, *ef*, and *gh*, thus obtaining the octagon or 8-sided piece as in fig. 998.

Essex Board Measure Table.—This table is shown in fig. 996, and appears on the back of the tongue on the Sargent square. In applying the table the inch graduations on the outer edge of the square are used in combination with the values along the five parallel lines.

After measuring the length and width of the board, look under 12 in. mark for the width in inches. Then follow the line on which this width is stamped toward either end until the inch marked is reached on the edge of

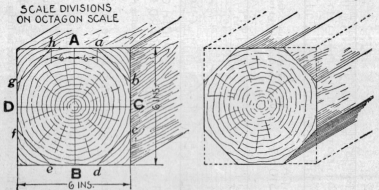

SCALE DIVISIONS
ON OCTAGON SCALE

FIGS. 997 and 998.—Square timber and appearance after being cut to octagon shape, showing application of octagon scale in laying sides of an octagon or eight-sided polygon.

the square where number corresponds with the length of the board in feet, and the number found under that inch mark on the line followed will be the feet and inches contained in the board. The first number is feet and second number inches.

Instead of a dash between the ft. and ins. numbers, some squares have the inch division continued across the several parallel lines of the scale appearing on one side of the vertical inch division lines and ins. on the other.

Example.—How many feet Essex board measure in a board 11 ins. wide 10 ft. long and 1 in. thick? 3 ins. thick? Under the 12 in. mark on the outer edge of the square (fig. 996) find 11, which represents the width of the board in ins. Then follow on that line to the 10 in. mark (representing length of board in feet) and find on line 9, 2 which means that the board contains 9 ft. 2 ins. board measure for thickness of 1 inch. If the thickness were 3 ins. then the board would contain (9 ft. 2 ins.) ×3=27 ft. 6 ins. B.M

CHAPTER 24

Joints and Joinery

In carpentry the term *joint* means *the union of two or more smooth or even surfaces admitting of a close fitting or junction*, as a joint between two pieces of timber. Joinery, or the art of joint making is an advanced branch of carpentry. It requires considerable skill to make a good joint, especially some of the complicated forms, because the parts must be shaped to dimensions with precision so that the fit will be accurate. It is work of precision and requires not only accurate tooling but accurate laying out.

Formerly, before the introduction of numerous iron fittings, joinery, especially in building construction, was practiced more than now. However, a thorough knowledge of joinery is still indispensable to the first class carpenter. There is a multiplicity of joints, all of which may be divided into two general classes according to the manner in which the joining pieces are brought together, as

1. Plain or butt joints.

a. Straight
b. Dowel pin
c. Corner { square, mitre
d. Mitre
e. Feather
f. Splice

2. Lap joints.

a. Dado (housed butt)
b. Scarf
c. Mortise and tenon
d. Dove tail
e. Wedge
f. Tongue and groove

1. Plain or Butt Joint

The term *plain* or *butt* joint signifies a joint in which the end or side of one piece is placed, or "butts" against the end of the other.

Straight Joint.—This is the simplest form of joint and has many uses, such as flooring, boat planking, etc. However, to

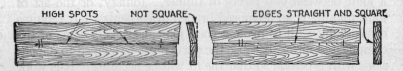

FIGS. 999 to 1,002.—Straight butt side joint. *First method, by fitting.* After planing with jack and jointer planes to square and straighten the edges, place the two pieces together as in fig. 999. Make marks, so they may be placed in same position each time the edges are tried. After the first planing the edges will probably not come together at all points because of high spots. The fit of the edges is tested by sighting, placing the pieces between the eye and light, the low spots being easily detected by the light coming through. The joint is made perfect by repeated planing and testing. Fig. 1,000 shows boards out of square, and figs. 1,001 and 1,002 the perfect joint.

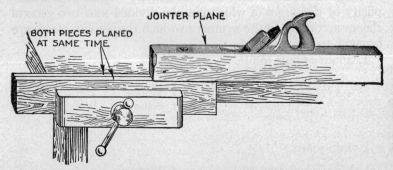

FIG. 1,003.—Straight butt side joint. *Second method, by planing both edges together.* This requires more skill in planing and it is necessary that the plane iron should be straight on the edge and carefully sharpened and adjusted.

make a good fitting butt joint requires skill in the use of planes. It may be made with or without the use of glue.

Straight butt joints may be classed as *side*, or *end*, according as the pieces are joined along their sides or ends.

To make the side joint, first square and straighten the edges with jack and fore or jointer planes, frequently testing the surfaces with try square and fitting until a perfect fit is obtained, as in figs. 1,001 and 1,002. Then if glue is to be used, apply to each of the edges good strong (fresh dissolved) hot liquid glue and, in some way, clamp and hold them tight together. If the wood be warmed better results are obtained as the glue is not chilled when it

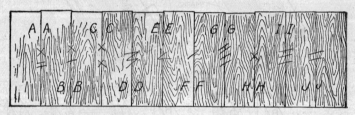

Fig. 1,004.—Narrow boards jointed and placed together showing system of marking so that the same edges will come together in assembling.

touches the surface. When dry, the adhesion will be permanent. This method is good for short, clean work, such as furniture, bottoms of drawers or light cabinet work, but for long, heavy and thick pieces, more labor, care and material becomes necessary.

Dowel Pin Joint.—This joint may be considered as a substitute for the mortised joint. If well made and not exposed to the weather it is an efficient substitute. A dowel point is simply a butt joint reinforced by dowel pins which fit tightly in holes bored in each member to align with each other. Fig. 1,013 shows dowel, the joint ready for assembly with dowel pins inserted. Figs. 1,014 and 1,015 show end view and plan of the joint.

Success in making a dowel pin joint depends upon the accuracy of marking and boring the holes for the pin, for unless the hole be bored in perfect alignment and straight it will be impossible to assemble the pieces, or when assembled, the pieces will not properly align. The method of making a dowel pin joint is shown in figs. 1,005 to 1,012.

In gluing dowels, the glue should be put in the holes and not on the dowels, otherwise it will be scraped off as the dowels are pushed in place.

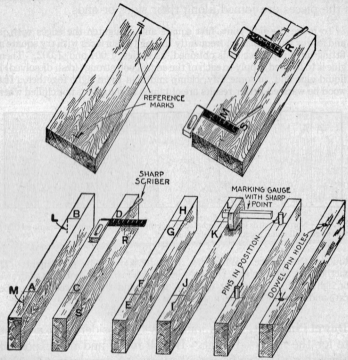

REFERENCE MARKS

SHARP SCRIBER

MARKING GAUGE WITH SHARP POINT

PINS IN POSITION

DOWEL PIN HOLES

Figs. 1,005 to 1,012.—Method of making a dowel pin joint. After jointing the two pieces reference marks are made as in fig. 1,005 so they can be placed in the same relative position. With the reference marks registering, scribe marks MS, and LR, at points where dowel pins are to be placed as in figs. 1,007 and 1,008. In scribing, use try square and sharp pointed scriber as shown. Square these lines across the edges by scribing lines A, B, C, D, as in figs. 1,007 and 1,008. Set marking gauge to half thickness of the boards and scribe lines EF, GH, IJ, and KL, as in figs. 1,009 and 1,010. At the intersections of these lines holes are to be bored with great accuracy. To center the bit at these intersections make small holes with a scratch awl. This will cause the bit to start true with the intersection, otherwise the spiral point of the bit would push to one side as it enters the wood. The dowels should be a nice fit in the holes. The size of holes depends on thickness of the boards, in general a trifle less than half the thickness. Thus, for ⅞ inch boards use ¾ inch dowels. Figs. 1,011 and 1,012 show holes bored and dowels in position.

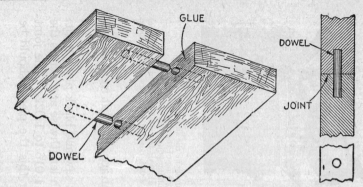

FIGS. 1,013 to 1,015.—Views of dowel pin joint. Fig. 1,013, parts ready to assemble, dowels in position. Figs. 1,014 and 1,015, end view and plan of joint.

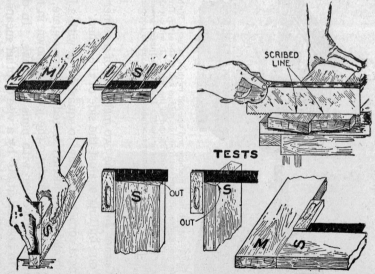

FIGS. 1,016 to 1,022.—Method of making a corner joint. First scribe right lines near the end of the pieces MS, as in figs. 1,016 and 1,017, using try square and sharp pointed scriber or knife. For small work the pieces may be placed on a bench hook with the scribed lines in line and both sawed in one operation with a back saw as in fig. 1,018. After sawing, the joint surface of S, should be block planed as in fig. 1,019, and continuously tested with try square as in figs. 1,020 to 1,022 until a perfect fit at right angles is obtained.

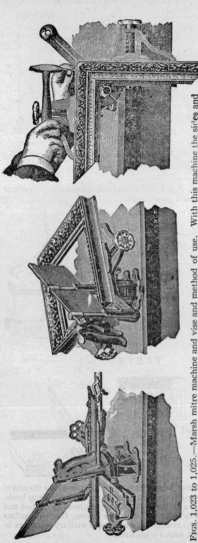

FIGS. 1,023 to 1,025.—Marsh mitre machine and vise and method of use. With this machine the sides and ends of a frame can be measured and cut from one side as well as the other, thus admitting of the machine being placed in any position at either side or end of the bench. It will cut the moulding equally as well from the *back* or *outside* as from the *front* or *inside*. Fig. 1,023 shows machine with back saw in position; fig. 1,024, position when sawing last mitre; fig. 1,025, position for boring and nai ing. It can be adjusted toward the right or left while either in a horizontal or perpendicular position.

Square Corner Joint.—The two members of a corner joint are joined at right angles, the end of one butting against the side of the other.

In making a corner joint saw to squared line with a back saw and block plane to fit. The work should be frequently tested with try square, both lengthwise and across the joint. The method of making the joint is shown in figs. 1,016 to 1,022. The joint may be fastened together with nails or screws. In doing this the pieces should be firmly held in position at 90° by a vise or other means.

FIG. 1,026.—Marsh picture frame vise. With this tool any frame can be held in proper position for nailing. It has a base with swivel attachment, allowing the frame to be swung or tipped in any position

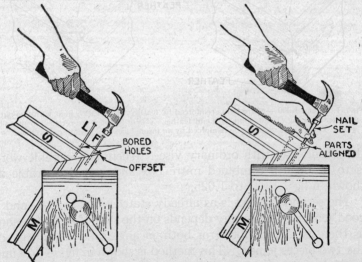

FIGS. 1,027 and 1,028.—Makeshift method of nailing mitre joint on picture frame by offsetting Holes are bored in the piece S, for the nails LF, and M, placed in the vise. The piece S, should be slightly *offset* as shown in fig. 1,027, so that when the nails are driven home by aid of nail set, S, will slide to the right as the pieces are brought closely together, thus bringing S, in alignment with M, as shown in fig. 1,028. Success in making a good joint by this method depends upon getting the right amount of offset and this is a matter of experience. The joint should be reinforced with glue.

Mitred Corner Joint.—This type of joint is used mostly in making picture frames. To properly make a mitred joint, a picture frame vise should be used in fastening the pieces together instead of the makeshift method of offsetting in nailing. In fact, a picture framing shop, to be worthy of the name, should be provided with a picture frame vise, one type of which is shown in fig. 1,026.

In cutting the 45° mitre, use a mitre box. After sawing, dress up and fit the ends with a block plane. There are two ways to nail a mitred joint: the correct way with picture frame vise and

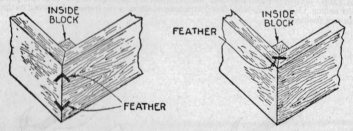

FIGS. 1,029 and 1,030 —Mitre joints reinforced by feathers Fig 1,029, joint with two outer edge feathers; fig. 1,030, joint with end feather These feathers are retained in place by glue. These joints may also be reinforced by an inside block as shown in dotted lines.

the wrong way with ordinary vise. Where considerable work is to be done a combined mitre box and vise is desirable as shown in figs. 1,023 to 1,025.

The second method is as already stated, a makeshift, and a good joint made this way depends on the skill of the workman, as there is chance for error both in angle and alignment of the two pieces joined. This method is shown in figs. 1,027 and 1,028.

Feather Joint.—In this form of joint a groove is made in each of the pieces to be joined and a tongue or *feather* made as a separate piece and inserted as shown in figs. 1,037 to 1,040. This form of feather joint has been largely replaced by the familiar tongue and groove joint used in flooring, but it is desirable to know how to make a feather joint in emergency.

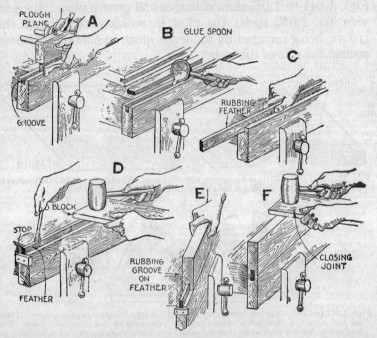

FIGS. 1,031 to 1,036.—Method of making a feather joint. After jointing the two boards to be joined, each board is grooved with a plough plane as at **A**, the depth of each groove being ⅓ half width of the feather. Next (after heating the boards) nearly fill one groove with hot glue using a glue spoon as at **B**. Insert feather (which should fit nicely but loose enough to slide easily) and rub feather back and forth to work in and remove excess glue as at **C**. Now tack stops at each end to prevent feather running out while rubbing; knock feather well into groove with mallet, using block to prevent denting feather; and apply hot glue to the edges and both sides of the projecting feather with glue brush as at D. Similarly applying hot glue to the other piece, rub it back and forth to work in and expel excess glue as at E. Finally, place boards in position and knock the joint well together as at F, and it will be advisable to place same in a vise, holding the boards firmly together until glue hardens.

The main reason for the feather joint seems to be that when jointing two pieces of soft wood, a hard wood feather (which for maximum strength should be cut across the grain) may be inserted, rendering the joint less liable to snap than if a tongue were cut on the soft wood itself and lengthwise with the grain. Figs. 1,041 to 1,045 show a tongue and groove plane; the end view fig. 1,045 shows the plow in position for cutting the groove, being centered by the fence which in planing is pressed against the side of the board.

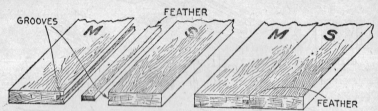

FIGS. 1,037 to 1,040.—Parts and assembly of feather joint. The feathers fit into the grooves in M, and S, and when assembled has the appearance as shown in fig. 1,040.

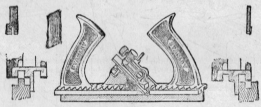

FIGS. 1,041 to 1,045.—Stanley double-end match planes for cutting tongue and groove. There are two cutters, a plow and a tongue tool, both governed by one permanent fence. The tongue tool has one edge wider than the other, which overhangs one side when tonguing on center. Both tongue and groove are cut by working the tool in the same direction, by reversing it end for end.

Splice Joint.—This kind of joint is similar to the familiar double strap butt joint used on the longitudinal seams of some shell boilers. The two pieces of wood to be joined are placed end to end and joined by *fish pieces* placed on each side and secured by through cross bolts, or nails as in fig. 1,046. These fish plates may be either of wood or iron and either plain or with projecting ends.

In gluing dowels, the glue should be put in the holes and not on the dowels, otherwise it will be scraped off as the dowels are pushed in place.

The plain type shown in fig. 1,046 is suitable when the stress is compression only, but when the joint is subject to tension the fish plates should be anchored to the main members by keys or projections as shown in figs. 1,048 and 1,049.

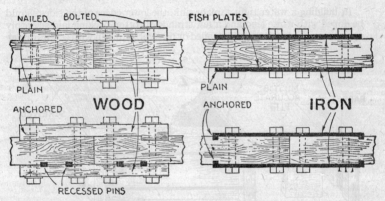

FIGS. 1,046 to 1,049.—Various splice or fish joints. Fig. 1,046 shows the plain joint with wooden fish plates. It may be either nailed or bolted, but in either case it is suitable only for compression stress. When subjected to tension stress the plates, if of wood, should be anchored by end projections on the plates or by keys as shown in figs. 1,048. The thickness of wooden plates should be at least half thickness of the main members. Fig. 1,047 shows plain iron plates and fig. 1,048 iron plates anchored by projections at the ends.

2. Lap Joints

In the various joints grouped under this classification one of the pieces to be joined laps over, or into the other, hence the name *lap joint*. There is a great variety of these joints, each of which will be briefly explained.

Housed Butt or Rabbetted Joint.—A rabbet is cut across the side of one of the pieces to be joined near the end to receive the end of the other piece as shown in fig. 1,050. This form of joint is easily made water tight and is therefore frequently used for tanks and sinks. It is not used where its appearance is considered because of the unsightly projecting end.

In making this joint, the rabbet should be cut accurately to size of the piece it is to receive especially when the joint must be water tight.

In building a water tight tank or sink, the lower edges of the sides should be doped with white lead and a few strands of cotton wicking laid smoothly upon them. The bottom being nailed or preferably put on with screws driven

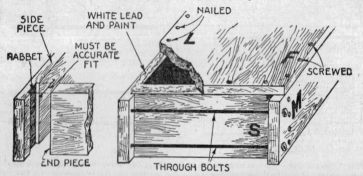

Figs. 1,050 and 1,051.—Housed butt, or rabbeted joint and wooden tank construction. Fig. 1,050 shows rabbet cut near end of the side piece. The end piece which is to fit in the rabbet, should be thicker than the side piece to permit nailing or fastening with screws without splitting and the end piece should accurately fit the rabbet. Fig. 1,051 shows assembly of a small tank with housed butt joint. The bottom may be either fastened with nails as at L, or with screws as at F. Part of the bottom is cut away showing white lead and cotton wicking placed on lower edge to make tight joint. The end piece may be fastened to the sides either with screws as at M, or by through bolts as at S. The latter makes a very strong construction. When through bolts are used, amply large washers should be provided to prevent heads and nuts cutting into the wood.

well home, will press tightly upon the wicking and caulk the joint. If the work has been properly done, the joint will be water tight.

Scarf Joints.—By definition a scarf joint is *an endwise lap joint made by beveling off, notching, or otherwise cutting away the sides of two timbers so as, when assembled, to form one continuous piece, usually without increased thickness, the two pieces being held together by bolts or sometimes by straps.*

There are various forms of scarf joint, and they may be classified according to the nature of the stresses they are to resist, **as** those designed for

1. Compression
2. Tension
3. Bending

4. Compression and tension
5. Tension and bending

Compression Scarf Joint.—This is the simplest form of scarf

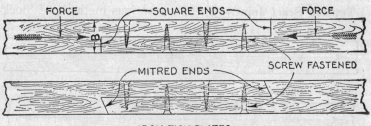

FIGS. 1,052 to 1,054.—Various compression scarf joints. Fig. 1,052, plain, square ends; fig. 1,053, plain, mitred ends; fig. 1,054, reinforced with iron fish plates.

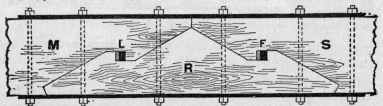

FIG. 1,055.—Butt and lap plate scarf joint, designed to avoid reducing the length of the joined timbers when the timbers are not long enough for a lap joint the piece R, is splayed onto the timbers M, and S, which are cut away correspondingly. The laps of M, and S, on R, are cut with notches and provided with wedges LF, to take any tension stress. The joint is bolted and sometimes reinforced by iron fish plates.

joint. As usually made, half of the wood is cut away from the end of each piece for a distance equal to the lap as in fig. 1,052, this process being called "*halving*." The length of the lap should be 5 to 6 times the thickness of the timber. Mitred ends, as in fig. 1,053 are better than square ends, as in fig. 1,052, where nails or screws are depended upon to fasten the joint.

For extra heavy duty iron fish plates are sometimes provided greatly strengthening the joint as in fig. 1,054. When these are used mitred ends are not necessary.

Tension Scarf Joint.—There are various methods of "lock-

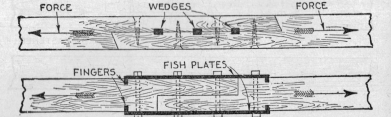

FIGS. 1,056 and 1,057.—Various tension scarf joints. Fig. 1,056, mitred ends fastened with screws and tension stress caused by wedges. Fig. 1,057, square ends bolted and reinforced by iron fish plates; tension stress caused by fingers on the fish plates.

FIGS. 1,058 to 1,060.—Key and wedges. Fig. 1,058, key; figs. 1,059 and 1,060, wedges.

ing" joints to resist tension as by means of keys, wedges or so-called keys, fish plates with fingers, etc. The difference between keys and wedges, as shown in figs. 1,058 to 1,060, should be noted. Keys are only permissible where only one key is used as in fig. 1,061, otherwise if the slots and keys were not perfect fits all the stress would be carried by one key as in fig. 1,062, rendering the other useless. Note how this is overcome by the use of wedges, even when the slots do not match as in fig. 1,063.

Bending Scarf Joint.—When a beam is acted upon by a

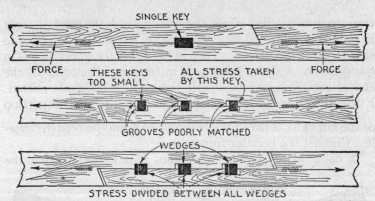

FIGS. 1,061 to 1,063.—Scarf joints with mitred ends illustrating the use of keys and wedges as explained in the text. Where two or more wedges are used in place of one key they can be made correspondingly smaller for equal strength to resist the tension stress, thus making the joint.

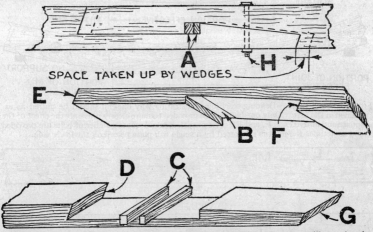

FIGS. 1,064 to 1,066.—Scarf joint with notch and half lap mitred; also mitred ends illustrating the placing and effect of wedges. Fig. 1,064 shows the two pieces joined together with the wedges **A**, driven home and cut off. The dotted lines show the amount of space closed when drawn into place by the wedges. It will be noticed in the next two illustrations which show the two pieces separated, that at **D**, and **E**, as well as at **F**, and **G**, the cut is mitred thus, if accurately made in seasoned timber it becomes a rigid joint. It is sometimes strengthened by a bolt through each section as at **H**.

transverse or bending stress, the side on which the bending force is applied is subjected to a compression stress and the opposite side to a tension stress. Thus in fig. 1,067 the upper side is in compression, and the lower side in tension. Hence at L, the end of the joint may be square but at F, it should be mitred. Evidently if this end were square (as at F', fig. 1,068), the portion of the lap of M between the bolt and F' would be rendered useless to resist the bending force.

In designing a bending scarf joint it is important that the

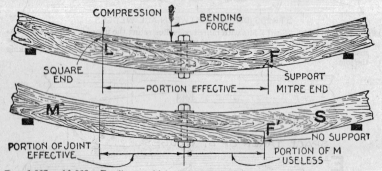

FIGS. 1,067 and 1,068.—Bending scarf joint illustrating why one end should be mitred as explained in the text. Only one bolt is here provided to more clearly illustrate the effect of the square and mitred ends F, and F'. *In practice*, an adequate number of bolts are provided and sometimes the joint is reinforced by a single fish plate placed on the lower side.

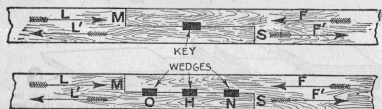

FIGS. 1,069 and 1,070.—Compression and tension scarf joints. Fig. 1,069, with key; fig. 1,070, with wedges. In fig. 1,069, unless the key be a tight fit, the compression stress LF, will be taken by the square lap ends M, and S, and the tension stress L'F', will be taken by the key. In fig. 1,070 the compression stress LF, is divided by the three wedges, O, H, M, and ends M, S, (if good fit); the tension stress L'F', being carried by the three wedges O, H, M.

thickness at the mitred end be ample, otherwise the strain coming at that point might split the support.

Compression and Tension Scarf Joint.—The essential requirements for this type of joint are flat ends to take the compression stress and notched lap with key, or wedges to take the tension stress as shown in figs. 1,069 and 1,070. For severe duty these joints are sometimes reinforced by iron fish plates with plain or fingered ends. When fish plates with fingers are used, a multiplicity of wedges is unnecessary.

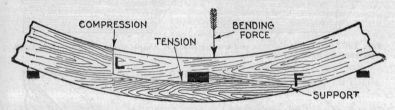

Fig. 1,071.—Tension and bending scarf joint. In making this joint the square lap end L, should be on the side which receives the bending force and the mitred end F, on the other side, otherwise when the joint is subjected to a bending force the result will be the same as in fig. 1,068.

Tension and Bending Scarf Joint.—This joint is similar to the bending scarf joint in that the lap end of one member is square, that of the other member, mitred. The lap is partly straight and partly inclined, as shown in fig. 1,071, a wedge being placed at the middle point fitted against notches to take the tension stress.

Mortise and Tenon Joints.—In carpentry, a *mortise* is defined as *a space hollowed out in a timber to receive a tenon or the like, and a **tenon** as, a projection, properly of rectangular cross section at the end of a piece of timber to be inserted into a socket or mortise in another timber to make a joint.*

Mortise and tenon joints are frequently called simply tenon

joints. The operation of making mortise and tenon joints some-times is termed tenoning which implies mortising also.

There is a multiplicity of mortise and tenon joints and they may be classified with respect to

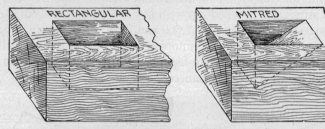

FIGS. 1,072 and 1,073.—Mortise and tenon joints. *1. Shape of the mortise.* Fig. 1,072, rectangular; fig. 1,073, triangular.

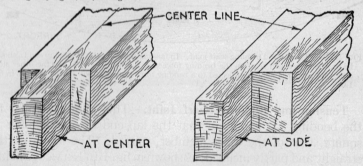

FIGS. 1,074 and 1,075.—Mortise and tenon joints. *2. Position of the tenon.* Fig. 1,074, at center; fig. 1,075, at side.

1. Shape of the mortise.
2. Position of the tenon.
3. Degree in which tenon projects into mortised member.
4. Degree of housing of mortise.
5. Number of tenons.
6. The shape of tenon shoulders.
7. The method of fastening the tenon.

The mortise and tenon must exactly correspond in size, that is, the tenon must accurately fit into the mortise. The position of the tenon is usually at the center of the timber, but sometimes it is located at the side, depending upon the *degree of housing*, except in special cases.

The tenon may project partly into, or through, the mortised timber.

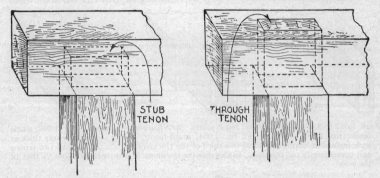

FIGS. 1,076 and 1,077.—Mortise and tenon joints. *3. Degree in which the tenon projects into the mortised timber.* Fig. 1,076, stub tenon; fig. 1,077, through tenon.

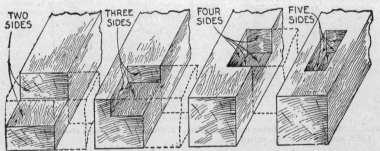

FIGS. 1,078 to 1,081.—Mortise and tenon joints. *4. Degree of housing of mortise.* Fig. 1,078, two sides; fig. 1,079, three sides; fig. 1,080, four sides; fig. 1,081, five sides. Figs 1,079 and 1,078 may be considered by some as lap joints.

When the tenon and mortise do not extend through the mortised timber it is called a stub tenon. This form of tenon is used for joining up the framework of partitions, and in work where the joint will not be subject to any tension.

The term "degree of housing" signifies the degree in which the tenon is covered by the mortise, that is, the number of sides of the mortise.

The number of tenons will evidently depend upon the shape of the timbers, whether square or rectangular with considerable width and little thickness.

The tenon shoulders are usually at right angles with the tenon as when

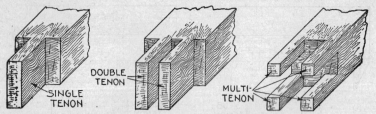

FIGS. 1,082 to 1,084.—Mortise and tenon joints. *5. Number of tenons.* Fig. 1,082, single tenon; fig. 1,083, double tenon; fig. 1,084, multi-tenon. When the wood is very thick or wide instead of having one tenon one-third of the thickness, it is usual to have two tenons and consequently two mortises. In this case the thickness of the tenon is about 1/5 that of the wood.

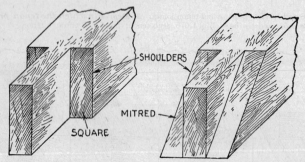

FIGS. 1,085 and 1,086.—Mortise and tenon joints. *6. Shape of the tenon shoulders.* Fig. 1,085, square; fig. 1,086, mitred.

the two timbers are joined at right angles, but they may be mitered to some smaller angle as 60° or 45° as in the case of a brace.

There are several ways of fastening mortise and tenon joints as with pins or wedges. The accompanying cuts illustrate the various points just mentioned.

In making a mortise and tenon joint the work is first laid out to given dimensions as in fig. 1,087.

Cutting the Mortise.—Select a chisel as near the width of mortise as possible. This chisel, especially for large work, should be a framing or mortise chisel.

Bore a hole same size as width of mortise at the middle point. If mortise be for a through tenon, bore half-way through from

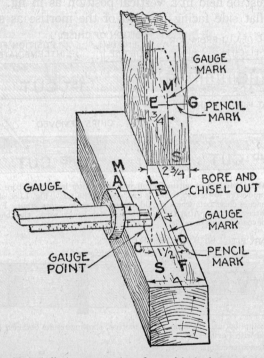

Fig. 1,087.—Method of laying out a mortise and tenon joint having mortise in the center of one timber and tenon at side of the other timber. Set gauge to ⅓ thickness of the timber to be mortised, then with gauge scribe line MS, and with gauge on opposite side of the timber, scribe line LF. These lines define the sides of the mortise. To complete the mortise lay out lines AB, and CD, using square and pencil. Without changing the setting on the gauge, scribe line M'S', for tenon on the other timber and EG, with square at correct distance from the end. In working on finished surfaces be careful not to scribe the lines MS, and LF, beyond the ends of the mortise as the scratches will show after job is completed. In such cases it is better to mark lightly with pencil AB, and CD, first.

each side. In the case of a large mortise, most of the wood may be removed by boring several holes.

In cutting out a small mortise with a narrow chisel, work from the hole in the center to each end of the mortise holding the chisel at right angles with the grain of the wood. At the ends the chisel must be held in a vertical position as in fig. 1,089, having the flat side facing the end of the mortise as shown.

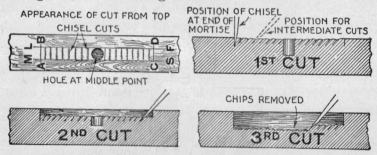

Figs. 1,088 and 1,091.—Method of cutting small mortise. After laying out, bore hole, fig. 1,088, at center and work toward each end as explained in the text. Fig. 1,088 shows layout and appearance of chisel cuts which should *always be made across grain*. Figs. 1,089 to 1,091 show successive cuts. After the first few cuts, for heavy work, the chisel can be driven an inch or more in pine or poplar.

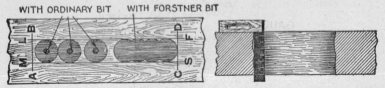

Fig. 1,092.—Method of boring in making a large mortise, showing results obtained by use of ordinary bit, and with Forstner bit.

Fig. 1,093.—End test after cutting mortise.

Always loosen the chisel by a backward movement of the handle, a movement in the opposite direction would injure the ends of the mortise.

Never make a chisel cut parallel with the grain as the wood as the side may split.

In cutting a through mortise, cut only half-way through on one side, and finish the cut from the other side.

After cutting test the truth of the sides by using a try square as in fig. 1,093; this will check the accuracy with which the work was laid out.

Cutting the Tenon.—A back saw is used for cutting out the wood on each side of the tenon and if necessary, a finishing cut

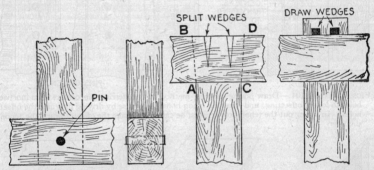

FIGS. 1,094 to 1,097.—Mortise and tenon joints. *7. Methods* of fastening the tenon. Figs. 1,094 and 1,095, side and end views showing tenon secured by pin. Fig. 1,096 shows tenon held by *internal or split wedges*, that is, wedges that are driven into the tenon splitting and spreading it as shown. By making the sides **AB**, and **CD**, tapering, the tenon becomes securely wedged into the mortise. In fig. 1,097 the tongue is extended beyond the mortise and rectangular holes cut into which *external wedges* are driven.

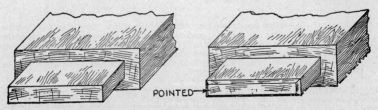

FIGS. 1,098 and 1,099.—Appearance of tenon before and after pointing.

may be taken with a chisel. After the wood is cut away the tenon should be pointed by chiseling all four sides.

Figs. 1,098 and 1,099 show appearance of tenon before and after pointing. The pointing is necessary, otherwise a tight fitting tenon would be difficult

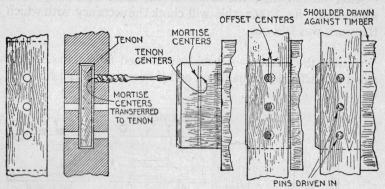

FIGS. 1,100 to 1,104.—Draw boring showing method of transferring pin centers from mortise holes to tenon, offsetting, and drawing tenon home in mortise by driving pins into the offset holes. In laying out the tenon hole centers, be careful to make the offset toward the tenon shoulder.

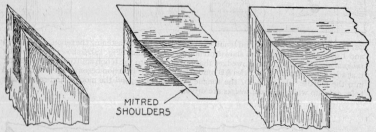

FIGS. 1,105 to 1,107.—Mortise and tenon joint with mitred shoulders. One timber has a mortise or slot cut down into the center until it squares through from the beginning o inside of the mitre, and on the other is formed a tenon to fit the slot so that the two will go snugly together as shown. In picture framing or light work where the materials are less than 2 ins thick, it will not be practical. It is all made with the saw except the bottom of slot which must be chiseled square through from inside of mitre.

to start into the mortise and would perhaps splinter the sides of the mortise when driven through. Do not cut off point until tenon is finally in place and pin driven home.

Making Pins.—Mortise and tenon joints are fastened as before explained, by pins or wedges. To make a pin select good grade straight grained wood. First square by chiseling to section slightly larger than diameter of finished pin, and bring to octagon form by taking off the corners. By careful chiseling

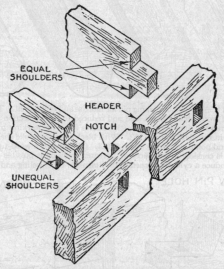

EQUAL
SHOULDERS

HEADER

NOTCH

UNEQUAL
SHOULDERS

Figs. 1,108 to 1,110.—Mortise and tenon joint suitable for headers and tail beams around well holes, chimney and scuttle openings. The header is notched out above the mortise to receive it, thus making a more rigid job where there is a tendency to twist, as in the tusk joint.

the cylindrical form may be approximated near enough to answer the purpose as in figs. 1,111 to 1,114.

Draw Boring.—The term draw boring signifies *the method of locating holes in mortise and tenon eccentric with each other so that when the pin is driven in it will "draw" the tenon into the mortise forcing the tenon shoulders tightly against the mortised timber.*

The holes may be located either by accurately laying out the centers as in fig. 1,102, or by boring the mortise and finding center for the tenon hole as in fig. 1,103. Considerable experience is necessary to properly locate the tenon hole for if too much offset be given an undue strain will be brought

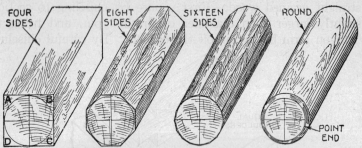

Figs. 1,111 to 1,114.—Method of making pin for mortise and tenon joint. The selected straight grained piece of wood should be scribed and reduced to square section ABCD (fig. 1,111), a trifle larger than the dimension circle (this allows for close working to size). Chisel to 8 and 16 sides as in figs. 1,112 and 1,113. With block plane or spoke shave reduce to scribed circular form, and point one end as in fig. 1,114. Of course, if a wood-turning lathe be available, the labor is considerably reduced and greater precision is possible as it takes considerable skill to produce a cylindrical surface to dimension by chiseling and planing.

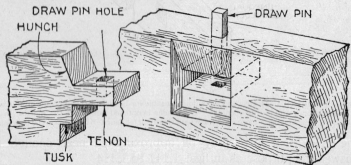

Fig. 1,115.—Mortise and tenon joint with tusk for floor beams, showing tusk, draw pin, etc. The object of this form of joint is to avoid the danger of too great a mortise and too small a tenon, and also of lessening the efficiency of either of the two pieces, in consequence of the tenon being placed too high or too low. It is used for horizontal bearings such as joists, binders, trimmers, beams, girders, etc. In this joint the body of the tenon is a little above the middle of the end, and runs out from two to four inches, as may be required. Below it protrudes the tusk and above it the shoulder is cut down at an obtuse angle with the horizontal line, thus giving to the tenon the strength of the whole depth of the timber above the under tusk, and giving it a bearing in a shallow mortise, while a greater depth of the mortised piece than that which the tusk rests on receives the body of the tenon, thus protecting its comparatively narrow margin from under pressure.

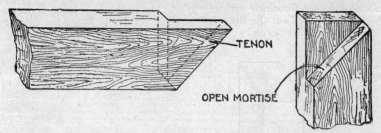

FIGS. 1,116 and 1,117.—Half, or open mortise and tenon joint (mitred). The ample glue surface and possibility of nailing makes it a strong and durable joint.

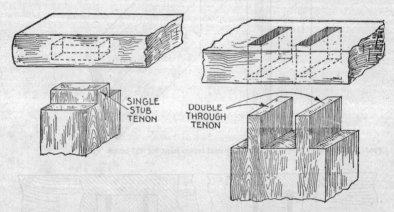

FIGS. 1,118 and 1,121.—Stub, and through mortise and tenon joints. Fig. 1,118, single stub joint; fig. 1,121, double through tenon joint.

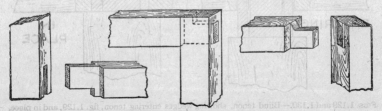

FIGS. 1,122 to 1,126.—Rebated mortise and tenon joints. Figs. 1,122 and 1,126, with mitred rebate; figs. 1,1248 to 1,126. with square rebate.

on the joint frequently sufficient to split the joint. It is much better to accurately lay out the work and make an accurately fitting pin than to depend on draw boring.

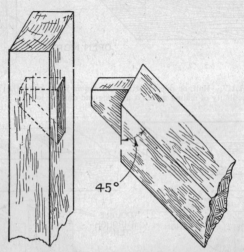

Figs. 1,127 and 1,128.—Mitred mortise and tenon joint for 45° brace.

ENTERING

IN PLACE

Figs. 1,129 and 1,130.—Blind tenon, showing wedges entering tenon, fig. 1,129, and in place, fig. 1,130. The mortise must be the exact shape of the tenon when the wedges are in place. All the lumber must be so well seasoned that there can be no shrinkage.

Dovetail Joints.—A dovetail joint may be defined as *a partially housed tapered mortise and tenon joint*, the tapered form of mortise and tenon forming a lock which securely holds the parts together. The word "dovetail" is used figuratively, the tenon expanding in width toward the tip resembling the fan-like form

FIGS. 1,131 to 1,133.—Notched mortise and tenon joint fastened with keyed strap. The bottom of the key hole is made lower than the wood so that when the wedges are driven to place, the timbers are drawn tight. The lower end is held by an angle dog. A plate is placed between the key and the wood to prevent the key cutting into the wood. With wedge adjustment, if the wood shrink, the slack may be taken up by driving the wedge in further.

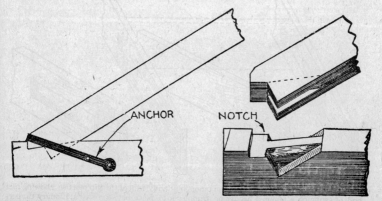

FIGS. 1,134 to 1,136.—Notched mortise and tenon joint fastened with anchor strap.

of the tail of a dove. The various forms of dovetail joint may be classed as

1. Common.
2. Compound.
3. Lap, or half-blind.
4. Mortise or blind.

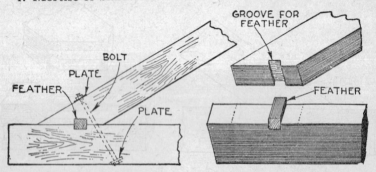

Figs. 1,137 to 1,139.—Butt joint anchored with a feather to prevent slipping under compression stress, and fastened with a bolt. In using bolts, the wood should always be protected by large washers or plates.

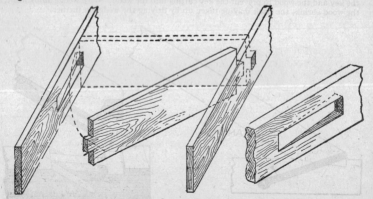

Figs. 1,140 and 1,141.—Slip mortise and tenon joint and detail of the slip mortise, showing method of swinging a tenoned header or trimmer into place between two stationary timbers. The operation is accomplished by a chase or slip mortise.

Common Dovetail Joint.—This is a plain or single *"pin"* joint.* Where strength rather than appearance is important, the common dovetail joint is used.

The straight form of this joint is shown in figs. 1,142 to 1,144, and the corner form in figs. 1,145 to 1,147, the proportions of the joint being shown in figs. 1,145 and 1,146.

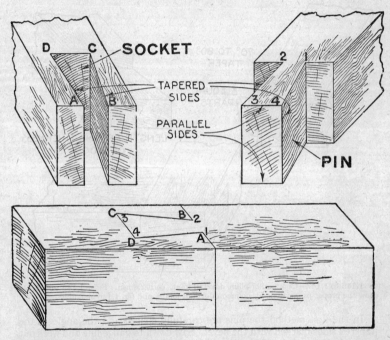

FIG. 1,142 to 1,144.—Common or plain dovetail joint, straight form. Fig. 1,142, socket; fig. 1,143, pin; fig. 1,144, assembly. By noting the positions of the letters and numbers, it is clearly seen how the parts go together.

Compound Dovetail Joint.—This is the same as the common

*NOTE.—In dovetail joints the tapered tenon is called the pin, and the mortised part, which receives this joint, the socket.

form but has more than one pin, adapting the joint to wide boards.

In making this joint, both edges are made true and square; a gauge line is run round one board at a distance from the end equal to the thickness of the other one, and the other board is similarly treated. Now, two methods are followed. Some mark and cut the pins first; others the sockets.

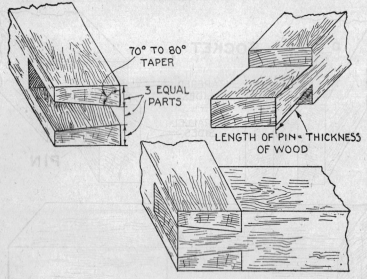

FIGS 1,145 to 1,147—Common or plain dovetail joint, corner form. Figs. 1,145 and 1,146 show the proper proportions for common dovetail joints, and fig. 1,146 assembly.

In the first method the pins are carefully spaced and the angles of the tapered sides marked with the bevel. Saw down to gauge line and work out spaces between with chisel and mallet. Then put B, on top of A (figs. 1,148 and 1,149), and scribe mortise. Square over, cut down to gauge line, clean out and fit together.

The second method is to first mark the sockets on A (sometimes on common work the marking is dispensed with, the mechanic using his eye as a guide); then run the saw in down to the gauge line, put A on B, and mark the pins with the front tooth of the saw; cut the pins, keeping outside of the saw mark sufficiently to allow of the pins fitting fairly tight; then both pieces may be cleaned out and tried together.

In cleaning out the mortises and the spaces between the pins, the wood worker must chop half way through, then turn the board over, and finish from the other side, taking care to hold the chisel upright, and not so as to cut under as shown in fig. 1,150, which is sometimes done to ensure the joint fitting on the outside. Another bad practice is to leave the pins long, and rivet them over with the hammer when the joint is glued up.

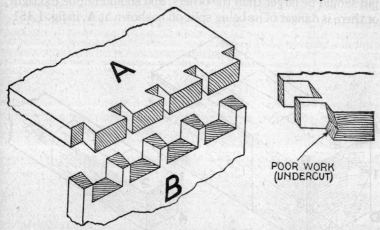

POOR WORK (UNDERCUT)

FIGS. 1,148 to 1,150.—Compound dovetail joint and detail (fig. 1,150), showing joint **poorly** cleaned out.

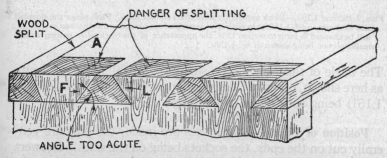

DANGER OF SPLITTING

WOOD SPLIT

ANGLE TOO ACUTE

FIG. 1.151.—Badly proportioned common dovetail joint showing results.

Spacing.—The maximum strength would be gained by having the pins and sockets equal; but this is scarcely ever done in practice, the mortise being made so that the saw will just clear at the narrow side, the space being from eight to ten times the width of the widest side. Small pins are used for the sake of appearance, but fairly large ones are preferable. The outside pin should be larger than the others, and should not be too tight or there is danger of its being split off as shown at A, in fig. 1,151.

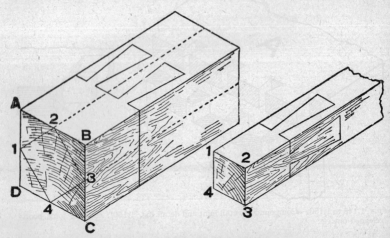

Figs. 1,152 and 1,153.—Block apparently dovetailed on four sides. Firs᠄ make the dovetail joint as shown in fig. 1,152, then with joint assembled cut block down so that section ABCD, will be changed in form to section 1234, the appearance of the block after cutting to this smaller section being shown in fig. 1,153.

The angle of taper should be slight (70° to 80°) and not acute as here shown, otherwise there is danger of the pieces L, F, (fig. 1,151) being split off in assembling.

Position of Pins.—When boxes are made, the pins are generally cut on the ends, the sockets being on the sides. Drawers have the pins on front and back, the rule being to have the tapered sides so that they are in opposition to the greatest stress that comes upon the piece of work to which the joint is applied.

Lap or Half-blind Dovetail Joint.—This is the joint used in

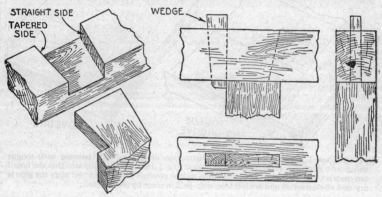

FIGS. 1,154 and 1,155.—Through half dovetail joint, or type in which one side is straight, and the other tapered. Evidently this joint is not suitable for a heavy tension stress as all the strain comes on one side.

FIGS. 1,156 to 1,158.—Through half dovetail joint with wedge. This joint even with inferior workmanship may be made a tight fit by driving in the wedge. Because of the tight fit thus secured it is better adapted for a tension stress than the simple half dovetail joint (figs. 1,156 and 1,157.

the construction of drawers upon the best grades of work. The joint is visible on one side but not on the other, hence the name "*half blind.*" As this form of dovetail joint is used so extensively

FIGS. 1,159 to 1,161.—Double socket feather dovetail joint, before and after placing feather in position. Evidently this joint could also be considered as a mitred butt dovetail feather joint.

in the manufacture of furniture, machines have been devised for making the joint saving time and labor.

TONGUE AND GROOVE

DOVETAIL

Figs. 1,162 and 1,163.—Drawing board construction illustrating end fastening with tongue and groove joint (fig. 1,162), and dovetail joint (fig. 1,163). It is readily seen that the board can contract and expand without checking, as the dovetail cleats are fitted after the glue is dry and all cleaned off and are left free, only held in place by the dovetail.

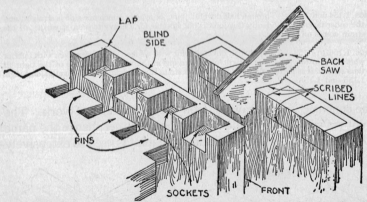

LAP

BLIND SIDE

BACK SAW

SCRIBED LINES

PINS

SOCKETS

FRONT

Figs. 1,164 and 1,165.—Lap or half blind dovetail joints and position of saw in sawing pins and sockets. Saw the pins as indicated and with a chisel cut out the rest of the wood in the spaces between the pins. The length of the pins must be less than the thickness of the front by an amount equal to the lap. When the side is completed it should be laid in position on the end of the front and the shape of the pins scribed. The sockets must be then carefully cut away with a chisel. Owing to the strain coming on the joint by the frequent opening of the draw it is of prime importance that the joint be well fitted.

Blind Dovetail Joint.—This is a double lap joint, that is, the joint is covered on both sides and on this account it is sometimes called a *secret* dovetail joint. The laps may be either

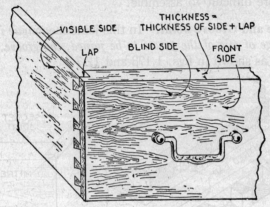

FIG. 1,166.—Detail of drawer showing lap or half blind dovetail joint.

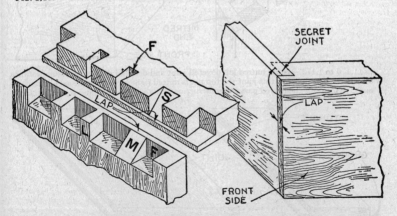

FIGS. 1,167 to 1,169.—Blind square lap dovetail joint and detail of draw showing appearance assembled. In figs. 1,167 and 1,168, two forms of pin and socket are shown, MS, mitred and LF, square. *In making* this joint, first cut the pins, then the lap and mark the sockets with a scriber.

square as in figs. 1,167 and 1,168, or mitred as in figs. 1,170 and 1,171. On account of the skill and time required to make these joints, they are used only on the finest work. The mitred form is the more difficult to assemble.

Tongue and Groove Joint.—In this joint the *tongue is formed on the edge of one of the pieces to be joined, the groove being in the other,* as shown in figs. 1,173 and 1,174.

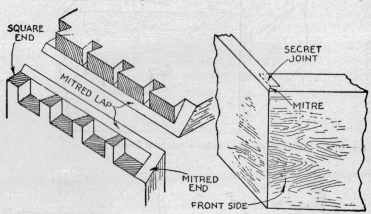

FIGS. 1,170 to 1,172.—Blind mitred lap dovetail joint and detail of draw showing appearance assembled. *In making* this joint the top pin is mitred right across, for the sake of appearance. Except for the mitred part the construction is the same as the blind square lap form.

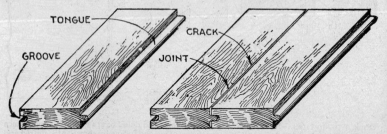

FIGS. 1,173 and 1,174.—Tongue and groove plank and assembly of two planks illustrating tongue and groove joint; the type of joint generally used for flooring.

CHAPTER 24A

Cabinetmaking Joints

The purpose of this chapter is to describe briefly, and illustrate some of the many joints and their application as used in cabinet work; in the hope that this information may be found useful to carpenters and others, when the occasion for such information arises.

The Tools.—Any good set of carpenters' tools is sufficient for most cabinet work. A few additions may be found necessary, such as:

1. Dovetail saw
2. Set of mortise and firmer chisels
3. Router plane
4. Plow plane

To these should be added:
1. Mitre box
2. Shooting board
3. Mitre shooting board
4. Bench hook
5. Set of hand-screws

These are described and illustrated, and a list of carpenters' tools given, under their respective headings in the fore part of this book.

The Bench.—A work bench having an end vise, in addition to the regular vise, for holding material between stops on top of the bench, will be found very convenient.

The great variety of joints used in cabinet work are usually classified according to their general characteristics, as: **A,** glued; **B,** halved and bridle; **C,** mortise and tenon; **D,** dovetail; **E,** mitred; **F,** framing; **G,** hinging and shutting.

Under each of these classifications is grouped a variety of joints, which will be considered separately, and briefly explained.

Glued Joints.—The term *glued joint* in cabinet work applies particularly to any "butt" joint held together with glue; although they are very often additionally secured. Under this head are grouped the following joints: 1, rubbed; 2, bevelled; 3, plowed and tongued; 4, hidden slot screwed; 5, dowelled; 6, coopered.

Rubbed Joints.—These joints, as the name indicates, are rubbed into position when gluing. They are the simplest kind of joints to make, and are used principally for material of fairly open texture where there is very little strain, and for thin boards.

Fig. 1 illustrates the simplest form of rubbed joint. The method of making it is fully described under "Straight Joint" on pages 378 and 379.

Gluing Up.—A satisfactory way of gluing up rubbed joints is to fasten one piece securely in the bench vise and place the edge of the other piece against it, as in fig. 2; apply glue thoroughly to both edges and put them together. To rub into position, take hold of the top piece at each end and rub steadily back and forth lengthwise as in fig. 3. As the air and glue are

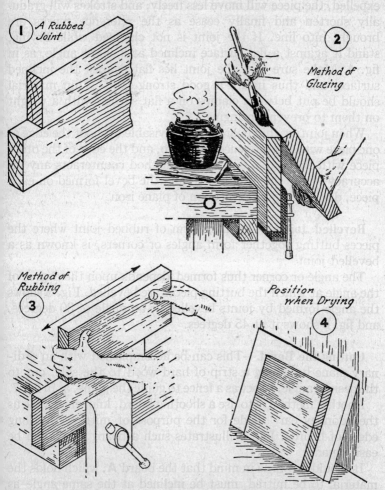

FIGS. 1 to 4—Rubbed joints and assembly methods.

expelled, the piece will move less freely, and strokes will gradually shorten and finally cease as the reference marks are brought into line. If the joint is not clamped while drying, stand it against a flat surface inclined at a slight angle, as in fig. 4. Make sure that the joint lies flat against the inclined surface, and thus insure a good strong joint. Thin material should be put between clamps on a flat surface with a weight on them to prevent springing.

When jointing thin boards, it is advisable to shoot the edge of one piece with the reference marks up, and the edge of the other piece with the marks down. This method counteracts any inaccuracy of the shooting board, and the bevel formed on each piece, due to unequal projection of plane iron.

Bevelled Joints.—Another form of rubbed joint where the pieces butting together form angles or corners, is known as a bevelled joint.

The angle or corner thus formed depends upon the degree of the angle at which the butting pieces are bevelled. Fig. 5 shows the angle formed by joints bevelled at an angle of 30 degrees, and fig. 6 shows it at 45 degrees.

Cutting the Bevel.—This can be accomplished with an ordinary plane by gluing a strip of hard wood to the sole, cut to the desired angle, to act as a fence to guide the plane, as in fig. 7.

Another method is to use a shooting board, known to some as the "donkey ear" made for the purpose of mitring the long edges of boards. Fig. 8 illustrates such a board which can be easily made.

It should be borne in mind that the board **A**, which holds the material to be mitred, must be inclined at the same angle as desired in the bevelled edge. In operation, the board is fastened in the vise and the material held firmly against the stop with the left hand, and with the right hand holding the plane on its right side, the edge is shot in the regular way.

When gluing these joints, it is usually found necessary to clamp them together while drying. A method for clamping is shown in fig. 72.

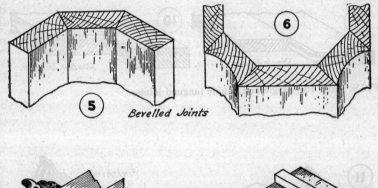

Bevelled Joints

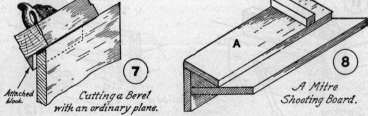

Attached block.

Cutting a Bevel with an ordinary plane.

A Mitre Shooting Board.

FIGS. 5 to 8—Various bevelled joints and methods of cutting the bevel.

Plowed and Tongued Joints.—This method of jointing is very commonly used in cabinet work and is very similar to the *feather joint* described on pages 384 to 386, except that in cabinet work the tongues are invariably hard wood cut across the grain. When the thickness of the material will permit, two tongues are used instead of one, as in fig. 10, because of the additional gluing surface afforded, and the increased strength to the joint. Feather tongues are cut lengthwise with the grain but are seldom used in cabinet work except for dry jointing.

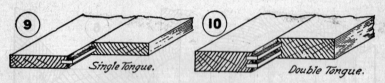

FIGS. 9 and 10—Single and double tongued joints.

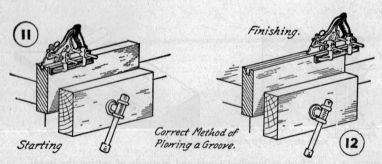

FIGS. 11 and 12—Method of plowing single tongued groove.

To make this joint successfully, the pieces should be properly faced and the edges squared and straightened with jointer so that they fit perfectly. Put reference marks on the face side so that the same edges will come together when finished. Set the plow with the iron projecting about ⅟₃₂ in. below the bottom. Set the depth gauge to half the width of the tongue, and adjust the fence so that the cutter will be the required distance from the edge between the two sides. Fasten the piece securely in the bench vise so that the groove can be plowed from the face side. Begin plowing at the front, fig. 11, and work backward, and finish by going right through from back to front, as in fig. 12. Hold the plow steady, otherwise an irregular groove will be the result.

For the cross grain tongue, shoot the end of a thin board of hard wood, mark and carefully saw off across its width a strip the required width of the tongue, about ¾ in. wide. Plane the tongue to thickness in a tonguing board. Assemble the parts and proceed to glue up as explained on page 385.

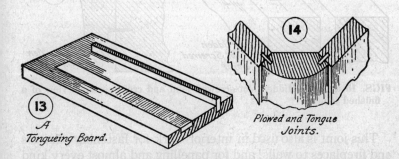

13 A Tongueing Board.

14

Plowed and Tongue Joints.

FIGS. 13 and 14—The tonguing board fig. 13 is a simple and handy device to overcome the difficulty of holding a narrow piece of thin material steady while placing. To make the board use ⅞ in. faced material, a piece about 8 or 10 ins. wide and longer than the tongues to be placed. Cut the grooves as indicated with tenon saw, clean out with chisel and router. The wider groove should be slightly deeper than the thickness of finished tongue to allow for planing both sides. Fig. 14 shows the application of the plowed and tongued joint to corner construction.

Hidden Slot Screwed Joints.—This joint is not often used as a glued joint, but is found to be an effective way of fastening brackets and shelves to finished work where the fastening must be concealed.

The joint consists of a screw driven part way into one piece, and a hole and slot cut into the opposite piece. The joint is effected by fitting them together with the head of the screw in the hole, and forcing the screw back into the slot. Fig. 15 shows the slot and screw in relation to each other. Fig. 16 gives a sectional view of a completed joint.

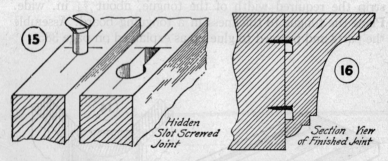

FIGS. 15 and 16—Hidden slot screwed joint and cross-sectional view of a finished joint.

This joint is also used in interior work for fastening pilasters and fireplaces to walls, and for panelling and almost every kind of fitting requiring secure and concealed fastening.

To make a joint as shown in fig. 16, gauge a center line on each of the pieces. Determine the position of the screws and put them in, to project about ⅜ in. above the surface. Hold the two pieces evenly together, and with a try-square, draw a line from the back of the screw shank across the center line of the opposite piece. From this line, measure off ⅞ in. forward on the center line; and with this point as center, bore a hole to fit the screw head a trifle deeper than the screw projects above the surface. Cut a slot from the hole back to the line from the screw shank, as wide as the diameter of the shank and as deep as the hole. For a general rule, the total length of the slot and hole should be slightly more than twice the diameter of the head of the screw.

The Shape of the Plug.

FIG. 16a—Plug to hold screw when hidden slot screwed joints are utilized on mortar and brick walls.

The process of fastening pilasters and fireplaces by this method is: First mark the position of the piece and the place on the wall for the screws. In brick and cement walls, wooden plugs are driven in flush with the surface to hold the screws. The plugs are shaped as illustrated, and pockets cut with a cold chisel in the brickwork. Plugs cut as shown seldom work loose.

Turn the screws into the plugs allowing them to project about ⅜ in. from the surface, and dab the heads with moist lamp-black. Put the piece in position pressing it against the heads, which leaves black impressions; bore holes to fit the heads about ⅝ in. below the impressions, and cut the slot to receive the shank of the screw. Replace the piece, with the heads in the holes, and force it down in position.

Dowelled Joints.—There are many variations of dowel jointing used in cabinet work. The basic principle and method of making a dowel joint is explained and illustrated on pages 379–381.

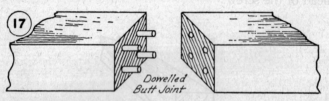

FIG. 17—Illustrates the use of dowels in a built joint such as is frequently used in cabinet work to lengthen large mouldings, etc., and where cross grain prevents tenoning.

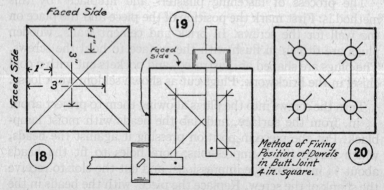

FIGS. 18 to 20—Method of marking position of dowels in a butt joint.

Placing the Dowels.—To accurately fix the position of dowels in a butt joint, make all measurements and gauge lines from the edge of the faced sides. For example, with material 4 in. square, mark diagonal lines from the corners with scratch awl, crossing at center. Then from the edge of the faced sides, mark off 1 in. and 3 in. as shown in fig. 18. From the same sides gauge the lines as in fig. 19. At the intersection of the lines is the center for the holes, as shown in fig. 20

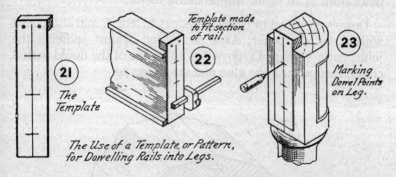

FIGS. 21 to 23—Shows method of using template for marking of dowel pin locations, where method described in figs. 18 to 20 can not conveniently be used.

Dowel Template.—In places where the ordinary means of aligning dowel holes cannot be used, a dowel template or pattern is used. It is made of a strip of zinc or veneer, having a small block of wood fastened to one end to act as a shoulder, and the position of the dowel points pierced through the zinc or veneer with a fine awl. Various types of templates are made and used as the occasion requires. Fig. 21 shows template for doweling rail in furniture.

It is made to fit the section of the rail as in fig. 22. While held in position, a line is gauged down through the middle and the position of the dowels indicated on the line. It is laid flat on a board, and the dowel points are pierced through the surface with a fine awl. When in use, it is placed in position on the piece, and the dowel positions are marked with an awl through the holes, as in fig. 23. A "bit gauge" regulating the depth of the bore should be used when doweling. Where much doweling is to be done a doweling jig which insures accurate boring of holes from ¼ to ¾ in. will be found useful.

Dowels are glued into one piece, cut to length and sharpened with dowel sharpener. As a precaution against splitting the joint, cut a V-shaped groove down the side of the dowel with a chisel; this permits the glue and air to escape.

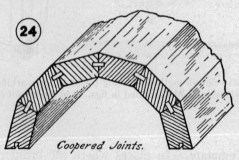

Coopered Joints.

FIG. 24—Typical coopered joints employed to form various curvatures in cabinet work.

Coopered Joints.—These are so named because of the resemblance to joints in barrels made by coopers, and are used for nearly all forms of curved work; they are usually tongued before gluing, though occasionally dowels are used.

Fig. 24 shows the joint in semicircular form, having the segments bevelled at an angle of 30 degrees. They are clamped after gluing, and planed to shape with a circular or compass plane.

Halved and Bridle Joints.—These are lap joints having each of the pieces halved and shouldered on opposite sides, so that they fit into each other. They are described as the simplest joint in cabinet work. Because they are strong and easily made, these joints are much used in constructing the skeleton framework, fastened to walls, which is necessary when tapestry or damask panels are required; also for faced up doors and panelling. These frames are also known as battens and are usually made of pine $3 \times \frac{3}{8}$ in. or $\frac{3}{4}$ in. as occasion requires.

Fig. 25 is the common halved angle, most frequently used. Fig. 26, the oblique halved for oblique connections. Fig. 28, the mitred halved useful when face of frame is moulded. Figs. 29, 30 and 31 used for cross connections having an outside strain. Fig. 32 is the blind dovetail halved, used in places where the frame edge is exposed.

Bridle or Open Tenon Joints.—These are used in connecting parts of flat and moulded frames. Fig. 34 is used where a strong framed groundwork is required, which is to be faced up. Fig. 36 is used as an inside frame connection.

Mortise and Tenon Joints.—Many variations of the mortise and tenon joints are used in cabinet work, differing in size and shape according to the requirements of the place and purpose for which it is used.

The most frequently used is the stub tenon; so called because it is short and penetrates only part way through the wood.

Fig. 37 is the type most generally used in doors and framing of furniture. Fig. 38 shows the stub tenon with the end mitred, which is often necessary when fitting rails into a corner post. Fig. 39 is the rebated or "haunched" tenon, considered a stronger joint by reason of the small additional tenon formed by

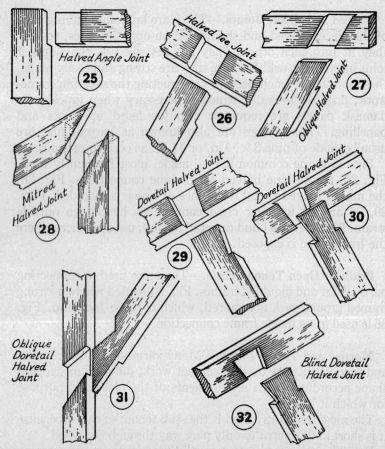

FIGS. 25 to 32—Various halved joints.

the rebate. It is often mitred as in fig. 40 to conceal the joint when used on outside frames. Fig. 41 is the same as that shown in fig. 39, but shouldered on one side only; it is sometimes called "barefaced" tenon, and is used when the connecting rail is

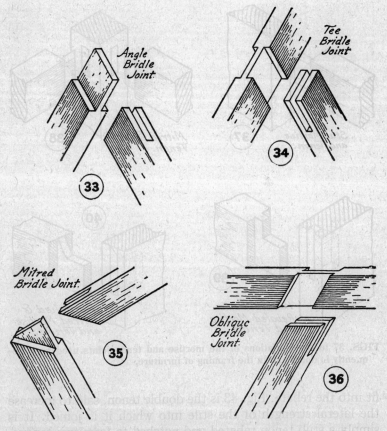

FIGS. 33 to 36—Halved joints generally used in the making of flat and moulded frames.

thinner than the stile into which it is joined. Fig. 42 shows the long and short shoulder tenon, the joint used when connecting a rail into a rebated frame. It has one shoulder cut back so as to

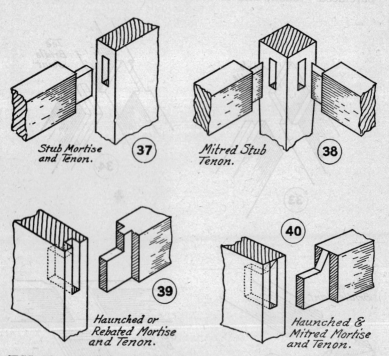

Stub Mortise and Tenon. (37)

Mitred Stub Tenon. (38)

Haunched or Rebated Mortise and Tenon. (39)

Haunched & Mitred Mortise and Tenon. (40)

FIGS. 37 to 40—Variations of the mortise and tenon joints used very frequently in doors and in the framing of furniture.

fit into the rebate. Fig. 43 is the double tenon, said to increase the lateral strength of the stile into which it is joined. It is simply a stub tenon rebated and notched to form two tenons, and when glued up, makes a very strong joint.

Fig. 44 is a type of through mortise and tenon which is sometimes used for mortising partitions into the top or bottom of wardrobes, etc. They are wedged across the tenon and glued.

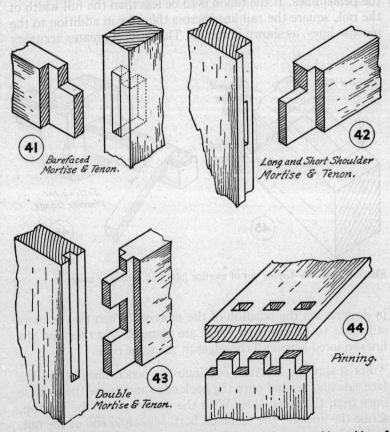

41 Barefaced Mortise & Tenon.

42 Long and Short Shoulder Mortise & Tenon.

43 Double Mortise & Tenon.

44 Pinning.

FIGS. 41 to 44—Another group of mortise and tenon joints used in making of furniture such as dresser drawers, etc.

Laying Out Mortise and Tenon.—The general practice when laying out a mortise and tenon is to square the mortise lines across the edge of the stile in pencil, and scribe the two lines for the sides of the mortise with a mortise or slide gauge, between the pencil lines. If the tenon is to be less than the full width of the rail, square the rail lines across the edge in addition to the mortise lines, as shown in fig. 45. This insures greater accuracy

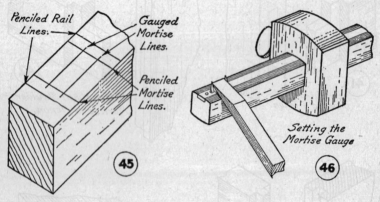

FIGS. 45 and 46—Laying out of mortise joint and setting of gauge.

in designating the position of the mortise. When two or more stiles are to be mortised, they are clamped together and the lines squared across all the edges at the same time.

For a through mortise, continue the pencil lines across the face side and around onto the back edge and gauge the mortise lines from the faced side. With the gauge set for the mortise, scribe the lines for the tenon on both edges and end of the rail, and with a try-square, mark the shoulder lines with a knife or chisel on all four sides.

The proportions of stub and through mortises and tenons are about ⅓ the thickness of the wood, and should be cut with a mortise chisel of the same size. If the chisel be not exactly ⅓ the thickness of the material, it is deemed better to make the mortise more than one third, rather than less.

Set the mortise gauge so that the chisel fits exactly between the points as in fig. 46; make a chisel mark in center of edge to be mortised and adjust the head of gauge so that the points coincide with the mark.

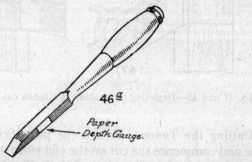

46 ᵃ

Paper
Depth Gauge.

FIG. 46a—Method of determining depth of joint by fastening a piece of paper or tape on side of chisel.

Cutting a mortise in cabinet work is usually done entirely with a mortise chisel, beginning at the center and working toward the near end with the flat side of the chisel toward the end, removing the core as you proceed, and then reversing the chisel and cutting to the far end, being careful to keep the chisel in a perpendicular position when cutting the ends.

Through mortises are cut half-way through from one side, and the material removed and cut through from the opposite side.

A depth gauge for stub mortises is made by gluing a piece of paper on the side of the chisel as in fig. 46a. If the method of boring a hole in the center from which to begin the cutting of the mortise be used for stub mortises, it is advisable to use "bit gauge" to regulate the depth of the bore. A small firmer chisel is used to clear out stub mortises.

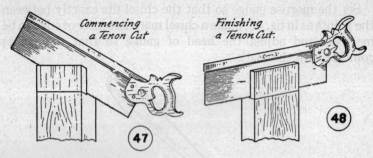

Commencing a Tenon Cut.

Finishing a Tenon Cut.

FIGS. 47 and 48—Depicting the making of a tenon cut.

Cutting the Tenon.—Fasten the piece firmly in the bench vise and commence the cut on the end grain and saw diagonally toward the shoulder line, as in fig. 47. Finish by removing the material in the vise, and cutting downward square with the edge as in fig. 48. The diagonal saw cut acts as a guide for the finishing cut and makes for greater accuracy. Very small tenons are cut with a dovetail saw.

Cutting the Shoulder.—After making the tenon cuts, and to overcome the difficulty in cutting the shoulders experienced by some, place the piece on the shoulder board or bench hook, and carefully chisel a V-shaped cut against the shoulder line, as in fig. 49.

Hold the work firmly against the stop on the board, place the saw in the chiseled channel and begin cutting by drawing it backward, afterwards pushing forward with a light stroke, holding the thumb and forefinger against the saw as in fig. 50, and keep the saw in an upright position. A straightedge is sometimes placed against the shoulder line as a guide in wide shoulders. In the case of very wide tenons and shoulders, a rebate and shoulder plane only are used, the straightedge used as a guide for the rebate plane.

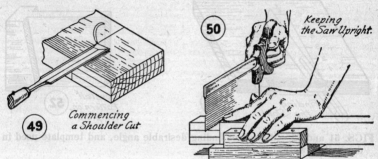

FIGS. 49 and 50—Arrangement of tools and material when making the shoulder cut.

Dovetail Joints.—The method of making dovetail joints is described in a previous chapter.

In common dovetailing it is a matter of convenience whether the pins or dovetails are cut first. However, where a number of pieces are to be dovetailed, time can be saved by putting them together in the vise and cutting the dovetails first.

The Angle of Dovetails.—For particular work where the joint is exposed, the dovetails should be cut at an angle of 1 in 8, and for heavier work, 1 in 6.

To find the angle, draw a line square with the edge of a board and divide it into 6 or 8 parts as desired; from the end of the line and square with it, mark off a space equal to one of the divisions and set the bevel as shown in fig. 51.

A dovetail template, as shown in fig. 52, will be found very handy where there is much dovetailing to be done. To make it, take a rectangular piece of ¾ in. material, any desired size, square the edges and with the mortise gauge set for a ¼ in. mortise, ¼ in. from the edge, scribe both edges and one end;

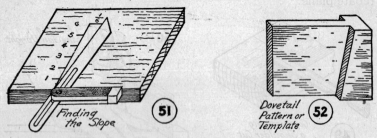

Finding the Slope **51**

Dovetail Pattern or Template **52**

FIGS. 51 and 52—Method of finding desirable angle, and template used in dovetailing work.

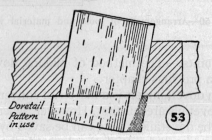

Dovetail Pattern in use **53**

FIG. 53—Method of laying out work, utilizing dovetail template shown in fig. 52.

with the bevel set as shown, mark the shoulder lines across both sides of the lower portion, and cut it with tenon saw, same as cutting a tenon. Make one for each of the two angles. It might also be made by gluing a straightedge, at the required angle, across both sides at one end of a straight piece of thin material.

Using a dovetail template saves time and insures uniformity. Place the shoulder of the template against the edge as shown in fig. 53, and mark along its edge one side of the dovetail; reverse it, put the other shoulder at the same edge and mark the other side of the dovetail.

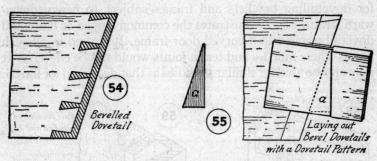

FIGS. 54 and 55—Bevelled dovetailing and method of laying out work with the assistance of dovetail template.

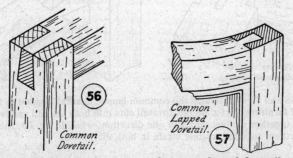

FIGS. 56 and 57—Details of common and common lapped dovetail.

Bevelled Dovetailing.—Fig. 54 is very frequently required in cabinet work, and a template is a great help in marking them out. To use the template for marking bevel dovetails, cut a wedge-shape piece of material as shown in fig. 55a, bevelled at the same angle as the bevel of the material to be dovetailed:

insert it between the edge of the material and the template, with its square edge to the shoulder of the template as in fig. 55; mark dovetail as described, but do not reverse the wedge-shape piece.

Fig. 56 shows the common or through dovetail, mainly used for dovetailing brackets and frames subject to heavy downward strain. Fig. 57 illustrates the common lapped or half blind dovetail applied to a curved door frame. It is used in all such places where mortise and tenon joints would not be effective. It may also be used for similar purposes as that described for fig. 56.

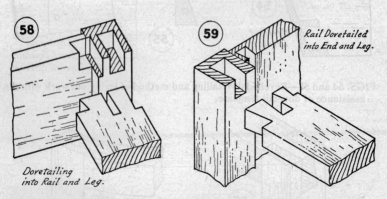

FIGS. 58 and 59—Illustrates the common lapped dovetail applied to the framing of furniture. In fig. 58 the dovetail cuts into both the rail and leg locking them together against strain in one direction, while in fig. 59, the dovetail locks them together against strain in both directions.

Fig. 60 shows the common housed dovetail, called "bareface" because it is shouldered on one side only. Fig. 61 which is shouldered and dovetailed on both sides, is another of the same type, having the dovetailing parallel its entire length. These are the simplest forms of housed dovetailing. Their application to framing of furniture is shown in fig. 73.

Fig. 62 illustrates a shouldered housing dovetail with the dovetail tapering in its length. Like the two preceding joints, it is shouldered on one or both sides. The tapered dovetail makes

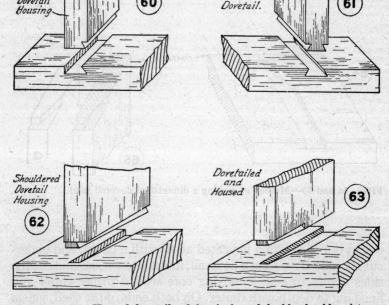

FIGS. 60 to 63—Housed dovetails of the single and double shouldered type.

it particularly adaptable to connecting fixed shelves to partitions. The dovetails prevent the partitions from bending. Fig. 63 illustrates a dovetailed and housed joint frequently called a "diminished" dovetail. It is principally used on comparatively small work, such as small fixed shelves and drawer rails.

Setting Out a Diminished Dovetail.—Square division lines across the ends into which the shelf is to be housed and dovetailed, as far apart as the thickness of the shelf, and gauge the depth of housing on back edge. Gauge lines ⅜ and 4½ in. from the front edge between the division lines; the space between these gauged lines brings the length of the actual dovetail as shown in fig. 64.

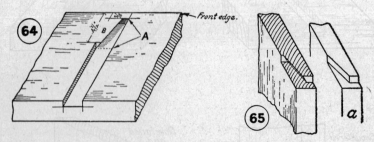

FIGS. 64 and 65—Method of making a diminished dovetail joint.

Cut out the section indicated at **A,** with a chisel, and undercut the side **B,** to form a dovetail; insert a tenon saw and cut the sides across to edge removing core with a firmer chisel and finishing to depth with router. On both ends of the shelf, gauge lines on side and end for depth of dovetail, and square across the end the distances from the front edge already given; cut away the surplus wood with tenon saw as shown at 65a, and finish with chisel, carefully testing until it fits hand tight. Fig. 65 shows completed end. The average length of the actual dovetail of this type is slightly less than ¼ of the total length of dovetail and housing.

Mitred Joints.—Mitring plays an important part in cabinet work in the framing of furniture, and in panelling where many difficult mouldings have to be mitred into place.

Fig. 66 illustrates a plain mitre with a cross tongue inserted at right angles to the mitre. It is principally used for mitring end grain, and is additionally strengthened by gluing a block to the internal angle, as shown in fig. 73.

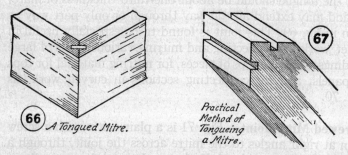

66 *A Tongued Mitre.*

67

Practical Method of Tongueing a Mitre.

FIGS. 66 and 67—Illustrates a tongued mitre joint and method of tonguing a mitre.

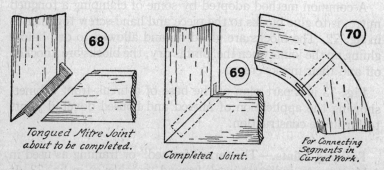

68

Tongued Mitre Joint about to be completed.

69

Completed Joint.

70

For Connecting Segments in Curved Work.

FIGS. 68 to 70—Showing the tongued mitre joint in various types of construction.

Tonguing a Mitre.—A very practical way of tonguing this joint, is to fasten two mitres together in a vise so as to form a right angle as in fig. 67, and thus provide an edge from which to gauge the position of the tongues and for plowing the grooves. If the pieces are not over 6 in. in width, the grooves are cut with dovetail saw and chiselled to depth.

Fig. 68 is a variation of plain mitring, and like the preceding joint, is most generally used for end grain jointing. For this joint, the tongue should be about one-third thickness of material, and may extend all the way through or only part way as shown in fig. 69. This joint is found to be especially useful in cabinet work for connecting and mitring various types of large mouldings round the tops of pieces, for mitring material for tops and panels, and for connecting sections in curved work, as in fig. 70.

Screwed Mitre Joint.—Fig. 71 is a plain mitre with a screw driven at right angles to the mitre across the joint, through a notch cut in the outside of the frame. It is used principally in light moulded frames.

A common method adopted by some of clamping a tongued mitre, is to glue blocks to the piece and hand-screw together as in fig. 72. The blocks are glued on and allowed to dry before gluing up the joint; when the joint is dry, the blocks are knocked off and their marks erased.

Fig. 73 is a part plan of the base of a break-front cabinet, showing the application of mitred and housed dovetail joints to furniture construction.

Framing Joints.—The term "framed" or framing as used in cabinet work, indicates work framed together as in fig. 73. It also refers to the "grounds" for fixing panelling to walls.

The following illustrations represent various joints used in connecting angles of panelling. Figs. 74 and 75 are identical except for the return bead which is worked on one of the pieces.

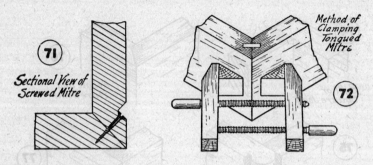

FIGS. 71 and 72—Screwed mitre joint and method of gluing up a tongued mitre.

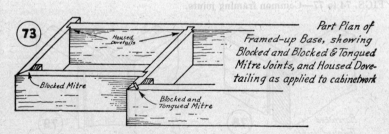

FIG. 73—Application of various forms of joints used in cabinet construction.

They are usually glued and nailed, but when used as an external angle, are secret-screwed before painting. That is, the screws are sunk below the surface and plugs or pellets of wood glued in the holes and bevelled off. Fig. 76 may be used to connect framing at any angle. The rebate prevents slipping while being nailed or screwed. Fig. 77, an ordinary rebated joint with the corner rounded off, and glued together. Because of its rounded corner it is often used in furniture for children's nurseries.

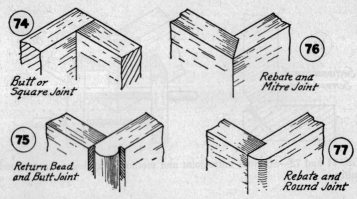

FIGS. 74 to 77—Common framing joints.

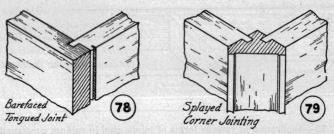

FIGS. 78 and 79—Barefaced tongued and applied corner framing joints.

Fig. 78 is shouldered on one side only. A bead is worked on the tongue piece to hide the joint. It is used for both internal and external angles, with or without the bead. Fig. 79 shows the bareface tongued joint used for joining sides into a pilaster corner.

Hinging and Shutting Joints.—The dust-proof joint and its application is considered a necessary part of cabinetmaking.

Fig. 80. The rebated dust-proof joint shown here is applied to a butt hinged double door closet. A bead is glued into the

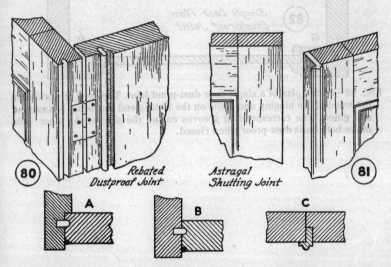

FIGS. 80 and 81—Showing hinging and shutting joints as used in cabinet construction.

rebated end back of the hinge, which is sunk flush, and a corresponding groove is cut in the door stile fitting over the bead when closed. The beads are sometimes covered with felt or rubber, making the joint absolutely dust-proof.

Fig. 81 shows the shutting joint with a beaded strip glued to the stile, and rebated to project over, and conceal any shrinkage in the adjoining stile. Diagram **A** shows the plain of joint at the hinge ends when closed. **B** shows plan of a plain butted hinged dust-proof joint. **C** is plan of the beaded shutting joint when closed, but with the astragal rebated into the stile.

FIG. 82—Shows plan of a single door dust-proof joint. The bead is worked on the wood of the hinging end while on the locking end the bead is inserted and glued. The corresponding grooves cut on the side of the door stile make both ends dust-proof when closed.

CHAPTER 24B

Wood Patternmaking

It is not to be assumed that this Chapter is intended to completely cover the subject of wood patternmaking in all its branches. The sole object is to present by means of description and illustration, its salient features and approved methods of obtaining satisfactory results.

The term *"patternmaking"* as applied here means the making of patterns to be used in forming molds for castings.

Patterns are made of different materials such as metal, plaster and wood. Most patterns are made of wood.

Patterns of every known kind of machine, from the smallest to the largest, are all made of wood. Therefore, this Chapter is confined to the subject of *"Wood Patternmaking."*

Wood patternmaking is regarded as the most important branch of the trade because of the greater amount of skill and technical knowledge required. It includes joiners work and the mastery of wood-working tools and machinery, a knowledge of wood carving and turning. The ability to read complicated blue prints and visualize the shape and form of the pattern from the print; also a thorough understanding of foundry and core work.

Although a pattern is defined as a model, its outward appearance does not always closely resemble the casting itself except in a simple casting, where the pattern is often a complete model. If, however, the casting is to have interior passages and external openings, its appearance will be changed by the addition of projections termed *"core prints."* These are so placed as to form bearing surfaces in the mold to support the sand cores used to form those passages or openings in the castings. These cores are usually formed in wooden molds called *"core boxes"* and the prints on the pattern are distinguished by being painted a different color from the pattern itself.

A pattern is given a certain amount of taper or *"draft"* to insure its easy removal from the molding sand; the removing process is called *"drawing."* A pattern is said to draw well or not, according to the amount of trouble experienced in removing it from the molding sand.

Patternmaker's Tools.—The first requisite of a patternmaker should be a complete set of good tools. The following list will be found adequate for a wide range of work:

Jack plane.

Block plane.

End-wood plane. (For planing long end-wood edges. It is 14 ins. long with the iron ground straight along the cutting edge. Often referred to as a *"jack plane".*)

Jointer plane.

Rabbet plane.

Router.

Circular plane. (Adjustable to both concave and convex surfaces.)

Core-box plane.

Paring chisel. (Fig. 1.)

Paring gouge. (Fig. 2.)

Outside ground gouge. (So called because it is ground on the outside or convex side. It is shorter and heavier than the paring gouge and is used for roughing work, and with the mallet when necessary.)

Carving Tools. (Those most commonly used are known as: *straight, short-bend* and *long-bend tools.* A number of different sweeps of each style.)

Bit brace (Ratchet.)

Hand drill.

Automatic drill.

Auger Bits. (In sizes from $\frac{3}{16}$ to 1 in.)

Gimlet bit. (For drilling screw holes.)

Center bit. (For drilling thin stock.)

Forstner bit. (For drilling flat bottom holes.)

Expansion bit.

Bit stock drills. (Standard twist drills with square shank to fit hand braces, $\frac{1}{16}$-$1\frac{1}{4}$.)

Screwdriver-bit.

Countersink bits.

Bit stop.

Back saw.

Key hole saw.

Coping saw.

Hammer (Patternmaker's). (Fig. 3.)

Claw hammer. (Medium size.)

Oil stones. And slip stones or "slips" of different shapes for sharpening the edge of cutting tools.)

Spoke shave. (Large and small.)

Hand screws.

Pinch-dogs. (Fig. 4.)

Bar clamps.

Distance marking gauge. (Monkey gauge.)

Panel gauge.

Turning tools.

Hermaphrodite calipers.

Outside calipers.

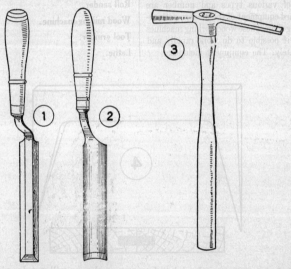

FIGS. 1 to 3—The paring chisel, fig. 1, is the patternmaker's principal tool. This is a long thin chisel varying in width from ⅛ to 2 ins. with square or beveled edges and straight or offset tangs. For general use, the ½ in. width is the most convenient, preferably with beveled edges and offset tang as illustrated. The paring gouge, fig. 2, like the chisel, is long and thin and varies from ⅛ to 2 in. in width, having three different curve sweeps known as "flat, middle and regular." They are called "inside-ground" gouges because they are ground on the inner or concaved side. Fig. 3 shows a patternmaker's hammer, especially designed to meet the requirements of the trade. The long slender end is used for driving nails in fillets and reaching corners that cannot be reached with the ordinary hammer.

Inside calipers.

Dividers. (Large and small.)

Trammels. (With inside and outside caliper points.)

Bevel square.

Combination square.

Screwdrivers.

Scribers.

Shop Machinery.—Power driven machine tools of various types and number are standard equipment of the modern pattern-making shop. These woodworking machines make it possible to do work rapidly and accurately. The equipment includes:

Circular saw.

Band saw.

Jointer.

Surfacer.

Trimmer.

Jig saw.

Sanding machines.

Disc sander.

Roll sander.

Wood milling machine.

Tool grinder.

Lathe.

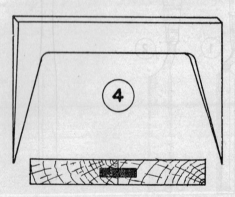

FIG. 4—In many cases where hand screws or clamps will not do, pinch-dogs, as shown, are used. The taper on the inside of the legs causes them to "pinch" when driven into two adjoining pieces.

Trade Terms.—There are certain *"Trade terms"* in common use in the patternmaking shop and in the foundry with which the prospective patternmaker should become familiar in order that he may have an intelligent understanding of his work. The most essential of these are:

Flask—A wood or metal frame made in two parts. Fig. 5.

Cope.—This term refers to the top part of the flask.

Drag.—This refers to the bottom part of the flask.

Bottom or Mold Board.—A board which lies under the drag on which the pattern rests while the mold is being rammed. It is also used on the top while rolling the mold over. Fig. 6.

Draft.—This is the taper put on the pattern so that it will "draw" easily out of the sand.

Boss.—A circular projection, knob or stud. Fig. 7.

Fillet.—Meaning a round corner used in patterns. Fig. 8.

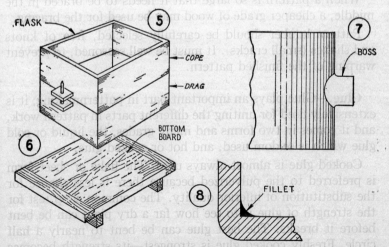

FIGS. 5 to 8—Here figs. 5 and 6 illustrate a patternmaker's flask. Figs. 7 and 8 show a boss and fillet respectively.

Materials

Lumber.—The most common varieties of wood used in patternmaking are: *White pine, mahogany, cherry, maple* and *birch.*

White pine is considered by far the best wood for all but the smallest patterns. It is soft and therefore easy to work, porous enough to take glue well, insuring strong glue joints, and when properly seasoned, is not much affected by exposure to heat, cold or dampness.

Cherry wood is used when greater strength is required in the pattern. It is also most generally used for small patterns.

Mahogany is used for patterns of light and thin construction, requiring strength and much hand work.

Maple and birch are too hard for economical hand tool work, but are well suited for small turned patterns.

When a pattern is so large that it needs to be braced in the middle, a cheaper grade of wood may be used for the bracing.

Pattern lumber should be carefully selected, free of knots and shakes (small cracks). It must be well seasoned, to prevent warping of the finished pattern.

Glue.—Glue plays an important part in patternmaking; it is extensively used for uniting the different parts in pattern work, and it comes in two forms and many grades, the liquid or cold glue which is seldom used, and hot or cooked glue.

Cooked glue is almost always used. The flake or sheet form is preferred to the pulverized because there is less chance for the substitution of inferior quality. The common shop test for the strength of glue is to see how far a dry piece can be bent before it breaks. The best glue can be bent to nearly a half circle. Freshly cooked glue is strongest—its strength becomes less with each successive heating and cooling.

Be sure to make the surfaces of the joint quite true before applying the glue, which should be thin enough to flow freely and penetrate the pores of the wood. Thick glue does not make a strong joint. Large surfaces should first be warmed and the glue applied to both surfaces quickly, and while very hot and rather thin.

End wood should always have a first coat of glue rubbed into the grain and a second coat applied before clamping together.

Shellac or Pattern Varnish.—Yellow shellac (commercially known as orange shellac) is used in pattern shops for varnishing finished patterns as a protection against atmospheric moisture and the wet molding sand, which would warp them, and to make them "*draw*" easier from the molding sand.

Pattern Colors.—It is a general shop practice to indicate core-prints and core-box faces by some given color, and to paint the patterns some recognized code of colors to correspond to the metals in which they are to be cast. As for example:

Pattern and core-box bodies for iron casting, are painted *black*.

Patterns and core-box bodies for steel casting are painted *blue*.

Patterns and core-box bodies for brass casting, are painted *orange*.

All core-prints and core-box faces are painted *red*.

Colored shellac is used for this purpose and is made by dissolving the powdered color in a little alcohol, and mixing it with the orange shellac.

Dowel Pins.—It frequently happens that some patterns must be put together in such a way that certain parts can be easily removed and replaced again as required; a split pattern is a typical example. Small dowel pins of wood or metal are used for this purpose. Wooden dowel pins are used if the pattern is to be used only a few times, but where there is much wear to a pattern, and on large patterns, metal dowels and dowel-plates are invariably used. Two styles of metal dowel plates commonly used are shown in figs. 9 and 10.

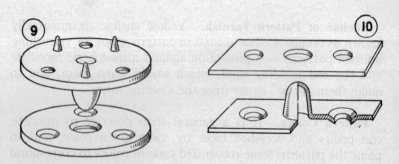

FIGS. 9 and 10—Illustrating two types of metal dowel plates.

Fillets.—Fillets or concave connecting pieces are used in the corners and at the intersection of surfaces of a pattern for the very important reason that they increase the strength of a casting by influencing the crystallization of the metal, and also to improve the appearance of the casting.

Fillets are of two types, "*stuck*" and "*planted*." A stuck fillet is one cut with a gouge out of the wood left on the pattern for that purpose, as in fig. 11. A planted fillet is one made separately and fitted in. Planted fillets are most commonly used and are made of wood, leather and wax (beeswax).

Wood fillets are used for corners of large radii and on straight work. A round plane and fillet board, figs. 12 and 13, are used for planing wood fillets. The stock is first reduced to a triangular section, fig. 14, on the circular saw, and cut to suitable lengths and the stock on the fillet reducing plane, with the round plane, with a screw head at the end so that it groove acts as a stop.

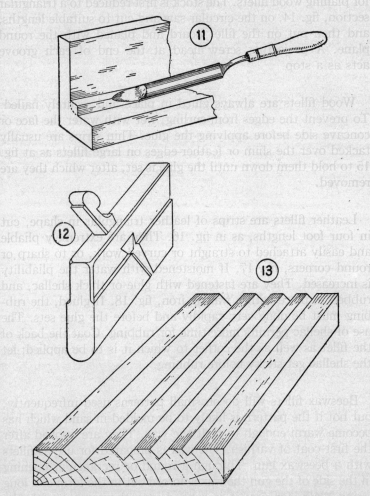

FIGS. 11 to 13—Showing tools and method used for shaping various types of fillets.

for planing wood fillets. The stock is first reduced to a triangular section, fig. 14, on the circular saw and cut to suitable lengths, and then put on the fillet board and planed with the round plane. A projecting screw head at the end of each groove acts as a stop.

Wood fillets are always glued in place and securely nailed. To prevent the edges from curling, wet with water the face or concave side before applying the glue. Thin strips are usually tacked over the shim or feather-edges on large fillets as at fig. 15 to hold them down until the glue is set, after which they are removed.

Leather fillets are strips of leather triangular in shape, cut in four foot lengths, as in fig. 16. They are extremely pliable and easily attached to straight or curved work, or to sharp or round corners, fig. 17. If moistened with water the pliability is increased. They are fastened with glue or thick shellac, and rubbed in place with a waxing iron, fig. 18. If glued, the rubbing must be done very rapidly and before the glue sets. The use of shellac permits more time for rubbing. Coat the back of the fillet as well as the corner to which it is to be applied; let the shellac get sticky before rubbing.

Beeswax fillets will do on small patterns used infrequently, but not if the pattern is likely to be molded in sand which has become warm enough to melt the wax. They are applied after the first coat of varnish. The wax is prepared for use as fillets with a beeswax gun. Through a round or rectangular opening in the side of the gun the wax is forced out in the form of a long string ready for use; it is rubbed into the corners with the waxing iron.

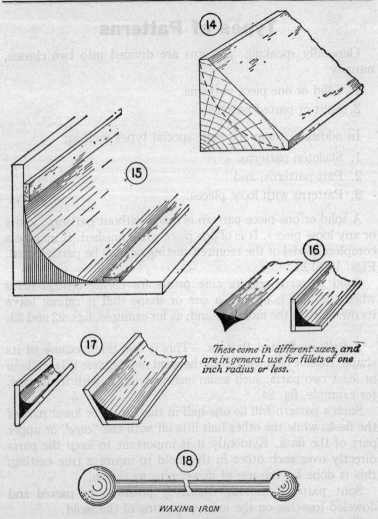

These come in different sizes, and are in general use for fillets of one inch radius or less.

WAXING IRON

FIGS. 14 to 18—Methods used in obtaining variously shaped fillets. Fig. 18 illustrates a typical waxing iron used in fillet construction.

Types of Patterns

Generally speaking, patterns are divided into two classes, namely:

1. Solid or one piece patterns.
2. Split or parted patterns.

In addition, there are some special types such as:

1. Skeleton patterns.
2. Part patterns, and
3. Patterns with loose pieces.

A solid or one-piece pattern is made without partings, joints or any loose pieces. It is of one piece when finished. It may be a complete model of the required casting or may be partly cored. Figs. 19 to 21.

Solid patterns require core prints for coring central holes when the hole is of such a size or shape that it cannot leave its own core in the molding sand, as for example, figs. 22 and 23.

A Split or Parted Pattern.—This is one that because of its shape, cannot be drawn from the sand mold unless it is made in at least two parts, such as an engine cylinder with its flanges, for example, fig. 24.

Such a pattern will lie one-half in the "*drag*" or lower part of the flask, while the other half lifts off with the "*cope*" or upper part of the flask. Evidently it is important to keep the parts directly over each other in the mold to insure a true casting; this is done by the use of dowel pins as shown.

Split patterns should, whenever possible, be parted and doweled together on the joint or parting of the mold.

Skeleton patterns are wooden frames used in framing a portion of the pattern in sand or clay. After the sand or clay is rammed inside the frame, it is worked to the required form by pieces of wood called "*strickles*."

Part patterns are sections of a pattern so arranged as to form a complete mold by being moved to form each section of the mold. The movements are guided either by following a line or by the use of a central pin or pivot. They are generally applied to circular work.

Patterns with "*Loose Pieces*" are patterns with projecting parts that form under-cuts which prevent their being drawn with the main body of the pattern without destroying the mold.

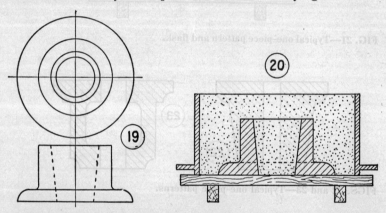

FIGS. 19 and 20—A very simple form of a "solid" or one-piece pattern. It is a complete model of the required casting including the control hole, which is large enough to let the molding sand stand in it as a "green sand" core to form the hole in the casting. The pattern is placed on the molding board with the larger side down and the bottom or "drag" part of the flask placed over it as in fig. 20. The surface of the pattern is covered with facing or fine molding sand which is rammed in and around it, and the drag filled with coarser sand which is rammed flush with the top. A bottom board is placed on top of the drag, which is then turned over and the first board removed. Parting sand is dusted over the exposed side of the drag and the "cope" side of the flask put in place, and rammed flush with the top as shown in fig. 21. The arrow indicates the direction in which the pattern is to be drawn from the mold.

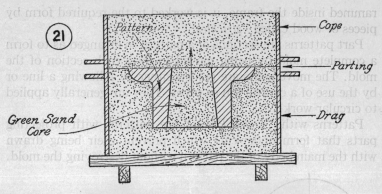

FIG. 21—Typical one-piece pattern and flask.

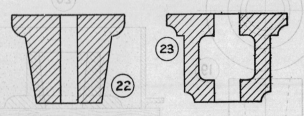

FIGS. 22 and 23—Typical one-piece patterns.

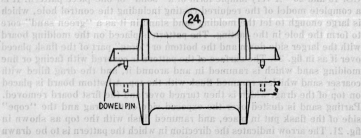

FIG. 24—Illustrating typical split or parted pattern.

The under-cutting projections are made as loose pieces, and fastened in place with loose dowels or "*skewers.*" By removing the skewers the pattern is freed; the loose pieces which remain in the mold when the pattern is drawn, are drawn into the cavity left by the pattern and removed from the mold; this is called "*picking in.*"

Cores, Core Prints and Core Boxes.—Core or dry sand core is a molded form made of sand mixed with a binder and baked until dry and firm. It is placed in the mold to form the interior passage or opening in the casting.

Green Sand Core.—The term used where the sand is allowed to stand in the mold and the metal run around it to form the interior passage or opening in the casting.

Core Prints.—When a casting is to be hollow, its pattern must be made with a core print as shown in fig. 25. This core print leaves a cavity or shelf in the sand mold, into which is laid a "*core*" as in fig. 26. When the metal is poured into the mold it surrounds the core and leaves an opening of its size and shape in the casting. The sand core is easily knocked out when the metal has cooled.

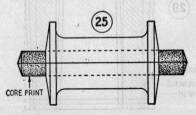

CORE PRINT

FIG. 25—Showing a split or parted pattern together with its core print used for hollow casting.

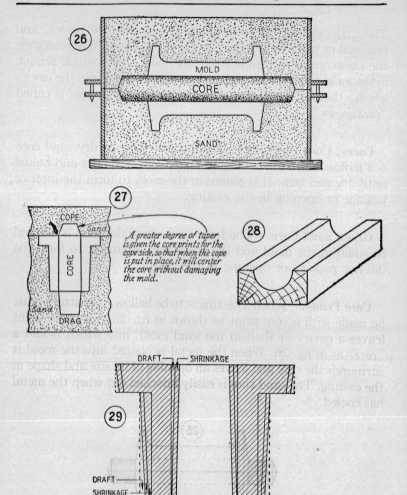

FIGS. 26 to 29—Illustrating various methods used in procuring a hollow casting. Fig. 29 illustrates the draft required on a pattern for a vertical casting.

There are two kinds of core prints, *vertical* and *horizontal*. Core prints should be given a taper in order to draw them from the sand, especially in the case of vertical prints. The usual core print taper is ⅛ in. per inch.

For vertical cores the lower core print should be longer than the upper one, as it practically supports the whole core; while the upper one serves only to keep the core from moving, fig. 27.

Horizontal cores usually have to be supported at both ends, as shown in fig. 26. The length of the core prints at these points is decided by the weight of the core; a heavy core requiring longer prints to give sufficient support to the cores, and to guard against the crumbling of the edges of the sand mold.

Core Boxes.—A core is molded to the required shape and size in a core box, as in fig. 28.

When both halves of a core are exactly alike, this type of half a core box is made to save the patternmaker's time. The core is made in two halves and pasted together after they are baked. If it is necessary to make a complete circular core box, the two parts are usually held together by dowels; thus making it easy to remove the core from the box.

In a core box for a large pattern, an allowance for expansion should be made, as cores expand in baking.

If the cores are not dried too quickly, the figure generally used for core box allowance is 1/16 in. per foot.

To insure good surfaces on the core, see to it that the face of the core box is smooth.

Draft.—A taper or "draft" must be given to vertical parts of a pattern, otherwise it would be impossible to "*draw*" it from the molding sand without damaging the mold. This tapering called the "*draft*" is shown in fig. 29.

The size and shape of a pattern determines the amount of draft to be allowed. However, it is good practice to allow one eighth of an inch to the foot of length.

Shrinkage.—When the molten metal is poured into a mold, it contracts as it cools and leaves the casting smaller than its mold. Therefore, in order to have the casting the required size, this shrinkage must be allowed for in making the pattern.

The shrinkage allowances usually employed by pattern-makers are:

Iron . . . . . . ⅛ in. per foot

Steel . . . . . . ³⁄₁₆ in. per foot

Brass . . . . . . ³⁄₁₆ in. per foot

Finish.—When any of the surfaces of a pattern are to be machined and finished off, an allowance for the finish must be made also, in addition to that for draft and shrinkage, as in fig. 29. The amount allowed for this varies from about ¹⁄₁₆ in. to ¼ in. according to the location and nature of the casting, the methods of machining it, and the degree of finish required.

A good general rule to remember for cast iron, small or medium sized work to be finished in lathe, planer or milling machine, is about ⅛ inch. For larger pieces, the allowance will vary from ¼ to ¾ inch.

An extra finish allowance is usually made on the cope side of patterns for large castings, to permit machining to the sound metal beneath the slag that always rises to the top of a mold.

If a casting is to be finished only on one end, the pattern should be marked so as to make that fact known to the foundry man. Some foundries paint the finished surfaces green.

Shrinkage Rule.—These are special rules with the shrinkage of the casting metal added. In appearance they are the same as an ordinary rule, except that they are longer. Thus, a two-foot shrink rule for ⅛ inch shrinkage to the foot, will be ¼ inch longer than the standard rule. They are made of wood or steel, in one-and two-foot lengths. These rules may be had for all the standard shrinkages.

Blueprints.—A blueprint is the plan of a casting from which the patternmaker is required to construct a pattern.

On standard blueprints there is a title block in the lower right-hand corner. It gives the *company's* name, and the *draftsman's* name. It tells whether the drawing is full size, half size, or quarter size, and also the kind of material to be used for the casting.

The notes on the blueprint should be carefully studied. When a drawing is to be scaled for dimensions, a standard scale should always be used on the work. If the dimension is marked thus, ¾ in., it means the drawing is out of scale. If holes are marked drill, this means the casting will be drilled. If marked bored, or with an "*f*", indicating finish, an allowance should be left on for this, the amount determined by the kind of material to be used for the casting.

On small work where the blueprint is marked spot face or disc grind, only about 1/32 in. finish allowance is added.

Joints and Joinery

Pattern Joinery.—Joinery is defined as: The art of a joiner. It is in fact, the art of joint making, and as such, is an important part of patternmaking. It is a work which requires the utmost skill, because of the precision and accuracy with which the parts must be shaped and fitted together.

It involves planing straight edges on the parts to be joined together, facing or forming true or plane surfaces on the sides of flat stock, cutting grooves, mortises and dovetails, planing, sawing or trimming edges to angles, fitting parts to circular or irregular forms, and many other like operations.

There are various forms of joints used in the construction of patterns and core boxes, and it is essential to know the different forms, and when and where to use them to the best advantage. They are:

1. Straight or butt.
2. Checked.
3. Half-lapped.
4. Tongue and groove.
5. Splined.

6. Rabbet
7. Dado
8. Mortise and tenon.
9. Dovetail!

The Butt Joint.—The butt joint, fig. 30, is the simplest form of joint and probably used most of all especially for light framework. It is not very strong even when properly glued, and should be reinforced whenever possible by nails, screws or dowels.

Checked Joint.—This joint, fig. 31, is also known as the housed, butt or rabbeted joint. It has an advantage over the butt joint in that it may be nailed or screwed from the edge. It is also adaptable to the formation of corner fillets.

The Half-Tapped Joint.—There are three kinds of this joint in general use; the corner lap, the cross lap and the center lap. The center lap is sometimes dovetailed, figs. 32 to 35. The half-lapped joint is considered the best all-around fastening for light frames. When properly glued and fastened with screws, it makes a very strong joint and is commonly used in the joining of ribs and webs.

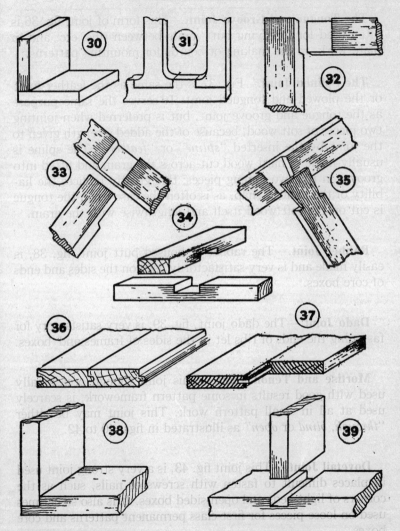

FIGS. 30 to 39—Various types of joints used in patternmaking.

The Tongue and Groove Joint.—This form of joint fig. 36 is often used for fortifying butt joints between ribs, etc. and in plate work, in the making of boards for mounting patterns.

The Splined Joint.—Fig. 37 is the same as the feather joint or the plowed and tongued joint. It serves the same purpose as the tongue and groove joint, but is preferred when jointing two pieces of soft wood, because of the added strength given to the joint by the inserted *"spline"* or *"feather."* The spline is usually made of hard wood cut across the grain and fitted into grooves in the two joining pieces; this greatly reduces the liability of the joint to snap, as is often the case when the tongue is cut on the soft wood itself and lengthwise with the grain.

Rabbet Joint.—The rabbet or housed butt joint, fig. 38, is easily made and is very satisfactorily used on the sides and ends of core boxes.

Dado Joint.—The dado joint, fig. 39, is very satisfactory for fastening the ends of ribs let in the sides of frames and boxes.

Mortise and Tenon Joint.—This joint though occasionally used with good results in some pattern framework, is scarcely used at all in small pattern work. This joint may be either *"through, blind or open"* as illustrated in figs. 40 to 42.

Dovetail Joint.—This joint fig. 43, is a very strong joint used in places difficult to fasten with screws or nails, such as the corners of light beds and open-sided boxes. It is also sometimes used on loose pieces for first-class permanent patterns and core boxes.

FIGS. 30 to 33—Various types of joints used in patternmaking.

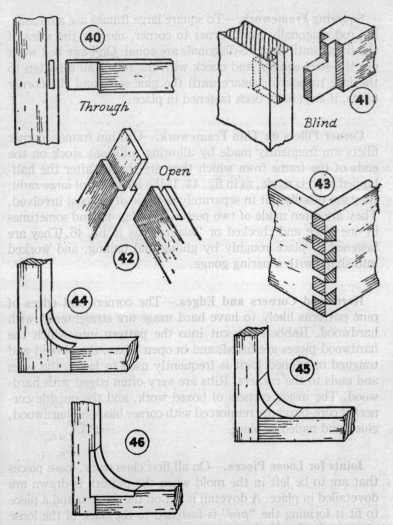

Squaring Framework.—To square large frames use a straightedge, and, generally, corner to corner, making sure that the two diagonals are equal. Or, square the frame with a . . . . and check w . . . . to the . . . . . square until the squa . . . . working . . . . it has . . . . been fastened in place.

Through

Blind

Open

Corner Fillets on Framework.—Certain frames and fillets are frequently made by allowing the . . . . stock on the ends of the frame from which . . . . after the half-ted . . . . . . made, as in fig. 44. Fillets . . . . . large radii . . . . in separately . . . . not involved. They are often made of two pie . . . . and sometimes in one piece and checked or . . . . as in fig. 46. They are . . . . place roughly by glu . . . . and worked . . . . with a bearing gouge.

Hard . . . Corners and Edges.—The corners and edges of pine patterns likely to have hard usage are strengthened with hardwood. Rabbeted . . . . . cut into the pattern into . . . the hardwood pieces a . . . . and in open . . . . and tongued or . . . . is frequently us . . . . and ends to . . . . Ribs are very often edged with hard-wood. The inside corners of boxed work, and the outside corners . . . . reinforced with corner blocks . . . hardwood, glued and nailed . . . .

Joints for Loose Pieces.—On all first class . . . . loose pieces that are to be left in the mold w . . . . . . tern is drawn are dovetailed in place. A dovetail is cut . . . the . . . . and a piece to fit it forming the "pin" is fastened to . . . . . . the loose

FIGS. 40 to 46—Various joints for square and curved–shaped patterns.

Squaring Framework.—To square large frames use a measuring rod diagonally from corner to corner, moving the sides of the frame until the two diagonals are equal. On large box work use the steel square, and check with the rod. Nail a batten to the face to hold it square until the glue sets, and the corner fillets, if any, have been fastened in place.

Corner Fillets on Thin Framework.—On thin frames, corner fillets are frequently made by allowing sufficient stock on the ends of the frame from which they are shaped after the half-lapped joint is made, as in fig. 44. If the fillets are of large radii, they are usually put in separately because of the cost involved. They are often made of two pieces, as in fig. 45, and sometimes in one piece and checked or *"housed,"* as in fig. 46. They are fastened in place roughly by gluing and nailing, and worked into shape with a paring gouge.

Hardwood Corners and Edges.—The corners and edges of pine patterns likely to have hard usage are straightened with hardwood. Rabbets are cut into the pattern into which the hardwood pieces are fitted; and in open boxes, the plowed and tongued or splined joint is frequently used to fasten the sides and ends to the corners. Ribs are very often edged with hardwood. The inside corners of boxed work, and the outside corners of core-boxes are reinforced with corner blocks of hardwood, glued and nailed in place.

Joints for Loose Pieces.—On all first class work, loose pieces that are to be left in the mold when the pattern is drawn are dovetailed in place. A dovetail is cut on the pattern and a piece to fit it forming the *"pin"* is fastened to the back of the loose piece, as in fig. 47. In laying out the dovetail, provide ample taper in the direction of the draw, as shown in fig. 48, and plane up the pin about half an inch longer and a trifle thicker than the depth of the dovetail from the face to the bottom; the additional length allows for cutting off of stock at the bottom if the dovetail should be cut a trifle too big and the added thickness permits planing the dovetail piece flush with the pattern face. A back saw is used to cut the dovetail socket, cutting as close to the line as possible and as far as the lines will allow. The stock is removed from the socket with a chisel, or finished to depth with a router.

Fillets on Loose Pieces.—Where fillets are required on loose pieces that are to be "*picked in,*" the loose piece is gained or grooved into the pattern, as in fig. 49, in order to give the fillet a thicker and stronger edge; thus eliminating the feather edge which is so easily broken. This thick edge is sometimes made in the form of a dovetail, as at **A,** fig. 49.

Pattern Details and Assembly

Patternmaker's Box.—The patternmaker's box, as shown in fig. 50, is used as a foundation in making many patterns, especially if they be of regular outline and rectangular form. It should be made so as to have as few pieces of end wood as possible in contact with the draw sides.

The top and bottom are fitted between the sides and ends to prevent them from extending beyond or falling short of the sides through shrinkage or other causes. As a support to the top and bottom the ends may be rabbeted and a central rib provided. This rabbet is sometimes formed by extra pieces glued and nailed to the inside of the box.

Shaping Parts Before Assembling.—Sometimes parts of patterns cannot be worked to shape after the pattern has been put together without great difficulty. In such a case, the parts should be laid out and cut as closely as possible to the lines before gluing. Framework that is to be shaped on the inside where machine finishing will be difficult after assembly, should be assembled for laying out and then taken apart and sawed. Screws or dogs may be used to fasten the work while being laid out. Pieces to be fitted in corners should be finished even to sandpapering before being fastened in place.

Fitting to Cylindrical Forms.—The usual practice when fitting to cylindrical pieces, is to chalk cylindrical parts, and rub and cut the piece to be fitted until it forms a tight joint. This fitting is principally done on the band saw; some additional fitting afterwards may be necessary, but don't spend much time in rubbing and hand fitting to make a perfect joint, because the fillet covers the joint. When making bosses, it is a good plan to use the thickest lumber on hand and fit as far as possible around the cylinder, and fill in with one or more pieces after the boss is fastened, as in fig. 51. This saves gluing large pieces. Figs. 52 and 53 illustrate an approved way of fitting a circular boss or branch to a cylindrical body.

Staved or Lagged Work.—Staved work is one of three methods used in constructing patterns and core boxes of the cylindrical type. The other two methods are known as stepped and segment work respectively.

A staved or lagged up pattern is constructed by the means of fastening barrow strips called "*staves*" or "*lags*" to foundation pieces called "*heads*." Fig. 54 shows the staves fastened to the heads of a pattern for half a regular cylinder that is to be

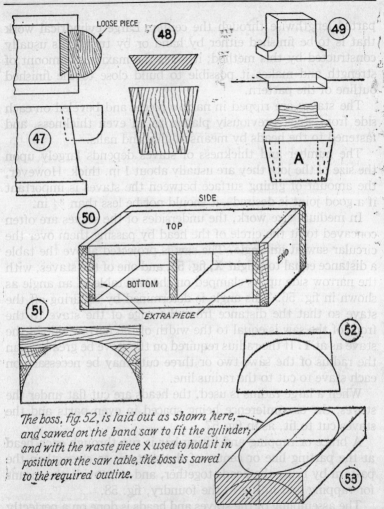

The boss, fig. 52, is laid out as shown here, and sawed on the band saw to fit the cylinder; and with the waste piece X used to hold it in position on the saw table, the boss is sawed to the required outline.

FIGS. 47 to 53—Joint details and a patternmaker's box are shown in figs. 47 to 50 respectively. Figs. 51 to 53 illustrate method of fitting a circular boss or branch to a cylindrical body.

parted lengthwise through the center. Large cylindrical work that is to be finished either by hand or by turning is usually constructed by this method; it gives the maximum amount of strength and makes it possible to build close to the finished outline of the pattern.

The staves are ripped in narrow pieces and beveled on each side from stock previously planed to an even thickness, and fastened to the heads by means of glue and nails.

The number and thickness of staves depends largely upon the size of the job; they are usually about 1 in. thick. However, the amount of gluing surface between the staves is important if a good joint is desired—it should not be less than ¾ in.

In medium size work, the undersides of the staves are often concaved to fit the circle of the head by passing them over the circular saw at an angle. The saw is projected above the table a distance equal to height **X**, fig. 55, and one of the staves, with the narrow side up, is clamped on the saw table at an angle as shown in fig. 56. This angle is determined by squaring off the stave so that the distance from the edge of the stave to the front of the saw is equal to the width of the narrow side of the stave as at **Y**. If the radius required on the stave be greater than the radius of the saw, two or three cuts may be necessary on each stave to cut to the radius line.

When a large radius is used, the heads are cut flat under the staves; the circumference being spaced in even parts and the staves cut to fit, as in fig. 57.

A brace or rapping and lifting bar is run through each head at the parting line or center of the pattern, to strengthen the pattern by tying the heads together, and to provide the means for rapping and lifting in the foundry, fig. 58.

The assembling of the staves and heads is done on a perfectly smooth, straight board having a straight edge. A center line is drawn parallel to the edge and lines representing the length of

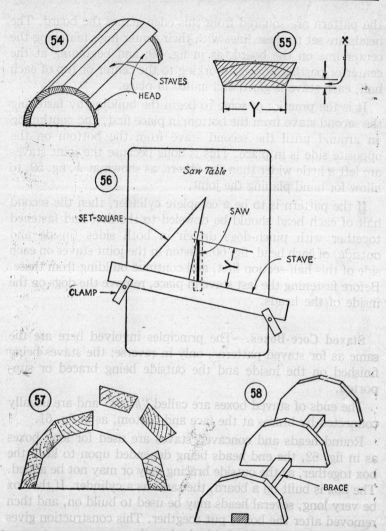

FIGS. 54 to 58—Illustrating staved work method to make cylindrical patterns.

the pattern are squared from this edge across the board. The heads are set to these lines with their center lines matching the center line on the board, as in fig. 59; and beginning at the center or parting line and working to the center or top of each half, each stave is glued and nailed in place.

It is the practice of some to begin the building by fastening the second stave from the bottom in place first, and continuing on around until the second stave from the bottom on the opposite side is in place. This is done because the joint staves are left a little wider than the others, as shown at **A**, fig. 59, to allow for hand planing the joint.

If the pattern is to be a complete cylinder, then the second half of each head should be doweled to the first and fastened together with pinch-dogs driven in both sides (inside and outside) of each head, fig. 60. Fasten in the joint staves on each side of this half-section first, and continue building from these. Before fastening the last stave in place, remove the dogs on the inside of the heads.

Staved Core-Boxes.—The principles involved here are the same as for staved patterns, only in reverse; the staves being finished on the inside and the outside being braced or supported.

The ends of staved boxes are called "*heads*" and are usually connected by braces at the face and bottom, as in fig. 61.

Round heads and concaved staves are used for long boxes as in fig. 62, the end heads being depended upon to keep the box together, as the outside bracing may or may not be added. The box is built on a board, the same as a cylinder. If the box be very long, several heads may be used to build on, and then removed after the box is put toegther. This construction gives a very true box, and is finished when the staves are put on.

Stepped work gets its name from the fact that the stock, when fastened together, resembles steps. It is the method used for constructing cylindrical forms such as straight and curved pipes up to 8 or 9 inches in diameter, that are to be finished in the lathe, and for elbows and bends of all sizes that are to be finished by hand.

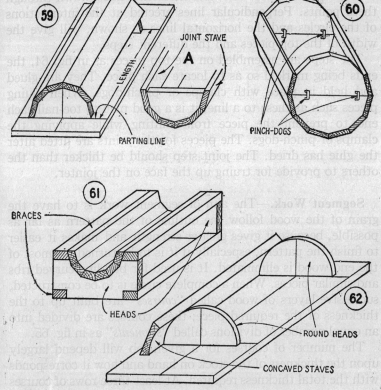

FIGS. 59 to 62—Staved core boxes and method of assembly.

Figs. 63 and 64 illustrate how a parted cylinder pattern is built by the stepped method. A lay-out is made of half the cylinder and the core-print as shown in fig. 63. The lumber used should be planed to thickness as the number of steps depends upon the thickness, and the two top pieces of the stock, and the different steps cut to width according to measurements taken on the lay-out. The outside diameter is divided into equal parts on the vertical center line, and horizontal lines drawn through these points. Perpendicular lines erected at the intersections of the circles and the horizontal lines as shown, will give the width of the top pieces and the different steps.

The steps are assembled on the top pieces as in fig. 64, the ends being marked so as to locate each piece. They are glued and held in place with clamps or pinch-dogs. When gluing pieces such as these to a line, it is a good plan to toe-nail each end to prevent the piece from shifting while applying the clamps or pinch-dogs. The pieces for the prints are fitted after the glue has dried. The joint step should be thicker than the others to provide for truing up the face on the jointer.

Segment Work.—The aim of segment work is to have the grain of the wood follow the outline of the pattern as far as possible, because it gives greater strength and makes it easier to finish the pattern, especially if it is to be turned, as most of the end wood is eliminated. It is used for building curved ribs and similar pieces. When a complete circle is to be constructed, successive layers of wood called "*courses*" are built up to the thickness of the required piece; these courses are divided into an equal number of divisions called "*segments*" as in fig. 65.

The number of courses for a given job will depend largely upon the thickness of the stock on hand and how it corresponds with the total thickness required. At least three rows of courses are necessary to avoid warping. An easy way to determine the number of courses is to make a layout of a section of the job, adding the necessary amount for finish, and divide this to suit the stock as shown at A, having 6 to each course. ██████ are six segments to a course, the length of each one is equal to the radius. The ████ ███████████

██ ████ ████ ██████ segment, 1-in. ████████ for ██████. The ████████████ is ███████ all ██████ then ████ laid up.

Sawing ████████ ██████ The band saw would be used in sawing segments, as close to the line as possible. The ends of the segments are cut to the ██████ ████ ██ the joining machine, which is equipped to ████ ██ ██████ the ██████ for a number of segments in a course, from three to twelve.

██████ ██████████████ segment, work are glued together with ██ segment lap on ███ course ████████ all works ████ up ███████. The above amount ██████ Quick glue is us██ ██████ be ████ ██████ the segments to size ████ ████████████ sure by nails, ██████ ██████ ████████

Coring, Construction. The ████████████████████ method of making a core box for square or ████████████████ ends with the ends dadoed into the sides and parti██████████ corners to release the core, fig. 67. The loose corners are fasten████ with screws ██████████████ or which ████████ a ████ black varnish, at the time that they are to be removed to ██████ box and released. ████████ dadoes ██ 1√4-in. ████████ usually ██ght on the shallow than those on the fastened corners in order to make the box ██████████ Corner blocks, securely glued and nailed in place, are used to reinforce the fastened corners. ████ corner blocks are ████████ ██ square ████████ ██████

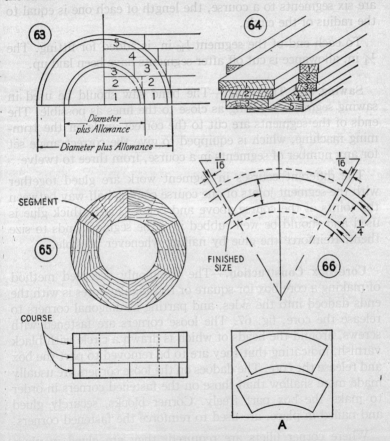

FIGS. 63 to 66—Figs. 63 and 64 illustrates construction of parted cylinder pattern by the stepped method. Figs. 65 and 66 show method of obtaining a cylindrical pattern by the segment method.

Laying Out Segments.—Fig. 66 shows the layout for a segment which is to be used as a pattern to mark the outline on the stock as shown at **A**, having 6 to each course. When there are six segments to a course, the length of each one is equal to the radius of the circle.

To each end of the segment 1/16 in. is added for fitting. The 1/4 in. allowance is cut off after segments have been laid up.

Sawing and Trimming.—The band saw should be used in sawing segments, cutting as close to the lines as possible. The ends of the segments are cut to the correct angle on the trimming machine, which is equipped to give the correct angle set for any number of segments in a course, from three to twelve.

The different courses in segment work are glued together with the segment joints of one course coming half-way between the joints of the course above and below. Fairly thick glue is used and should be well rubbed into the segment ends to size them. Reinforce the glue by nailing whenever possible.

Core-Box Construction.—The commonly accepted method of making a core box for square or rectangular cores is with the ends dadoed into the sides, and parting at diagonal corners to release the core, fig. 67. The loose corners are fastened with screws, around the heads of which is drawn a circle with black varnish, indicating that they are to be removed to part the box and release the core. The dadoes on the loose corners are usually made more shallow than those on the fastened corners in order to make the box part freely. Corner blocks, securely glued and nailed in place, are used to reinforce the fastened corners.

Where corner fillets are required, they are glued in place at the fastened corners, but at the parting they must be made a part of the side of the box, as shown in fig. 68.

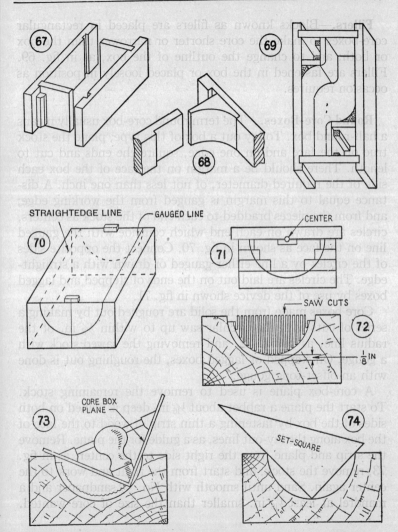

FIGS. 67 to 74—Illustrating various core-boxes and details of construction.

Fillers.—Blocks known as fillers are placed in rectangular core-boxes to make the core shorter or narrower than the box or both; and to change the outline of the box, as in fig. 69. Fillers are fastened in the box or placed loosely in position as occasion requires.

Round Core-Boxes.—The term round core-box usually means a half-round box. To lay out a box of this type, plane the stock true on the face and on one edge, square the ends and cut to length. There should be a margin on the face of the box each side of the required diameter, of not less than one inch. A distance equal to this margin is gauged from the working edge; and from the pieces bradded to each end of the stock as centers, circles are drawn on each end which coincide with the gauged line on the face as shown in fig. 70. Connect the opposite sides of the circles by a line either gauged or drawn with a straight-edge. The circles are laid out on the ends of stepped and lagged boxes by use of the device shown in fig. 71.

Core boxes made from the solid are roughed out by making a series of cuts with the circular saw up to within ⅛ in. of the radius line, as in fig. 72, and removing the sawed stock with a gouge. On stepped or lagged boxes, the roughing out is done with an offset-tong gouge.

A core-box plane is used to remove the remaining stock. To start the plane a rabbet about ⅟₁₆ in. deep is planed on both sides of the box by fastening a thin strip of wood to the face of the box along the lay-out lines, as a guide for the plane. Remove the strip and plane from the right side to the center, as in fig. 73, remove the stock, and start from the right and work to the center again. Sand until smooth with No. ½ sandpaper and a mandrel at least ⅟₁₆ in. smaller than the size of core wanted.

CHAPTER 25

Furniture Suggestions

Although not every mechanic has sufficient skill to make really fine furniture, yet there are a great many simple pieces which can be easily made. In general it is better to make the simplest things first, and when greater proficiency has been attained in the handling of tools and working wood, the more intricate and difficult pieces may be undertaken.

Tool Box.—It may be assumed that the amateur who desires to make things will first want a good tool box where his tools may be placed and locked. There is a great variety of tool boxes which may be obtained on the market, but to build one is the aim of the amateur who desires not only to save money but to increase his skill in the use of tools by using them.

Fig. 1,175 shows a tool box of simple design, which, with a little extra expense for materials and care in making is at once a work of art. The dove tail joints shown may be undertaken by those sufficiently advanced. This joint is not only the strongest, but considerably improves the appearance of the box. If desired, the construction may be simplified by mitre joints reinforced by inside corner pieces. However, the dove tail joint as shown is a good exercise in joint making. Before cutting the dove tails and pins (especially if costly wood be used for the box), it is better to make one or two practice joints, first with ordinary wood to avoid chance of spoiling one of the pieces for the box.

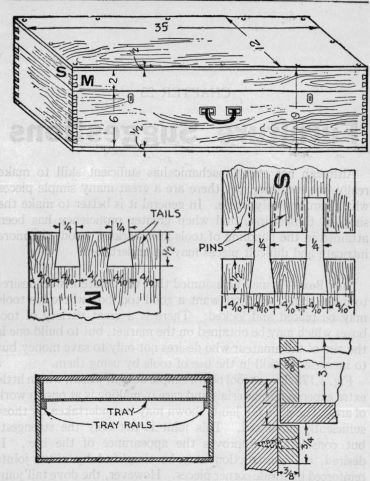

... mechanic has sufficient skill to make ... there are a great many simple pieces ... . In general it is better to make the ... when better appliances has been ... of tools than where the more intricate and difficult pieces may be ...

... It is assumed that the ... desires ... want a good ... tools ... may be ... and locked. There is a ... tool boxes which may be obtained on the market, but to build one is the ... amateur who desires not only to save money but to ... skill in the use of tools by using them. ...

... a tool box ... little extra ... work of art ... his own ... undertaken those sufficient ... This joint is the strongest, but ... improves the appearance of the box. If desired, ... the corner pieces. However, the dove tail joint ...

TAILS

PINS

TRAY

TRAY RAILS

Figs. 1,175 to 1,179.—Tool box and details of construction. Fig. 1,175, general view of box with overall dimensions; figs. 1,176 and 1,177, dove tail joint; fig. 1,178, section through box showing arrangement of tray; fig. 1,179, detail of tray. Figs. 1,175 and 1,176, show dove tail joint for top (M, and S, corresponding to the same letters in fig.1,175), but the spacing for sides of the box is the same. *Lumber required for box:* 4 piece 6'×12"×½":

... wood to avoid chance of spoiling one of the pieces for the box

In making the box any kind of wood desired may be used, but in considering the amount of time spent in making the dovetail joints only the finest wood should be used, as for instance mahogany. The length of box is such that there will be practically no waste of material. The top and bottom are fastened with flat head brass screws. These should be put in carefully so that the heads are exactly flush with the wood.

Figs. 1,176 and 1,177 give details of the dove tail joints; the spacing is the same for both the top and sides of the box.

A tray may be provided to hold small articles as shown in fig. 1,178. This

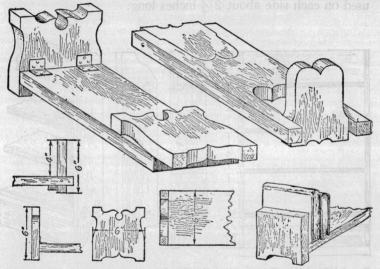

FIGS. 1,180 to 1,186.—Book rack and details of construction.

tray may extend across the box or only part way. If a half tray be made the rails may extend the length of the box so that the tray may slide from one end to the other. An important point in design of tray is that it should extend up to the top so that when the box is closed and turned up in carrying, small articles as nails, etc., will not drop out of their compartments into the box. Any number or arrangement of compartments may be provided as desired. Butt hinges, locks, grips, etc., may be obtained from any large hardware house.

Book Rack.—A simple design for a book rack is shown in

figs. 1,180 to 1,186. It may be made from remnants as the
pieces are very small, requiring but 3 pieces, in all less than
18″ of lumber unless the body is made longer than 12 inches″.
Fig. 1,180 shows the upright end pieces hinged to the top
face of body, so that when folded they lay on the top. The ends
may either be cut to a design or left plain. The ends are pivoted
by passing a rod through as shown or a round head screw may be
used on each side about 2½ inches long.

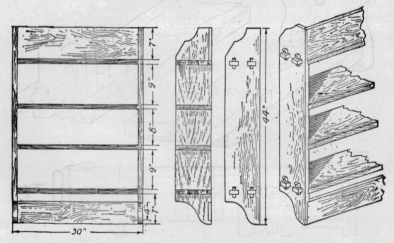

FIGS. 1,187 to 1,190.—Cabinet wall shelf rack and details of construction. The shelves are
rabbetted in ⅛ in.; they are ¼ in. narrower than the sides so that the rabbet does not show
on the front. The top and bottom shelf is keyed through the sides, as shown thus binding
all together so that the only nailing necessary is to fasten on the two strips on the back.

The design to which these ends are cut is such that when opened they
stop at an erect position, however, to insure this in case the sawing out has
left too much play, the strip shown in fig. 1,182 is nailed to the under side.
A little sand papering after these cuts are made is usually sufficient to fur-
nish enough play.

Cabinet Wall Shelf Rack.—A simple design of wall rack is shown in figs. 1,187 to 1,190, which gives practice in making wedge form of mortise and tenon joints. Do not try to improve this design with fancy scroll work as that form of ornamentation is out of date. The shelf is fastened with hook and eyes, the latter being screwed into the underside of shelf and engage the eyes wihch are screwed into the side wall, thus supporting the cabinet. These hook and eyes are spaced 16 ins. so that the hooks may screw into studs. In order for the cabinet to hang plumb

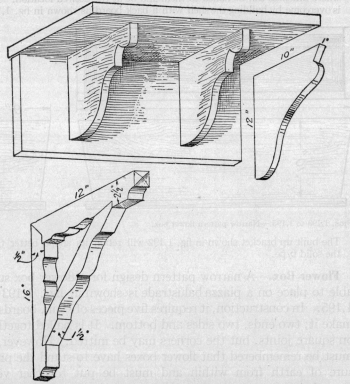

it is important, indeed necessary, that the wall eyes are at the same elevation.

Bracket Shelf.—Very often it is desired to erect a shelf in a room on plastered walls, and in most instances for appearance, it should be placed center equi-distant from other objects such as possibly two windows.

It is seldom that the studs which are spaced 16 ins. centers are located where brackets can be nailed to them and be at the desired location. This is overcome by building the shelf with a back board as shown in fig. 1,191.

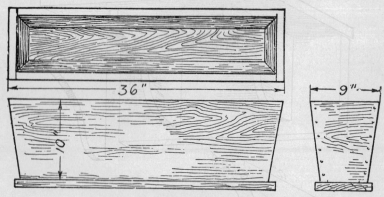

Figs. 1,193 to 1,195.—Narrow pattern flower box.

The built up bracket shown in fig. 1,192 will retain its shape better than the solid type.

Flower Box.—A narrow pattern design for a flower box suitable to place on a piazza balustrade is shown in figs. 1,193 to 1,195. In construction, it requires five pieces of $7/8$ in. boards to make it, two ends, two sides and bottom. It is nailed together on square joints, but the corners may be mitred. However, it must be remembered that flower boxes have to stand the pressure of earth from within and must be put together very strongly.

Fig. 1,196 is an isometric view of the same style box made 3 ins. wider.

Cedar or Moth-proof Chest.—In making a moth-proof chest cedar is used because some property of the wood, probably its aroma, keeps the moths away. Figs. 1,197 to 1,200 show design and details of construction of a cedar chest of convenient size.

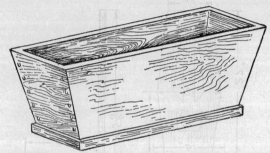

Fig. 1,196.—Isometric view of flower box made 3 ins. wider than in figs. 1,193 and 1,195.

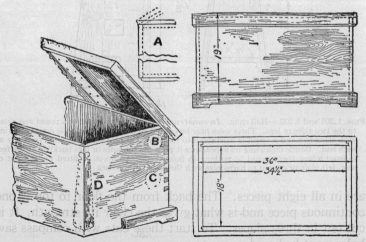

Figs. 1,197 to 1,200.—Moth proof cedar chest and detail of construction.

It has an apron lid or cover, and a base which lifts the bottom from the floor enough for ventilation.

The covers of the chest, may be put together as in fig. 1,198, square dove tail as at B, or mitre dove tail as at C. Another method is the butt joint reinforced and ornamented with metal trimming as at D.

Hall Chair.—In the design shown in figs. 1,201 and 1,202, there

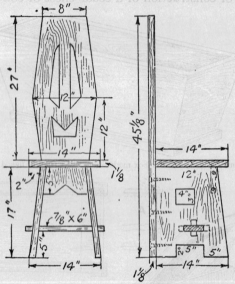

FIGS. 1,201 and 1,202.—Hall chair. *In construction,* the seat is nailed or screwed and glued to the two sides or legs. These sides may be cut out to a pattern fitting the design. A ring with shoulders and a tenon is mortised into the sides and held secure in place by a key at each end. Beside improving its appearance it prevents the sides or legs buckling at the feet in front where there would be nothing to hold them. An apron is fitted under front of seat, left plain or cut out to harmonize with the design of the back.

are in all eight pieces. The back from the floor to top is one continuous piece and is what gives the chair its strength. It is cut out in three places. To start these cuts with compass saw holes must be bored.

It can all be made of $\frac{7}{8}$ in. oak or other suitable wood, but looks better if of $1\frac{1}{8}$ in. material, being more massive and dignified in appearance, or a compromise, making the back and seat of $1\frac{1}{8}$ in. and the remainder of $\frac{7}{8}$ in.

Tabouret.—A design for a tabouret which will be found a

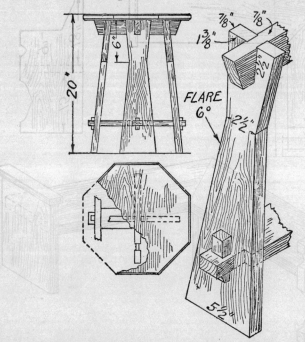

FIGS. 1,203 to 1,205.—Tabouret. Fig. 1,203, elevation; fig. 1,204, plan; fig. 1,205, enlarged view of one leg showing joints.

good exercise in joint making is shown in figs. 1,203 to 1,205. A detail of one of the legs is shown in fig. 1,205, drawn to larger scale to show more clearly the joints at top and bottom of the legs.

Cosey Corner.—In the design of cosey corner shown in figs. 1,206 to 1,208, the aim was to illustrate a simple construction easy to make. The seat is mitred at corner with a leg under the joint. Sometimes a butt joint is used.

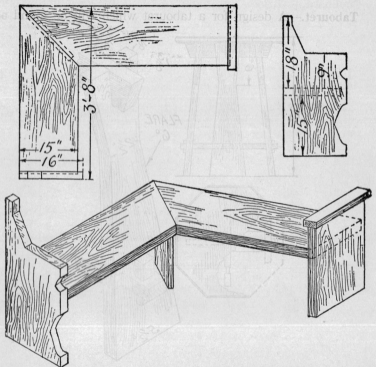

FIGS. 1,206 to 1,208.—Cosey corner. Fig. 1,206, plan; fig. 1,207, detail of end; fig. 1,208, isometric view.

Built-in Construction.—The accompanying cuts (figs. 1,210 to 1,213) are interesting as showing some of the numerous built-in features with which the kitchen may be equipped. Some of these conveniences, in design, are quite simple and ordinary and some are truly unique, but all of them will be found to constitute particularly desirable auxiliaries, if space will permit of their being used.

Cupboard.— A good example of built-in construction is

FIG. 1,209.—Built in table and benches for breakfast nook adjoining butler's pantry.

shown in figs. 1,225 and 1,226. The general proportions are shown in the figures. The counter height should be about 32 ins. And the counter opening not less than 12 ins., as shown

Framing for Drawers.—This is a job of precision, and it can not be expected that the drawers will move in and out without sticking or jambing unless first class lumber be used and all

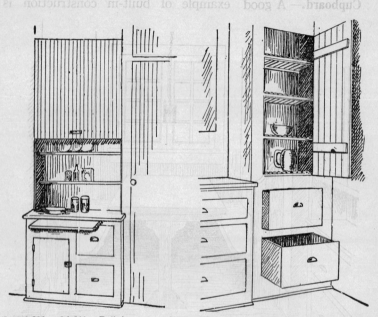

FIGS. 1,210 and 1,211.—Built in construction I.—Fig. 1,210, a combination of conveniences. Fig. 1,211, draught cooler which serves an excellent purpose as a feature of kitchen equipment.

the work be square and straight, and the parts properly fitted. Figs. 1,214 to 1,216 show frame construction.

The guides A, should be of hard, smooth wood. Here C, is made wider than A, this would only be necessary if much greater strength might be required.

FIGS. 1,212 and 1,213.—Built in construction II.—Fig. 1,212, ordinary cupboard and drawers, including nine little spice drawers. Fig. 1,213, folding ironing board.

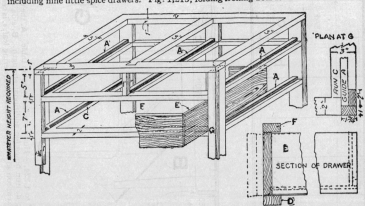

FIGS. 1,214 to 1,216.—Frame for draws. Fig. 1,214, assembly; fig. 1,215, detail of drawer end showing bevel D. and action of same. Full lines show draw closed. and dotted lines, position in opening.

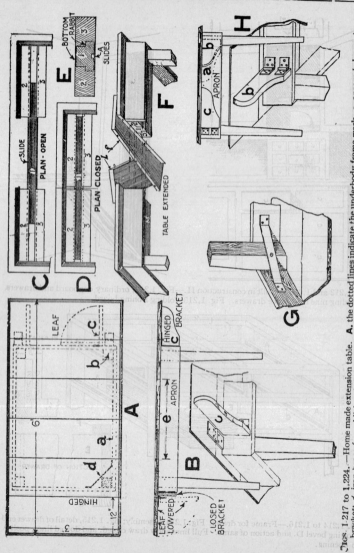

Figs. 1,217 to 1,224.—Home made extension table. **A**, the dotted lines indicate the underbody frame work, *a*, apron; *b*, leg; *c*, lap bracket; *d*, iron brace for additional strength. **B**, side elevation showing leaves raised and held in position with bracket *c*, *e*, hinged to apron so as to fold back for lowering leaf; *c*, is center and that part of apron omitted when made an extension table. **C**

Figs. 1,225 and 1,226.—Cupboard. Fig. 1,225, front view; fig. 1,226, end sectional view.

The run guides A need not be larger than ⅝ in. square. Their face must be flush with the inside of frames forming drawer space.

In the detail of draw front (fig. 1,216) it is seen at D, that the bottom

Figs. 1,217 to 1,224.—*Continued.*

to F, show construction without hinged leaves but as an extension table, the extra leaves being omitted. The slides 2 and 3 are fastened to the underside of top; when closed the ends of the apron meet. The rabbeted strips 2 and 3 are best fastened by screws. Strip 1, moves freely in these and is pulled to position by a stop screwed to table and engaging in a slot. Strip 1 (in E), if of hard wood may be as small as 2⅛″ × 1⅞″. F, side view, showing table extended and leaves ready to go in. G, shows corner of table inverted, illustrating iron strap reinforcement binding leg to apron. H, end elevation, showing the leaf brackets open at *b*, and folded at *c*, the operation being indicated by dotted outline *b, a*. Two ways of hinging are shown at *b* and *c*, the better way being shown at *b*.

of the front is beveled so that as the drawer closes the top of drawer rises, practically making a closed joint at F. The side of the drawer E is ⅛ in. lower than the front so that there can be no possibility of the drawer binding until it is closed. The dotted lines show that as the drawer moves out, the bevel at D, lowers it ⅛ in. so that it will run free. Hence, if the front binds from swelling, this bevel releases it.

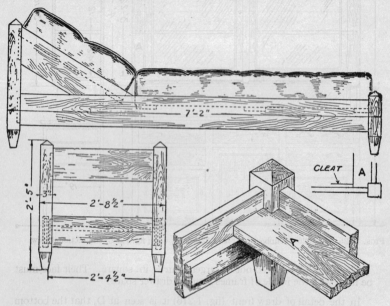

Figs. 1,227 to 1,230.—Home made couch with details of construction. The design shown is of the severe mission style, simple and easy to build. The piece A, resting on a cleat, ties the frame of couch together. The side elevation shows that there are three more of these cleats, one holding the head cushion in place, the others the long upholstery frame.

☐ GUETHS MECHANICAL DRAWING $1

A CONCISE DRAWING COURSE. 150 pages, 50 plates, size 6 x 9, flexible cover.
A complete instructor and reference work on: Drawing tools and their use, drafting room and shop practice, laying out sheets and lettering, important rules for working drawings, three views and isometric simple models, joints and carpentry work, machine drawing, projections, sections, intersections, warped surfaces, method of plan of elevation, method of vanishing point, shades and shadows, points, lines and planes, prisms and pyramids, spheres, screw surfaces, shadow perspective. How to use the slide rule.

☐ ROGERS DRAWING AND DESIGN $2

MECHANICAL DRAWING SELF TAUGHT.
506 pages, 600 illustrations (many full page drawings), flat-opening.
A standard work, with all details so clearly explained that this valuable training is easily obtained without an instructor. Covers terms and definitions, how to use drawing board—instruments, T square, triangles, how to do lettering, shade and section lining, geometrical drawing, development of surfaces and isometric, cabinet and orthographic projections, working drawings, explains how to do tracing and make blue prints, how to read prints, machine design. Reference index, with valuable tables. How to use the slide rule. A STANDARD STUDY TEXT FOR DRAFTING ROOM AND SHOP.

☐ AUDELS MILLWRIGHTS & MECHANICS GUIDE . $4

PRACTICAL LATE INFORMATION ON PLANT INSTALLATION, OPERATION & MAINTENANCE.
1200 pages, completely illustrated, 5 x 6½ x 2, flexible covers, fully indexed. 1000 facts at your fingertips.
For millwrights, mechanics, erecting maintenance men, riggers, shopmen, service men, foremen, inspectors, superintendents.
Section 1: Mechanical power transmission—2: millwrights and mechanics tools and their use—3: building and construction work—4: plant operation and maintenance—5: installation and maintenance of electrical machinery—6: practical calculation and technical data—how to read blue prints.

☐ AUDELS CARPENTERS & BUILDERS GUIDES

A PRACTICAL ILLUSTRATED TRADE ASSISTANT ON MODERN CONSTRUCTION FOR CARPENTERS, JOINERS, BUILDERS, MECHANICS AND ALL WOODWORKERS.
Explaining in practical, concise language by illustrations, diagrams, charts, graphs and pictures, principles, advances, short cuts, based on modern practice. How to figure and calculate various jobs.
Vol. 1—Tools, steel square, saw filing, joinery, furniture—431 pages—1200 illustrations.
Vol. 2—Builders mathematics, drawing plans, specifications, estimates—455 pages—400 illustrations.
Vol. 3—House and roof framing, laying out, foundations—255 pages—400 illustrations.
Vol. 4—Doors, windows, stair building, millwork, painting—448 pages—400 illustrations.
4 VOLS., 1600 PAGES, 3700 ILLUSTRATIONS, FLEXIBLE COVERS, $6. EACH VOLUME POCKET SIZE. SOLD SEPARATELY $1.50 A VOL.

☐ AUDELS PLUMBERS & STEAMFITTERS GUIDES

A PRACTICAL ILLUSTRATED TRADE ASSISTANT AND READY REFERENCE FOR MASTER PLUMBERS, JOURNEYMEN AND APPRENTICE STEAM FITTERS, GAS FITTERS AND HELPERS, SHEET METAL WORKERS AND DRAUGHTSMEN, MASTER BUILDERS AND ENGINEERS.
Explaining in plain language and by clear illustrations, diagrams, charts, graphs and pictures the principles of modern plumbing practice.
Vol. 1—Mathematics, physics, materials, tools, lead work—374 pages—716 diagrams.
Vol. 2—Water supply, drainage, rough work, tests—496 pages—6126 diagrams.
Vol. 3—Pipe fitting, ventilation, gas, steam—400 pages—900 diagrams.
Vol. 4—Sheet metal work, smithing, brazing, motors.
4 VOLS.—1670 PAGES—3642 DIAGRAMS—FLEXIBLE COVERS, $6. EACH VOL. POCKET SIZE. SOLD SEPARATELY $1.50 A VOL.

☐ AUDELS MASONS & BUILDERS GUIDES

A PRACTICAL ILLUSTRATED TRADE ASSISTANT ON MODERN CONSTRUCTION FOR BRICKLAYERS—STONE MASONS—CEMENT WORKERS—PLASTERERS AND TILE SETTERS.
Explaining in clear language and by well-done illustrations, diagrams, charts, graphs and pictures, principles, advances, short cuts, based on modern practice—including how to figure and calculate various jobs.
Vol. 1—Brick work, bricklaying, bonding, designs—266 pages.
Vol. 2—Brick foundations, arches, tile setting, estimating—245 pages.
Vol. 3—Concrete mixing, placing forms, reinforced stucco—259 pages.
Vol. 4—Plastering, stone masonry, steel construction, blue prints—345 pages.
4 VOLS.—1100 PAGES—2067 ILLUSTRATIONS—COMPLETE SET, $6. EACH VOL. (POCKET SIZE, FLEXIBLE COVER) $1.50 A VOL.

☐ AUDELS TELEVISION SERVICE MANUAL ☐ . . $2

Gives practical information on Installing, Trouble-Shooting & Repairing. This greatly needed fact-finding manual is easy to understand, 384 pages, more than 225 illustrations & diagrams covering operating principles of modern television receivers.

Covers T.V. information at your finger ends. Shows good receiver adjustment and How to get Sharp, Clear Pictures. How to Install Aerials—Avoid Blurs, Smears and How to test. Explains color systems and methods of conversion. 1001 FACTS—18 CHAPTERS.

☐ AUDELS ELECTRIC MOTOR GUIDE $4

Covers the construction, hook-ups, control, maintenance and trouble shooting of all types of motors including armature winding. Explains entire subject in every detail. A Handy Guide for Electricians and all Electrical Workers.

Over 1000 Pages of Information—31 Instructive, Interesting Chapters—617 Diagrams, hook-ups and drawings. All types of motors fully illustrated and indexed for ready reference.

☐ AUDELS QUESTIONS & ANSWERS FOR
ELECTRICIANS EXAMINATIONS $1

A PRACTICAL BOOK TO HELP YOU PREPARE FOR ALL GRADES OF ELECTRICIANS LICENSE EXAMINATIONS. A Helpful Review of all the fundamental principles underlying each question and answer needed to prepare you to solve any new or similar problem, which while being asked differently still calls for the same answer and knowledge.
Covering the National Electrical Code, Questions and Answers for License Tests; Ohm's Law with applied Examples; Hook-ups for Motors; Lighting and Instruments; 250 Pages. Fully Indexed and Illustrated. Pocket Size. Flexible Covers. A COMPLETE REVIEW FOR ALL ELECTRICAL WORKERS.

☐ AUDELS WIRING DIAGRAMS FOR
LIGHT & POWER $1

Electricians, wiremen, linemen, plant superintendents, construction engineers, electrical contractors and students will find these diagrams a valuable source of practical help.
This book gives the practical man the facts on wiring of electrical apparatus. It explains clearly in simple language how to wire apparatus for practically all fields of electricity. Each diagram is complete and self-explaining—210 pages, illustrated. A PRACTICAL, HANDY BOOK OF HOOK-UPS.

☐ AUDELS HANDY BOOK OF PRACTICAL
ELECTRICITY $4

FOR MAINTENANCE ENGINEERS, ELECTRICIANS AND ALL ELECTRICAL WORKERS.
1340 pages, 2600 illustrations.
A quick, simplified, ready reference book, giving complete instruction and practical information on the rules and laws of electricity—maintenance of electrical machinery—A.C. and D.C. motors—armature winding and repair—wiring diagrams—house lighting—power wiring—cable splicing—meters—batteries—transformers—elevators—electric cranes—railways—bells—sign flashers—telephone—ignition—radio principles—refrigeration—air conditioning—oil burners—air compressors—welding, and many modern applications explained so you can understand.
THE KEY TO A PRACTICAL UNDERSTANDING OF ELECTRICITY.

☐ AUDELS ELECTRONIC DEVICES $2

TELLS WHAT YOU WANT TO KNOW ABOUT THE ELECTRIC EYE.
Covering photo-electric cells and their applications. Includes easily understood explanations of the workings of the electric eye, amplifiers, anodes, candlepower, color temperature, illumination, frequencies, photo tubes, grid basis, voltage, photo-electric tubes, photocell, vacuum tubes, the oscillator, electron tubes, electrons versus atoms, Ohm's Law, wiring diagrams.
A PRACTICAL BOOK ON ELECTRONICS.